THE LITERACY MYTH

*Literacy and Social Structure
in the Nineteenth-Century City*

An Ontario common school. *"The March of Intellect,"* sketched by William Elliot in 1845. [John Ross Robertson Collection, Metropolitan Toronto Library Board, JRR 3338.]

THE LITERACY MYTH

Literacy and Social Structure

in the Nineteenth-Century City

Harvey J. Graff

School of Arts and Humanities
The University of Texas at Dallas
Richardson, Texas

ACADEMIC PRESS   New York   San Francisco   London
A Subsidiary of Harcourt Brace Jovanovich, Publishers

This is a volume in

STUDIES IN SOCIAL DISCONTINUITY

A complete list of titles in this series appears at the end of this volume.

ACADEMIC PRESS, INC.
111 Fifth Avenue, New York, New York 10003

United Kingdom Edition published by
ACADEMIC PRESS, INC. (LONDON) LTD.
24/28 Oval Road, London NW1 7DX

Library of Congress Cataloging in Publication Data

Graff, Harvey J
    The literacy myth.

    (Studies in social discontinuity)
    Includes bibliographical references.
    1. Illiteracy––Ontario––History. 2. Education,
Urban––Ontario––History. I. Title. II. Series.
LC154.2.06G72   301.44'5   79–51702
ISBN 0–12–294520–4

PRINTED IN THE UNITED STATES OF AMERICA

79 80 81 82   9 8 7 6 5 4 3 2 1

FOR VICKI

Contents

List of Illustrations
and Abbreviations

ILLUSTRATIONS

ABBREVIATIONS

List of Tables and Figures

TABLES

FIGURES

Preface

In the fall of 1975, newspaper and news broadcasts announced that "one in five U.S. adults lacks skills to cope in life." A substantial number of schooled adult citizens and workers, an Office of Education study reported, were deficient in the basic educational skills required to function competently in job, marketplace, community, and personal affairs. In addition to these underprepared 35 million, an additional 39 million were considered "functional, but not proficient."[1]

In the fall of 1977, the U.S. Secretary of Health, Education, and Welfare, Joseph Califano, announced that the federal government, in recognition of continuing evidence of surprisingly high levels of functional illiteracy and recent declines in basic skill levels of students, was beginning a broad investigation. In addition to asking why those examined failed to perform well on tests of basic literacy skills, he dedicated the federal government to breaking with traditions of local educational initiative, and to helping to develop plans for improving basic skills.[2] Six months later, an educational supplement to the *New York Times* added to this repeated identification of the literacy problem, pointing to frustrations of life for the illiterate as well as to the common theme of continuing failures in the national educational system's efforts toward a universal, useful literacy.[3] Simultaneously, and significantly, the U.S. Postal Service issued a new stamp. Bordered around the display of quill pen and ink well, the message proclaimed: "The ability to write. The root of democracy."

These are only samples of recent commentary that has become com-

[1] *Dallas Times Herald,* 12 October 1975.
[2] *Dallas Times Herald,* 25 October 1977.
[3] Spring Survey of Education, 30 April 1978.

monplace. The recent bombardment of woeful tales of literacy decline, drops in Scholastic Aptitude Test scores, low levels of preparation for fulfilling and productive lives, and illiterate high school graduates can too easily obscure the significance that lies behind these familiar words. A deeper meaning, the importance of which transcends the present moment and its discontents, must not be lost. I point to the value that our society, and our western tradition, places on primary schooling and literacy, and the high expectations we attach to them. It is precisely this value that lurks behind the fears so often expressed today, the roots of which lie in a legacy firmly and unquestioningly carried forth from previous times. Contemporary discussions about literacy, basic skills, and mass schooling are hardly unique; to anyone knowledgeable in the history of western social thought, education, or literacy, they ring out with familiarity. They are at once reflective and derivative of ideas and assumptions rooted especially in the eighteenth-century Enlightenment, but also in the Reformation and Counter-Reformation of the sixteenth century. These are ideals that permeate the trans-Atlantic western cultural heritage and influence social thought broadly and deeply: in our assumptions and theories of society, economy, culture, religion, as well as education. Indeed, their commmonplaceness and ordinariness, I fear, have reduced their significance to many.

There can be no doubt about the place of literacy in this key complex of notions that influences our thought, understanding, and behavior. For at least several centuries, the acceptance of the primacy of print and the abilities to read and reproduce it has advanced to universality, with an instructive degree of consensus. While the uses of literacy are still debated, its basic value is not.[4] Although interpretations of the story can violently differ, its outlines are standard: The rise of literacy and its promulgation through different agencies of schooling is associated firstly with a positive evaluation of mass access to the tools of reading and writing. It is seen as one of many eighteenth- and nineteenth-century social reforms that sought the improvement of society and the human condition within it. Overwhelmingly, to be literate and to spread literacy were considered more and more important; all opposition was branded reactionary and overcome (in theory if not in fact). Literacy, it was held, carried benefits to individuals as well as to societies, nations, and states. Ambiguities and contradictions are minor, especially when

---

[4] See, for example, Léon Bataille, ed., *A Turning Point for Literacy: Adult Education for Development* (New York: Pergamon Press, 1976); Robert Disch, ed., *The Future of Literacy* (Englewood Cliffs, New Jersey: Prentice-Hall, 1973). For full bibliographic information on much of what follows, see my *Literacy in History: An Interdisciplinary Research Bibliography* (Chicago: The Newberry Library, 1976, 2nd ed., 1979).

viewed in terms of the association of mass schooling with progress and enlightenment in all spheres of life and development. Value to the community, self- and socioeconomic worth, mobility, access to information and knowledge, rationality, morality, and orderliness are among the many qualities linked to literacy for individuals.[5] Literacy, in other words, was one critical component of the individual's road to progress. Analogously, these attributes were deeply significant to the larger society in which the educated man or woman resided and to which he or she contributed. From productivity to participation, schooled workers and citizens were required if the best path to the future and its fulfillment were to be followed.

Literacy, thus granted its valuable role in the process of individual and societal progress, itself became identified with that process and its success, acquiring a cultural endorsement that it easily maintains. This of course is highly simplified and too schematic, as the pages that follow will illustrate; nonetheless, at least an awareness of the broadest context in which an understanding of literacy must be placed and an awareness of the implications of the history of literacy for the present are required for this work to be fully assimilated. The story is not a simple one, as we shall shortly observe.[6]

Most accounts that relate to literacy's history fall well within the usual context. The rise of literacy and its dissemination to the popular classes is associated with the triumph of light over darkness, of liberalism, democracy, and of universal unbridled progress. In social thought, therefore, these elements relate to ideas of linear evolution and progression; literacy here takes its place among the other successes of modernity and rationality.[7] In theory and in empirical investigation, literacy is conceptualized—often in stark and simple fashion—as an important part of the larger parcel of factors that account for the evolution of modern societies and states. The centrality of literacy is found in its expected

[5] See, Introduction, below, as well as the examples provided by Alex Inkeles and David H. Smith, *Becoming Modern* (Cambridge, Mass.: Harvard University Press, 1974).

[6] I plan to develop these points more completely and at greater length in a forthcoming volume on the theme, "literacy in history," an interpretative essay on the place of literacy in modern western history. For a partial excursion into some of these relationships, see my "Literacy Past and Present: Critical Approaches in the Literacy–Society Relationship," *Interchange* 9 (1978), 1–21.

[7] See, as one example, Robert Nisbet's important *Social Change and History* (New York: Oxford University Press, 1969).

[8] For two representative and illustrative cases, see Richard D. Altick, *The English Common Reader* (Chicago: University of Chicago Press, 1957); Daniel Lerner, "Towards a Communication Theory of Modernization," in *Communication and Political Development,* ed. Lucian W. Pye (Princeton: Princeton University Press, 1963), among his many works.

place in historical works as well as sociological ones.[8] Whether it is assigned a role as cause or consequence, independent or dependent function, its value is seldom doubted. Primary schooling and literacy are necessary, it is so often repeated, for economic and social development, establishment and maintenance of democratic institutions, individual advancement, and so on. All this, regardless of its veracity, has come to constitute a "literacy myth."

The sanctity of this traditional and normative interpretation of the modern history of the western world is no longer as secure as once thought.[9] Nor, as this study and other recent works reveal, is the analysis of the role of literacy within the larger complex that comprises social development, any more secure. Modern historical scholarship, along with related research in other social sciences, is now in the midst of a challenging period of reevaluation and revision. This volume seeks to contribute to several aspects of this larger intellectual movement. Consequently, this study of literacy and its social correlates in the nineteenth century commences from a critical and revisionist stance. The data that I have gathered, analyzed, and interpreted do not fit easily within traditional thinking about literacy, nor do they correspond with previous ideas about the course of social development or the operation of social processes. The examination of a variety of factors central to those components of society will make this clear. The importance of these findings is relevant to those of us who seek to comprehend our contemporary world in its relationship to its past. It is for these reasons that I wish to make my own orientation clear.

I began this research with some reservations about certain aspects of this "received wisdom," and with a great many questions about literacy: its distribution, transmission, social and economic significance, relative values to different levels of social aggregation and to different layers within the social order, and its meaning and utility. I did not find myself persuaded by the small amount of previous scholarship that pertained directly to my questions. In particular, I was troubled by the dependence of earlier inquiries on informal and anecdotal approaches to the issues represented by literacy and to the very nature of literacy itself. Equally problematic were the regular appearance of the normative and progressive assumptions. Influenced certainly by Lawrence

---

[9] Among a large and growing critical literature, see Ian Weinberg, "The Problem of the Convergence of Industrial Societies," *Comparative Studies in Society and History*, 11 (1969), 1–15; Dean C. Tipps, "Modernization and the Comparative Study of Societies," *Comparative Studies in Society and History* 15 (1973), 199–226; Ali A. Mazrui, "From Social Darwinism to Current Theories of Modernization," *World Politics*, 21 (1968), 69–83; Nisbet, *Social Change*.

Stone's seminal review of English literacy and by Roger Schofield's major statistical study (which continues today),[10] I was convinced of the need to develop an explicitly empirical and numerical approach to literacy in order even to attempt to resolve the kinds of questions I found most important. This was my purpose in developing the data upon which much of this study rests: manuscript censuses, tax assessment rolls, employment contracts, jail registers. It is essential to note that literacy is both a quantitative and a qualitative attribute, one whose measurement continues to raise countless difficulties; nonetheless, it is equally apparent that a great many of the important issues can only be approached numerically. Moreover, my studies have led me to conclude that qualitative questions, which may be ultimately of greater consequence, may only be tackled from a solid empirical basis. Other recent research has only made my conviction firmer.[11]

To illustrate my intentions, a preview of what follows will serve well; let us turn to the structure of the book. Following a brief introduction, which sets this study in the context of earlier researches into historical and contemporary literacy and which reviews their deficiencies, we shall evaluate the nineteenth-century consensus on the significance and provision of primary schooling. The focus will be, as in much of what follows, on persons and processes in mid-nineteenth-century Ontario, Canada. Here, as wherever possible, comparative material will be used to supplement and support the principal findings and arguments, extending the explicit comparative thrust and establishing a framework for future comparative explorations. In considering the framing of a "moral basis of literacy" and the progress of a "literacy myth," contemporary expectations and institutional mechanisms for literacy provision are laid bare for detailed questioning of the social realities that accompany this rhetoric.

The chapters of Part One, "Literacy and Social Structure," therefore examine the lives and livelihoods of illiterate and literate men and women in three cities, Hamilton, London, and Kingston, in comparative study. Their experiences in work, wealth, migrations, mobility, and family patterns form the core of this section. The conclusions, which require the qualification of conventional understanding and normative, progres-

---

10 Stone, "Literacy and Education in England, 1640–1900," *Past and Present*, 42 (1969), 61–139; Schofield, "Dimensions of Illiteracy, 1750–1850," *Explorations in Economic History*, 10 (1973), 437–454.

11 Especially, Kenneth A. Lockridge, *Literacy in Colonial New England* (New York: W. W. Norton, 1974); François Furet and Jacques Ozouf, *Lire et écrire: l'alphabétisation des français de Calvin à Jules Ferry* (Paris: les editions de Minuit, 1977); Lee Soltow and Edward Stevens, "Literacy and the Rise of the Common School," unpublished manuscript, 1977.

sive social thought, reveal a reality much more complex than one might expect. In the first place, a number of discontinuities and contradictions are apparent, showing the role of literacy to be much less direct and clear-cut than typically thought. Moreover, systematic patterns of inequality and stratification—by origins, class, sex, race, and age—were deep and pervasive, and relatively unaltered by the influence of literacy. The social hierarchy, we will see, even by mid-century in modernizing urban areas, was ordered more by the dominance of social ascription than by the acquisition of new, achieved characteristics.

The promise of education, and the rhetoric of school promoters, so strong since the end of the eighteenth century, is contradicted by the experiences of these common men and women. In many ways, traditional structural factors remained dominant, as indeed we now find increasing amounts of recent evidence suggesting that these patterns have yet to be universally reversed.[12] The story is even more interesting, for the data also question other traditional historical stereotypes and relate to other elements of social thought. For example, despite common notions that many immigrants to North America were the dregs of their societies of origin and were rooted in cultures of poverty, we shall see that their levels of literacy were well above average for those places and that they were calculating individuals, able to use their resources and traditions for adaptation, survival, and sometimes for advantage in new, alien environments. Finally, there are important indications that by the second third of the nineteenth century, the society had not developed to the stage at which literacy was a requirement for social and economic advancement or for the intergenerational mobility of children. After the evidence is presented and interpreted, the implications of these patterns will be considered in the conclusion.

Part Two of the study, "Literacy and Society," leaves these urban residents to continue several important themes in the relationships among literacy, development, order, discrimination, and the uses of literacy in the same period. Centering on the Ontario experience, supplemented again with other North American and Western European evidence, literacy's role in work and economic development will first be examined. A case is made for questioning traditional assumptions, as the argument suggests that the connections joining industrialization, eco-

---

[12] See, for example, Ivar Berg, *Education and Jobs* (Boston: Beacon Press, 1971); Christopher Jencks *et al, Inequality* (New York: Basic Books, 1972); Raymond Boudon, *Education, Opportunity, and Social Inequality* (New York: John Wiley, 1974); Pierre Bourdieu and Jean-Claude Passeron, *Reproduction in Education, Society, and Culture* (Beverly Hills: Sage Publications, 1977). This is of course a highly controversial area.

nomic progress, and literacy are hardly as direct as most discussions imply. Theories and investigations supportive of these views, we shall discover, hold little systematic evidence when examined carefully. Once more, the need for reconsideration and revision should be apparent.

A further chapter inquires into the relations tying illiteracy to criminality, another firm element in our "received wisdom" and literacy myth. Close textual analysis and a re-analysis of a nineteenth-century gaol register indicate that these typical causal patterns may be less than conclusive. Reiterating themes from Part One, we shall see the influence of social hierarchy and the pervasiveness of structural inequality both counteracting and simultaneously reinforcing the roles of literacy and illiteracy. The possibility and the potential utility of alternative formulations will be indicated, as these chapters amplify the themes and conclusions of the earlier analysis.

A final chapter attempts to confront systematically, for the first time, questions of the qualitative nature of literacy at that time. A topic obviously much less amenable to numerical treatment for the past than the other themes, this part of the inquiry adopts a different strategy. When taken together, a variety of indirect indicators, from observers' and proselytizers' remarks to methods of reading instruction, point to significant patterns in abilities and in the uses to which those abilities were put. For example, we find indications that accompanying the high levels of literacy prevalent in this society were lesser degrees of qualitative skills and probably relatively low levels of use. Literacy abilities, I suggest, while broadly disseminated and quite probably sufficient for many everyday needs, were less than that required for other needs.

Through the series of interrelated examinations that comprise the substance of this book and the elaboration of these arguments, I attempt to illustrate both the significance of the study of literacy and the necessity for rethinking and reinterpretation. While I shall neither belabor the relevance of this research for better comprehension of contemporary events, nor reduce the integrity of the past to suit the present, I do not wish to ignore these implications either. I shall return to this in my conclusions. To summarize, then, the study that follows offers a contribution to comparative urban and social history, the history of education and schooling, and to social theory. By revealing problems in traditional formulations along with the discontinuities, contradictions, and complexity of the subject matter itself, I hope to place literacy and the literacy myth in a new perspective. Literacy, in its social context, is neither simple, direct, nor unambiguous; the ways in which it relates to social processes and social structures reveals its significance alone. That, as we shall see, is only one part of the story.

Acknowledgments

Some of the material presented in Chapters 5 and 6 has appeared elsewhere. An earlier version of Chapter 5 was published in *Essays in Canadian Working Class History*, edited by Gregory Kealey and Peter Warrian (Toronto: McClelland and Stewart Ltd., 1976), under the title, "Educated and Profitable Labour: Literacy, Jobs and the Working Class in the Nineteenth Century." Much of Chapter 6 appeared as " 'Pauperism, Misery and Vice': Illiteracy and Criminality in the Nineteenth Century," *Journal of Social History*, 11 (Winter, 1977–1978).

This book has been in the making for several years. In that time, I have accumulated a great many debts—too numerous to list completely here. Nonetheless, there are some persons and institutions who deserve special mention, and I want to express my gratitude to them. Certainly none of them bear any responsibility for this work.

For financial assistance, I gratefully acknowledge the fellowships and grants awarded by the Woodrow Wilson Foundation, the Ontario Institute for Studies in Education and the University of Toronto, the Urban Affairs Fellowship program of the Central Mortgage and Housing Corporation of Canada, the National Endowment for the Humanities, the Swedish Institute and Umeå University, and, for a grant-in-aid that allowed final work and covered manuscript costs, the American Council of Learned Societies. For research grants, keypunching, computer time, and ancillary services, the Department of History and Philosophy of Education and especially the Canadian Social History Project of the Ontario Institute for Studies in Education, University of Toronto, have been more than generous. Without their aid and support, this work would undoubtedly remain unfinished. The department and the project, under both Michael Katz's and Ian Winchester's supervision, created an environment in which I was free to begin this broad, and expensive, undertaking with a minimum of bureaucratic and intellectual constraint.

For technical advice and assistance in preparing the quantitative data and in programming, I thank John Tiller, Gloria Kissin, Inno Dubelaar, Rick Mason, Martha Coutts, and Ron Hipfner (all of whom are or have been associated with the Ontario Institute, often in the invaluable work-study program).

Many librarians and archivists have aided me with their understanding and generosity, and often rewarded me with their interest. I acknowledge in particular the assistance of Isabelle Gibb of the Ontario Institute, the Inter-Library Loan staff of Northwestern University, the Center for Research Libraries in Chicago, Barbara Craig and Marion Beyea of the Province of Ontario Archives, Edward Phelps of the Regional History Collection of the University of Western Ontario, the staff of the Queen's University Archives, and Robin Taylor and Vickie Bullock of the University of Texas at Dallas Library. Nancy Weissman, Eileen Tollett, and Vicki Graff provided indispensable assistance in the preparation of the manuscript.

Fellow students and colleagues have been especially supportive, encouraging, and more than willing to read, listen, and criticize; I want to record my sincere thanks to Alison Prentice, Ian Davey, Michael Doucet, and Greg Kealey. Other scholars have assisted me with encouragement, ideas, advice, and in some cases the examples of their work; Kenneth Lockridge, Roger Schofield, Egil Johansson, and Lee Soltow merit special mention. I also appreciate the support and interest of Jill Conway, Ian Winchester, Maurice Careless, Charles Tilly, Bob Black, Paul Monaco, Gerald Soliday, and Steven Weissman.

Finally, my major intellectual debt is to Michael Katz, who supervised the first version of this manuscript as a dissertation. The first paper I wrote on the history of literacy originated in his kitchen; his interest has yet to diminish. As both mentor and friend, Michael has taught me a great deal, and he has been unfailing and uncompromising in his support and in his invaluable criticism.

To my parents and my brother go my special thanks. My debts to them are too many to acknowledge. Last, but not least, I thank Vicki Graff, my most loyal supporter and most vocal critic, for whom there are no appropriate words of gratitude. She will understand. I alone accept responsibility for what follows, of course.

THE LITERACY MYTH

Literacy and Social Structure
in the Nineteenth-Century City

Introduction

Literacy and History

What would be the effect if reading was abolished by some stroke of arbitrary authority, while the radio, records, cassettes, were available very cheaply? I am still not clear why you think the act of reading is so important.

ANDREW SCHONFIELD
The Listener, 25 July 1974

In most urban and suburban communities, most children will pick up the printed code anyway, school or no school. . . . It is likely that teaching destroys more genuine literacy than it produces. But it is hard to know if most people think that reading and writing have any value anyway, either in themselves or for their use, except that they are indispensable in how we go about things. Contrast the common respect for mathematics, which are taken to be about something and are powerful, productive, magical; yet there is no panic if people are mathematically illiterate.

PAUL GOODMAN
Speaking and Language: in Defense of Poetry (1971)

And when we consider the first use to which writing was put, it would seem quite clear that it was first and foremost connected with power: it was used for inventories, catalogues, censuses and instructions; in all instances, whether the aim was to keep a check on material possessions or human beings, it was the evidence of the power exercised by some men over other men and over worldly possessions.

CLAUDE LEVI-STRAUSS
*in Georges Carbonnier,
Conversations with Claude Levi-Strauss (1969)*

1

I

A literacy myth surrounds us. Literacy is considered a basic human right and a tool for productive citizenship and fulfilling lives, yet world illiteracy continues at a high rate. Although literacy is closely associated with basic western values and key elements of our social thought, tests reveal that many high-school graduates and college students are illiterate and that children are not learning to read. Other observers portend the end of traditional print literacy; some disclaim even the frequent cries of literacy decline. Our uncertainty and anxieties are striking.

Nonetheless, a new book is published every minute, and the world's reading population has more than doubled in 20 years. Eight billion volumes are printed each year—the distribution and circulation are, however, unequal and unbalanced. The developed countries suffer from a glut of print and other parts of the world suffer from a scarcity amounting to what has been termed "book hunger." Ironically, in the developed or industrialized nations many who can read very often do not. In Italy and Hungary, for example, 40% of the population do not read to any appreciable extent; in France, 53% do not; and in the United States, with low levels of absolute illiteracy, "functional" illiteracy is quite high: estimates range up to a full 50% of adults![1]

That a literacy problem exists seems certain. Its dimensions, causes, and comprehension are, however, less than clear. Many reasons and explanations for its existence have been offered. Specialists such as Baker and Escarpit point to the competition and distraction of audiovisual media and to school and preschool experiences—two common areas of censure. They argue that "the child who meets books for the first time when he goes to school tends to associate reading with the school experience especially if no reading is done at home. . . . More often than not the child comes to dislike reading and drops it altogether when he leaves school." [2] Others point to instructional methods and materials, classroom settings, problems of motivation and relevance, external influences, social changes, and home environments. Despite the quantity of print devoted to this topic, one of the few justifiable conclusions is

[1] *Toronto Star*, January 2, 1974; George Steiner, "After the Book," in *The Future of Literacy*, ed. Robert Disch (Englewood Cliffs, N.J.: Prentice-Hall, 1973); Escarpit, *The Book Revolution* (New York: UNESCO, 1966); David Harmon, "Illiteracy: An Overview," *Harvard Educational Review*, 40 (1970), 230; "Functional Illiteracy Found High in U.S.," *New York Times*, May 20, 1970.

[2] *Toronto Star*, January 2, 1974; see also, M. M. Lewis, *The Importance of Illiteracy* (London: Harrap, 1953).

that common understanding of literacy is inadequate and incomplete. This is as true for past as for present considerations of the subject.

Discussions of literacy are confused and ambiguous—an ironic, and even startling, phenomenon, which contrasts sharply with the high value we assign to the skills of reading and writing. Vagueness pervades virtually all efforts to discern the meaning of literacy; moreover, there is surprisingly little agreement on or specific evidence for the benefits of literacy, whether socially or individually, economically or culturally. Rather, assumptions preempt criticism and investigation, and agencies and specialists whose business it is to promote literacy shrink from asking fundamental questions in their campaigns to disseminate skills.

Definitions and conceptualizations are obviously basic to these considerations; recognition of persistent problems with them can illuminate the most significant issues. As David Harmon recounts, until the 1950s most governments equated the abilities of reading, writing, and ciphering with individual literacy, and UNESCO summarized: "A person is literate who can, with understanding, both read and write a short simple statement on his everyday life." During the 1950s, however, efforts were made to distinguish between a literate and a functionally literate person, thereby complicating measurement and evaluation. New definitions issued. Functional literacy meant "the essential knowledge and skills which enable [one] to engage in all those activities in which literacy is required for effective functioning in [one's] group and community, and whose attainments make it possible for [one] to continue to use these skills towards [one's] own and the community's development." But nowhere are "effective functioning," "knowledge and skills," or "development" defined or discussed. The relativism of these conceptualizations is important, for literacy's role changes with time, place, and circumstances; nonetheless, these definitions are less than useful.

In response to such complications, most governments employ little more than a loose definition, often similar to the one just quoted, in conjunction with a grade-completion equivalency (commonly, the fourth or fifth grade is taken as a standard). Agencies ranging from the U.S. Census Bureau, the Army, and the Navy to the census authorities of Statistics Canada and the United Nations follow this common practice, but usually admit that the completion of a particular grade of school does not warrant a presumption of the attainment of literacy—a disheartening and debilitating comment on efforts at measurement. Thus, comparisons of literacy rates are contradicted, too, over units large or small, and even the implications of reading and writing a message are, apparently, seldom considered. Without the specification of a context in which literacy is to serve either the individual or society, attempts to establish a valid concept of functional literacy cannot succeed. Moreover, even in the present decade, those fostering renewed literacy campaigns, such as the "right-to-read" movement, still do not define "functional competencies" (i.e., of reading, writing, and computing) or "requirements for adult living" although they rely on such terms to justify their efforts.[3]

Investigators focusing on units of analysis smaller than nations or international units pursue other alternatives in defining and measuring literacy. Some, for example, administer tests. In the Schuman, Inkeles, and Smith East Pakistan (Bangladesh) study, each subject was first asked if he could read (i.e., Bengali). If the response was yes, a short newspaper-level passage was given to him to read. His comprehension was rated as follows: *cannot read, reads only a few words, reads slowly but understands,* or *reads well.*[4] DeYoung and Hunt, in a Philippine study, defined functional literacy as ability to read and comprehend sufficiently to communicate their understanding to another. To test functional literacy, they graded individuals on responses to questions about a text, scoring them "nonfunctional" (no comprehension), "poor," or "good in comprehension."[5] In a third study, Rogers and Herzog assessed the ability of Columbian peasants to read or write well enough for them to carry out the functions of their roles in the social system. The peasant's functional literacy was assessed according to the number of words he or she read and comprehended from a sentence consisting of six words of varying difficulty. This represented, to the researchers, a measure of literacy viewed as a continuous variable (with many levels of ability); if literacy was seen as a dichotomous attribute (literate or illiterate only), they add, only those who read all six would be functionally literate.[6]

These examples represent a clear improvement over the census-style measures. Nevertheless, the definitions employed do not fit closely with styles of testing. For instance, a reference to writing forms a portion of

[3] Harmon, "Illiteracy: An Overview," 226–229; UNESCO, *Literacy as a Factor in Development* (Paris, 1956), 7.

[4] Howard Schuman, Alex Inkeles, and David H. Smith, "Some Social Psychological Effects and Non-effects in a New Nation," *Economic Development and Cultural Change,* 16 (1967), 2.

[5] John E. DeYoung and Chester L. Hunt, "Communication Channels and Functional Literacy in the Phillipine Bario," *Journal of Asian Studies,* 22 (1962), 69–70.

[6] Everitt M. Rogers and William Herzog, "Functional Literacy among Columbian Peasants," *Economic Development and Cultural Change,* 14 (1966), 192–194. All three studies report that their tests showed "close congruity" with self-reporting, thus census-type surveys of literacy may be considered reasonably accurate when compared with tests.

each definition, but writing ability is never evaluated. More importantly, work and social functions are neither specified nor related to test questions, for no attempt is made to relate literacy to a hierarchy of job or social skills or to the specific needs of the circumstances of life. Insights, like that of Rogers and Herzog that literacy is a process, different for different roles, and with requirements shifting as individuals and society change, are not incorporated into measurement or analysis. The meanings and uses of literacy are more complex and diverse than these typical questions or tests allow. Popular confusion and scientific ambiguity are not resolved by the strategies thus far adopted; the crux of conceptualization and definition is not satisfied, nor is the myth dispelled.

Vagueness and ambiguity of definition and measurement not surprisingly influence forms of analysis and research questions. Functional necessities, interestingly and importantly, are often translated into matters of attitudes and values rather than of behavior or skill. Rogers and Herzog, for example, inquire about such abstractions as empathy, achievement motivation, and "cosmopoliteness," instead of isolating the roles played by literacy in work or life chances. Few of their questions, in fact, relate to functional skill in ways that might correspond to the definitions usually offered.

David Harmon, for one, has attempted to surmount the limitations of these definitions, so it should not be construed that no efforts have been made to do so or that this critique is wholly novel. He has offered a three-stage conceptualization of literacy: as a tool, as a skill attainment, and as an ability having applications. "Each stage," he concludes, "is contingent upon the former; each stage is a necessary component of literacy." A useful beginning, undoubtedly, Harmon's model nevertheless continues to make key assumptions without support or rationale; while maintaining the required flexibility, he does not succeed in dispelling the vagueness and confusion which beset discussions of literacy. Literacy is rightly assumed to be a tool and a skill, but we must ask, What kind of tool and for what uses? Today, as previously, the understanding of literacy remains at the level which it has held for a century. As Harmon remarks, "Few would dispute the significance of literacy for either individual or national development." [7] This, need I add, is hardly an advancement in comprehension; the literacy myth is pervasive. Its influence weighs upon analysis both past and present.

This obstacle to understanding is not recent in origin. It dates from at least the previous century, and as Robert Disch usefully summarizes, "The assumption that literacy and progress were identical had become a

[7] Harmon, "Illiteracy: An Overview," 228.

dogma of progressive thought. Many thinkers believed that universal literacy was no less than the final milestone on the road to Utopia." He continues, reflecting my position,

> Subsequently the twentieth century inherited a mystique of literacy born out of two tendencies. One, essentially utilitarian, was committed to the functional uses of literacy as a medium for the spread of practical information that could lead to individual and social progress; the other, essentially aesthetic and spiritual, was committed to the uses of literacy for salvaging the drooping spirit of Western man from the death of religion and the ravages of progress.[8]

Nor, as we shall see, is this all. The main point, of course, is that some disputation of the significance and mystique of literacy is possible; we will shortly consider the nineteenth century anew. Moreover, it might also be useful for other, more contemporary analysts to reexamine the current implications of this major legacy.

II

A review of the major conclusions of contemporary literacy studies offers a heuristic perspective and orientation. As has been indicated, these findings often relate to attitudes and values, suggesting that therein may lie literacy's most important influences. For example, functionally literate adults (as they have been defined here) are, research reports, more empathetic, more innovative in agriculture and at home, more achievement motivated, and more cosmopolitan than illiterates; they also have larger farms, greater exposure to media and political information, and more often serve as opinion leaders. Literates, in addition, identify more often with a nation than a community or ethnic group, aspire to postsecondary education for sons, and are more aware of new opportunities. Urban places of residence may intersect with literacy, moreover, in promoting such attitudes as acceptance of birth control and technological awareness. Whether these attitudes result from literacy, or literacy from these or other influences, remains unclear.[9]

[8] Disch, *Future of Literacy*, 4–5.

[9] Rogers and Herzog, "Functional Literacy," 198–202; see also Daniel Lerner, "Literacy and Initiative in Village Development," in *Rural Development Research Project*, ed. F. W. Frey (Cambridge, Mass.: M. I. T., Center for International Studies, 1964), "Toward a Communication Theory of Modernization," in *Communication and Political Development*, ed. Lucian Pye (Princeton: Princeton University Press, 1963); Schuman *et al.*, "Some Social Psychological Effects," 4–5; 8–10.

Negative findings, often unexpected ones, are equally important. Literacy is found to bear no relationship, for instance, to growing material self-interest in East Pakistan, whereas urbanization may; neither does it relate to the recognition of differing opinions among one's fellow men. In fact, literacy is correlated negatively with contentment with material possessions. Researchers have also found that literacy does not correlate highly with media exposure (including print media), a finding that suggests that literates do not read to a significant extent and that illiterates have access to information sources. Illiterates often buy newspapers (48% of illiterates in one report) and have them read to them. Moreover, among Columbian peasants, most households contain at least one literate resident. Sources of information and new ideas are available to those without reading skills; and, individuals, in fact, not the media, are considered the best sources of information. Opinion leaders, finally, are far from 100% literate.[10]

These findings are important. The contradictions and paradoxes are no less significant than the expected results. Not only do they reflect the problems considered here, they also reinforce the need for reconsideration. Nevertheless, this lack of consistency in research findings does not reduce the influence of the literacy myth, nor does it occasion a questioning of the centrality of literacy to development, whether of individuals or of societies. Consider the ingenuous response of Schuman, Inkeles, and Smith to several aspects of this predicament. Evading issues of functions and skills, they argue, "Rather than finding literacy to be a factor which completely pervades and shapes a man's entire view of the world, we find it limited to those spheres where vicarious and abstract experience is essentially meaningful. The more practical part of a man's outlook, however, is determined by his daily experiences in significant roles." There is no mention of the functional or concretized contributions of literacy; its impact is construed as symbolic, abstract, and not practical. Moreover, both the correlates and noncorrelates of literacy seem to be explained at least in part by such factors as urban residence and industrial work. For instance, some attitudinal changes occur "most completely" in the presence of both literacy and urban-industrial experience, requiring the new experience of the latter and what they call the "ideational sophistication" of the former. Literacy, therefore, does not enter into all psychological changes, and when it does, its impact is influenced by other, contextual and structural factors. Thus, Schuman *et al.* argue vaguely, literacy specifically, and education more generally,

[10] Schuman *et al.*, Some Social Psychological Effects," 6–10; Rogers and Herzog, "Functional Literacy," 196–197, 201; DeYoung and Hunt, "Communication Channels," 74.

open minds to new ideas and change attitudes little dependent on concrete situations.[11] Literacy's role has shifted perceptibly and significantly.

This is not all; for enter here Alex Inkeles' "modern man": the
culmination of a "set of personal qualities which reliably cohere as a
syndrome and which identify a type of man who may validly be described
as fitting a reasonable theoretical conception of modern man." The central elements of this "syndrome" remarkably parallel literacy's imputed
influences: an openness to new experiences, an assertion of independence,
a belief in the efficacy of science, an ambition for one's self and one's
children's success in education and work, a dependence on planning, an
interest and involvement in politics, and an effort to be aware of issues
larger than local ones. The connection lies in the setting in which these
attitudes are learned: the school, first, and then the factory. As Inkeles
explains,

> If attending school brings about such substantial changes in these funda-
> mental personal orientations, the school must be teaching a good deal more
> than is apparent in its syllabus on reading, writing, and even geography.
> The school is evidently also an important training ground for inculcating
> values. It teaches ways of orienting oneself towards others, and of conducting
> oneself, which could have bearing on the performance of adult roles in the
> structure of modern society.

The effects of the school, and of the factory too, Inkeles concludes,
"reside not mainly in its formal, explicit, self-conscious pedagogic activity, but rather in its informal, implicit, and often unconscious
program. . . ."[12]

Literacy, then, as a measure of modernity, on either the individual
or the societal level, becomes a symbol—and just as its benefits are
located in the areas of abstraction and symbolism, so are its functions.
Important questions need to be considered, however. In the first place,
causation, direction, and weight of influence are uncertain. As Tilly
argues, structural settings need not relate directly to the type of learning taking place in them or to its outcomes in attitude and behavior;
neither in fact must attitude and behavior be in lock-step conformity.
The relationships might be very different. In addition, there are good
reasons, for past and present both, to contradict Inkeles' insistence on
the unconscious nature of the results of schooling on attitudes and

---

[11] Schuman *et al.*, "Some Social Psychological Effects," 7–11.

[12] Inkeles, "Making Men Modern: On the Causes and Consequences of Individual
Change in Six Developing Countries," *American Journal of Sociology*, 74 (1969), 210,
213; Inkeles and Smith, *Becoming Modern* (Cambridge, Mass.: Harvard University
Press, 1974), *passim*.

values; these influences can be far more direct, and yet equally subtle. And finally, the modernity syndrome's coherence and causes, and its very relationship to literacy, suffer from both conceptual and empirical limitations.[13]

The evidence remains nonetheless suggestive. For, in the nineteenth century, literacy's role and the expectations held for it paralleled in significant ways elements of these patterns, yet it also symbolized a somewhat different set of changes. The ambiguity and confusion between skills and values remain important aspects of continuity, and continuing obstructions to understanding. Curiously, literacy—and schooling—are held to represent a complex of attitudinal changes, related in some measure to modernity. In part, this is a result of the acquisition and possession of literacy, but perhaps it is more directly the result of the processes that accompany the dissemination of that ability: the values and organization of the school. This duality is not often recognized, but may comprise the essence of schooling's contribution to development and modernization. It may also explain the frequency with which researchers isolate attitudes while neglecting functional skills.

Recognition of this conceptual confusion about the purposes that literacy serves aids in understanding the place accorded it in notions of societal modernization and change. Not surprisingly, literacy is accorded a pervasive role. Economists, sociologists, planners, and governments inform us that literacy rates correlate with scores of factors, ranging from individual attitudes to economic growth and industrialization, per-capita wealth and GNP, political stability and participatory democracy, urbanization and vital rates, communications and consumption—to list only a few of the correlations reported.[14] There is a certain logic behind many of these correlations; however, no convincing or documented explanations or analyses correspond to them. The assumptions, ambiguities, and contradictions implicit in these approaches attract criticism, so we need not repeat that debate. What need to be stressed are the limitations

[13] Charles Tilly, "Talking Modern," *Peasant Studies Newsletter*, 6 (1977), 66–68; Robert Dreeben, *On What Is Learned in School* (Reading, Mass.: Addison-Wesley, 1968); Kenneth Lockridge, *Literacy in Colonial New England* (New York: Norton, 1974). Lockridge in a tentative test of the Inkeles conclusions locates little evidence of literate persons exhibiting more modern attitudes, using charitable giving as his measures, 32–37. See also, *Becoming Modern*, 138, 246, *passim.*, for complications in testing education's contribution to modernity.

[14] For a summary, see Bruce M. Russet *et al.*, *World Handbook of Political and Social Indicators* (New Haven: Yale University Press, 1964); see also, Lerner, "Towards a Communication Theory"; Carlo Cipolla, *Literacy and Development in the West* (Harmondsworth: Penguin, 1969); H. H. Golden, "Literacy and Social Change in Underdeveloped Countries," *Rural Sociology*, 20 (1955), 1–7.

of the literacy–modernization–development sequence, especially as it relates to historical time. One valuable example is Flora's refutation of
Daniel Lerner's sequences-of-development theory with literacy at its
center; Flora has offered evidence *dis*connecting urbanization and industrialization from literacy.[15] The vagueness that surrounds the meaning
of literacy, the failure to specify the contexts of its role, the power of
the literacy myth, and, crucially, the ignorance about the functional
benefits to the individual and society of literacy skills debilitate these
macrosociological correlations, along with many of the individual-based
approaches.

Assumptions remain simplistic and deterministic; explanation and
critical understanding are rare. The implications of these criticisms are
severe for common notions about literacy and its centrality in social
theory and western values. The need for reexamination, and a direct
confrontation of theory with the facts of historical development and
modernization, is compelling. Our current "crisis" makes this examination imperative. These concerns, and their ramifications, must be recognized, finally, by historians, whose own studies of literacy have only
recently begun. Regardless of our position regarding the myth or the
crisis, we cannot ignore literacy's own history, one which intersects vitally
with the course of social change and development—especially in the
centuries since the invention and spread of printing. Nor can we neglect
the relevance of that history to modern social thought.

III

The volume and pace of historical studies of literacy has increased
dramatically since Roger Schofield lamented, in 1968, "Despite its relevance to many kinds of historical study, literacy does not feature very

[15] Peter Flora, "Historical Processes of Social Mobilization: Urbanization and
Literacy, 1850–1965," in *Building Nations and States,* ed. S. N. Eisenstadt and Stein
Rokkan (Beverly Hills: Sage Publications, 1973), 213–258; see also, François Furet and
Jacques Ozouf, "Literacy and Industrialization: the case of the Départment du Nord
en France," *Journal of European Economic History,* 5 (1976), 5–44; Jack Goody, "Lit-
eracy and the Non-Literate in Ghana," in *The Future of Literacy,* 45; and Paulo
Freire, *Pedagogy of the Oppressed* (New York: Herder and Herder, 1970). For more
general critiques, see Dean C. Tipps, "Modernization Theory and the Comparative
Study of Societies: A Critical Perspective," *Comparative Studies in Society and History,*
15 (1973), 199–226; Manfred Stanley, "Social Development as a Normative Concept,"
Journal of Developing Areas, 1 (1967), 301–316; and Robert Nisbet, *History and Social
Change* (New York: Oxford University Press, 1969).

often in historical discussion, and when it does appear, a certain vague-ness surrounds its meaning." [16] Only in the past decade have systematic studies of historical literacy been seriously initiated. This development derives in part from a recognition of the role of primary education and lit-eracy in society; that is, the factors that influence their growth, stagnation, or decay and the ways in which changing levels of literacy and education affect social change. Lawrence Stone has sketched most forcefully the relations between schooling and the influences on it. In a seminal essay, Stone identified several factors that determine the social structure of education and educational opportunities: patterns of social stratification, job opportunities, religion, theories of social control, demographic and family patterns, economic organization and resources, and political theory and institutions. General as his discussion was, it stimulated in-terest in and research on a largely neglected problem.[17] Contemporary social research provided another impetus as historians now attempt to apply or test social theories with the evidence of historical development. A third source is the fortuitous byproduct of the recent tendencies of social historians to examine large bodies of routinely generated records, which in some cases include measures of literacy.

Literacy, despite its place in legacy and thought, was almost totally ignored in traditional historical writing. A search through histories of education or social histories is seldom rewarded by a passing reference to it.[18] The topic appeared, nonetheless, in a few works. These may be grouped into three categories, interesting in themselves: studies of elites or special groups, studies in which literacy levels are deduced indirectly rather than measured, and, ironically of more value than either of the preceding, studies in which literacy remains peripheral to the main themes.

Our first category includes much of the oldest work on the subject and has included studies of medieval English kings, early Methodist preachers, upper-middle-class and aristocratic library subscribers, the laity in the Middle Ages, and individual markers, whose stylized marks do

---

[16] "The Measurement of Literacy in Pre-Industrial England," in *Literacy in Tra-ditional Societies,* ed. Jack Goody (Cambridge: Cambridge University Press, 1968), 312. For a detailed discussion, see my *Literacy in History: An Interdisciplinary Research Bibliography* (Chicago: Newberry Library, 1976; second edition, 1979).

[17] "Literacy and Education in England, 1640–1900," *Past and Present,* 42 (1969), 69–139.

[18] There are welcome exceptions which are signs of change, for example Lawrence Cremin's *American Education: The Colonial Experience* (New York: Harper and Row, 1970) and some very recent surveys; they are few and far between however. Cremin, for example, typically perpetuates the myth.

not signify an inability to write or read.[19] These studies' limits need not be elaborated, for tests of literacy for such samples need not be direct and generalization is almost totally prohibited. Before the 1950s, they represented the historical study of literacy.[20] Private surveys of the nineteenth century and government statistics were seldom noted, although contemporary writers made use of them.

The next generation of researchers matured in the 1950s. Their conceptualization of literacy was still vague; evidence was primarily literary or anecdotal but research was conducted on a wide, if ill-defined, front. Contemporary comments were taken, regardless of context, as indicators of the extent of literacy, without reference to age, sex, status, or residence.[21] More importantly, these students cited the volume and types of current publications, and deduced from any increase in their numbers a sign of growth in rates of literacy. In some cases such a judgment may be warranted—although not, as is commonly argued, for mid-eighteenth- to early nineteenth-century England. There are in fact grave difficulties in the method and the assumptions behind it. There is no necessary relationship between the volume of production and size of audience. The number of readers per copy can not be assumed to stay constant. And changes in quantity are also influenced by factors other than rates of literacy: technological changes in printing, printers' legal status, distribution systems, and size of editions, as well as modifications in governmental fiscal policy, such as the imposition of stamp duties on periodicals.

This generation also associated the institutional history of schooling with literacy levels. Growth in facilities, regardless of kind or quality was equated, invalidly, with dramatic increases in readers. A knowledge

---

[19] For each group, I will provide several examples only; my *Literacy in History* includes more complete listings. V. H. Galbraith, "The Literacy of the Medieval English Kings," *Proceedings of the British Academy*, 21 (1935), 201–238; Paul Kaufman, *Libraries and Their Users* (London: Library Association, 1969); J. W. Thompson, *The Literacy of the Laity in the Middle Ages* (Berkeley: University of California Press, 1939).

[20] The work of J. W. Adamson in English history is an exception to these generalizations, for he has drawn on widely scattered sources to discuss *The Illiterate Anglo-Saxon* (Cambridge: Cambridge University Press, 1946).

[21] See, as prime examples, R. D. Altick, *The English Common Reader* (Chicago: University of Chicago Press, 1957); Victor E. Neuberg, *Popular Education in Eighteenth Century England* (London: Woburn Press, 1971); John McLeish, *Evangelical Religion and Popular Education* (London: Methuen, 1969): Ålvar Ellegard, "The Readership of the Periodical Press in Mid-Victorian Britain," *Gotesborgs Universities Årsskrift*, 63 (Goteborg, 1957).

of such matters is certainly valuable for an understanding of the nature of the transmission of reading, writing, and other learning, but it fails to supply reliable estimates of the level of development of the skills attained. Rates and regularity of attendance were rarely examined or questioned, nor was the quality or effectiveness (of "dame" schools, for example) or the purposes of instruction (in, for example, Sunday Schools). Informal instruction was ignored, whether in the home, the church, the village, or on the streets, even though we do not know the significance of these modes of instruction.

The greatest advance made by this generation of researchers was the study of surveys produced by government investigations, and educational and statistical societies, in the nineteenth century. Robert Webb has made the best use of this material in his studies of the English and Scottish working class. But such evidence remains of restricted value because of its definitional vagueness, problems of its comparability, and the lack of systematic collection procedures when it was gathered. Nonetheless, direct evidence was examined, largely for the first time, the examination constituting an important contribution.[22]

The inclusion of literacy as a topic peripheral to another subject makes for a third category of studies. This research has gone on simultaneously with the others, but more recently it has reflected the renewal of interest in direct studies of literacy. Importantly, much of this work focuses on working class history (much of it English), although demographic history increasingly places literacy among its variables. This tendency dates from the studies of the Hammonds in the early twentieth century, and has included those of E. P. Thompson, E. J. Hobsbawm, Edward Shorter, Stephan Thernstrom, Charles Tilly, Sune Åkerman, and Maris Vinovskis, among many others. Literacy has been treated anecdotally, descriptively, and analytically, and important contributions have been made to the study of it. These studies inform direct inquiries of literacy and also aid in posing questions and forming hypotheses. The relationship of literacy to migration, mobility, vital rates, social structure, collective activities, and communications, for example, has been highlighted. A wide variety of sources have been exploited by these studies: aggregate and published data as well as more isolated information.

This summary marks the state of the history of literacy until the

[22] Webb, "Working Class Readers in Early Victorian England," *English Historical Review*, 65 (1950), 331–351, "Literacy among the Working Class in Nineteenth Century Scotland," *Scottish Historical Review*, 32 (1954), 100–114; M. Fleury and P. Valmary, "Le progrès de l'instruction élémentaire de Louis XIV à Napoléon III," *Population*, 12 (1957), 71–92.

mid-1960s. Research begun in the past decade, much of it unpublished to date, treats literacy as the central topic for analysis (work in the third category has proliferated, too); these studies are principally in the area of systematic and quantified social history. Drawing its impetus from important trends in current historiography, this development derives from the renaissance of educational history, the use of social science techniques and the computer, the critical appraisal of social theory with retrospective data, and a willingness to confront large bodies of historical materials which contain measures of literacy.[23]

Especially striking is the wide variety of sources tapped by students of literacy (see Appendix A). Illustrating a characteristic of a developing field of research, this makes for both a challenge and a central problem, for the comparability of results from records with differing measures of literacy is a matter that has yet to be resolved satisfactorily or systematically. For example, it is unclear how the ability to place a signature, the most common historical indicator of the presence of literacy, compares with reading abilities, how different levels of reading and comprehension compare with signing, or how responses to census-type questions compare with it. Consequently, most studies of literacy are forced to treat reading and writing as a dichotomous attribute: either one had both abilities or one had neither. Usually, this means that the significance of differing literacy abilities is ignored, although an attempt is made in Chapter 7 to deal with this issue. Nonetheless, problems remain, including that of joining different measures for sets of individuals in order to provide a full analysis and a more complete test of these records' reliability. Definitions of literacy are problematic, for the past as the present, although historians show great sensitivity to the issues.[24]

This is not the place for a full assessment of these first studies. What has been achieved thus far lies, for the most part, on a descriptive plane, as a skeletal view of literacy's course over time and space is being delineated and fleshed out. Regional, sexual, and occupational variations are isolated, as are the effects of events, such as the French Revolution, or processes, such as the Industrial Revolution. Research in this mode has commenced in a small number of areas, principally literacy in

[23] See also my "The 'New Math': Quantification, the 'New' History, and the History of Education," *Urban Education,* 11 (1977), 403–440.

[24] See, however, Schofield, "The Measurement of Literacy"; Lockridge, *Literacy in Colonial New England;* my "Notes for Studying Literacy from the Manuscript Census," *Historical Methods Newsletter,* 5 (1971), 11–16, "What the 1861 Census can tell us about Literacy," *Histoire Sociale,* 8 (1975), 337–349, summarized in Appendix B.

England,[25] France,[26] Sweden,[27] the United States,[28] and Canada.[29] Concentrating on the period from the seventeenth to the nineteenth century, this work draws on available sources and seeks to illuminate the modern rise of literacy—"the literacy transition," as it has been called. The beginning of the course of literacy's dissemination among various social groups in these places is now outlined. Present and future efforts aim to complete the time series, to expand the coverage, and to attempt explanation for these changes and their significance.

Important findings have resulted from this as yet early research. In addition to the establishment of time series and group differentials,

[25] Stone, "Literacy and Education"; Schofield, "Dimensions of Illiteracy, 1750–1850," *Explorations in Economic History*, 10 (1973), 437–454; Michael Sanderson, "Literacy and Social Mobility in the Industrial Revolution in England," *Past and Present*, 56 (1972), 75–104; V. A. Hatley, "Literacy at Northampton, 1761–1900," *Northampton Past and Present*, 4 (1966), 379–381; W. P. Baker, *Parish Registers and Illiteracy in East Yorkshire* (York, 1961); D. A. Cressy, "Education and Literacy in London and East Anglia, 1580–1700," unpublished Ph.D. Dissertation, University of Cambridge, 1972, "Literacy in pre-industrial England," *Societas*, 4 (1974), 229–240, "Levels of Literacy in England, 1530–1730," *Historical Journal*, 20 (1977), 1–23, "Literacy in Seventeenth-Century England," *Journal of Interdisciplinary History*, 8 (1977), 141–150; Richard T. Vann, "Literacy in Seventeenth Century England: Some Hearth-Tax Evidence," *Journal of Interdisciplinary History*, 5 (1974), 287–293; various notes in *Local Population Studies*; T. W. Laqueur, "The Cultural Origins of Popular Literacy in England, 1500–1800," *Oxford Review of Education*, 2 (1976), 255–275.

[26] François Furet and Jacques Ozouf, *Lire et Écrire* (Paris: Les éditions de Minuit, 1977), summarizes earlier studies; Michel Demonet, Paul Dumont, and Emmanuel le Roy Laduire, "Analyse factorielle des recènsements militaires de 1819–1830," *Historical Methods Newsletter*, 7 (1974), 147–160; the work of Jean Meyer, Michel Vovelle, Alain Corbin, Michel Fournaux, Jacques Houdaille, etc.

[27] Egil Johansson, ed., *Literacy and Society in a Historical Perspective: A Conference Report* (Umeå, Sweden: Umeå University, 1973), *En Studie Med Kvantitativa Metoder av Folkundervisningen I Bygdeå Socken, 1845–1873* (Umeå: Umeå University, 1972), *The History of Literacy in Sweden* (Umeå: Department of Education, 1977).

[28] Lockridge, *Literacy in Colonial New England*, "L'alphabetisation en Amérique," *Annales; e,s,c*, 32 (1977), 503–518; Cremin, *American Education*; Alan Tully, "Literacy Levels and Educational Development in Rural Pennsylvania, 1729–1775," *Pennsylvania History*, 39 (1972), 301–312; Lee Soltow and Edward Stevens, "Economic Aspects of School Participation," *Journal of Interdisciplinary History*, 8 (1977), 221–244, and their forthcoming book.

[29] Graff, "What the 1861 Census," "Towards a Meaning of Literacy: Literacy and Social Structure in Hamilton, Ontario," *History of Education Quarterly*, 12 (1972), 411–431, "Literacy and Social Structure in Elgin County, Canada West, 1861," *Histoire sociale*, 6 (1973), 25–48, "Approaches in the Historical Study of Literacy," *Urban History Review*, 1 (1972), 6–11; the unpublished work of Lee Soltow.

conclusions stress the dynamic role of religion, especially Protestantism, in the spread of literacy, the significance of population concentration and distance from schools, and the role of social stratification and inequality. The French Revolution is sometimes seen as having been a stimulus to literacy, whereas the Industrial and urban revolutions are not. The assumed links between education, on the one hand, and industrialization, modernization, and urbanization, on the other, are questioned, but it is agreed that literacy does make economic contributions to the individual and society. Rates of fertility and mortality influence levels of literacy, and vice versa. Overall, variability marks the pace of literacy's growth both within and among nations throughout the west.

The importance of these beginnings is clear, their relevance to both historical analysis and social theory undoubted. However, research is far from complete, the implications of findings are not always precise and certain, and controversy rises rather than abates. Many agree that an important reevaluation has begun, yet we are far from new syntheses and reinterpretations: This is the intellectual context to which the present work seeks to contribute.

Concomitant with this research, moreover, has come the realization that the contexts of literacy, the needs for and uses of it, are far more interesting and important than the raw series of data on changes over time. Literacy requirements, we now understand, vary among different social and economic groups, regions, and communities. What is equally significant, we see that levels of literacy do not always relate to demands for them and that literacy can be in some cases nonfunctional. It is these differences in achieved literacy and the need for or use of literacy that historians must now explain. Thus, measures of literacy must be comparative; and a focus on individuals rather than on trends in gross rates best allows these questions to be confronted. The research conducted thus far represents only a beginning.

Peter Laslett states well what needs to be done: "The discovery of how great a proportion of the population could read and write at any one point in time is one of the most urgent of the tasks which face the historian of social structure, who is committed to the use of numerical methods. But the challenge is not simply to find the evidence and to devise ways of making it yield reliable answers. It is a challenge to the historical and literary imagination." [30] To meet the challenge, students must move beyond the numerical data, a prodigious task in itself. To consider any of the ways in which literacy intersects with social, political, economic, cultural, or psychological life (as it is held to do) requires

[30] *The World We Have Lost* (London: Methuen, 1971), 207.

excursions into other records. Aggregative statistics, for example, are useful,[31] and traditional historical sources offer opinion on the value attributed to literacy and on the uses to which it may be put. We note also the value of literary sources and the continuing usefulness of literary approaches, despite the complications noted above. Rather than debate the contribution of each approach, as Neuberg unfortunately does,[32] we are better served by a marriage of approaches, combining sources and methods toward a more complete analysis of literacy. To list the materials which would inform the questions is pointless, but their importance should be obvious. Quantitative materials yield only a certain return, no matter how cleverly they are exploited. The parameters of literacy's relationships are too broad, and questions of motivation, perception, institutions, and culture are not always amenable to numerical inquiry. The quality of individual literacy, finally, can be directly derived only from rare sources—for example, the Swedish catechetical examinations. In studying other societies this remains perhaps the most difficult problem.[33]

IV

In the chapters which follow, I offer the results of my own foray into aspects of literacy's past. The basis of my approach is quantitative, and is supplemented by a number of other sources; I have drawn upon a wide range of numerical materials in order to examine literacy's place in a variety of the spheres of social life. The time is the mid-nineteenth century; the focus is on the city; and the society is most often that of North America, with Ontario (called Upper Canada or Canada West in much of the period) as the empirical center. Comparative perspectives complement this concentration. Not only are these cities—Hamilton, London, and Kingston—typical examples of nineteenth-century urban development, but excellent literacy data for their residents have survived as well.

Part One focuses upon these cities and their populations; it presents a systematic exposition of the place of illiterate and literate adults and

[31] See, for example, Fleury and Valmary, "Le progrès"; Cipolla, *Literacy and Development*.

[32] Neuberg, *Popular Education*, 96–98.

[33] The brilliant essay by Daniel Calhoun, *The Intelligence of a People* (Princeton: Princeton University Press, 1973), however, shows how a wide variety of materials can be employed to provide some statements about the quality of literacy.

their families. Literacy's social correlates—its significance for social placement and stratification and its relationship to other structural factors—
integrate the analysis.

Hamilton, Kingston, and London were relatively small commercial
cities, in many ways typical of nineteenth-century patterns of growth
and development. The population of each was growing, although Kingston, the oldest, declined in relative importance throughout the century,
mainly as a result of its geographic position between the metropoles of
Toronto and Montreal and its failure to gain the capital and adminis-
trative functions of Upper Canada. Each city was an immigrant reception
center; most adult residents were born in the British Isles. London, the
farthest west and the youngest, had the most mixed population: the fewest
Irish and the most United States-born. Commercially based, each city
was to a large extent a market center, dependent on an agricultural
hinterland. This was most important to the local economy of London.
Hamilton, however, was the most economically advanced in commerce,
trade, finance, and protoindustrialization. It was also the largest, as it
would remain; and it was the first to industrialize, in the 1870s and
1880s. All three cities, moreover, were important transshipment centers:
Hamilton and Kingston were ports, on Lake Ontario and the St. Lawrence River, respectively, and London became the center of the shipping
and commerce in southwestern Ontario. Hamilton and London advanced
with the coming of the railway in the 1850s and 1860s, both prospering
throughout the sixties, as Kingston continued its decline in economic
importance and remained relatively stagnant. Nevertheless the same
forces shaped each city—working in differing circumstances and degrees,
of course—but the three cities provide a valid basis for comparative
studies of literacy.

Part Two expands the focus, taking up selected problems related
to the social roles of literacy: crime, work, and the quality of literacy.
Important matters to contemporaries, these topics merit critical reexamination. These topics of course do not compose an exhaustive list of
matters of importance.

The argument elaborated in these chapters takes a critical stance.
I will challenge the usual historical interpretations of literacy and illiteracy and raise questions about normative social theory and social
thought regarding literacy, popular education, and the literacy myth.
In so doing, I will urge that literacy, in the past and, by implication,
in the present, can not be understood until new perspectives are developed and outmoded conceptualizations rejected. The data and their
interpretation allow of no other consistent conclusion.

My emphasis in these inquiries centers on neither the rates of literacy, their changes over time, nor on regional variations, although these are all discussed. The focus, instead, is on individual men and women in society and the meanings of literacy to them. The study of literacy, I urge, is important not only in and for itself; it also illuminates the dynamics of society and provides penetrating insights into how its processes functioned—for example, in stratification, in mobility, or in family adjustment. Literacy study therefore constitutes a valuable mode of analysis for students of society. Moreover, it forms one way of confronting directly the literacy myth, the value assigned to literacy, and its place in social theory. It enables us to examine critically the legacy of literacy's centrality in social and economic life and its relationship with institutional responses such as the public school, productivity, criminality, and the like. The findings, we will see, contradict much of our received wisdom and expectations, with respect to social ascription and its relationship to achievement, mobility, economic development, social order, and broader cultural themes.

Literacy did carry certain benefits to those who possessed it, although its possession often signified attributes other than the abilities of reading and writing. The social and cultural hegemonic functions of schooling were closely tied to the carefully designed transmission of literacy and to the transformation of society. Literacy was both act and symbol; it was neither neutral, unambiguous, nor radically advantageous or liberating. Its value, in fact, depended heavily on other factors, from ascribed social characteristics such as ethnicity, sex, or race, to the institutional, social, economic, and cultural contexts in which it was manifest. The role of literacy in the life of individual and society is contradictory and complex.

The society examined here is a literate society, with rates of literacy in excess of 90%, but literacy—a phenomenon suggestive of equality—contributed regularly as an element of the structure of inequality, reinforcing the steep ridges of stratification, and also as a force for order and integration. It also served as a symbolic focus of other forces of inequality: ethnicity, class, sex, and age. Literacy, then, did not universally serve to benefit all who had attained it, but neither did it disadvantage all those who had not. Tensions and discontinuities of social contradictions emanated from the varied demands for and uses of literacy, its unequal social distribution, and the divergent realities which accompanied its roles. Perceptions, and expectations, could differ greatly from those realities, and they differed among the classes and cultures within the society as well. These contradictions need to be confronted, their relative contribution to literacy's myth and reality evaluated.

1

The Moral Bases of Literacy:
Society, Economy,
and Social Order

Morality is worthy of the attention of the economist.

J. P. KAY
*The Moral and Physical Condition of the Working
Classes Employed in the Cotton Manufacture
in Manchester (1832)*

In general terms, literacy opens up innumerable possibilities in the way of individualized response in the intellectual, moral, spiritual, and political spheres. But in the concrete case, the institution which provides literacy training at the same time exercises a determining influence by narrowing the range of choices and possibilities open to the subject.

JOHN MCLEISH
Evangelical Religion and Popular Education (1969)

The case of literacy is more complex. The ability to read and usually (though not always) to write was, of course, an aim of all nineteenth-century educators. Yet it is important to stress that literacy . . . was embedded in all kinds of other aims which predominated in the minds of providers.

RICHARD JOHNSON
*"Notes on the Schooling of the English
Working Class, 1780–1850" (1976)*

I

By the end of the first third of the nineteenth century, opposition to the universal institutional schooling of the masses had largely vanished in Anglo-America and in much of western Europe. Though the nature of the opposition had differed from place to place, from Great Britain to the Canadian provinces and the American republic, the educational solutions reached early in the century were similar in goals and content, if not always in structural forms. Changes in social context, involving the transformation of economic and social relations, joined with new modes of social response to promote new roles for education, and a new place for literacy within them. Now, largely gone were traditional elite attitudes, stressing fears of an educated poor and laboring class, discontented with its traditional position of deference. Rather, the masses should be schooled properly.[1] Mockery and caricature now became the common responses to notions that "it should be deemed an offense to teach the child of an English laborer to write his own name," or that "boys or girls, designed for domestic service, ought not to have the powers of reading their masters' or mistresses' letters if founding about." [2]

The new consensus, and its institutional forms, stressed schooling for social stability ·and the assertion of appropriate hegemonic functions; these dominated the goals of educational reformers and their supporters throughout Anglo-America. This view emphasized aggregate social goals—the reduction of crime and disorder, the instillation of proper moral values and codes of conduct, and, to a more limited extent, increased economic productivity—rather than the more individualistic ends of intellectual development and personal advancement.[3] Dominat-

---

[1] On such attitudes, see Victor E. Neuberg, *Popular Education in Eighteenth Century England* (London: Woburn Press, 1971), Chapter One. Of course, this applied to the white masses and not to those like slaves in the American south. For important elements of continuity and discontinuity, see David Cressy, "Educational Opportunity in Tudor and Stuart England," *History of Education Quarterly,* 16 (1977), 301–320; Gerald Strauss, *Luther's House of Learning* (Baltimore: Johns Hopkins University Press, 1978).

[2] Central Society of Education, *Papers* (London, 1837–1839; reprinted New York: Kelly, 1969), 1838, 356.

[3] See Carl F. Kaestle, "Between the Scylla of Brutal Ignorance and the Charybdis of a Literary Education: Elite Attitudes toward Mass Schooling in Early Industrial England and America," in *Schooling and Society,* ed. Lawrence Stone (Baltimore: Johns Hopkins University Press, 1976), 177–191; Rush Welter, ed., *American Writings on Popular Education in the Nineteenth Century* (Indianapolis: Bobbs-Merrill, 1971), Introduction; J. F. C. Harrison, "Education in Victorian England," *History of Education Quarterly,* 10 (1970), 485–491, reviewing contemporary writings.

ing the rhetoric promoting the creation of systems of mass schooling, these goals represented the primary motives for the controlled training of children (and sometimes of adults) in literacy. The central questions became: Why (and how) should the population be´ provided with literacy? What uses will these skills serve to individual and society? What place does literacy have in the promotion of schooling? To borrow a phrase from Richard Hoggart, we ask, What were the "uses of literacy"?[4]

An answer, which this chapter addresses, lies in the confluence of morality, derivative of nondenominational Protestantism, with social change and the need for control.[5] Of the panoply of reasons offered by school promoters in this period, the inculcation of morality was supreme; this represented one issue on which virtually all agreed. Literacy, the medium for training, consequently was rarely seen as an end in itself. More often, its possession or absence was assumed to represent either a symbol or a symptom of the progress in moral training or an index of what remained to be accomplished through the creation of educational systems embracing all the children of the community. Schooling in literacy was useful for the efficient training of the masses to the social order and the reassertion of hegemony; its provision ideally signified that the process was underway. Literacy alone, however,—that is, isolated from its moral basis—was feared as potentially subversive. Rather, the literacy of properly schooled, *morally restrained* men and women represented the object of the school promoters. As Susan Houston summarizes, "The campaign against ignorance (and the mandate of the school system) encompassed more than reading; illiteracy was deplored, but more as a visible sign of that other ignorance that was the root of personal and social deviance," [6] and a threat to the emerging capitalist order.

An emphasis on the controlled provision and use of literacy was not novel to these spokesmen for institutionalized schooling who rushed to build systems. Efforts with similar purposes predated their own, the source of which was sectarian: religious groups who agreed on the need to morally uplift the poor and working classes and competed for their souls. Religion, and in particular a reforming Protestantism, was the dynamic force in those few societies that achieved near-universal adult

---

4 Richard Hoggart, *The Uses of Literacy* (Boston: Beacon Press, 1961).

5 See Alison Prentice, "The School Promoters: Education and Social Class in Mid-Nineteenth Century Upper Canada," unpublished Ph.D. Dissertation, University of Toronto, 1974 (published as *The School Promoters* [Toronto: McClelland and Stewart, 1977]); see also David Tyack, "The Kingdom of God and the Common School," *Harvard Educational Review*, 36 (1966), 447–460; John McLeish, *Evangelical Religion and Popular Education* (London: Methuen, 1969).

6 "The Victorian Origins of Juvenile Delinquency: A Canadian Experience," *History of Education Quarterly*, 12 (1972), 259.

literacy before the nineteenth century. "In all this world," concludes Lockridge, "the only areas to show a rapid rise in literacy to levels approaching universality were small societies whose intense Protestantism led them to offer to compel in some way the education of their people. . . . The motive force behind this action was the common Protestant impulse to bring all men the Word of God . . . [along with] the conservation of Piety. . . ." Reading the Bible was the vehicle for this impulse, for religious indoctrination derived from the moral message of this print. This was not so much an intellectual or a liberating action as it was a ritualistic one. The level of literacy, in fact, could be quite low: a proper understanding of the words was not in itself essential. Literacy, however nominal, signified in theory the observance of an ordained and approved social code.[7]

By the mid-nineteenth century, diverse educational promoters and religious groups, among others concerned with schooling, agreed in their motives for literacy training; their goals were institutionalized in developing systems for mass education, regardless of sponsorship. Schoolmen, while proclaiming that education should be nonsectarian, continued to stress Christian ethics and moral training as central to schooling.[8] The increasing secularization, and indeed the subtle transformation, of morality can only be understood in the context of the larger changes occurring at this time.

The views accorded the place of literacy in schooling and society may be usefully characterized as the moral bases of literacy. The concept of moral bases both relates to and represents a crucial shift in and development from a traditional moral economy, as is explicated best by E. P. Thompson. To Thompson, the moral economy was "grounded upon a consistent traditional view of social norms and obligations of the proper economic functions of several parties within the community, which taken together, can be said to constitute the moral economy." In his usage, this was largely the view of the poor and the crowd in eighteenth-century England. He found it possible to locate in every crowd action a legitimizing notion, such that those involved held the belief that they acted in defense of traditional rights and customs and, in so doing, were supported by a wider popular consensus.[9]

Economy, in the usage employed here, involves at once the rules that

----

[7] Kenneth A. Lockridge, *Literacy in Colonial New England* (New York: Norton, 1974), 99–101; Richard Altick, *The English Common Reader* (Chicago: University of Chicago Press, 1957).

[8] J. M. Goldstrum, *The Social Context of Education, 1808–1870* (Shannon: Irish Universities Press, 1972).

[9] *Past and Present*, 50 (1971), 79, 78.

govern or control a person's mode of living or regimen and the administration of the resources of a community or larger unit with a view to orderly conduct and productiveness. Moral economy, thus, is analogous to but not synonymous with political economy, which the *Oxford English Dictionary* defines thus: "Originally the art or practical science of managing the resources of a nation so as to increase its material prosperity." As a political economy replaced a moral economy, morality continued to comprise the core or base of this management, with its regulation and reforming orientation, although the context and the means of management changed. A religious frame of reference naturally informed the uses of the concept and its terminology, for morality of course derived from Christian ethics. Nonetheless, an emphasis on the purely theological or narrowly sectarian aspects of morality restricts appropriate conceptualization and can trivialize the meaning. Morality, we note, represented a mode of conduct and a way of life: habits, values, attitudes, which were based by this time on the cultural necessities of progress and the requirements of society.[10] Political economy did not supplant morality as a valued instrument toward social organization.

The moral bases of literacy accompanied the shift from a *moral* economy to a *political* economy in the late eighteenth and early nineteenth centuries, developing in response to a sweeping societal transformation and efforts to comprehend and interpret those changes. Literacy, we will see, was expected to contribute vitally to the reordering and reintegration of the "new" society of the nineteenth century; it represented one central instrument and vehicle in the efforts to secure social, cultural, economic, and political cohesion in the political economy of the expanding capitalist order. As J. P. Kay reminds us, "Morality is worthy of the attention of the economist"; indeed, popular behavior and the presumed needs for social learning attracted the attention of many concerned individuals, including those dedicated to the reform of society and the reformation of the masses comprising that society. In their many activities which sought to reestablish integration and recreate social order, they developed a conception of a literacy rooted in morality and of literacy as an instrument of social stability in a time of change, facilitating both progress and development without threat of disorder. As the political economy replaced the moral economy, the moral bases of literacy evolved. A "moral economy" of literacy itself was articulated; it lay behind new educational innovations and mass schooling as it expressed the dominant social assumptions of the controlling

10 See Richard Johnson, "Educating the Educators: 'Experts' and the State, 1833–9," in *Social Control in Nineteenth Century Britain,* ed. A. P. Donajgradzki (London: Croom Helm, 1977), 90–91.

interests and integrated their efforts at maintaining order and control. Consequently, literacy could not be promoted or comprehended in isolation from morality.

Moral economy, which in the presuppositions of the mid-nineteenth century underlay the foundations of social order, government, economy, and preparation for work, involved the management of the masses, their adaptation to the requirements of the new order. As education increasingly became a dominant tool for social stability and hegemony, morality formed the basis for tutelage in literacy. Instruction was properly to teach and inculcate the rules for social and economic behavior in a changing and modernizing society; and literacy became a crucial vehicle for that process. Morality and literacy were intertwined and they were to be taught together: literacy speeding and easing moral instruction, morality guiding and restraining the potentially dangerous uses of literacy.

Indeed, the transformation of society required more than ever before the use of literacy to aid in instruction and integration. With the breakdown of traditional patterns of deference, in the face of capitalism's social transformations, the inculcation of morality and its behavioral attributes without literacy was increasingly seen as impossible. Education now substituted for paternalism as a source of order, cohesion, and hegemony in a society stratified by social class rather than by rank. Traditional desires and needs for control and assimilation had to be maintained but the form of the emerging social order demanded that the agencies and their functions be different. The need arose for the creation of institutions, like the school, to provide carefully structured, morally based tutoring in literacy. A unified attitude toward the place of schooling in society developed, and moral values formed its core with literacy its vehicle.

The moral bases of the political economy and of literacy embraced by school promoters and their supporters differed from that of the eighteenth century. Their morality was not that of the poor, but rather was one of the middle class and a new economic order that the poor and the working class were to be taught to share. To educational spokesmen, it represented a central legitimizing notion in the rhetoric of common school promotion, one which they felt was widely embraced. Yet, in their recognition of social changes, their realization that traditional rights and customs were being transformed, and their ambivalence and anxiety about these changes, the values they made central were not strictly traditional. While their concepts were grounded on a consistent view of social norms and obligations, their goals of harmony and order had shifted from traditional rural ideals. What they sought was the reestablishment of stable patterns of social and economic relations in a new and different society.

Moreover, the promoters of education were hardly naive about the possibility or the usefulness of restoring the social order of the past. Men like Egerton Ryerson, the first Chief Superintendent of Education for Upper Canada, were well aware of the transitional state of their society; they feared that rampant commercialism, materialism, and urbanism carried the seeds of the destruction of their civilization. Nevertheless, the same men also sought social and economic change and development, never quite grasping that these ideals of progress were intimately connected to the social disorder they feared. They did realize, however, that urgent measures were required to elevate the minds and morals of the populace. Formal education, through the structured provision of literacy, was intended to elevate and assimilate the population and insure peace, prosperity, and social cohesion. An efficient and necessary substitute for deference, education would produce discipline and aid in the inculcation of the values required for an urban and industrial society. Here the moral economy was central, and morality and restraint were essential to proper education. As Alison Prentice aptly put it, "secular learning without [morality] was like a 'steam engine without its safety valve.' " [11]

Changing modes for training in social morality and restraint, and with them a new role for education, were responses to complex social and economic changes rooted in the transition from a pre-industrial to a mercantile and, later, an industrial capitalist order. Michael Katz states the connection:

> The most characteristic and important feature of capitalism for the development of institutions, including public school systems, was its utilization of wage-labor and the consequent need for a mobile, unbound labor force. The shift in the nature of social organization consequent upon the emergence of a class of wage-laborers, rather than industrialization or urbanization, fueled the development of public institutions.

[11] See, for example, Ryerson, "Report on a System of Public Elementary Instruction for Canada," in *Documentary History of Education in Upper Canada (DHE)*, ed. J. George Hodgkins, 6 (Toronto, 1899); Prentice, "School Promoters," Chaps. 2, 6; quote from 200. (I will cite only the more complete, dissertation edition of this important work.)

As Charles Tilly has observed, interpretive schemes which pit morality against secular learning are versions of Durkheim's classic theories of social integration and disintegration. These clear expressions of nineteenth-century thought are still with us, as Samuel P. Huntington's *Political Order in Changing Societies* (Princeton: Princeton University Press, 1968), among others, illustrates. On this and related points, see Tilly, *From Mobilization to Revolution* (Reading, Mass.: Addison-Wesley, 1978). Ch. 2.

In much of the western world, and especially in Anglo-America, a new context for social life and social relations was forming; the role of schooling and literacy can be appreciated only in this context. New requirements and new demands resulted, to which institutions responded. These included the need to meet the perceived threats from crime, disorder, and poverty; the need to counteract cultural diversity; the need to prepare and discipline a work force; and the need to replace traditional popular culture with new values and habits. These problems, especially that of disciplining the work force and that of countering crime, disorder, and cultural heterogeneity, interacted with one another to heighten the need for action and to hasten the pace of institutional response. This sequence may be located throughout the Anglo-American world.[12]

Culturally, customary routines and rhythms had to be replaced by the punctuality, regularity, docility, and orderliness required by the new society. Socially, the place of traditional expectations of inheritance of position was preempted by a promise implicit in education: the triumph of achievement over ascription, or at least the need for individual attainments. Despite this new ideal, neither specific occupational skills nor cognitive traits were stressed; these remained less critical than character, behavior, habits, or attitudes in the moral economic formulations. Literacy's role in this process was complex, for the way in which it was to be acquired and the setting for instruction were obviously crucial. Both method and structure were elements in the inculcation of morality, in education's creation of proper restraint and modes of conduct. These processes, and literacy's place within them, were those of control and hegemony, as social relations and work patterns were reformed in accord with other transformations. The theorist of hegemony, Antonio Gramsci, aptly summarized the process in discussing education: "Its aim is always that of creating new and higher types of civilisation; of adapting the 'civilisation' and the morality of the broadest popular masses to the necessities of the continuous development of the economic apparatus of production; hence of evolving even physically new types of humanity." [13]

Schooling therefore, in its institutional role, held out an obvious attraction to many. A traditional force in society, especially in its moral orientation, education could be remolded and redirected to serve its new

[12] "The Origins of Public Education: A Reassessment," *History of Education Quarterly*, 16 (1976), 391, see also 381–408; Johnson, "Notes on the Schooling of the English working class, 1780–1850," in *Schooling and Capitalism: A Sociological Reader*, ed. Roger Dale, Geoff Esland, and Madeleine MacDonald (London: Routledge and Kegan Paul, 1976), 44–54.

[13] *Selections from the Prison Notebooks of Antonio Gramsci*, ed. and tr. Quentin Hoare and Geoffrey Nowell Smith (London: NLB, 1971), 242; see also Johnson, "Notes"; Katz, "The Origins"; Johnson, "Educating."

social roles, not the least of which was the resurrection of restraint and control in times of rapid and disruptive social change—for stability and cohesion, and now for progress. The language of morality reveals a continuity of concern for hegemony and control—albeit in new forms and for new goals—and an emphasis in social thought and perception on the moral failings of individuals and classes as sources of society's severe problems. Despite resistance and conflict, efforts to reimpose control in these ways were swiftly established, succeeding in embracing the great mass of children and in providing them with some measure of schooling. And here, literacy had an important function to serve.

II

Popular education, as Richard Johnson has stressed, formed "one of the strongest of early Victorian obsessions"; this was equally true for Upper Canadians. Particularly striking in the educational development of Upper Canada is the speed and ease with which the school system was established (nor was this exceptional). This transformation, as Gidney illustrates, "was due, rather, to the growth during the 1830s and early forties of a consensus among public men about the importance of mass education to society—to the growing conviction that it was in the national interest to ensure that all children received some schooling." This conviction saw Upper Canadians closely following developments in both the mother country and the American republic, and resulted in conservatives, radicals, reformers, as well as diverse clergymen, in remarkably similar arguments, depicting education as promoting loyalty and order, good government, contented labor, and national progress. Sharing the values of the moral bases of literacy, they believed that "intellectual improvement was more than a source of material prosperity, it was also a powerful moral agent." [14] Education divorced from morality was not education; morality divorced from education was not morality—the morality required for hegemony in a time of change.

Egerton Ryerson, the province's educational chief, addressed this broadly held conviction and enunciated this moral basis in his "Report

[14] "Educational Policy and Social Control in Early Victorian England," *Past and Present,* 49 (1970), 96; "Upper Canadian Public Opinion and Common School Improvement in the 1830's," *Histoire sociale,* 5 (1972), 48–56, "Elementary Education in Upper Canada: A Reassessment," *Ontario History,* 65 (1973), 169–185; Susan Houston, "Politics, Schools and Social Change in Upper Canada," *Canadian Historical Review,* 52 (1972), 249–271.

on a System of Elementary Education for Upper Canada," of 1846. He commenced by defining education, as "not the mere acquisition of certain arts, or of certain branches of knowledge, but that instruction and discipline which qualify and dispose the subjects of it for their appropriate duties and enjoyments of life, as Christians, as persons of business and also as members of the civil community in which they live." Three years later, he expanded on these notions, adding that by education he included all that is inculcated and acquired: principles, habits, character, in the apprenticeship for life and for eternity. Education, of which literacy was the medium, comprised Christian duties, character and habit formation, and discipline. Morality was at the core of education, as Ryerson never failed to repeat throughout the two and one-half decades of his tenure as Chief Superintendent and principal architect of the school system. He, in his representative opinion, simply did not regard any instruction or attainment as education that did not include Christianity and morality. "High intellectual and physical accomplishments may be associated with deep moral and public debasement," he argued. Rather, "It is the cultivation and exercise of man's moral powers and feelings which forms the basis of social order and the vital fluid of social happiness." [15] This indeed was common schooling—moral, Christian, and nondenominational—that pivoted on the moral bases of literacy.

Moral education of course was not the only education these school promoters provided. Man, they knew, was a physical, an intellectual, and a moral being. The physical side, a source of consternation and even fear, was to be curbed; the inculcation of moral restraint was required. Other dimensions of human development, however, were more central to the social goals of mid-century educators, receiving far more attention and a greater expenditure of energy. Consider intellectual development. Intellectual progress without moral development was simply not proper education; mental as well as moral training contributed to social order, and these two kinds of training should reinforce each other. Intellectual development, moreover, related to literacy, but not necessarily to individual advancement or to job preparation. As Ryerson saw it, a mechanic, for example, "will be a member of society; and as such, he should know how to read the language spoken by such society. . . ." Why reading? To be acquainted with ordinary topics of social intercourse. And why writing? Writing, which should be correct and intelligible, was "the vehicle of his thoughts, the instrument of all his intercourse

[15] Ryerson, "Report", 142; "Canadian Mechanics and Manufacturers," *Journal of Education for Upper Canada (J.E.),* 2 (1849), 19; "The Importance of Education to an Agricultural People," *DHE,* 7, 148.

with his fellow men and with the histories of other nations and of the past ages." [16] Noble goals, undoubtedly; useful skills—that is open to question.

Literacy's benefits were primarily social and integrating, and only rarely connected with job pursuits. Nonetheless, literacy could be essential, for the promise of the school had to be conveyed: "Every man, unless he wishes to starve outright, must read and write, and cast accounts, and speak his native tongue well enough to attend to his own particular business." These were ominous tones, but the implications of these needs were nowhere elaborated: did the individual benefits from the everyday uses of literacy make the worker more skilled, more knowledgable about his work? Yes, but only partly so; educated labor, it was claimed, was more productive than uneducated labor. The educated mechanic was not disruptive; he was superior because he was orderly, punctual, and content.[17]

These moral functions of schooling intersected with work in another way, too. Schooling had the additional important task of assuring that manual workers did not aspire to rise above their station in life. Farmers or agricultural workers, for example, must be educated *not* to view their activities as narrow or regard them with contempt and disgust; they were not to be schooled so that they would want to leave their work, "in order to attain to a position of importance and influence." Education meant the cultivation of the workers (that is, if properly conducted) not the alienation of them from their positions. They were taught that labor did not deaden their mental faculties. Therefore, through the moral bases, "the proper education of the mechanic is important to the interests of society as well as to his own welfare and enjoyment." Social order, progress, and restraint were the goals of intellectual education, although the balance between the benefits to the individual and the benefits to society could seem ambiguous. Yet to consider the value of schooling to individuals in isolation from the value of it to society distorts the meaning of the educational purpose and confutes the goals of schooling. Ryerson considered this question, and his emphasis, the common one, was clear. "And if the intended mechanic should be trained to a mastery of his native tongue, he should, on still stronger grounds, be instructed in the nature of his social relations and duties. If he should be taught to speak correctly, he should be taught to act uprightly. He should be correct in his actions as well as in his words. He should surely be not less grounded in the principles of

[16] See Prentice, "School Promoters," Chap. 1; Chap. 5, below; Ryerson, "Canadian Mechanics and Manufacturers," 19.

[17] *J.E.,* 7 (1854), 134.

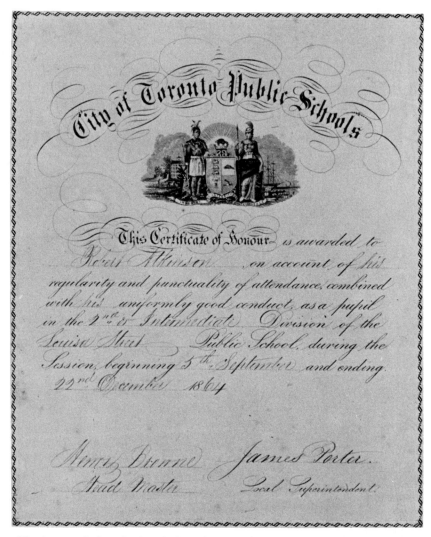

The lessons of the school and the values rewarded—regularity and punctuality of attendance, uniformly good conduct. *"Certificate of Honour,"* City of Toronto Public Schools, 1864: Robert Atkinson. [Records and Archives Centre, Toronto Board of Education]

honesty. . . ." [18] Here indeed are the intentions of schooling; here are the moral bases, and the results of control. Rather than literacy, knowledge, or skills, social morality (Ryerson's Christian virtues) formed the

[18] "The Importance of Education to an Agricultural People," 143; Prentice, "School Promoters," 160–167; *J.E.*, 3 (1850), 20, quoting the Port Hope *Watchman*.

proper basis of education, and of social and individual happiness. Literacy had its place, for if morally controlled, it was the most effective vehicle for the creation and maintenance of the moral economy and the moral society.

These virtues were not only central to education, they were an intrinsic part of orderly civilization. The inculcation of them was "to habituate our children from early life to the rules of order, and to teach men justice, sobriety, industry, truth and the fear of God. . . . Whatever, in the education and training of your children, goes to restrain and subdue bad passions, is so much gained on the score of civil liberty and social order." Assimilation to a new manner of conduct was the end sought by the school; and the processes included molding and elevating, breaking and taming, governing and ordering, and managing, calming, restraining—all so that the individual could "live according to the best rules." Representing what Ryerson often called education for the duties of life, these were not professional or occupational attainments.[19] They were rather the goals of the moral economy, the re-creation of hegemony through literacy and schooling.

Moral virtues influenced other actions too. Education supported the moral underpinning of democratic rights in a time of insecurity and social change; it also "unites the whole population in one common brotherhood by a community of interest and of brotherhood." The proper instillation of literacy insured these results, and though literacy alone did not guarantee the best use of these rights, the expected results of its teaching represented at once "the poor man's elevation and rich man's security." If free and universal schooling prevailed, the classes would be united; public education and public liberty would stand or fall together.[20] Children would attend the school, not through force or coercion, but as their free right; none would be stigmatized or isolated as either uneducated or educated through charity.

In the school, all children would be taught the "mutual relations and obligations" of the various classes, gaining mutual affections and "feelings of social oneness." The aim of common schooling, as many schoolmen noted, was the closing of the gap between the classes and the elimination of conflict (but not of inequality). Superintendent Henderson, of Kingston, put it nicely: "Education is to be the lever, that will not only show the deformity of vice, but that will elevate the social state

19 *J.E.*, 1 (1848), 49, 180; for the context, set in Ryerson's view of human nature, see Prentice, "School Promoters," Chap. 1; "Obligations of Educated Men," *J.E.*, 1 (1848), 161.

20 "The Importance of Education to a Manufacturing, and a Free People," *J.E.*, 1 (1848); Editorial, *J.E.*, 1 (1848), 151; "The Importance of Education."

of the poor—assimilating them in habits, thoughts, and feelings to the rich and the educated—giving them the same intellectual tastes and pleasures and embuing them with the same social sentiments and feelings." Community and oneness, the bases for cohesion and hegemony, would be well advanced in common and correct schooling. The classes— rich and poor alike—would share habits and values once more, respect one another, and the lower class would become respectable and self- respecting. Of course, neither the classes nor the social order need be disturbed; attitudes would change from those represented by exclusion and hostility to those represented by sharing and cooperation. In this way, the poor and the working class would be taught the values of the middle class: Christian love, social morality, respect for property, har- mony, and work discipline.[21] This was the practice of the moral bases, toward prosperity and communication in shared goals.

This was also the re-creation of cultural and ideological hegemony. Represented in the process of such schooling is Gramsci's conception of the circumstances in which assimilation and control develop: The con- sent of the masses arises in response to "the direction imposed on social life by the dominant fundamental group." Involving neither conscious choice, coercion, nor deliberate deception, predominance derives from consent, or "the spontaneous loyalty that any dominant social group ob- tains from the masses by virtue of its social and intellectual prestige and its supposedly superior function in the world of production." Hegemony, which was to obtain from correct and proper moral schooling, there- fore, represents the social order in which one way of life and pattern of behavior becomes dominant; in which one concept of reality is dif- fused throughout society in its institutional and private functions; and which informs tastes, morality, customs, religious and political prin- ciples, and all social relations, "particularly in their intellectual and moral connotations." Hegemony consequently is the result of complex and subtle processes—conscious and unconscious—of control, in which the predominance of one class is established over others, by consent rather than by force. In this formulation, it is achieved by the institu- tions of civil society.[22]

This is precisely what Egerton Ryerson and other promoters of

---

[21] "The Social Advancement of Canada," *J.E.*, 2 (1849), 179; *Annual Report of the Chief Superintendent. . .* , 1852, 130; Prentice, "School Promoters," Chap. 5; Ryerson, "Report on a System," 142–158.

[22] *Selections from the Prison Notebooks*, 12; John M. Cammett, *Antonio Gramsci and the Origins of Italian Communism* (Stanford: Stanford University Press, 1967), 204; Gwyn Williams, "The Concept of 'Egemonia' in the Thought of Antonio Gramsci," *Journal of the History of Ideas*, 21 (1960), 587.

education sought to provide through their work; this lay at the heart of their efforts to reform and systematize schooling to embrace all the children in controlled instruction. The development of hegemony, they learned, depended on a "level of homogeneity, self-consciousness, and organization" reached by a social class. Neither narrowly economic nor crudely imposed or conspiratorial, their actions derived from a sure recognition of the needs of society and of the oneness of social interests, and the identification of their own requirements with those of others. Their task was to achieve this; the school and literacy were the instruments—through a dissemination of the message of the moral economy—for stability and cohesion.

Literacy's roles, as we will shortly observe, were several, but in general it was the medium and the carrier of the elements of the hegemonic culture, or as E. J. Hobsbawm writes, "the only culture that operates as such through literacy—the very construction of a standard national language belongs to the literate elite. The very process of reading and schooling diffuses it, even unintentionally." We will return to this aspect of the process, but even in this sketch it is possible to grasp the intentions of the educators and the mechanisms for the development of control in the moral economy. The popular acceptance of public education gave meaning to the process and represented public consent to the efforts, such as those of Ryerson, made to re-establish and maintain hegemony—apart from any public recognition of the values or assumptions that underlay those efforts.[23]

That Ryerson grasped this development, however unclearly or unconsciously, cannot be doubted. For in addition to his other insights, he saw that success required the cooperation of all classes, but especially the higher responsibilities of educated and prosperous men. Aside from the awareness of self-interest, school promoters depended on the recog-

[23] Hobsbawn, "Religion and the Rise of Socialism," *Marxist Perspectives*, 1 (1978), 22. My interpretation owes much to the writings of David B. Davis, *The Problem of Slavery in the Age of Revolution, 1770–1823* (Ithaca: Cornell University Press, 1975), 348–362; Aileen S. Kraditor, "American Radical Historians on Their Heritage," *Past and Present*, 56 (1972), 136–153; Eugene Genovese, "On Antonio Gramsci," in his *In Red and Black: Marxian Explorations in Southern and Afro-American History* (New York: Pantheon, 1971), 391–422, *Roll, Jordan, Roll: The World the Slaves Made* (New York: Pantheon, 1974). See also, R. W. Connell, *Ruling Class, Ruling Culture* (Cambridge: Cambridge University Press, 1977). For pioneering application to educational history, see Katz, "The Origins"; Johnson, "Notes," "Educating." See also, E. P. Thompson's remarks, "Eighteenth-century English Society," *Social History*, 3 (1978), 133–165, which appeared after this chapter was written. It should be clear, finally, that this interpretation is offered as an explanation sketch, not as a fully detailed synthesis. While this is sufficient for the present purposes, much more remains to be done.

nition of the obligations of the educated to their society and to the lower class. Ryerson realized the need for their full support, maintaining that "one of the most formidable obstacles to the universal diffusion of education and knowledge is class isolation and class exclusiveness. . . ." The functions of schooling could not succeed if men of liberal education looked down on the education of the masses; they, as trustees of the social inheritance, had to be interested and involved, as moral agents, employing their powers, possessions, and advantages. As active leaders and material contributors, in addition to their personal stake in their own children's common schooling, they would contribute morally, too. These were in fact their obligations, the fulfillment of which was required if Canada was to rise and not sink: "What order and beauty [would arise] from chaos and desolation . . . what an intellectual, a moral, a social transformation would ensue." [24]

The attributes that educational promoters attempted to instill in their pupils, particularly the children of the poor and the laborers, constitute what I have called the moral bases of literacy—the primary purpose of common school education. These moral values, central to nineteenth-century educators and to the society for which schooling was to prepare men and women, reveal the perceived connections between the school, the society, and the economy. Morality, in other words, underlay social relations, social order, economic productivity, and the development of hegemony. The inculcation of values, habits, or attitudes to transform the masses, not skills, was the task of schooling and the legitimating notion of the moral economy. Literacy properly served as the tool for this training in a close and reinforcing relationship with morality. This was the source of cohesion and order, and the defense of progress, in a developing and modernizing capitalist society.

III

Ryerson was hardly the sole spokesman for the moral bases of literacy, which amounted to a consensus view throughout Anglo-America. Examples of this are legion. Others in Upper Canada, particularly the clergy, often addressed the same ends; but this agreement has too easily been obscured by attention to differences in tactics and procedures. Often, bitter disagreements over sponsorship and control, as well as ten-

[24] *Annual Report,* 1857, 49; *Annual Report,* 1850, 215; "Obligations of Educated Men," 194, 196, 166, 165; see also, John William Dawson, *The Duties of Educated Young Men* (Montreal, 1863).

dencies to interpret their moral opinions as much more narrowly sectarian and theological than social, obstruct an understanding of the larger point. The religious press was an important voice in nineteenth-century Upper Canada, quite widely read and circulated, and the degree to which its statements, regardless of denominational affinities, amplified basic elements in a shared world view is instructive. Nor should it be forgotten that here, as elsewhere, the architects of the educational system were clergymen: the Anglican John Strachan and the Wesleyan Methodist Ryerson. This convergence of opinion is all the more striking when one notes the number of denominations in agreement, regardless of differences over doctrine, organization, the place of the Bible in school, control, or support.[25] Their consensus, a shared consciousness, fostered the legitimation of the moral economy and the development of hegemony. Their views provide further insight into the parameters of schooling's purposes.

Ryerson's own denomination, the Methodists, trumpeted loudly in support of morality in common schooling, in their weekly, *The Christian Guardian,* which Ryerson edited before he was appointed superintendent. From its first numbers, the *Guardian* expressed the moral economy, for the Methodists were certain that "A young Christian ought to aim at the highest degree of intellectual improvement [for] his Christian character will rest on what he knows." The usefulness, happiness, safety, and devoutness of any person could only follow, they argued, upon the eradication of ignorance. Morality, and Christianity, grew from education and literacy; the schools' "greatest glory," as it was put, lay in the provision of, first, moral development and, second, intellectual. And, as a result, free schools, common schools, would "level" the social hierarchy, producing a society "in which the multitude shall not be looked down upon as an inferior race." [26]

Moral instruction, continued the *Guardian,* would also prevent crime, for unless the moral advanced with the intellectual progress, there would be "no increase from our increased education, but an increased capacity for evil doing." But with correct schooling, this

[25] On religion and sects in Upper Canada, see for example, John Moir, *Church and Sect in Canada West* (Toronto: University of Toronto Press, 1959); C. B. Sissons, *Church and Sect in Canadian Education* (Toronto: Ryerson Press, 1959); S. D. Clark, *Church and Sect in Canada* (Toronto: University of Toronto Press, 1948); Gerald Craig, *Upper Canada, The Formative Years* (Toronto: McClelland and Stewart, 1963); J. M. S. Careless, *Union of the Canadas* (Toronto: McClelland and Stewart, 1967); F. A. Walker, *Catholic Education and Politics in Upper Canada* (Toronto: University of Toronto Press, 1955).

[26] *Christian Guardian (CG),* Jan. 23, 1830; Jan. 15, 1834; on the politics of the *Guardian* see Goldwin French, *Parsons in Politics* (Toronto: Ryerson Press, 1972).

28

LESSON XX.

claw	jaw	shawl
crawl	law	spawn
dawn	maw	straw
haw	paw	thaw
hawk	raw	yawn

The beef is quite raw; will you roast it? A flail is used to part the grain from the straw. The hawk takes its prey with its claws. A worm can crawl, but a hare can run. Heat makes the ice thaw. I will rise as soon as day dawns. What part of a bird is the maw? Haws are the fruit of the thorn. Why do you yawn? Pull the tooth from my jaw. A fish spawns. Fine shawls are made from the hair of the goat. Puss has hurt her paw.

God gave this law to men, that they should love him more than all things in the world.

29

LESSON XXI.

cause	fraud	pause
clause	gauze	sauce
daub	laud	vault

James daubs his clothes with clay. Pause at the stops or points. It is fraud to take what is not yours. To laud is to praise. Read this clause. Jane has torn her gauze frock; that is the cause of her tears. Let me have sauce to my fish, if you please. It is not my fault, if you do not learn to read. Paul is a man's name. Wine is kept in vaults. *You must not vaunt or boast of your skill.*

LESSON XXII.

cloud	ground	proud
couch	hound	shout
flour	mount	sour
gout	mouse	south

This fruit is sour; I found it on the

Inculcating the message and the purposes of formal education. "*First Book of Lessons, for the Use of Schools,*" authorized by the Council of Public Instruction for Upper Canada, Series of National School Books, Montreal and Toronto: James Campbell and Son, 1867, pp. 28-29. [Record and Archives Centre, Toronto Board of Education]

would not result. Moreover, Sunday schools could also serve this end. The *Guardian* saw them as solely for religious and moral instruction according to the Word of God. Proper education, in sum, revolved around the nature of man, for man was a moral being, not only an intellectual one. Morality, therefore, formed the only safe basis for popular education. Pupils, as this journal approvingly quoted an American educator, "need some central governing power to rule the conscience, regulate the pulsations of the heart, and restrain the passions [, for] knowledge is power to do evil as well as good." Both intellect and emotion needed moral circumscription; alone or unrestrained by appropriate education they could only be harmful to society's interests. Consequently, the processes of control must begin early in life.[27]

The need to control the use of literacy itself led the *Guardian* to specify what should and should not be read, extending the moral bases beyond the classroom with the products of its influence. "No part of education," it announced, "is of greater importance than the selection of proper books. . . . No dissipation can be worse than that induced by the perusal of exciting books of fiction . . . a species of a monstrous and erroneous nature." Novels, especially, were "pernicious" to man as intellectual and moral; they made few appeals to reason and engendered an aversion to profound and controlled thought—even threatening its loss. Novel reading was proscribed for young and unmarried women, and a religious newspaper was recommended for the needs of all, especially for a poor family. Best of all, of course, was the Bible, which, along with religious literature, formed the primary source for moral, Christian reading.[28]

More specifically, the press offered "Advice to Apprentices." Often too young to choose what was best for themselves, they were to seek out "a friend to select for [them] the best books," on morality and religion, the liberal arts, and the profession likely to be theirs, in that order. The emphasis is clear; morality came first, then came the more practical arts and sciences. Tastes and manners were not neglected; for they were a sign of morality and they contributed to discipline.[29] Thus morality impinged on the passive employments of leisure.

Its applications, in fact, were broader, as few forms of leisure could

[27] *CG.*, July 2, 1834; Dec. 2, 1835; Oct. 16, 1844; Apr. 15, 1840; June 7, 1848; May 1, 1850. For another view on Sunday Schools, see T. W. Laqueur, *Religion and Respectability: Sunday Schools and Working Class Culture, 1780–1850* (New Haven: Yale University Press, 1976). For an extensive discussion of crime, see Chap. 6, below.

[28] *CG.*, July 31, 1850; see also Altick, *Common Reader*, Chap. 5, and Chap. 7 below; *CG.*, Nov. 17, 1849; Jan. 16, 1850; Feb. 19, 1840; May 24, 1848.

[29] *CG.*, Dec. 13, 1867.

be left to individual freedom. The development of institutions for the
controlled transmission of literacy coincided with the transformation of
more active forms of popular recreation. Traditional activities, whether
fairs, work holidays, bearbaiting, or cockfighting, were in the first half
of the nineteenth century replaced by morally sponsored, socially accepted activities. Robert Malcolmson comments, "A closer regulation
of popular behavior, an improvement in the common peoples' tastes
and morals, a reform of their habitual vices, the instilling in them of
discipline and orderliness: these were some of the principal objectives
of the movement for the reformation of manners which arose [in En-
gland] in the later 1780s and matured during the following half century."
This activity, aimed at the transformation of culture, stemmed from
many of the same goals that led to the establishment of school systems
and the propagation of the moral bases of literacy: the promotion of
order, the maintenance of respect for property, propriety, the diminution of conflict, the assimilation into society of the poor and
working class, the maintenance of control and discipline in new urban
and industrial environments.

Morality was injected into play activities, in the establishment of
hegemony, as into the curriculum; and, "it came to be assumed . . . that
'if recreation was permissable at all, it must be "rational" and must
prepare mind and body for work instead of being an end in itself.' "
In the attempt to reestablish order and cohesion in a society changing
from the rural and paternalistic to the urban and capitalistic, recreation,
like literacy, had to be transformed and controlled. As with schooling
too, concern for labor discipline and conduct was central; "the more
popular diversion could be controlled and restrained, the more would
the national economy be strengthened and expanded; habits of leisure
had to be brought into line with the requirements of efficient and orderly
production." [30] Neither literacy nor leisure was neutral to the reforming
spirit; their regulation by morality was required. Indeed, if controlled,
one could reinforce the best use of the other.

That there were debates among the different denominations should
not be allowed to obscure their consensus on the proper functions of
education. Acrimonious struggles over sponsorship, legal arrangements,

[30] Malcolmson, *Popular Recreations in English Society, 1700–1850* (Cambridge:
Cambridge University Press, 1973), 169, 167, 98, *passim.* J. F. C. Harrison, *Early Vic-
torian England* (New York: Schocken, 1971), 135–139; Brian Harrison, "Religion and
Recreation in Nineteenth-Century England," *Past and Present,* 38 (1968), 98–125. But
see also Gareth Stedman Jones, "Working Class Culture and Working Class Politics in
London, 1870–1900: Notes on the Remaking of a Working Class," *Journal of Social
History,* 7 (1974), 460–508.

procedures, doctrinal interpretations, and the like, fill the pages of the religious press and the interpretations of the early years of school promotion.[31] Nonetheless, despite such disagreements, which could be significant, a primary agreement was more important; this held that schooling without morality simply was not proper education. Upper Canada's Anglicans, the opponents of the Methodists and Ryerson on so many educational issues, made the consensus clear in their journal, *The Church*. To them, moral and religious education was important to schooling anywhere, but particularly so in Upper Canada; their complaints centered on legislation—not on the place of the moral economy. Fearing that the Bible and morality would be neglected, they worried that it might be replaced with the writings of Tom Paine and Voltaire, and that free schools were republican, even socialistic.[32] Considering the desires of the chief superintendent, there was little danger of this.

The Anglicans, like the superintendent and his Methodists, therefore saw correct education, with morality at its core, as the formation of the social order. Their educational first premise held Christian morality "naturally and essentially" favorable to inquiry and cultivation. More fundamentally, moral schooling alone would properly equip the masses for their duties and guide them away from disturbance and commotion. Lacking the ties of property, pleasure, fashion, character, honor, or refinement, the poor, if not trained to be lawful and orderly, were dangerous and threatening to peace. Herein was reflected the Anglican faith. *The Church*, finally, was equally adamant about the choice of reading matter, advocating the control of books as well as the development of the ability to read them, and censuring many kinds of improper literature. Morals, they felt, could be as easily corrupted as properly molded by the use of bare literacy. The moral bases meant the regulation of transmission as well as use.[33]

The province's Roman Catholics also embraced the moral economy, despite their rejection of common, nondenominational (Protestant) schooling. While they struggled to develop a school system of their own, they argued over means rather than ends. Schooling, even if separate, would be "suitable to [one's] station in life," producing the "faithful Christian . . . [a] better Man, and a more useful member of Society." Man, born in weakness and ignorance, required instruction, a schooling that provided at its base a sense of moral duty.[34] These groups, consti-

[31] See, for example, *CG.*, Oct. 26, 1853; *The Church*, July 28, 1843. (*TC*)

[32] *TC.*, May 30, 1850; May 26, 1838.

[33] *TC.*, Feb. 12, 1852; May 20, 1852; Oct. 12, 1839; Oct. 27, 1843.

[34] *The Catholic Citizen*, Jan. 5, 1854; *The Catholic* (Kingston), July 1, 1831; *The Catholic* (Hamilton), June 7, 1843; for continuing statements, see Rev. D. H. Macvicar,

tuting the province's major denominations, held education to be necessary to society and their place within it; their views moreover placed
morality and religion at the core of education. All subscribed to the
moral bases—their subscriptions very similar—as they accepted the
hegemonic functions of schooling.

IV

How were the moral bases propagated and inculcated; how was
hegemony developed through the school? We must turn briefly to the
classroom itself, for the moral bases were operative in diverse schoolrooms and transmitted in several ways, both consciously and unconsciously, subtly and unsubtly. The provincial board of education, the
Council of Public Instruction, for example, ruled in October, 1850, that
all common schools should open and close daily with religious exercises.
The exercises consisted of the Lord's Prayer and Bible reading, and the
Ten Commandments were also taught in the common school. After their
incorporation in 1853, similar rules were devised for grammar schools.
Morality, therefore, would be central in the classroom, as it was in the
minds and intentions of the schoolmen. "Christianity, it was pointed
out," Prentice notes, "in connection with these regulations, was the basis
of law and order, as well as the cement and ornament of society." [35] If
proper education was to succeed, the message of the school had to be
in the air, in the ears of the pupils, and on their lips.
    Was this mere lip service? The superintendent attempted to insure
the contrary; Ryerson's education office also stressed the importance of
morality in the classroom, regularly requiring information as to whether
it was being adequately promoted. For his annual reports, Ryerson asked,
Did the day open with prayer, Was the Bible in use, OF what denomination is the teacher? Summarizing the responses in his reports, he attempted to prove, to critics who thought his system godless, that the
schools as they developed became progressively more religious. Local re-

---

"Moral Culture, an Essential Factor in Public Education," an address delivered before
the Ontario Teachers Association, Toronto, August 14; John Eaton, "Illiteracy and its
Social, Political and Industrial Effects," an address to the Union League Club, New
York City (New York, 1882).
    [35] "Religious Instruction in the Common Schools, 1859," *DHE,* 14, 267; "Pro-
gramme of Public Instruction in Upper Canada," *J.E.,* 8 (1855), 24.

ports illustrate the success of his efforts, as Prentice reveals in her cita-
tion of a typical report. This claimed that "all the schools" in one city
" 'now opened and closed by the teacher reading aloud a portion of the
Scriptures and the Lord's Prayer;' and that in almost all cases, the
children voluntarily repeated the prayer with the teacher." [36]

The texts in use also demonstrate the centrality of morality, and
the frequency and intensity of its message, in the classroom. Approved
books spread the doctrines of order, harmony, and progress, ignoring
conflict and inequality. Here lay one key role for literacy. Yet we must
also recognize that the child did not need to be proficiently literate to
read and comprehend the moral message and thus be instilled with the
desired values. At mid-century, before silent reading was valued as a
pedagogical tool—and for some years thereafter—oral reading dominated
the classroom: reading to the class by the teacher with pupil recitation
and repetition. The constant repetition of passages would surely dent
the minds of the young, regardless of the level of their own ability to
decipher the written word. Hearing would advance the necessary purpose, though literacy would surely ease the process of reinforcement and
internalization.

The Irish National Readers constituted the texts for the Ontario
common schools following Ryerson's endorsement and adoption in 1846.
In a useful analysis of the series, J. M. Goldstrum concluded that school
reform in both England and Ireland was moralistic in orientation, and
permeated by the belief that individuals could be made over or radically
changed by being taught correct social values. "School readers played a
crucial role in this system because the scantily-educated teachers relied
heavily on them," their authors and sponsors thought. Nevertheless,
teachers were expected to be moral agents and to emphasize the moral
economy in classroom behavior, management, and teaching.[37] Demanding order, respect, industry, and diligence, they were to reinforce the
moral order of society. They were to insist on conformity to rules and
regulations and respect for property, whether through discipline hard
or soft, external punishment, or the inculcation of internal restraint.
Barbara Finkelstein, in studies of nineteenth-century American teachers,
calls this "pedagogy-as-intrusion": "The way these primary teachers

---

[36] Prentice, "School Promoters," 201.

[37] Goldstrum, *The Social Context*, 1, 2, passim.; see also Ruth M. Elson's analysis
of school books used in the United States, *Guardians of Tradition* (Lincoln, Neb.: University of Nebraska Press, 1964); Sherwood Fox, "School Readers as an Educational
Force," *Queen's Quarterly*, 39 (1932), 688–703. Chap. 7, below, elaborates some of these
points.

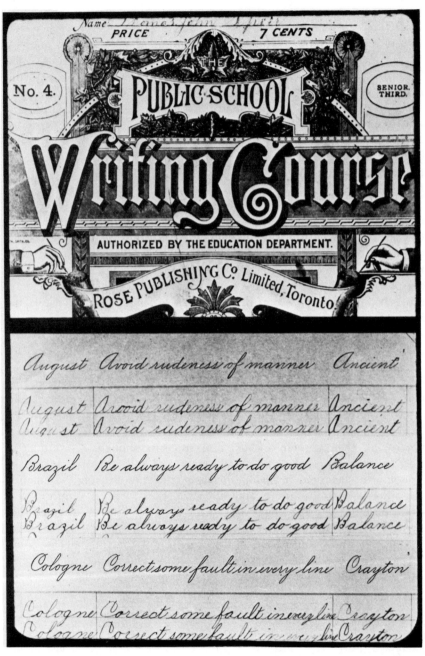

Learning the moral bases of literacy by repetition, example, and practice. *"Thomas Speer Copy Book,"* Public School Writing Course, No. 4, Senior Third Level, authorized by the education department. [Records and Archives Centre, Toronto Board of Education]

taught suggests that they believed that the main function of education was instilling restraint," tying intellectual and moral instruction firmly together in the service of character development.[38] In these ways, in text, teaching style, and classroom management, teachers and the authorities worked to maintain control of ideas and conduct, especially given the short stay of many pupils.

The National Readers followed closely upon the heels of the creation of a national educational system in Ireland, as their adoption accompanied the erection of Upper Canada's system of schools. The values expressed, and promoted, were secular, but they were at once morally and religiously imbued, permeated by Christian ethics. Though they might no longer contain Biblical passages or moral tales, the heroes of the tales and fables were inevitably good Christians. In these daily lessons, pupils were taught the rationales for government, military and police, private property, rich and poor, and the interdependence of the social classes. By explicit example and description, the duties of citizens, the necessity of obedience, cleanliness, industriousness, sobriety, honesty, and frugality were brought home to them.[39] By drill, repetition, and memorization, youngsters absorbed a code for social behavior.

Moreover, self-help and personal advancement were presented modestly; no large prospects of upward mobility were put forth, inasmuch as the continuation of the two classes—the rich and the poor—was justified. Poverty, pupils were instructed, was the consequence of moral failings: a lack of self-restraint, indolent and intemperate behavior, or early and improvident marriage. The poor were taught that to succeed, they must be self-restrained, obedient, and cooperative; the rich would then treat them with respect. The poor, of course, were not encouraged to nurture social ambitions. So, for the inculcation of correct standards of behavior and attitude, "a sound moral is conveyed in almost every lesson." As the *Thirteenth Report* of the National Society, 1841, emphasized, the diffusion of knowledge cannot, perhaps, be stopped, but it can be directed into the least dangerous channels: "He cannot hinder the people from obtaining Knowledge, but he can do something towards making that knowledge the safest and the best." Of course, other groups and denominations produced competing readers, but "all the books show one very important fact—the religious societies felt the same about

[38] Barbara Finkelstein, "Pedagogy as Intrusion," *History of Childhood Quarterly*, 2 (1975), 349–378, "The Moral Dimensions of Pedagogy," *American Studies*, 15 (1974), 79, 79–89. See also Katz, *The Irony of Early School Reform* (Cambridge, Mass.: Harvard University Press, 1968), Part II; Prentice, "School Promoters," *passim*.

[39] Goldstrum, *The Social Context*, 67, 68, Chap. 2. On the Irish schools, see Donald Akenson, *The Irish Education Experiment* (New Haven: Yale University Press, 1969).

Time-Table for a School 6, 7, or 8 Grades.

Recitations.	Hours.	Time.	STUDY.			
			D Division.	C Division.	B Division.	A Division.
Opening Exercises......	8.50– 8.57	7 min.	....	....	....	....
Roll Call.	8.57– 9.00	3 "	....	....	....	....
D Reading.............	9.00– 9.15	15 "	{ Copying Lesson	Reading	Reading	Arith ....
C Reading..	9.15– 9.30	15 "	with help of an	....	Reading	Arith ....
B Reading.'	9.30– 9.50	20 "	older pupil*. }	Copying Lesson.....	....	Lang. or Read†......
A Lang. or Read...... ...	9.50–10.10	20 "	Busy Work..........	Arith..............	Arith..............	Arith ....
D Number.....	10.10–10.25	15 "	....	Arith..............	Arith..............	Write notes on Les..

Recess 15 Minutes.　　　　　　　　10.25 to 10.40.

C Arithmetic	10.40–10.55	15 "	Reading	....	Language..........	Arith........ ...
B Language..	10.55–11.10	15 "	Read to Tutor*.....	Arith.............	Arith	Geog. or Hist...... .
A Geog. or Hist..........	11.10–11.35	25 "	Writing	Arith.............	Arith	Map Drawing.......
D Reading.............	11.35–11.50	15 "	....	Arith. with Tutor..	Geog. or Hist......	Map Drawing.......
Singing taught.........	11.50–12.00	10 "	....	....	....	....

Noon 60 Minutes.　　　　　　　　12 to 1.

Roll Call	1.00–1.05	3 "	....	....	....	....
B Geog. or Hist........	1.05–1.25	22 "	Number	Lang	....	Arith.............
C Language...........	1.25–1.45	20 "	Read to Tutor*.....	....	Map Drawing......	Arith.. ... .
Singing	1.45–1.50	5 "	....	....	....	....
Writing or Drawing. ..	1.50–2.20	30 "	Nat. Les. to Teacher...	. , ...	....	....

Recess 10 Minutes.　　　　　　　　2.20 to 2.30.

D Reading..............	2.30–2.45	15 "	....	Reading...........	{ Write outline {	Alg. or Arith.......
C Reading	2.45–3.00	15 "	Copy Lesson........	....	of Geog. or Hist }	Alg. or Arith.... ...
B Arith.............	3.00–3.20	20 "	{	DIS-	MISS.	{	Arith......... ...	Geom...... ....
A Geom. or Arith........	3.20–3.40	20 "	{		{	Arith......... ...	....
A and B Nature Lessons.	3.40–4.00		....	....	....	....

* In a large ungraded school it will be necessary frequently to utilize some of the older pupils as tutors. Let it be looked upon as a privilege, perhaps the reward of good work.

† For the highest class, reading three times a week, and language or grammar twice, will be sufficient. So, also geography, three times a week, and history twice. Writing and drawing the same, alternately.

Note.—It will sometimes happen that the 6th Grade can work with the 7th in history or geography. In various circumstances many minor changes of that kind may be desirable.

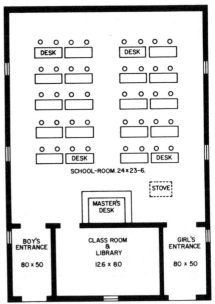

The ordering of time and the ordering of space—two aspects of carefully controlled and structured learning. (above) *"Time Table for a School, 6, 7, or 8 grades,"* The Education Review (Quebec), 5–6 (1891–1893), p. 220. [Public Archives of Canada] (right) *"Ground or Floor Plan,"* for school rooms, *Eighth Annual Report of the Chief Superintendent of Schools for New Brunswick*. Fredrickton, New Brunswick, 1860.

education and the poor." [40] With proper instruction, the dangers of unrestrained literacy, or of illiteracy, could be neutralized; in learning to read, children would be taught the rules of social order and correct behavior and the principles of economic advancement.

Important as they are, these were not the only ways in which the moral bases and hegemony were developed. Hegemony involves, we recall, the unwilled and unselfconscious consent so the direction that the predominant group imposes on social life—on morality, principles, and all social relations—through public institutions such as the school. The school, in addition to its curriculum, in ways beyond its stated goals and intents, is an environment conducive to training in approved patterns of conduct, and the inculcation of normative behavior. The organization of the institution, it seems, acts as a "hidden persuader" that implicitly contributes to learning the rules of personal action. Consciously and unconsciously, formally and informally, the organization of work and social life is implicitly encapsulated in the microcosm of the school. The school-as-microcosm, in fact, forms a mechanism of socialization frequently neglected by scholars.

In their internal organization, schools reflect social relations and ideology and serve as key agents of transmission, at once legitimating the social order and assimilating to it their charges. Dreeben, for one, illustrates the outcomes of schooling in learning to accept norms and authority, in a sensitive exploration of the structural aspects of education. Focusing on the "peculiar," noncognitive properties of schooling, he shows how the experiences of learning link the students to the larger social structure, teach them to "participate in authority relations based on inequalities," "link the family with the public institutions of adult life," and integrate schooling with work and politics. Bowles and Gintis further document this complex process, concentrating also on the noncognitive behavioral and attitudinal aspects of the correspondence between the social relations of school and the requirements of work. Emphasizing submission to authority, temperament, and internalized control, their discussion informs our understanding of how hegemony is transmitted through the institutions of education. In these ways, the moral bases gained vital enforcement from the very environment built to transmit it.[41]

---

[40] Goldstrum, *The Social Context*, 80, Chap. 2; 104; 129; for examples from the readers, see Chap. 2.

[41] Alex Inkeles, "Making Men Modern," *American Journal of Sociology*, 75 (1969), esp. 213, "The School as a Context for Modernization," *International Journal of Sociology*, 14 (1973), 163–179; Robert Dreeben, *On What Is Learned in School* (Reading, Mass.: Addison-Wesley, 1968), 144–145, *passim;* Samuel Bowles and Herbert Gintis,

Carefully guided instruction in literacy represented one central theme in the practical elaboration of the moral bases that bound school promoters to a specific notion of education in the past century. Reading and writing were seldom seen as ends in themselves or valued as individual attainments; indeed, undirected they were thought to be very dangerous and subversive. If, however, their provision in formal institutions were properly controlled and efficient, literacy could be the vehicle for the transmission of the moral message and the development of hegemony. The purpose of literacy was to integrate society through binding men and women in it and instilling in them the principles of correct behavior. The importance of print and of the ability to read was grasped by those most interested in social order and progress. They saw, on the one hand, that more and more people were becoming literate, and thus potentially able to use their literacy without restraint. On the other hand, there were the illiterate, especially among the young. Both elements constituted a threat, a barrier to the spread of the values considered essential to social order and economic progress. The result, of course, was the determination to seize upon print and literacy as socializing agents, to provide them in environments specifically and carefully structured for their dissemination, and to teach the moral code and the approved uses of literacy. Literacy was now necessary for moral control and control was required for literacy; progress would be advanced through the behavior of properly schooled persons. Given the vast importance attached to literacy and the values that accompanied it, what did literacy mean to *individuals* in Upper Canadian society? We address this question in the chapters that follow.

Schooling in Capitalist America (New York: Basic Books, 1975), Chap. 5; Gintis, "Education, Technology and the Characteristics of Worker Productivity," *American Economic Review,* 61 (1971), 266–279.

I

LITERACY AND SOCIAL STRUCTURE IN THE NINETEENTH-CENTURY CITY

Who are the illiterates? In what respects do illiterates—apart from their illiteracy—differ from the rest of the population? The answer, surprising though it may seem, is that the majority of illiterates, especially functional illiterates, are, apart from their illiteracy, not markedly different from other men and women.

—M. M. LEWIS
The Importance of Illiteracy (1953)

Literacy is there to a large extent to create an illusion of equality . . . the literacy is not functional, it's only a statistical artifact for large groups of the population.

JOHAN GALTUNG
"Literacy, Education and Schooling—For What?" (1976)

It is impossible to define the characteristics of an illiterate man. It seems that almost any type of person—gay, or morose, lively or sluggish, intelligent or unintelligent may fall within the category. Indeed, illiterates are occasionally found who belong to really high intelligence groups.

R. C. SAWYER
Adult Education (1944)

2

Illiterates and Literates
in Urban Society:
The Mid-Nineteenth Century

Social, political, and emotional commentators—today as in the past century—persistently point to a *problem* of illiteracy. Their arguments are often vague and ambiguous, sometimes contradictory, especially concerning the more concrete aspects of literacy's presumed advantages and illiteracy's alleged disadvantages. They result, nonetheless, in a dramatically unfavorable assessment of the position of the illiterate as compared with that of the literate. In fact, since the early to mid-nineteenth century, as we have seen, those without the experience of education and without its badge of literacy, have been perceived as inferior and pathetic, alien to the dominant culture, subversive to social order, unequipped to achieve or produce, and denizens of self-perpetuating cultures of poverty. As exceptions to the processes that provide the vast majority of their fellows with literacy, illiterates are seen as different in attitude and social attributes. In 1933, M. C. McLean, reviewing retrospective census tabulations, offered an unemotional summary that stands as well for 1845 as 1979: "The illiterate class is below par in every attribute for which they were tested except one—tendency to crime—and . . . they show certain attributes which may or may not be antisocial but in any case are different from those shown by literate classes." [1]

This is the stuff of which myths are made; and, as with all myths, some important evidence does exist in support of these common conclusions. This and the two following chapters, which comprise Part One,

[1] See Chs. 1, 5 and 6 herein; H. E. Freeman and G. C. Kassebaun, "The Illiterate in American Society: Some General Hypotheses," *Social Forces*, 34 (1956), 371–375; M. C. McLean, *Illiteracy in Canada* (Ottawa, 1933: King's Printer, 1931 Census Monograph), 584.

shall present nineteenth-century evidence that lends some credibility to aspects of the literacy myth. Although these data cannot be neglected, they do not form a basis for a complete understanding of the social relations grounded in literacy in mid-nineteenth-century cities. Literacy's role was neither as simple nor as direct as contemporary opinion would predict. In a variety of ways, which intersect significantly with the larger parameters of social and economic life of the men and women who lived and worked in cities such as Hamilton, London, and Kingston, Ontario, in 1861, the possession or the lack of literacy had not the determining consequences that school promoters' rhetoric and middle-class moral proselytizing declaimed so frequently. Despite some points of accuracy, which undoubtedly contributed to the acceptance of the moral bases and the development of hegemony, literacy or illiteracy only infrequently carried an independent and distinct meaning. Rather, literacy's role was more typically a reinforcing or mediating one, which can only be understood in the specific context of social structural processes. Isolated from its social relationships, literacy takes on a reified and symbolic significance unwarranted by its own, more restricted influences. More-over, when examined in this context, the analysis of literacy advances a more sensitive interpretation of the social structure itself and the place of the school. This forms the primary theme of this part of the study.

This interpretation of literacy-in-context questions traditional for-mulations, while suggesting the need for further comparative examina-tion, and the potential for revision of the myth—the limits of the case-study approach employed here. Especially important are the issues that lie in the confluence of historical understanding and modern social theory, however infrequently the former are expressed in terms of the latter or how uncomfortably they may join. Regardless, the point at issue, which much of the following addresses, relates to the normative ex-pectations and the normative comprehension of the presumed importance of literacy, an importance based more on theoretical expectations (as the earlier analysis indicates) than on empirical inquiries. This conjuncture is itself important, though hardly surprising; nonetheless, central ideas about literacy inform nineteenth-century opinion, historical thinking, and modern social thought, forming a broad and pervasive continuity. A brief review will establish the framework for our historical investigation.

As noted above, literacy is commonly, and ambiguously, held to be critical to the processes and evolution of modern society and the place within them of modern men and women. Its role is taken as central and deterministic, a requirement, in fact, of development, both in the aggregate and in respect of individuals. A number of diverse theoretical strands, unite to form this tenet of progressive social thought; many of them relate to this analysis. They cohere principally around notions about migration, social organization and integration, stratification and mobility, adjustment and assimilation, and social and economic progress.

Illiterates, those without the benefits of primary schooling in skills, values, and attitudes, it is held, are distinct and separate culturally and socially, perhaps even composing a "class," or "culture" (in today's jargon) such as McLean suggests. Alien to the dominant or "host" society, they are typically migrants from a different and "inferior" place of origin (with an emphasis on their ethnic or racial characteristics). Ill- or under-equipped to meet the demands made on them, their response is one of social disintegration, retreat, disorganization, or disruption. In this manner, their condition—and their lack of requisite abilities and attributes—severely restricts their own progress, as it hinders the larger social unit in which they reside. Trapped in a paralyzing poverty, they are, ironically, seen as unstable and rootless, either immobilized in pockets of penury or aimlessly moving about. Overwhelmingly, their condition is one of disorganization, an inability to adjust to demands or to assimilate the values and behavior required for normative success and advancement. Maladjusted and irrational in conduct and in the way they employ their resources, the illiterates' culture is synonymous with a "culture of poverty." In their segregation, personal and material resources, family life, cohesion, and communication, the poor illiterates are distinctive, degraded, detrimental, and self-perpetuating.[2]

Their dire position leaves the illiterates outside the dominant social processes as well, exacerbating their own disadvantages and enlarging the loss they represent to the society and the economy. Without skills, normative values, or approved patterns of conduct, their contribution is much more negative than positive (aside from the example they present to others), a drain on rather than a contribution to resources and production. Moreover, their existence threatens the function of internalized controls and the successful operation of a democratic, participatory social order. Comprising either a real or a symbolic threat, or both, to social progress, they are targets of abuse and denigration, which can

[2] See, for example, David Ward, "The Victorian Slum: An Enduring Myth?," *Annals of the Association of American Geographers*, 66 (1976), 323–336; S. L. Schlossman, "The 'Culture of Poverty' in Ante-Bellum Social Thought," *Science and Society*, 38 (1974), 150–166; Charles A. Valentine, *Culture and Poverty* (Chicago: University of Chicago Press, 1968); Michael Anderson, *Family Structure in Nineteenth Century Lancashire* (Cambridge: Cambridge University Press, 1971); Eleanor Burke Leacock, ed., *The Culture of Poverty: A Critique* (New York: Simon and Schuster, 1971), among an important revisionist literature.

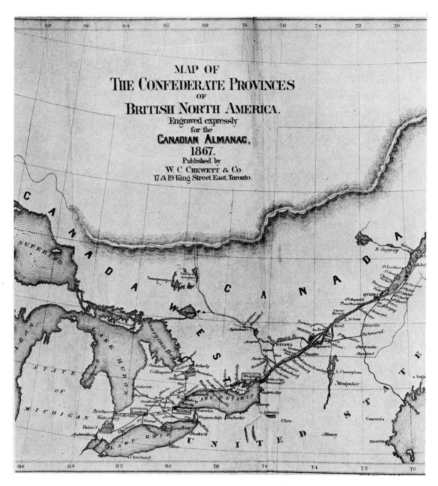

"*Map of the Confederate Provinces of British North America,*" engraved expressly for the *Canadian Almanac, 1867,* published by W. C. Chewett & Company, Toronto. [Map Collection, Archives of Ontario, Toronto]

in many cases become attacks upon their social existence—in rhetoric, in policy, or in action.

Finally, it is assumed illiterates do not profit from the promises of modern life and the benefits society can bestow upon them. Without the advantages of education, they are dominated by the fact of their lowly origins, unable to substitute educational achievement and its accompanying influences for ascribed characteristics and attributes. This failing—the putative result of their own weaknesses, not of the social structure—reinforces their station, prevents advancement and escape, and challenges the premises of modern society. Attainment is prohibited inasmuch as they can not rise above their inheritance, but must persist as they are, with all the consequences for themselves and society.[3]

Rapid as this review has been, we may recognize here the main elements—but presented within an interpretation quite contrary to the more common, progressive and positive one—of much of modern thought, and of nineteenth-century commentators too. This is the context that must inform our inquiry—the focus of Part One.

A facile examination of the illiterate adults resident in Hamilton, Kingston, and London, 1861, might lead the investigator to concur in the common progressive view. Here are a body of men and women in significant if not large numbers who reveal common attributes in their social characteristics. Less than 10% of those above the age of 20 in each of the cities as counted by the census,[4] they present similarities in ethnic, demographic, and economic characteristics, in ways that the above might lead one to expect. When compared with literate adults (the literates of Hamilton, who serve as a control group), they seem to share a significant series of disadvantages. This congruence of compositional and situational features is revealing about the social structure of these places, their economies, and the immigration processes that fed them. Nevertheless, if viewed only superficially and in the aggregate, it is less revealing about the importance of literacy to social life and work. Maintaining analysis only at this level precludes an understanding of literacy's more complex role and merely reinforces the contemporary perceptions and their legacy in thought and theory.

[3] The shift from a predominant emphasis on ascriptive or inherited characteristics to achieved or acquired ones is of course a central tenet of modern social development, as well as one promise of education. See, among a large literature, Christopher Jencks et al., Inequality (New York: Basic Books, 1972); Raymond Boudon, Education, Opportunity, and Social Inequality (New York: Wiley, 1974); Barbara Jacobson and John M. Kendrick, "Education and Mobility: From Achievement to Ascription," American Sociological Review, 38 (1973), 439–460; Dorothy Wedderburn, ed., Poverty, Inequality, and Class Structure (Cambridge: Cambridge University Press, 1974); Gregory D. Squires, "Education, Jobs, and Inequality," Social Problems 24 (1977), 436–450; Ivan Berg, Education and Jobs (Boston: Beacon Press, 1971); Michael Olneck and James Crouse, "Myths of the Meritocracy: Cognitive Skill and Adult Success in the United States," Institute for Research in Poverty, University of Wisconsin-Madison, Discussion Paper, 485-78 (1978). On Canada, see Lorne Tepperman, Social Mobility in Canada (Toronto: McGraw-Hill Ryerson, 1975); Carl Cuneo and James Curtis, "Social Ascription in the Educational and Occupational Attainment of Urban Canadians," Canadian Review of Sociology and Anthropology, 12 (1975), 6–24; Allan Smith, "The Myth of the Self-made Man in English Canada, 1850–1914," Canadian Historical Review, 59 (1978), 189–219.

[4] On the use of the census as a source for the study of literacy, see Appendix B.

Despite the confluence of opinion on literacy's fundamental contributions, its influences are far less direct and linear. Much more contradictory and complex, they require reexamination with new approaches. Therefore, in confronting those diverse elements of thought about literacy, this chapter examines five aspects: the social origins of illiterates; the process of immigration; work, wealth, and reward; homeownership, property, and residence; and family formation. As we will observe, the facts of mid-nineteenth-century life challenge many common views. The facts of immigration, for example, do not support contemporary reformers' perceptions nor do those of social-structural inequality. Migrants were selected individuals with important resources on which to draw. Immigrants represented no distinct class in themselves, but were socially ordered in ways that strikingly paralleled those of the larger population. Hardly an independent or dominating factor, literacy interacted with ethnicity, age, occupation, wealth, adjustment, and family organization, reinforcing and mediating the primary social processes that ordered the population, rather than determining their influences.

Furthermore, despite the widespread diffusion of literacy, social ascription—not achievement—remained dominant among the factors contributing to structural inequality. The illiterates themselves, finally, were neither all trapped in cultures of poverty nor all unable to attain some measure of success in wealth and work. They reveal themselves to be resourceful in the use of assets, personal and material, adapting to their new environments and surviving despite the circumstances militating against them. In sum, the facts of social reality contrast strikingly and significantly with social perceptions and social theories.

I. The Origins of Illiteracy: Ethnicity, Race, Sex, and Age

An analysis of the place of literacy in these Upper Canadian cities requires first the identification of those with and those without literacy. Who are these presumably disadvantaged persons, these exceptions to the social process that allotted some education to a majority of their fellows? What is their social composition? Exceptional men and women in ways that observers failed to note, illiterates were not randomly distributed among the adult population, nor did they numerically dominate any of its segments. Their characteristic identities are more regular and patterned—in ethnicity, race, age, and sex—indicating the critical connections tying literacy to the social structure and to processes of social inequality. These were the factors that contributed most significantly to the numbers of the illiterate, and to their composition across the cities.

Ethnic origins form the first fact about the illiterates. Their composition is remarkably consistent in each of the cities: in their share of the total population and among the illiterate themselves (Table 2.1).[5] Ethnicity, a function of the joint influences of place of birth and religion, was predominant among the factors contributing to the conforma-

Table 2.1
Ethnicity of Adults, 1861

	Hamilton literates	Percentage illiterate	Hamilton illiterates	Kingston illiterates	London illiterates	Total illiterates
Irish Catholic						
N	1,292		547	334	140	1,021
%	15.0	29.7	60.6	66.1	37.8	57.4
Irish Protestant						
N	1,188		83	71	44	198
%	13.8	6.5	9.2	14.1	11.9	11.1
Scottish Presbyterian						
N	1,417		23	10	21	54
%	16.4	1.6	2.5	2.0	5.7	3.0
English Protestant						
N	2,045		64	16	42	122
%	23.7	2.9	7.1	3.2	11.4	6.9
Canadian Protestant						
N	1,153		29	15	17	61
%	13.4	2.5	3.2	3.0	4.6	3.4
Canadian Catholic						
N	181		7	22	4	33
%	2.1	3.7	0.8	4.4	1.1	1.9
Nonwhite/black						
N	94		86	4	29	119
%	1.1	48.0	9.5	0.8	7.8	6.9
Others						
N	1,246		64	33	73	170
%	14.5	4.9	7.1	6.5	19.7	9.6
Total						
N	8,616		903	505	370	1,778
%	100.0					
Population (total)	19,096			13,743	11,555	

[5] Those desiring more detailed numerical discussions, tables, and references may consult my "Literacy and Social Structure in the Nineteenth-Century City," unpub. PhD. Diss., University of Toronto, 1975.

tion of the illiterate, much as it was among the larger population of these places. The result of similar processes of settlement and social placement in each city, ethnic origins stratified the educational attainments of adult populations. Not surprisingly, given usual expectations, in each city, those of Irish Catholic origin were most often unable to read and write. Members of one of the largest immigrant groups, they were overrepresented among the illiterate, compared to their share of the total. Their religion, moreover, importantly influenced their disadvantaged status, as the contrast with Protestants of Irish birth shows. These Protestants were slightly underrepresented among the illiterate, but nonetheless also added a large number of illiterates. Irish births, first, contributed most significantly to illiterate numbers, as over 70% of those who were illiterate shared this origin; religion, however, differentiated their numbers inasmuch as Protestantism provided a greater impetus to literacy than Catholicism—a link that historians should well expect. In the ethnic factor lay the confluence of these culturally inseparable influences.

No other ethnic group played the role of the Irish and the Irish Catholic in determining the origins and social structure of illiteracy, yet ethnicity and race served to distinguish the experiences and social position of other groups too. The United States-born were also disproportionately present among illiterates; in Hamilton and London, they were the second largest numerical group among them. For these individuals, race was the determining factor. A great many of the U.S.-born migrants were black, a group whose 48% rate of illiteracy was by far the highest, almost twice that of the Irish.[6] Black adults, in fact, accounted for 10% of Hamilton's illiterates and 8% of London's, while constituting less than 2% of the cities' populations. Blacks, and U.S.-born whites too, belonged predominantly to Methodist and Baptist churches, overrepresented denominations. The whites alone, however, were neither disproportionately present nor exceptional in frequency of illiteracy. In this way, race joined with Irish birth and Catholicism to form the primary factors contributing to illiteracy in these mid-century cities.

The Scottish-born added few to the illiterate. Significantly, birth and religion again coupled as Presbyterian and Church of Scotland communicants held the lowest rates of illiteracy; rates were higher in London, for example, where other Scots resided. Those from an area with a long tradition of primary schooling, a state church, and a religious impulse that manifested itself partly through a favorable attitude

---

[6] As elsewhere, there is a high probability of underenumeration of blacks in the Canadian censuses; see Robin Winks, *The Blacks in Canada* (New Haven: Yale University Press, 1971), 484–496.

toward universal literacy could not be expected to be often illiterate, reinforcing the crucial role of religion in the spread of literacy.[7] The English and Welsh, by comparison, were larger groups in each city. As one result of their numbers, they supplied the third-largest group of illiterates, but they were not disproportionately present among them nor among their share in the population.

In this largely immigrant society, native-born Canadians added few illiterates. A plurality of the cities' total population, many native-born persons were under the age of twenty; the adults among them nonetheless were underrepresented among the illiterates. As with the Irish, a Protestant–Catholic religious differential was important, as Canadian Catholics (including many of French origin) had higher levels of illiteracy than Canadian Protestants, although the degree of difference was much less. Among the Quebec-born, higher rates of illiteracy are found in Kingston, much nearer the provincial boundary, than in London, which suggests the possibility that migratory distances may relate to literacy.

In ethnic origins we find the first factor among the determinants of illiteracy; later we will consider the intersection of ethnicity with social-structural inequality in evaluating the functions of literacy. Here we note two points: the similarity among illiterates in each of the commercial cities and the origins of the great majority in places in which educational opportunities were restricted and rates of illiteracy were high—rural, poverty-stricken Ireland and the U.S. South, with its large population of slaves. Ethnicity (and race), while first, was not the only important factor.

The role of ethnic origins, and the disproportionate and undoubtedly highly visible place of the Irish and the Catholic among the illiterate, obscures one fundamental conclusion. Despite the facts of predominance and ethnic stratification, the great majority of the Irish were *literate*: in Hamilton only 20% of all Irish-born were illiterate, and estimates suggest a slightly lower rate in London and Kingston. Among Catholics, 70% were literate, as were 93% of Protestants. They represented, to be sure, a majority of all illiterates, and much of this analysis will focus on them. Nonetheless, we must not—as contemporaries did— neglect the fact that the greatest numbers were able to read and write. Despite the plethora of contemporary and more recent opinion, these immigrants stand out as special individuals with a surprisingly high rate

---

[7] See Ch. 1 above; Kenneth Lockridge, *Literacy in Colonial New England* (New York: Norton, 1974); Lawrence Stone, "Literacy and Education in England, 1640–1900," *Past and Present*, 42 (1969), 61–139; Carlo Cipolla, *Literacy and Development in the West* (Harmondsworth: Penguin, 1969).

of literacy; dominant images are based in error and social myths and fears not founded in social realities.[8]

Age and sex were also critical factors in the composition of illiteracy, and as with ethnicity, a common pattern among the cities emerges. In each case, illiterates were older, 4 or 5 years on the average, than the literate adults of Hamilton, with illiteracy increasing with age (Table 2.2). More revealing than this small gap (which indicates that illiterates were not elderly remnants of a time with less educational opportunity) is the cohort distribution. Only among the youngest adults (20–29) were they largely underrepresented; illiterates closely resembled the distribution of those 30–39. After that age, they were overrepresented to a relatively constant but small degree. Expansion in education was a recent phenomenon, as the literacy rates of youngest adult cohorts point directly to the period of international mass-educational impulses: from the late 1830s to the 1850s, assuming that most schooling occurred before the age of 15.[9] Importantly, this is the only break in distribution; those under 40 faced no such discontinuity but had a more common experience. Old age and the effects of mortality were levelers, closing the gaps without indication of greater age-specific mortality for illiterates. The function of age, finally, was one shared by the ethnic groups.

The contribution of sex to illiteracy is much more distinct, although it intersects significantly with the role of aging. Most obvious is a sharply imbalanced sex ratio: a 3–2 differential female disadvantage in each city (Table 2.3). Women predominated among the illiterate, one important sign of their unequal status in this society, reflecting sexual inequality in educational opportunity through and past mid-century. Sex represented another, inherited characteristic that influenced the structure of illiteracy. Sexual imbalances, moreover, have become a common finding in historical literacy studies, with the important exception of Sweden, which had a long tradition of home education. The degree of imbalance could differ, apparently, through migration and regional effects; rural areas in Upper Canada, for example, in some cases show near-parity ratios and even female ratio-advantage. The latter cases are, however, rather rare.[10]

---

[8] See, for example, S. C. Johnson, *A History of Emigration from the United Kingdom to North America, 1763–1912* (London, 1913), 320.

[9] See, as one example, R. D. Gidney, "Elementary Education in Upper Canada: A Reassessment," *Ontario History*, 65 (1973), 169–185. See also, Michael B. Katz, "Who Went to School?" *History of Education Quarterly*, 12 (1972), 432–454; Ian E. Davey, "Educational Reform and the Working Class: School Attendance in Hamilton, Ontario, 1851–1891," unpub. PhD. Diss., University of Toronto, 1975.

[10] See Katz, *The People of Hamilton, Canada West* (Cambridge, Mass.: Harvard University Press, 1975), Ch. 2; Carroll Smith Rosenberg and Charles Rosenberg, "The

Table 2.2
Ages of Adults, 1861

Age	Hamilton literates	Hamilton illiterates	Hamilton total adult population a	Kingston illiterates	Kingston total adult population a	London illiterates	London total adult population a
20–29							
N	3,264	221	3,501	97	2,480	83	2,149
%	37.9	24.5	37.5	19.2	37.7	22.3	37.8
30–39							
N	2,447	249	2,705	168	1,814	102	1,596
%	28.4	27.5	29.0	33.3	27.6	27.4	28.0
40–49							
N	1,545	211	1,768	114	1,205	78	1,014
%	17.9	23.4	18.9	22.5	18.3	21.0	17.8
50–59							
N	806	130	824	68	575	59	563
%	9.4	14.4	8.8	13.5	8.7	15.9	9.9
60–69							
N	403	63	368	38	331	39	261
%	4.7	7.0	3.9	7.5	5.0	10.4	4.6
70+							
N	152	29	172	20	168	11	108
%	1.8	3.2	1.9	4.0	2.6	3.0	1.9
Total							
N	8,617	903	9,338	505	6,573	372	5,691
%	100.0	100.0	100.0	100.0	99.9	100.0	100.0
Mean Age	35.9	39.8	—	40.5	—	41.2	—

a Data are from published census tabulations.

Table 2.3
Sex of Adults, 1861

	Hamilton literates	Hamilton illiterates	Hamilton total adult population[a]	Kingston illiterates	Kingston total adult population[a]	London illiterates	London total adult population[a]	Total illiterates
Male								
N	4,202	341	4,897	194	3,161	147	2,820	682
%	48.8	37.8	52.4	38.5	48.1	39.7	49.6	38.4
Female								
N	4,414	561	4,441	310	3,412	223	2,871	1,094
%	51.2	62.2	47.6	61.5	51.9	60.3	50.4	61.6
Total								
N	8,616	902	9,338	504	6,573	370	5,691	1,776
%	100.0	100.0	100.0	100.0	100.0	100.0	100.0	100.0

[a] Data are from published census tabulations.

The ethnic factor exacerbated the role of gender, as females in the largest group of illiterates, the Irish-Catholic and Protestant, suffered the greatest and most constant imbalance in sex ratios. Exceeding virtually all other groups, over ⅔ of Irish women were educationally disadvantaged; only the Canadian-born showed a comparable educational disadvantage. Such was the place of women born in Ireland, and the process of educational opportunity in that impoverished land. Women's position differed greatly, with no disproportion, among two other groups, however: the English Protestants and the blacks. This is significant, for as we will see, illiterate members of these groups fared relatively well economically, suggesting a connection between some success in society and a more equal distribution of education. Nonetheless, women dominated among the illiterates. Unequal allotment of schooling in an unequal society missed them most often; the structure of illiteracy was punctuated by sex, as it was by ethnicity.

Not all women suffered this differential equally. Age and sex were not independent influences on the origins of illiteracy in these cities; they intersected crucially in determining the structure of illiteracy. The youngest cohorts of women were most severely disadvantaged, exceeding their overall disproportion and climbing to largest disparities among those aged 20–29, declining thereafter (Table 2.4, Figure 2.1). Importantly, these were precisely the ages at which the effects of increased educational opportunity were detected. The broader chances for schooling, at least at first, were not shared by the sexes, but were ones in which males dominated. In Hamilton, for example, women of these ages continued to have restricted opportunities, regardless of ethnicity. The gender gap narrowed, with the aging of the cohorts, approaching near equality only among the very oldest. Illiteracy embraced a larger share of women at virtually all ages than it did men; the experience of the oldest probably reflects age-specific mortality differentials rather than any earlier time of greater equality. The pattern, finally, held among all ethnic groups, as the sexual imbalances were a common theme even if the degree could differ. Sex, in this way, mediated against a potentially levelling impact of aging, contributing to a lower status and greater disadvantage for women, among the illiterate and throughout

Female Animal: Medical and Biological Views of Woman and Her Role in Nineteenth Century America," *Journal of American History*, 60 (1973), 332–356; Davey, "Trends in Female School Attendance in Mid-Nineteenth Century Ontario," *Histoire sociale*, 8 (1975), 238–254. Lockridge, *Literacy;* Cipolla, *Literacy;* on Sweden, see Egil Johansson, "Literacy Studies in Sweden· Some Examples," *Canadian Social History Project, Report*, 5 (1973–74), 89–123. Graff, "Literacy and Social Structure in Elgin County, Upper Canada, 1861," *Histoire sociale*, 6 (1973), 25–48.

Table 2.4

Age by Sex, 1861 (Three Cities Combined)

Age	Literates			Illiterates		
	Male	Female	Total	Male	Female	Total
20–29						
N	1,413	1,851	3,264	130	271	401
%	33.6	41.9	37.9	19.1	24.8	22.6
30–39						
N	1,280	1,166	2,447	195	322	517
%	30.5	26.4	28.4	28.6	29.4	29.1
40–49						
N	804	741	1,545	151	252	403
%	19.1	16.8	17.9	22.1	23.0	22.7
50–59						
N	416	390	806	106	151	257
%	9.9	8.8	9.3	15.5	13.8	14.5
60–69						
N	207	196	403	74	65	139
%	4.9	4.5	4.7	10.9	5.9	7.8
70+						
N	82	70	152	26	33	59
%	2.0	1.6	1.8	3.8	3.0	3.3
Total						
N	4,202	4,414	8,617	682	1,094	1,776
%	100.0	100.0	100.0	100.0	99.9	100.0

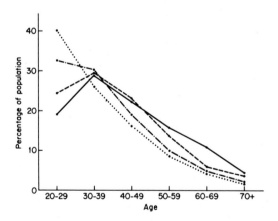

Figure 2.1   Age–sex structure, 1861. (——) Illiterate males; (– – –) illiterate females; (– • – •) literate males; (• • •) literate females.

the society. Changes in the provision of education affected males more than females, as sex continued to shape the origins of illiteracy in striking fashion.

Ethnicity and race, age and sex—these represent the major structural features of illiteracy in urban Ontario in 1861. The ascribed characteristics of Irish birth, Catholicism, color, and female sex, as they intersected with age, constituted the dominant forces among the origins of illiteracy. Identifying the illiterate, these factors interacted with the facts of everyday life, work, residence, and family to shape the role that literacy played.

II. Literacy and the Migration Process

Central to ethnic origins was the experience of migration, the process which pushed and pulled these men and women, literate or illiterate, from their homelands to these and other urban places in North America. Literacy's contribution to migration was important and direct, constituting one of its clearest influences. Migrants to these cities, and probably to places throughout North America, were selected individuals whose rate of literacy was higher than that found among those living in their birth places, regardless of origins, age, or sex. Immigrants, students have come to recognize, were special kinds of people; literacy was among their distinctive characteristics.[11]

Consider the Irish first, the group with the largest representation among the illiterates. As already noted, only 20% of them were illiterate. In Ireland, though, according to the 1841 census, 54% could neither read nor write, or 56% if only nonurban places (the origins of most migrants) are considered.[12] Since these populations comprised all those

---

[11] See Barbara A. Anderson, "Internal Migration in Modernizing Society: The Case of Late Nineteenth Century European Russia," unpub. Ph.D. Diss., Princeton University, 1973; Larry H. Long, "Migration Differentials by Education and Occupation: Trends and Variations," *Demography*, 10 (1973), 243–258; Sune Åkerman, "Mobile and Stationary Populations: The Problem of Selection," in *Literacy and Society in a Historical Perspective: A Conference Report*, ed. Egil Johansson (Umeå: Umeå University, 1973), 67–81.

[12] T. W. Freeman, *Pre-Famine Ireland* (Manchester: Manchester University Press, 1957), 133. Complications arise in the comparability of data. There is little information on the regions within the places of origin, and literacy rates varied tremendously within national areas; we are left with national rates. Bases for comparison differ as well, from census data to signatures, marriage registers, surveys by educational and statistical societies, prison records. A final complication is the timing of migration, which

aged 6 or more years, adult illiteracy would probably be underestimated, for the new Irish educational emphasis, in the form of the National System, was beginning to be felt by this date. So, the Irish immigrants rated especially high in their literacy ability, whether they are compared with rates in rural or in urban Ireland. As with all illiterate immigrants, females from Ireland predominated, with a greater than 10 percentage-point difference. Not until the late 1870s and the 1880s, in fact, did the Irish national literacy levels begin to approximate those of the urban Canadian Irish: a gap of 30 or 40 years in educational advantage for the migrants, as most of them arrived during the famine exodus of 1845–1852.[13]

Projecting, retrospectively, from 1871 marriage registers, religious differences may be assessed. A greater gap separated Catholic and Protestant illiteracy in Ireland than in places like Hamilton (40 to 14%, respectively, in Ireland; 30 to 7% in Hamilton), and the migrants exhibited higher levels than co-religionists who stayed behind.[14] In literacy ability these migrants were special persons, whose experience indicates an important relationship. And of course, this selection process resulted in a very highly literate immigrant population, even among the economically depressed Irish Catholics.

Literacy influenced not only the selection of the immigrants but also the distance they migrated. The Irish provide one clear example of this. A great many migrated only as far as Great Britain; that is, across only the Irish Sea and not the Atlantic, forming a major migratory stream to urban and rural work and with both seasonal and permanent tributaries. Researchers such as Robert Webb have located areas of Irish residence with higher illiteracy rates than those of predominantly native-born districts and Irish parishes with higher illiteracy rates than mixed areas. Educational-society surveys of two London areas in 1837, for example, reported 49 to 55% of adults (parents) unable to read.[15] If these rates are compared to those from the 1841 Irish Census, we find that

---

obscures attempts to pinpoint a baseline for the date of migration. Only general tendencies may be established, to await detailed confirmation.

[13] See Donald Akenson, *The Irish Education Experiment* (New Haven: Yale University Press, 1970); see also, R. E. Kennedy, Jr. *The Irish: Emigration, Marriage and Fertility* (Berkeley: University of California Press, 1973); Freeman, *Ireland,* 133; Cipolla, *Literacy,* 124, 73; Oliver MacDonagh, "The Irish Famine Emigration to the United States," *Perspectives in American History,* 10 (1976), 357–446.

[14] Cipolla, *Literacy,* 73; Freeman, *Ireland,* 133, *passim.*

[15] Freeman, *Ireland;* Webb, "Working Class Readers in Early Victorian England," *English Historical Review,* 65 (1950), 333–351. On Irish settlement in London, see Lynn H. Lees, "Patterns of Lower Class Life: Irish Slum Communities in Nineteenth Century London," in *Nineteenth Century Cities,* ed. Stephan Thernstrom and Richard Sennett (New Haven: Yale University Press, 1969), 359–385.

short-distance migrants had literacy levels at best only marginally above those of people at home; the difference does not compare with that of those who made the lengthier and more arduous journey to North America.

The proportion of illiterate migrants and their share of the migratory stream seems to have decreased proportionately to the distance moved, and decreased radically when the Atlantic was confronted. The relationship of literacy to opportunity, awareness, and motivation remains obscure and many without literacy were able to make major movements. Nonetheless, it may well be, as Barbara Anderson has argued, that illiterate migrants came from regions of above-average literacy, in which their position would be enhanced. Their absolute illiteracy and its potential disadvantages in comparison with the position of literates could have been mediated by place of residence and proximity to information, reducing relatively the effects of their illiteracy.[16] They too would be "selected" migrants. Regardless, literacy related directly to migration, and levels of literacy interacted with distance of movement.

The relationship is supported by the experience of the other migrants. English-born immigrants to the cities also had substantially lower levels of illiteracy. In Hamilton and the other cities, only 3.2% were illiterate, while rates in England remained much higher, judging from marriage registers from 1800 to 1861. In 1800, for example, about 50% could not sign their names (40% of males; 60% of females), and in 1861, the rate was still 30% (25% men; 35% women).[17] Migration selected a special segment of the adult population in terms of their literacy.

The Scottish immigrants reveal the same patterns. The most literate of all migrants, they left a land of very high literacy. In 1851, 80% of adults (10 years or over) in Scotland were able to read and write, and between 1855 and 1861, only 15–18% of newlyweds were illiterate (men 10–12%; women 21–25%).[18] In Hamilton, however, only 1.8% of the Scottish-born were illiterate, with perhaps a few more in the other cities. Once again, the evidence, however imperfect, strongly indicates that immigration was selective of literates among Scotland's population, and

---

[16] B. Anderson, "Internal Migration."

[17] Roger Schofield, "The Measurement of Literacy in Pre-Industrial England," in *Literacy in Traditional Societies*, ed. Jack Goody (Cambridge: Cambridge University Press, 1968), 311–325, "Dimensions of Illiteracy, 1750–1850," *Explorations in Economic History*, 10 (1973), 445, Figure 2. See also, Webb, "Readers". For data after 1839, see Great Britain, *Annual Reports of the Registrar General of Births, Deaths, and Marriages*.

[18] Cipolla, *Literacy*, 18, 115; Lockridge, *Literacy;* Webb, "Literacy among the Working Classes in Nineteenth Century Scotland," *Scottish Historical Review*, 33 (1954), 114, 100–114.

that migrants had special characteristics. To their new homes these immigrants brought skills and personal resources, a contribution which needs to be further emphasized in studies of immigration and social development.

U.S.-born migrants, by contrast, exhibit the pattern noted for shorter-distance journeys, such as those of the Irish to England and the French Canadians to Ontario. These adults, white and black together, had an illiteracy rate of 17% in Hamilton, similar to that in the other cities. The impact of race must be distinguished here, for only 11% of whites were illiterate. U.S. census data from 1840 (which may underestimate illiteracy) reveal a 9% level of illiteracy; the 1850 Census found 10% for native-born whites.[19] The areas from which most immigrants to Canada came were even more literate places: New England, New York, the old Northwest. These migrants, we may judge, show no exceptional abilities with regard to literacy; selectivity apparently did not function over a short distance—perhaps it was not required.

Assessments of the literacy levels of blacks from the United States are much more difficult, for there exist fewer data on which to draw. However, it seems that literacy played a more significant role in their movements than it did for whites. Blacks obviously came for different reasons and responded to different pressures. In Hamilton, 48% of black adults were illiterate in 1861, a rate similar to that in London and Kingston. Black illiteracy was first reported in the 1850 U.S. census: 43% of free blacks and, what is doubtful, 100% of slaves.[20] It remains impossible to distinguish the free blacks from the fugitive slaves resident in Canada, yet it is known that many ex-slaves migrated via the Underground Railroad. Very possibly, black migrants to these cities were, as a group, more often literate than U.S. blacks; some degree of selection may well have been at work in determining who came, although we can not precisely evaluate its significance.

Literacy, we may now conclude, served an important function in the process of migration and the peopling of these cities, especially for the longer distance migrations. This relationship, in fact, is not peculiar to North America: studies of nineteenth-century European Russia and Sweden and contemporary surveys point to the same phenomenon in those countries. Anderson, for one, found evidence of selection of mi-

---

[19] U.S. Commissioner of Education, *Annual Report,* 1870, 478–479; and the Census volumes for those years. For data from wills, to 1790, see Lockridge, *Literacy.*

[20] See Winks, *Blacks.* On attitudes toward education in the South, see William R. Taylor, "Toward a Definition of Orthodoxy," *Harvard Educational Review,* 36 (1966), 412–426; Eugene Genovese, *Roll, Jordon Roll* (New York: Pantheon, 1974); Thomas Webber, *Deep Like the Rivers* (New York: Norton, 1978); Willie Lee Rose, *Rehearsal for Reconstruction* (Indianapolis: Bobbs-Merrill, 1964); note 19 above.

grants (literate or not) from areas of high literacy, concluding that literacy ranked among the key explanatory variables in accounting for differential migrations. Migrants, as well, tended to come from areas of what has been called "cultural modernization" and had more characteristics indicative of modernity, skill, or sophistication than nonmigrants. Even illiterates, she concludes, if they were originally from an area with higher literacy levels, were likely to have more and better information and to be more receptive to new ideas than illiterates from other places. Indeed, they might hold some advantage over literate persons from less-advanced areas.[21] Perhaps then many North American immigrants were these kinds of exceptional persons regardless of their own literacy or illiteracy. Anderson's analysis indicates that the most modern came to the cities, a finding adding another important implication for the study of literacy and North American development. The data for the further exploration of these ideas do not now exist; however, the issues raised here could well be the subjects of future interpretive studies.

An analysis of shorter-term movement than the Russian case further supports our conclusions. Sune Åkerman, studying nineteenth-century Sweden, and Larry Long, researching the contemporary United States, also link education to migration distance. Both find that short-distance migrants reveal no educational advantage.[22] The mid-nineteenth-century migration patterns, with their direct relationship to literacy, were hardly unique; immigrants were exceptional, selected men and women. They were overwhelmingly literate in comparison with the people in their places of origin; they were not the dregs of their society that contemporaries and school promoters were so quick to conclude they were. The Irish in particular stand out. In sum, migrations brought to the cities a population with some definite skills, undoubtedly offering them important advantages for social and economic development. The illiterates too gained through selectivity. They also were primarily selected by their inherited characteristics, reflecting the structures of social inequality.

III. Work, Wealth, and Reward

The relationship between schooling and success and the relative importance of achievement over ascription undoubtedly constitute two of the most profound issues in modern social science and social theory.

[21] B. Anderson, "Migration", Chapter X, 8–9.
[22] Long, "Differentials"; Åkerman, "Populations".

In pursuit of these matters, more words are written and more data are collected, I suspect, than in any other area of social inquiry. This is hardly surprising, for the centrality of education in the attainment of prestigious work and its commensurate rewards, and the dominance of achievement over social ascription is at once a major component of modern society with its stress on equality (of opportunity, at least) and an emotionally charged ideal of democratic social progress. The existence and the maintenance of opportunities through access to education and the continued ability to substitute attainment for origins, largely as a result of schooling, represent the progressive evolution of the social organization, even while they insure its future. The premise of these social principles lies in the interpretation that before modernization and mass education—in traditional societies—rewards were distributed more on the basis of ascriptive, inherited characteristics than on the basis of achieved ones. Social placement derived from continuity and succession—primarily natal. The transition—in theory, a major and irreversible shift—occurred with the impact of modernization, and its concomitant institutions, on the social structure. The school, in these formulations, became the setting for much more equal opportunities to advance, as the substitution of achievement for ascription triumphed in social theory as the ideal (and presumably an actualized one) for a new distribution of rewards and positions. The line separating theory and rhetoric from social reality continues to be a difficult and debated one, as both contemporary and historical studies reveal; regardless, the dominance of democratic ideology based upon educational achievement remains firmly in place.[23] (One might add, as well, that students of the relationships between schooling and success are also, by and large, professional educators, who have professional and personal investments in the value of education.)

Nineteenth-century commentators and school promoters appear even more certain of the necessity of education for achievement than modern students and theorists; they had little doubt at all. Egerton Ryerson put it quite plainly when he asked, "How is the uneducated and unskilled man to succeed in these times of sharp and skilful competition and

[23] The literature on these questions is mammoth and growing daily. See however, the works cited in note 3 above, and Peter Blau and O. D. Duncan, *The American Occupational Structure* (New York: Wiley, 1967); W. H. Sewell and R. M. Hauser, *Education, Occupation, and Earnings* (New York: Academic Press, 1975); Sewell, Hauser, and D. L. Featherman, eds., *Schooling and Achievement in American Society* (New York: Academic Press, 1976). For an introduction to the historical literature, see Katz, *Class, Bureaucracy, and Schools* (New York: Praeger, 1975); Diane Ravitch, "The Revisionists Revised," *Proceedings of the National Academy of Education*, 4 (1977), 1–84 (revised ed. pub. in 1978 by Basic Books).

sleepless activity?" Answering his own rhetorical question, he was certain that "everyman, unless he wishes to starve outright, must read and write, and cast accounts. . . ." [24] This interpretation followed from Ryerson's prototypical view of the components and content of schooling (discussed in Chapter 1); its connection with more recent affirmations is clear. Based on the claim that the attainment of some measure of schooling is instrumental, and required, for occupational and economic success, it was promoted widely and frequently. The attainment of literacy, or at least the acquisition of some education, is considered necessary and sufficient for individuals to overcome their other ascribed characteristics, including those stemming from ethnic origins, family and class background, and sometimes sex and race. Achievement, therefore, is held out as an avenue to those who seek to surmount the handicaps of their social and cultural inheritance, as the poor and immigrant were often expected (or were hoped) to do. The school, of course, in its new institutional structure was offered as the agency best suited for this task. The ideal of success and mobility, however, cautiously presented or qualified in the rhetoric of school promotion, aided, no doubt, the work of formal education in support of the moral economy.

The economic experience of the illiterates, whose origins have been examined, provides an appropriate opportunity for evaluating the promises of modern achievement. Their positions, we would expect, were determined directly by their lack of educational attainment as reflected by their illiteracy. Without this accomplishment, their opportunities for success should be severely restricted, if not totally obstructed. To the superficial observer, in fact, their occupational and economic situations affirm expectations and reinforce the understanding that literacy laid the basis for advancement.

That conclusion, which this section challenges, is incomplete. Regardless of the promise of achievement-through-education (and the probable results of a simple examination of the status of illiterates), qualities such as education and literacy proved insufficient, by themselves, to negate facts of birth, inheritance, and structural inequality. The continued dominance of ascriptive characteristics and a rigidly stratified social structure were far more important influences on economic rewards than educational achievement and literacy.[25] The process

[24] Ryerson, "The Importance of Education to a Manufacturing and a Free People," *Journal of Education*, 1 (1848); *Journal of Education*, 7 (1854), 134; see also Ch. 5.

[25] My perspective on stratification and inequality is indebted to the work of Michael Katz in particular. See *The People of Hamilton, C. W.* esp. Chs. 1, 2, 3, in addition to the literature cited above and modern sociological inquiries, such as those of D. Trieman, E. Laumann, S. Lipset and R. Bendix, B. Barber, M. Tumin, R.

of stratification related directly to ascribed characteristics, which overwhelmingly determined the structures of occupation and wealth. Much
as ethnicity influenced the social distribution of education, as we have
seen, it also predominated in determining economic position and
rewards. Social stratification, consequently, seldom related directly to
literacy: most rewards were based on ethnicity, age, and sex. The resulting disparity between promise of achievement and social processes shows
literacy to be a mediating and reinforcing factor, not an autonomous
or determining one. For many individuals, the attainment of literacy
had relatively little effect; for others, though, it could matter. Differential rewards accrued to members of different ethnic groups whether
they achieved literacy or not. Only through an intensive analysis of the
distribution of occupation and wealth does a clear picture of the complex role of literacy emerge.

The relationship of literacy and schooling to occupational success,
with its requirements of skill and performance, is seldom questioned,
despite the contradictory results of many empirical examinations. Not
surprisingly, illiterate workers clustered in the lower-ranking levels of
unskilled work in the three mid-century cities of Hamilton, Kingston,
and London (Table 2.5).[26] Highly stratified, more than half of employed illiterates were unskilled common laborers; many others held
semiskilled positions. They were not overrepresented, however, in this
transitional level, as they were among the lowest ranking. On the sur-
face, we have strong evidence for affirming the expected relationship
of illiteracy to low skill and low status. The social reality, though, was
not so simple. For example, note that, according to the tabulations,
illiterate workers were not a majority at any occupational level. Although
the proportions of illiterates increased with lower-class position, significantly, less than one fourth of even the unskilled and only 7% of the
semiskilled were illiterate. Despite the disproportionate clustering of
the uneducated, a full ¾ of the laborers and 93% of the semiskilled
possessed literacy skills. Their achievement was insufficient to influence

---

Collins, and S. Ossowski. A good review is E. C. Laumann, ed., *Social Stratification*
(Indianapolis: Bobbs-Merrill, 1970). Recent historical work while mixed, is important
too, especially that of S. Thernstrom, C. Griffen, T. Hershberg, R. S. Neale, J. Foster,
G. Stedman Jones, E. P. Thompson, E. J. Hobsbawm.

26 I employ the Five Cities Occupational Scale, as determined by Katz, Stuart
Blumin, Laurence Glasco, Clyde Griffen, and Theodore Hershberg for comparison of
their data on nineteenth century cities. A copy appears in Appendix C. On problems
associated with the use of occupations, see Katz, "Occupational Classification in History," *Journal of Interdisciplinary History*, 3 (1972), 63–88; Clyde Griffen, "Occupational Mobility in 19th Century America: Problems and Possibilities," *Journal of Social
History*, 5 (1972), 310–330.

Table 2.5

Occupational Hierarchy, 1861

	Hamilton literates	Percentage illiterate	Hamilton illiterates	Kingston illiterates	London illiterates	Total illiterates
		Six categories				
Professional/ proprietor						
N	306		3	1	—	4
%	3.6	1.0	0.3	0.2	—	0.2
Nonmanual/ small proprietor						
N	768		21	13	6	40
%	8.9	2.7	2.3	2.6	1.6	2.2
Artisanal/ skilled						
N	1,467		72	34	29	135
%	17.0	4.8	8.0	6.7	7.8	7.6
Semiskilled						
N	959		75	85	32	192
%	11.1	7.3	8.3	16.8	8.6	10.8
Unskilled						
N	638		216	107	84	407
%	7.4	25.3	23.9	21.2	22.6	22.9
None/Others [a]						
N	4,479		516	265	221	1,002
%	52.0	10.3	57.2	52.5	59.4	56.3
Total						
N	8,617		903	505	372	1,780
%	100.0		100.0	100.0	100.0	100.0
		Five categories (employed)				
Professional/ properietor						
N	306		3	1	—	4
%	7.4	—	0.8	0.4	—	0.5
Nonmanual/ small proprietor						
N	768		21	13	6	40
%	18.6	—	5.4	5.4	4.0	5.1
Artisanal/ skilled						
N	1,467		72	34	29	135
%	35.4	—	18.6	14.2	19.2	17.4
Semiskilled						
N	959		75	85	32	192
%	23.2	—	19.4	35.4	21.2	24.7

(continued)

Table 2.5 *(continued)*

	Hamilton literates	Percentage illiterate	Hamilton illiterates	Kingston illiterates	London illiterates	Total illiterates
Unskilled						
N	638		216	107	84	407
%	15.4	—	55.8	44.6	55.6	52.3
Total						
N	4,138		387	240	151	778
%	100.0		100.0	100.0	100.0	100.0

a Largely women (wives, widows).

occupational position or to benefit them; other factors were more important.

Many other illiterates, in fact, fared better, despite their lack of schooling. Almost one fifth gained artisan or skilled work, and they were distributed across a broad range of jobs. Blacksmiths, cabinet makers, carpenters, dealers, engineers, masons, tailors, and watchmakers—these positions illustrate the significant fact that skilled work did not always presuppose schooling and that illiterates were by no means disqualified from jobs exceeding the least skilled places in urban society (for a complete list, see Appendix D). Literacy may well be important to some artisan traditions; but no evidence exists that it is central in their work processes. Learning a job surely remained empirical—by seeing and doing and gaining experience on the job; manual dexterity, "knack," and good sense contributed more to job skills than a common-school education. Technical literacy undoubtedly differed from literary skills, as artisan's accounts make scant mention of the practical uses of literacy in their work.[27] If literacy facilitated the gaining of skilled positions, its benefits lay elsewhere, we may surmise. Thus, these urban illiterates were only underrepresented by half compared with the distribution of literates. Nonetheless, in recognizing the success of some uneducated, their small share (5%) of skilled positions can not be overlooked: literacy did carry some importance, albeit by virtue of an often indirect influence.

At the upper levels of the occupational hierarchy, access for illiterates was, expectedly, more restricted; commercial, clerical, and pro-

---

[27] See, for example, John Burnet, ed., *Useful Toil: Autobiographies of Working Men From the 1820's to the 1920's* (Harmondsworth: Penguin, 1974); George Sturt *The Wheelwright's Shop* (Cambridge: Cambridge University Press, 1923); and Edward Shorter, ed., *Work and Community in the West* (New York: Harper and Row, 1973).

fessional roles surely demanded literacy more than other work did. Yet, 40 uneducated persons (including a Hamilton merchant and clergyman—a black leader) found a niche above the skilled and manual level. No doubt as a result of significant striving and savings, they became small storekeepers, inn- or tavernkeepers, or public servants (even "gentlemen") without the advantage of literacy.[28] For them, apparently, literacy was not a requirement for commercial life nor for public responsibility. Clearly exceptional individuals who escaped the fate of most illiterates, their occupational success challenges the achievement-emphasis of contemporary and later interpreters, demonstrating, with the skilled workers, that in mid-nineteenth-century commercial centers, gains could come without education. For many of them, ascriptive characteristics counteracted any disadvantage that illiteracy might represent. For many others, though, the achievement of education brought no occupational rewards at all; inherited factors cancelled the potential of advancement through literacy.

Sex continued to be an element of social inequality independent of literacy, as the pervasiveness of sexual inequality restricted virtually all women who sought to work. Illiterate women workers compared relatively favorably to literate ones in an economic system in which few women worked officially and fewer could hope for independence. Overall, illiterate women were only slightly disadvantaged: almost 90% of each group were semi- or unskilled. Faced with sexual stratification, women found very few benefits in education. (However, one must note the very real opportunities that the mid-century feminization of the teaching force presented to women.)

Ethnicity, more than any other factor, influenced the structure of inequality in these cities, and in so doing overwhelmingly determined the place of illiterates. This was a class society, with class divisions rooted in ethnic differences.[29] As it governed the incidence of literacy itself and the success enjoyed by literates, ethnic origin directly affected the status of the uneducated; and ascription dominated the effects of education. Contradicting any presumably independent role for literacy as a social structural determinant, this interpretation carries important

[28] For examples of this kind of mobility, see Stephen Thernstrom, *Poverty and Progress* (Cambridge, Mass.: Harvard University Press, 1964); Clyde and Sally Griffen, *Natives and Newcomers* (Cambridge, Mass.: Harvard University Press, 1978). On achievements of illiterates in Marseilles, see W. H. Sewell, Jr., "Social Mobility in a Nineteenth-Century European City," *Journal of Interdisciplinary History*, 7 (1976), 213–234.

[29] See, in particular, Katz, *The People of Hamilton*, Ch. 2; Stanley Leiberson, "Stratification and Ethnic Groups," in *Social Stratification*, ed. Laumann, 172–181, provides a sound introduction to the importance of ethnic stratification.

implications. It further demonstrates the integration of the illiterates into the primary social processes; they were neither segregated nor isolated from the major functions of stratification. Moreover, that the same processes operated among illiterates and literates brings literacy's own role into proper context. For among the uneducated, social stratification differentiated the status of members of the various ethnic groups, as ranking among them strikingly paralleled the ordering of the literate members in its social influences, with ethnicity mediating the influence of literacy and literacy reinforcing that of origins. Both literacy and illiteracy were strongly determined by ethnic origins; illiteracy could be a handicap, especially in its ascriptive associations, as literacy by itself was no advantage.[30]

Despite their common illiteracy, the occupational status of the members of different ethnic groups varied widely (Table 2.6). Ethnic stratification differentiated their occupational attainments quite similarly in each city, to the effect that the groups form a clear hierarchy. As a result, instead of a common depressed profile, we find that whereas 73% of Canadian Catholics, 60% of Irish Catholics, and 50% of Irish Protestant illiterates were unskilled, only 35% of English Protestants, 33% of blacks, 28% of Scottish Presbyterians, and 26% of Canadian Protestants were. In proportions skilled or higher ranking, the order is reversed, with the English and the blacks improving their place over the Canadian Protestants, who were much younger. The handicap of illiteracy clearly was not shared equally.

The role of ethnicity, with its parallels in both illiterate and literate experience, is seen more easily through the use of a simple index of occupational standing. Subtracting the sum of the percentage of those at skilled or higher levels from the total of those with a lower rank isolates the unskilled membership of each group. High index numbers indicate an excess in lower positions; low to negative scores signify

---

[30] To establish this case even more firmly, the data analysis should advance from the cross-tabulations and contingency tables presented here to multivariate procedures. Unfortunately, as I began to replicate the analysis with Multiple Classification Analysis (MCA), the University of Texas at Dallas Computing Center *lost* my data tape; back-up copies disappeared in a relocation of facilities at the University of Toronto. Multivariate replication, to my great regret, proved impossible. Although it is insufficient to "prove" my case, I can, however, point to my first, incomplete results and to unpublished tabulations on Hamilton by Katz's York Social History Project, 1976–77. Katz did find that literacy, by itself, reduced a person's probability of becoming a laborer by only 3%, that it increased the chances for skilled work by 6%, and that it did little to increase wealth. In contrast, illiteracy was more depressing: a 24% greater chance of being a laborer. Literacy's impact was greater on occupation than on wealth. Personal communications from Katz, 1976–1977.

parity to higher standing. Drawing a line at the skilled level permits the further exploration of the relationship of literacy to skills and provides flexibility. The use of this scale facilitates a direct comparison among the groups (Table 2.7). It shows more clearly the distinct profiles of the separate groups and their stratification. In rank order, the English came first (−3.0), the only ones among the illiterates with a majority of skilled or higher ranking, followed by blacks and native-born Protestants, and Scots. A widening gap separated these groups from the Irish, both Protestant and Catholic (54.2 and 62.6), and the Catholics, both Irish and Canadian, those most concentrated in lowest positions. The rank ordering is significant, and it is very consistent across the cities.

Explicit in these distributions is the differentiated experience of illiterates, proving that they were not a homogeneous lot, equally depressed, as their contemporaries often implied. A recognition of this variation brings us much closer to the meaning of literacy, whose potential advantages were shared no more equally than the disadvantages of illiteracy. Ethnicity directly influenced their occupational placement, cutting deeply into any contribution that literacy might make. Literacy, correspondingly, supported these processes of stratification, reinforcing the lines between groups, as the ordering of the illiterates paralleled, and derived from, the inequalities in the larger, literate society. English Protestants, for example, ranked high in each city (second to the younger, native Protestants in Hamilton), whereas Irish Catholics stood even more consistently lowest. (The few Canadian Catholics' position resulted from their older age.) Significantly, the only group able to improve its relative position when illiterate was the blacks. To them, illiteracy was hardly a material handicap when added to that of racial status and discrimination; consequently, among illiterates they stood relatively well, while ranking lower among literate adults.

The process of ethnic stratification and its relationship to literacy emerges most clearly from a systematic comparison of the literates and illiterates of each group. Irish Catholics ranked lowest, whether illiterate or not, but their disadvantage was not shared equally (scores of 63 and 41). More of the uneducated were unskilled and more stood below the skilled level, although the difference was not great: three-fifths to two-thirds. Two conclusions follow. First, regardless of education, the overwhelming numbers of Irish Catholics did poorly. Unable to escape their ascriptive bonds, literacy brought only the slightest of benefits and a very small chance for skilled work. Second, the handicap of illiteracy proved greater than the advantage of literacy. To be Irish and Catholic was to be severely disadvantaged, regardless of education. Irish Protes-

Table 2.6
Occupation by Ethnicity, 1861 (Three Cities Combined)

Ethnic group	Professional/proprietor (1)	Nonmanual (2)	Skilled (3)	Semiskilled (4)	Unskilled (5)	4 + 5 (%)	1,2,3 (%)	N
Irish Catholic								
Literate								
N	9	59	139	226	272			705
%	1.3	8.4	19.7	32.1	38.5	70.6	29.4	
Illiterate								
N	1	11	50	109	261			432
%	0.2	2.5	11.6	25.2	60.4	85.6	14.4	
Irish Protestant								
Literate								
N	57	91	170	152	98			568
%	10.0	16.0	29.9	26.8	17.3	44.0	56.0	
Illiterate								
N	0	5	12	20	37			74
%	—	6.8	16.2	27.0	50.0	77.0	23.0	
Scottish Presbyterian								
Literate								
N	47	145	295	195	69			751
%	6.3	19.3	39.3	25.9	9.2	35.1	64.9	
Illiterate								
N	0	8	8	13	8			29
%	—	27.6	27.6	44.8	27.6	72.4	27.6	
English Protestant								
Literate								
N	62	194	467	139	105			967
%	6.4	20.0	48.3	14.4	10.9	25.3	74.7	

									Total
Illiterate										
N	1	10	24	9	24					68
%	1.5	14.7	35.3	13.2	35.3		48.5	51.5		
Canadian Protestant										
Literate										
N	71	142	130	85	9					442
%	16.2	32.5	29.7	19.4	2.1		21.5	78.5		
Illiterate										
N	0	5	4	8	6					23
%	—	21.7	17.4	34.8	26.1		60.9	39.1		
Canadian Catholic										
Literate										
N	0	18	30	28	10					86
%	—	20.9	34.9	32.6	11.6		34.2	65.8		
Illiterate										
N	0	0	1	3	11					15
%	—	—	6.6	20.0	73.3		93.4	6.6		
Black										
Literate										
N	0	7	17	22	17					51
%	—	11.1	26.9	34.9	26.9		61.8	38.2		
Illiterate										
N	1	1	23	18	21					64
%	1.6	1.6	35.9	28.1	32.8		60.9	39.1		
Others										
Literate										
N	60	112	219	112	58					561
%	10.7	19.9	39.0	19.9	10.3		30.2	69.8		
Illiterate										
N	1	8	13	12	39					73
%	1.4	10.9	17.8	16.4	53.4		69.8	30.2		

Table 2.7
Index of Occupational Standing [a]

	Hamilton literates	Illiterates			Total illiterates
		Hamilton	Kingston	London	
Irish Catholic	41.2	64.5	64.0	73.8	62.6
Irish Protestant	−11.8	57.1	54.8	46.8	54.2
Scottish Presbyterian	−29.8	10.0	71.4	81.8	45.0
English Protestant	−49.4	− 4.6	40.0	− 4.4	− 3.0
Canadian Protestant	−57.0	23.2	25.0	0.0	21.8
Canadian Catholic	−11.6	100.0	33.4	100.0	86.6
Black	23.6	21.6	−33.3	40.0	21.8
Others	−39.6	8.6	57.8	57.0	39.8
Total	−22.8	50.4	60.0	53.6	54.2

[a] Index: (percentage unskilled + percentage semiskilled) − (percentage skilled + percentage nonmanual + percentage professional/proprietor).

tants, in comparison, were less socially and economically depressed than the Catholics, and more of them rose to skilled or higher ranking positions. If their disadvantage was less, they too fared poorly, whether illiterate or literate. Education could only marginally cancel the effects of their origins.

English Protestants, in sharp contrast, met some success, whether educated or illiterate. The highest ranking among illiterates—by a wide margin—over half gained skilled or nonmanual work. Among literates, they also stood well, second only to Canadian Protestants. For the English illiterates, the fact of their ethnic origins reduced the significance of education as a career determinant, as they benefitted from the advantages of birth. A lack of education could handicap them—illiterates more often were unskilled, but their opportunities for higher status remained good. Above the line of skilled work, for example, the differential was not large: 50% of illiterates, 68% of literates. Canadian Protestants, the closest rivals to the English in accomplishment, reveal the same factors of ascription outdistancing achievement. Indeed, it was only the Canadians' relative youthfulness that allowed the English to fare better among the illiterate.

The experience of blacks differed radically from that of the others, yet it did not run counter to the facts of stratification. Compared with virtually all other illiterates, uneducated blacks were quite successful, ranking second, while their literate peers stood only second to the lowest.

In fact, the distributions of literate and illiterate blacks are extremely similar, much more so than those of any other group; chances to gain skilled or higher status posts were the same. To a racial minority, faced with racial discrimination, education brought no discernible benefits, and illiteracy no detriments; race carried an independent influence. Among these groups, education was far from a primary component in the stratification of their society. In the attainment of occupation, ethnic origins proved far more influential and powerful than literacy. Although education undoubtedly contributed to inequality, its contribution was not direct; rather, the extent to which its absence was detrimental or its possession was advantageous followed from the individual's ethnic group membership. The achievement of schooling simply did not often contradict the facts of birth in this society.

Age also influenced the process of stratification and occupational success in these cities, especially as it intersected with ethnicity. Another dynamic in the process, aging reinforced the dominant patterns of ethnic determination, differing in its importance to members of different groups only to a small extent. As the evidence of the social-structural integration of illiterates suggests, aging had a similar impact on all workers; regardless of education, their chances for success rose in the younger to middle years, then diminished with advancing years (Figure 2.2.). These data, and the patterns of the ethnic groups, demonstrate that in the relationship connecting occupational success, social inequality, and the life course, literacy had remarkably little impact. Illiterates, with few exceptions, shared the experiences of their ethnic peers more than they followed different career paths. To the extent that aging intersected with illiteracy, it lay in the depressing fact of their older ages rather than any more direct influences; at most, it accentuated the effects of ethnicity.

There were several small, but revealing, exceptions to these trends, which advance an understanding of the nature of the handicap presented by illiteracy. Patterns of access to skilled work and to nonmanual ranks for illiterates diverged somewhat from those of literates. For the skilled, success came to the uneducated slightly earlier in life (especially in the thirties, with 40% of all skilled illiterates), a less gradual attainment than for others. Their rising to this level—their most frequent point of success, and a real success—apparently involved a greater role for youthfulness and may have also reflected earlier entry into work. Starting to work earlier, they obtained their skills and experience at less advanced ages than many literates. In addition, they may have migrated while younger and consequently benefitted from lengthier periods of residence in and adaptation to their new homes. Estimates of age at migration, while very approximate, provide some evidence that illiterates

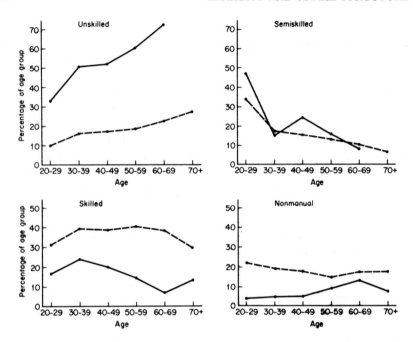

Figure 2.2 Occupation by age, 1861 (percentage of age group in each occupation). (- - -) literate; (——) illiterate.

who gained skilled or even higher ranking work migrated at relatively youthful ages (before their mid-twenties) and were not newcomers to North America by this point in their careers. These estimates also suggest that skilled illiterates may well have migrated earlier in life than the unskilled.[31] For some then, the interaction of career, selective migration, and life course could partially compensate for the effects of ethnicity and illiteracy. This was especially true for a group such as the Irish Catholics in their struggles to overcome the barriers to their success. For, the more disadvantaged the group, the greater the depressing role of advancing age; the influences of inequality did not diminish across the life course for the greatest majority.

For a very few illiterates, the timing of success differed. Contrary to the experience of most literates, those who reached nonmanual and small proprietary positions were older, holding this rank most often in their forties and fifties. For them, this position meant not a transitional

[31] These estimates of age at migration were made for illiterate heads of household who had children living at home, at least one of whom was born abroad and one in North America. They involve a minimum and maximum range of probable times of migration. While quite imprecise and difficult to summarize, they support my argument. For full details, see "Literacy and Social Structure," unpub. PhD. Diss. University of Toronto, 1975, 118–120, 206–207, 485–488.

stage as it did for many literates, but the peak of success, no doubt the end of a long striving for security To an illiterate, these occupations probably represented a greater accomplishment. Analogously, at the semiskilled level—another transitional stage in occupational succession—illiterates also gained work more often at older ages, especially their forties, than literates. In the world of lower class status and poverty, this level could mean a real gain, and not merely a transitional rank.[32] Overall, though, these variations are small, if revealing; aging primarily reinforced the structure of inequality and the dominance of ethnicity, its impact greatest for those who faced the largest obstacles to their success.

In their quests for occupational success in these mid-nineteenth-century commercial cities, most illiterates fared poorly; they stood among the lowest ranking, as many expected. Despite their lowly positions, it was *not* their lack of education that determined social placement. Social ascription, primarily their ethnic origins and sometimes their sex or age, remained most responsible. Their illiteracy contributed to their depressed status, but was not an independent influence, as their origins were. Nonetheless, many without education climbed above the skilled level, as literacy by itself proved even less of an advantage than illiteracy proved an obstruction.

Important as these insights into the social structural correlates of literacy are, our understanding of the processes remains incomplete. Occupation as a measure of status, class, or rewards, despite its frequent use in stratification research, provides only one indicator; and its employment is complicated by the variation in rewards which come to the same occupational levels.[33] To this evidence we must add that of wealth, advancing the analysis of the economic standing of these individuals. Measures of wealth, importantly, validate the interpretation developed here, reinforcing it, while permitting a deeper understanding of the social context of literacy in nineteenth-century urban society. Ascription outweighed the importance of educational achievement, with regard to wealth as to occupation, as the distribution of rewards was determined directly by ethnicity—which literacy did not contravene. Literacy probably played an even smaller role. The structure of inequality is manifest, and the benefits of literacy to the great many seem even dimmer.

Before proceeding, it is necessary to note that the population under

---

[32] Katz, *The People of Hamilton*, Ch. 3. Thernstrom, *Poverty and Progress*.

[33] See esp. Katz, "Occupational Classification in History," *The People of Hamilton*, Chs. 2–3. Thernstrom, *The Other Bostonians* (Cambridge, Mass.: Harvard University Press, 1973); W. A. Armstrong, "The Use of Information About Occupation," in *Nineteenth Century Society*, ed. E. A. Wrigley (Cambridge: Cambridge University Press, 1973), 191–335, make the case for the use of occupations.

examination is reduced. The census manuscripts supply no direct information on wealth-holding, so we examine only those heads of households found also in the city assessment rolls of 1861.[34] Fewer illiterates, in fact, were traced to these rolls, compiled 3 months after the census: only 50% of heads of households compared with 80% of literate heads. Indicative of illiterates' greater transiency, discussed in the next chapter, the analysis is obviously biased toward the stable elements of the population, as any examination built upon record-linkage must be. The predominance of poverty among even persistent illiterates reduces any chances of additional distortion, I believe. Finally, in discussing wealth, the assessment category of *total annual value* is used; it provides the most inclusive data amenable to comparison. The data are available for Hamilton and Kingston (there was no comparable category for London), and the literate population of Hamilton continues to serve as the control group.

The poverty of illiterates stands out dramatically among the patterns of wealthholding (Table 2.8). Ryerson's view that a man would starve outright if unable to read or write appears to be vindicated; over 70% of assessed illiterates fell below the 40th percentile, the line taken to represent poverty in Hamilton.[35] Only 36% of Hamilton's literate population were poor; therefore, an illiterate's chances of poverty were twice as great. Yet many uneducated persons did escape poverty's boundaries. In the middle ranks, they fared better, with 22% among the 40th–79th percentiles, and compared more favorably in the third quintile, the level above the poor. And, despite their rather pronounced underrepresentation at the highest levels, those few who did succeed (e.g., 10 in the 80th–89th percentiles in Hamilton) represented slightly more than half the proportion of literates. These were exceptional men, illiterate but wealthy. Overall, as we would expect, poverty and lower class status befell the illiterates; however, as we should now expect, this was not merely a function of their lack of education.

It is significant, too, that of *all* the poor in Hamilton—with its pervasive inequality—only 13% were illiterate. One certainly did not have to be uneducated to be poor. Illiterates made up only a tiny percentage of the poor; therefore any rhetoric or social analysis aimed at their condition was obviously not based upon their numbers. Their economic plight was shared by a great many others who could read or write—almost 90% of all of Hamilton's poor.

Equally important is the role of ethnic origins in determining the

[34] The record linkage is described in Appendix E and persistence is analyzed in Chapter 3. References to nominal record linkage will be found there as well.

[35] See Katz, *The People of Hamilton,* Ch. 2.

Table 2.8
Wealth: Total Annual Value, 1861
Linked Heads of Household (Census–Assessment)

Dollars	Hamilton literates	Percentage illiterate	Hamilton illiterates	Kingston illiterates	Total illiterates	Percentile
0–23						
N	329		76	16	92	0–19
%	12.9	18.8	40.6	22.2	35.5	
24–42						
N	609		62	36	98	20–39
%	23.9	9.2	33.2	50.0	37.8	
43–71						
N	447		22	11	33	40–59
%	18.7	4.7	11.8	15.3	12.7	
72–168						
N	593		15	8	23	60–79
%	23.2	2.5	8.0	11.1	8.8	
169–375						
N	230		10	1	11	80–89
%	9.0	4.2	5.3	1.4	4.2	
376–700						
N	141		1	—	1	90–94
%	5.5	0.7	0.5		—	
701–2367						
N	117		1	—	1	95–98
%	4.6	0.4	0.5		—	
2368–9999						
N	55		—	—	—	99
%	2.2	0.0				
Total	2,521		187	72	259	
Mean	$ 98.8	6.8	53.6	38.9		

distribution of wealth. Gaining economic rewards, much as succeeding in occupation, derived most directly from ascriptive characteristics. Success in this stratified society went hand-in-hand with ethnicity. The results of systematic structural inequality therefore functioned similarly among literate and illiterate alike; the same dynamics divided the population. Economic differentiation among the illiterates followed from their ethnicity primarily, and to some extent from their sex and age, in noticeable parallel to stratification within the larger society. The achievement of literacy only occasionally counteracted the force of other factors. Accordingly, English Protestants ranked first among the assessed literates, and also stood first among the uneducated (Table 2.9). Con-

Table 2.9
Percentage Poor (0–39th Percentiles), 1861
(Census–Assessment Linked)

| | Hamilton literates | Illiterates | | Total illiterates |
		Hamilton	Kingston	
Irish Catholic				
N	399	109	48	157
%	64.6	78.0	70.8	75.8
Irish Protestant				
N	359	13	8	21
%	39.3	77.0	87.5	80.9
Scottish Presbyterian				
N	678	4	1	5
%	36.8	75.0	100.0	80.0
English Protestant				
N	690	24	4	28
%	26.8	62.5	75.0	64.3
Canadian Protestant				
N	215	5	2	7
%	17.2	60.0	100.0	71.4
Canadian Catholic				
N	23	—	3	3
%	34.7	—	100.0	100.0
Black				
N	42	17	—	17
%	59.5	64.7	—	64.7
Others				
N	353	15	4	19
%	31.4	73.3	50.0	68.4
Total				
%	36.8	73.8	72.2	73.3

versely, Irish Catholics were extremely depressed among both literate and illiterate, while the blacks, when illiterate, equalled the position of their literate fellow blacks. In this measure of rewards, we find first the same process relating to literacy as found previously; the uneducated were not equally handicapped and ethnicity punctuated their experience.

The pattern of intraethnic differences shows the processes of inequality and social differentiation even more clearly.[36] Among the Irish Catholics, the largest and poorest group, literacy brought little benefit;

36 *Ibid.*

65% of the literate and 76% of the illiterate were poor, those with some education hardly gaining (these are smaller differences than those in occupation). The difference was even smaller in the middle ranges of reward, a scant 6 percentage-point advantage (28 to 22%) to the readers, and very few fared better than this regardless of literacy. To the Irish Catholic pursuit of survival and success the acquisition of education was largely irrelevant; social forces worked against them, with poverty the most common outcome. Education meant even less to blacks. Among them, even less distance separated the position of literates from that of illiterates, with virtually equal proportions poor (60 and 65%) and middling (33 and 35%). The disadvantages with which ethnicity and race confront these groups were simply too great for education to reduce significantly, or for illiteracy to handicap much more.

English Protestant illiterates, not surprisingly, gained from their origins. Ranking second among literates (to Canadian Protestants), they stood first among the uneducated: fewer than two-thirds were poor. Ethnic advantage outweighed their handicap—a situation in contrast to that of other illiterates; nonetheless, they did not succeed as often as literate English, only 27% of whom fell into poverty. Their experience illustrates the nature of ascriptive advantages, which, if most important, were still limited by a lack of education. Ethnicity was not powerful enough to erase totally an absence of achievement; literacy's significance derives from its relationship with the other factors. As noted before, a lack of literacy, in this social order, depressed more forcefully than its acquisition contributed to success. In the interaction lies the meaning of literacy. English illiterates, as a result, gained greater financial (and occupational) rewards than other illiterates while unable to match their literate peers. In the middle ranks, the difference continued: 50% of educated to 18% of uneducated. Despite this restriction, these illiterates succeeded at the highest levels; in the 80th–99th percentiles ranked 19% of them, as compared with 24% of literates. The exceptional individual could still draw upon ascriptive advantage for high attainments, even in the absence of education. Literacy's role, we again discover, was rarely direct or independent; it did not counteract the dominant patterns of inequality but largely reinforced them.

With sex as well, ascription could only be slightly moderated by achievement. All women were heavily restricted by virtue of gender, and one-half of those literate and 70% of those illiterate were poor. The advantage of literate women continued into the middle range (48 to 23%); however, few attained independence. Wealth quite often derived from the husband's property and was not of a woman's own making. Literacy perhaps aided some women to a limited extent, in a society with little opportunity for work outside the home or remunerative roles for them. Sex, therefore, largely constituted an independent influence.[37] As with ethnicity, the achievement of education could not cancel the disadvantages of birth. Literacy, overwhelmingly, supported the social structure, with little independent contribution to advancement, and, conversely, greater disability from its lack. Contrary to contemporaries' claims, the greatest numbers of unskilled and poor were nonetheless literate, while real success came to small numbers of the illiterate.

The limited significance of literacy appears most dramatically in the financial rewards of work. The relationship between occupation and wealth, while fairly direct, was not a perfect one; both individual positions and job levels were variably rewarded, with nomenclature sometimes disguising the nature of skill and status.[38] Significantly, in economic returns, very little difference separated the literate from the illiterate among the unskilled or semiskilled (Table 2.10). Seven percentage points divided the unskilled: 85% of illiterates were poor and 78% of literates. Among the semi-skilled, the returns were even smaller: a 2 percentage-point benefit to the educated. Possession of literacy for workers at these levels brought no rewards; education made remarkably little difference to their wealth. The effects of ethnicity, moreover, were only reinforced. If one was Catholic or Protestant or black, literacy scarcely boosted one's standing (Table 2.11). Percentage poor hardly differed among the semi- and unskilled of these groups; Irish Catholics sharing common poverty, Protestants benefitting only slightly (unskilled: 78% of literates, 89% of illiterates poor), blacks showing no differences at all.

Biographical examples from the total population of illiterates and literates nicely illustrate these processes. Consider the Lawlor, Alexander,

Table 2.10
Percentage Poor by Occupation, 1861
(Census–Assessment Linked)

	Hamilton	Illiterates		Total
	literates	Hamilton	Kingston	illiterates
Unskilled	78.3	85.5	82.2	85.6
Semiskilled	47.6	45.5	75.0	50.0
Skilled	37.3	69.2	41.7	62.8
Nonmanual	17.5	20.0	80.0	40.0

[37] *Ibid.*, 55–60.
[38] On the nature of this complex relationship, see Katz, *The People of Hamilton*, Chs. 2, 3; see also notes 25, 26, above.

Table 2.11

Percentage Poor by Occupation and Ethnicity, 1861
(Census–Assessment Linked)

	Unskilled	Semiskilled	Skilled	Nonmanual
Irish Catholic				
Hamilton literates	82.3	52.2	48.2	35.7
Total illiterates	82.3	54.5	69.6	50.0
Hamilton illiterates	84.3	25.0	80.0	0.0
Kingston illiterates	76.9	71.4	50.0	66.0
Irish Protestant				
Hamilton literates	78.2	61.5	39.2	20.0
Total illiterates	88.9	100.0	100.0	100.0
Hamilton illiterates	83.3	100.0	—	—
Kingston illiterates	100.0	100.0	100.0	100.0
English Protestant				
Hamilton literates	72.0	28.5	29.5	7.2
Total illiterates	100.0	0.0	62.5	0.0
Hamilton illiterates	100.0	0.0	62.5	0.0
Kingston illiterates	100.0	—	—	—
Blacks				
Hamilton literates	72.8	66.7	53.9	—
Total illiterates	66.7	50.0	55.5	—
Hamilton illiterates	66.7	66.7	62.5	—
Kingston illiterates	—	0.0	0.0	—

and O'Brien families, all resident in Hamilton in 1861. John Lawlor was an Irish Catholic laborer; aged 52, he was married, living with his wife and son in a rented one-story frame house. The 14-year-old son neither attended school nor reported an occupation. Lawlor and his wife were unable to read or write, and they were quite poor (0–19th percentiles in wealth ranking).

The Alexanders were a family of 11. James and his wife lived with their 9 children (3 boys and 6 girls) in a two-story frame house. The family head was a Scottish-born, Free Church Presbyterian, aged 50; he worked as a carpenter. Five of the Alexander children attended school: girls aged 6, 8, 10, 13, and 15. The boys, aged 17, 19, and 21, worked as carpenters and glaziers, probably in their father's construction business. The Alexanders not only owned their home, they were quite well-to-do, ranking in 80th–89th percentiles of Hamilton's assessed population. Mr. Alexander, we note, was illiterate.

Finally, the O'Briens were a famiy of 6: husband, wife, 2 sons, and 2 daughters. Mr. O'Brien, 30 years of age, was Irish and Catholic; he was a railroad laborer. The family rented a one-story frame house,

sent no children to school, and ranked among Hamilton's poor (20th–
29th percentiles). O'Brien was in fact able to read and write—Irish,
Catholic, literate, and a poor laborer.

The realities of the working world of the mid-nineteenth-century city
contrasted sharply with the rhetoric of school promoters. What sense
did Ryerson's assertions make to the people situated in them, so many
educated but still in poverty? And irony punctuated assurances such as
Horace Mann's that "very few, who had not enjoyed the advantages of
a Common School education, ever rise above the lowest class of operative." This was true, but of course neither did a great many others who
had some education. Education, and literacy, certainly did not insure
success, a social rise, or social mobility. One answer, which links these
findings to those of Chapter 1, lies in Ryerson's view that the "proper
education of the mechanic is important to the interests of society as well
as to his welfare and enjoyment." For enjoyment perhaps, for society
certainly; to his own welfare much more questionably. Promises of success through schooling held little truth for these workers. The ever
increasing school attendance of their children therefore derived from
other perceptions, including the moral bases and some special hopes for
success, related to realities other than their own.[39]

In fact, the skilled worker who was literate did have greater chances
for financial rewards, very possibly providing an example to others.
More skilled illiterates remained poor (63% across the three cities, but
only 42% in Kingston) than skilled literates, of whom 37% were poor.
A meaningful difference apparently lay in the economic returns to
schooling from artisanal or skilled positions. Literacy aided in boosting
men into skilled work and commensurate rewards, which parents saw
and—in hopes for their children—accepted the school's hegemony. Ethnicity of course influenced these economic gains, as more Irish and
black artisans stayed poor, regardless of education. For blacks, literacy
continued to make no difference, although it boosted the status of the
Irish (48 to 70% poor). English Protestants fared best, whether educated
or not, but within this ethnic group, literates most often escaped poverty (only 30% poor) and exceeded the position of illiterates (62% poor).
At this level, literacy, while reinforcing the influence of ethnicity,
brought rewards which may well have attracted a response from others

[39] Mann, *Annual Report of the Secretary of the Board of Education*, 5 (Boston,
1842), 89. Chapter 3 details the social mobility of the illiterates. *Journal of Education*,
2 (1849), 20. See Ch. 5, and Ch. 4, below, on school attendance, and Ian Davey's Ph.D.
Diss. (note 9) on school attendance throughout the period.

who did not themselves share in them, especially for the uneducated who attained skilled work but not a fairer return.

For the much smaller number who gained nonmanual, largely small proprietary posts, literacy carried less importance, especially in Hamilton. Although the numbers are tiny, only 2 of 10 illiterates at that level remained poor, compared with 18% of literates; 6 in fact attained the 80th–89th wealth percentiles, a tremendous success for one unable to read. No doubt such success resulted from lengthy periods of efforts and savings. In three ranks, the unskilled, semiskilled, and nonmanual, very slight differences in wealth separated the educated from the illiterate; to these workers schooling's benefits were not important ones and the returns to the illiterate were nearly equal. Conversely, literates at these ranks gained little from their education alone. Nevertheless, at the skilled level, the difference was greater and it carried more significance, very possibly affecting the educational responses of others. Illiteracy created barriers to the skilled ranks, and even more to its rewards, despite its reduced and indirect effects elsewhere.

In the acquisition of wealth and in the rewards of work, age made remarkably little difference. Literates and illiterates alike improved their economic standing as they grew older; those aged 50–59 were the least often in poverty (25% of literates, 66% of illiterates). At every age, in fact, regardless of ethnicity, illiterates were poorer, although the differences were quite small among the most depressed groups. The passage of life did not benefit those who were disadvantaged ethnically or educationally. Age only reinforced the dominance of the facts of birth in a society so deeply stratified.

In these three mid-nineteenth-century commercial cities, ascription was the first and most important fact of inequality and social position. Ethnic origins, primarily, determined the processes of social differentiation, and in so doing, their impact was shared by literate and illiterate. Neither homogeneous nor equally depressed, the illiterates were not a distinct and separate class in society. They either gained through their origins or suffered a common disadvantage. Literacy, consequently, reinforced rather than countered the structures of inequality: achievement did not replace social inheritance. Literacy's one contribution came at the level of skilled work and its rewards—and it is a revealing one, especially in the social meaning that might be drawn from it and its probable support to the school. Overall, literacy by itself influenced remarkably little one's life-chances, as illiteracy in its ethnic relations proved to many a real handicap.

IV. Homeownership, Property, and Residence:
Urban Adaptation (1)

Despite their common plight of frequent poverty and low occupational standing in a deeply unequal urban society, the illiterates and the poor adjusted to urban life, sometimes with real success. Handicapped by illiteracy and heavily burdened by ascriptive characteristics, these men and women often proved themselves resourceful in their ability to settle, survive, form families, and make their way in environments new and alien to them. Drawing on their traditions as well as devising other strategies, even those without the advantage of education found adaptation and integration, in a variety of ways, within their grasps. This evidence allows us to go beyond the analysis of work and wealth, which while central to their experiences and to the meanings of literacy, allow an incomplete understanding of the illiterates' place in society. By examining their patterns of property and homeownership, residence, and, in the final section of this chapter, family formation, a more complete and even more complex social and cultural dynamic emerges into view, permitting deeper insight into the social processes and the place of literacy within them. This section and the next complement the argument, underlining the limits of literacy, the resourcefulness of illiterates, and the contradictions between social perceptions and social reality.

The analysis of the illiterates' adjustment and adaptation in mid-nineteenth-century Hamilton, Kingston, and London further challenges nineteenth- and twentieth-century thought about the culture, values, and abilities of the uneducated, the illiterate, and the poor. In both centuries, as we have seen, opinion commonly emphasized a pervasive culture of poverty among these elements of the population. The poor, in these views, often immigrant and alien to North American Protestant culture and ill-prepared for the demands of modern urban life, are disorganized, unintegrated, unstable; constituting a serious challenge to social order, they restrict productivity and impede progress. Public schooling, the carefully structured provision of literacy, has been proclaimed as the solution to the problems posed by the unassimilated and unprepared. As discussed in Chapter 1, arguments for education and many of the goals of proper schooling stress the social integration of the poor, the immigrant, and the lower class. Unattended, they would retain their foreign ways and distinct culture, remaining isolated from the dominant middle-class norms and moral economy that reformers and school promoters held essential for cohesion, development, and advancement. Illiterates, especially, represented a threat to these goals, maintaining a gap between the classes and reproducing increasing numbers of unintegrated, socially disorganized poor.[40]

In sharp contrast, the evidence presented here shows the illiterates, overwhelmingly poor immigrants, to be successful in adapting to these urban environments. Hardly disorganized, they used their resources to gain some security in the cities, by purchasing homes and also by modifying their family organization, in useful and sensible ways. A different interpretation follows: Without literacy and with limited assets, these illiterates were able to adapt resourcefully; they were not trapped in a culture of poverty. On several measures, they reveal success in adjusting to urban life, through adapting traditional rural customs or through calculating strategies.

Predominant poverty excluded most illiterates from maintaining a business establishment of any kind. Compared with 18% of Hamilton's literates, only 3 to 5% of illiterates reported themselves to be proprietors of businesses to the census-takers. However, much as illiteracy did not prohibit artisanal or proprietary work, it did not preclude ownership and operation of an enterprise, however small or localized. Illiterates ran groceries, craft shops, inns, and taverns, along with one prosperous manufactory (which produced vinegar). Twenty-seven persons without education were able to succeed in this manner: 5 in London, 6 in Kingston, 16 in Hamilton. Their attraction to inn- and tavernkeeping is important, too. Not only was small shop and pubkeeping one prized path of mobility for the lower class, but pubs were also local centers of news and information.[41] It is instructive that illiterate men and women could have this role; illiteracy did not prevent them from acquiring the capital or the means necessary for such operations. No direct evidence indicates that literacy skills were required to run a shop in cities where commerce was king, and the accomplishment of these persons is a virtual rejoinder to the received wisdom that reading, writing, and shopkeeping must march linkstep. If, in fact, literacy were needed for conducting business, others in the family, or employees, could lend their skills. A small number of illiterates (15) also owned carriages, a sign of high status in these cities that only 5% of households

---

[40] See preceding text, and note 2.

[41] The returns of business establishments in the 1861 census were incomplete. The numbers reported here are, therefore, not inclusive, but rather indicative of trends. There is no reason for a difference in underenumeration between literates and illiterates. On the social and cultural importance of pubs, see Brian Harrison, *Drink and the Victorians* (London: Faber, 1971), "Pubs," in *The Victorian City*, ed. H. J. Dyos & M. Wolff (London: Routledge, Kegan Paul, 1973), 161–190.

the heads of which were literate claimed. Lack of literacy did not prevent these forms of property ownership and the successful integration they represent.

These individuals clearly represented exceptions to the dominant experience of illiterates. For the greater numbers, there were other ways to adapt to the city and to fend off the perils of poverty. To keep livestock was one; and it was seized more often by families headed by an illiterate. Twenty per cent of literates, and 25% of Hamilton's illiterates, 40% of London's, and 15% of Kingston's kept animals in their urban residences; they probably also grew other foodstuffs. Rural and traditionally oriented, stock-keeping was one strategy with which to confront urbanism and poverty. Illiterates' stock was lower in monetary value, suggesting that they more likely used animals for self-sufficiency than for investments. This was one way for the poor to mitigate their circumstances in their search for security, adapting older customs to new places; illiterates made it work for them.[42]

Of greater significance than these measures are the homeownership patterns of illiterate household heads, representing perhaps their most important approach to adjustment and security. Homeownership, as recent scholarship has demonstrated, constituted an important and complex process among residents of nineteenth-century cities. Ownership patterns derived from the interaction of social class, demographic behavior, and ethnicity; property-holding thus related to cultural values, inequality, persistence of residence, and power.[43] It was more than a linear consequence of wealth. To this imposing roster, we add literacy, for homeownership served an especially important function for the illiterates who settled in the three cities. Illiterates, in their struggle to survive, tried and apparently succeeded more often than many literate

---

[42] See, for examples of traditional values in adjustment, Virginia Yans McLaughlin, *Family and Community: Italian Immigrants in Buffalo, 1880–1930* (Ithaca: Cornell University Press, 1977); Josef Barton, *Peasants and Strangers* (Cambridge, Mass.: Harvard University Press, 1975); John W. Briggs, *An Italian Passage* (New Haven: Yale University Press, 1978); John Bodnar, "Immigration and Modernization," *Journal of Social History*, 10 (1976), 44–71; Herbert Gutman, *Work, Culture and Society in Industrializing America* (New York: Knopf, 1976). See also, Louise Tilly's comments on Yans McLaughlin's earlier work, *Journal of Social History*, 7 (1974), 452–459.

[43] See Katz, *The People of Hamilton*, Chs. 2,3; Thernstrom, *Poverty and Progress*; Mark Stern, "Homeownership," qualifying research paper, York University, 1976; Michael Doucet, "Building the Victorian City," unpub. Ph.D. Diss., University of Toronto, 1977; Daniel Luria, "Wealth, Capital and Power: The Social Meaning of Home Ownership" *Journal of Interdisciplinary History*, 7 (1976), 261–282; the unpublished research of David Hogan. Chapter 3, below, explores the relationship of persistence and ownership for the illiterates.

household heads in obtaining their own homes. In this behavior, they reflect the responses of many of the Irish, and, equally importantly, they did not act as marginal, disorganized, or unstable individuals. Rather, their behavior represented the calculating, culturally influenced strategies of men and women who, in climbing above crises of subsistence and poverty, sought to protect themselves and their dependents from the vagaries of an unequal market economy. Exhibiting a great desire for property, illiterates in this way found security and successful adjustment. (As with the analysis of wealth, the population under study narrows to those heads of household, literate and illiterate, who were linked between the assessment and census of 1861.)

Despite their overwhelming poverty, illiterates across the cities owned their homes at least as frequently as the literates: 29% of illiterates to 27% of literates (Table 2.12).[44] Twenty-four per cent in Hamilton,

Table 2.12
Homeownership, 1861 (Census–Assessment Linked Heads)

	Own	Rent
Hamilton literates		
N	695	1,856
%	27.2	72.8
Hamilton illiterates		
N	45	142
%	24.1	75.9
Kingston illiterates		
N	16	56
%	22.2	77.8
London illiterates		
N	34	38
%	46.6	53.4
Total illiterates		
N	95	236
%	28.7	71.3

[44] Their homes were, of course, not as substantial as those of some higher-ranking literates. Fewer lived in stone or brick homes, while most families, literate or illiterate-headed, resided in frame dwellings. On working class housing in Hamilton, see Michael J. Doucet, "Working Class Housing in Hamilton," in *Essays in Canadian Working Class History*, ed. G. S. Kealey and P. Warrian (Toronto: McClelland and Stewart, 1976), 83–105; more generally, S. D. Chapman, ed., *Working Class Housing: A Symposium* (Devon: David and Charles, 1971); Enid Gauldie, *A History of Working Class Housing* (London: Unwin, 1974).

22% in Kingston, and 47% of illiterates in London succeeded in the saving, sacrifice, and effort required to purchase the property on which they lived. London represents the extreme case, as the illiterates' achievement undoubtedly reflects higher rates in that city. The accomplishment of illiterates in all three cities is remarkable, given their economic and occupational situations. Owning their homes must have had a special meaning to these individuals, who with far fewer material resources equalled the property-holding rate of literates. In large measure, their success was influenced by ethnicity, wealth, and age, resembling the relationships among the literate heads of households. Homeownership, in fact, among either the educated or the uneducated, was to a degree independent of direct socioeconomic influences. Constituting a mark of security, individual power, and personal independence, it involved cultural traditions as well as assets. Among illiterates, these functions combined to produce a special emphasis on ownership which obviously represented a deeply held value and a significant goal. For these disadvantaged persons, possession of their own homes carried a peculiar significance, which exaggerated more general ethnic, economic, and life-course tendencies. Some, particularly the Irish, perhaps escaped for the first time their age-old subservience to a landlord. Illiteracy, a sum, neither limited their ability to transact the business of ownership nor narrowed their vision into a headlong and early rush to own property. Cultural values intersected with wealth and age, all encouraging an adaptive response to the urban environment.

Illiteracy, consequently, did not reduce significantly the propensity of any ethnic group to purchase homes (Table 2.13). Among three groups, of widely different standing, illiterates obtained property more often: Irish Catholics (31 to 22%), English Protestants (40 to 30%), Scottish Presbyterians (33 to 27%), though these comparisons suffer from tiny numbers. The Irish and English are most interesting. Despite their ascriptive differences, both exceeded the proportions of literates owning homes by 10%, revealing the special significance of ownership and their success in it. The Irish rate is all the more remarkable considering their overwhelmingly depressed position, but only the English with their advantages exceeded that rate. When Irish Protestants are added to the Catholics, the great success of the Irish-born becomes one shared by all Irish, regardless of literacy or religion, a discovery common to studies of several nineteenth-century cities. The "Five Cities" analysis, for example, while finding that the lowest class most often lacked property, concluded that the experience of Irish laborers contradicted their generalization. Ethnicity and cultural values, thus, blurred a clear link between class and property. When occupation was held constant, the

Table 2.13

Homeownership by Ethnicity, 1861 (Percentage Owning) (Census–Assessment Linked)

	Irish Catholic	Irish Protestant	Scottish Presbyterian	English Protestant	Canadian Protestant	Canadian Catholic	Black	Others
Hamilton literates								
N	87	130	125	204	59	2	10	78
%	21.8	36.2	26.6	29.9	27.4	8.7	23.8	22.1
Hamilton illiterates								
N	30	2	2	6	—	—	4	1
%	27.5	15.4	50.0	25.0	—	—	23.5	6.7
Kingston illiterates								
N	10	3	—	2	1	—	—	—
%	20.8	37.5	—	50.0	50.0	—	—	—
London illiterates								
N	19	2	1	8	—	—	1	3
%	59.4	33.3	25.0	66.7	—	—	20.0	23.1
Total illiterates								
N	59	7	3	16	1	—	5	4
%	31.2	26.9	33.3	40.0	12.5	—	20.8	12.5

Irish more often owned property.[45] With the Irish, cultural norms and traditional values very likely combined with the need to gain some measure of security in cities dominated by ascribed status, inequitable rents, and discriminatory labor markets. Their native-Irish experience of landlessness and exploitation, in the context of a cultural heritage rooted in the possession of land, pushed them to acquire property in the new world, giving them at once a goal more attainable and a strategy for additional security and independence. This gave them a stake in the cities, increasing their likelihood of staying as well. Shared by literate and illiterate alike, opportunities for success were not handicapped by illiteracy, and among Catholics, illiterates succeeded more often than literates.

The English experience is analogous. Benefitting from their social structural advantage, both illiterate and literate household heads were able to purchase very often. The poorer illiterates among this ethnic group also sought security and protection for themselves and their families, with the result that they too more often bought property: 40% across the cities, with rates of 50 and 67% in Kingston and London, respectively.

For both literates and illiterates, economic position as measured by wealth related directly to property acquisition (Table 2.14).[46] Clearly visible is interaction between the economic handicap represented by a lack of education and the illiterates' exceptional emphasis on homeownership whenever possible. While members of each group increased their proportions owning homes directly with levels of wealth, illiterates responded far more readily to rising from poverty. Equalling the literates' rate among the poor (0–39th percentiles), the illiterates leaped into ownership upon reaching the middle ranks of wealth-holding; over half (53%) owned homes at these levels, contrasting with 28% of literates. A modicum of financial status—at least a movement up from poverty— was for most a prerequisite of ownership. The urge toward security and the cultural stress on property therefore did not push them toward ownership at all costs; owning represented instead a more rational decision based upon the utilization of available resources. Security, in

---

[45] Theodore Hershberg, Michael Katz, Stuart Blumin, Laurence Glasco, and Clyde Griffen, "Occupation and Ethnicity in Five Nineteenth Century Cities: A Collaborative Inquiry," *Historical Methods Newsletter*, 7 (1974), 204, 203–207. See also, Katz, *The People of Hamilton*, Ch. 2; Thernstrom, *Poverty and Progress*.

[46] Occupation had little affect on homeownership with only the exception of the semiskilled (largely Irish Catholic) in Hamilton. The implications of this are drawn in Chapter 3.

Table 2.14
Homeownership by Wealth, 1861 (Percentage Owning) (Census–Assessment Linked)

Percentile	0–19	20–39	40–59	60–79	80–89	90–94	95–98	99–100
Hamilton literates								
N	24	124	119	186	94	63	60	25
%	7.3	20.4	24.9	31.4	40.9	44.7	51.3	45.5
Hamilton illiterates								
N	6	12	14	10	3	—	—	—
%	7.9	19.4	63.6	66.7	30.0	—	—	—
Kingston illiterates								
N	3	7	4	2	—	—	—	—
%	18.8	19.4	36.4	25.0	—	—	—	—
Total illiterates								
N	9	19	18	12	3	—	—	—
%	9.8	18.6	54.5	52.3	30.0	—	—	—

other words, followed savings. The importance of gaining this measure of security, moreover, led some of them to value it more highly than their children's schooling, as will be discussed in Chapter 4. That was another aspect of their adjustment and survival strategies. And, of course, it was the Irish Catholics who led in this adaptive behavior; over 60% of them owned homes at the middle levels of wealth. Illiteracy did not preclude homeownership, nor did the plight it might entail lead them blindly into early and unstable actions; it did not prevent calculating responses to their circumstances and efforts to ameliorate their positions.

The final determinant of homeownership is the life course, represented here by household heads' age and family size. Among the literates, both aging and increasing numbers of children at home were directly associated with higher rates of ownership. These factors obviously worked through their relationships with wealth, on the one hand, and domestic needs, on the other. For all families, illiterate- or literate-headed, aging was accompanied by greater opportunities for purchasing their residences; this was one regular feature of the life course (Table 2.15). Illiterates, however, were less influenced by family size in their decisions and abilities to purchase homes (Table 2.16). In fact, family size made remarkably little difference to their actions, hardly the direct impact it had among literates. With fewer resources to spare or expend, and living in tighter circumstances, family formation carried a different and more severe meaning for the illiterates. Larger families, as noted

Table 2.15
Homeownership by Age, 1861 (Percentage Owning) (Census–Assessment Linked)

	20–29	30–39	40–49	50–59	60–69	70 +	N
Hamilton literates							
N	35	206	235	134	67	17	695
%	9.5	22.7	34.8	37.2	38.5	28.3	27.2
Hamilton illiterates							
N	1	12	6	20	6	0	45
%	5.3	23.1	14.3	42.6	30.0	0.0	24.1
Kingston illiterates							
N	2	5	3	4	2	0	16
%	16.7	29.4	17.6	23.5	28.6	0.0	22.2
London illiterates							
N	2	8	10	7	6	1	34
%	33.3	40.0	50.0	52.9	66.7	100.0	46.6
Total illiterates							
N	5	25	19	31	14	1	95
%	13.5	28.1	24.1	38.3	38.9	14.3	28.9

Table 2.16
Homeownership by Family Size (Number of Children), 1861 (Percentage Owning) (Census-Assessment Linked)

	Small (0–2)	Medium (3–5)	Large (6+)	N
Hamilton literates				
N	1,393	883	227	2,503
%	23.0	32.6	37.9	
Hamilton illiterates				
N	106	66	15	187
%	23.6	25.8	20.0	
Kingston illiterates				
N	43	26	3	72
%	25.6	15.4	33.3	
London illiterates				
N	41	27	5	73
%	46.3	44.4	60.0	
Total illiterates				
N	55	33	7	332
%	28.9	27.7	30.4	

in Section V, were not virtual signs of success in occupation and wealth among illiterates as they were among many literates; rather they pressed harder upon limited assets, preventing ownership by channelling resources away from savings. The strategies that could succeed toward homeownership for them were circumscribed so their path was often a narrow one. The restraints on their actions heighten the significance of the achievement that the illiterates made in their rates of homeownership, considering their handicaps in both ascriptive and achieved characteristics. Overall, their success in gaining security and protection through property, which equalled that of literates, is impressive. In conjunction with the evidence of other indicators, we may conclude that these uneducated, often poor immigrants were hardly the disorganized, maladjusted persons of contemporary judgments and cultural stereotypes. They exhibited important indications of a more adaptive, calculating approach to their environment and to the use of their resources, human and material, in finding security and stability in the cities. Their approach to family formation shows similar tendencies.

This conclusion is reinforced by their patterns of residential settlement in the three cities, further highlighting the potential for adaptation and integration.[47] Spatially, the mid-nineteenth-century cities were complex places,[48] and illiterate men and women were not residentially segregated or isolated within them. In Hamilton, Kingston, and London, illiterate individuals and families headed by illiterates resided in every area of the cities. Their apparent clustering in some wards and districts derived not surprisingly from ethnic patterns of congregation, and not from rigid separation by class or wealth. Areas in which large numbers of illiterates of one ethnic group resided, especially Irish Catholics, in-

---

[47] The importance of residential patterns has recently been reinforced by John Foster, *Class Struggle and the Industrial Revolution* (London: Weidenfield and Nicholson, 1974), "Nineteenth Century Towns—A Class Dimension," in *The Study of Urban History*, ed. H. J. Dyos (London: Edward Arnold, 1968) 281–299. See also, Alan Armstrong, *Change and Stability in an English County Town* (Cambridge: Cambridge University Press, 1974).

[48] See in particular, the work of Michael J. Doucet and Ian Davey in *The People of Hamilton*, Appendix, among Doucet's work. See also, Peter Goheen, *Victorian Toronto* (Chicago: University of Chicago, Department of Geography Research Papers, 1970); David Ward, *Cities and Immigrants* (New York: Oxford University Press, 1971), "The Internal Spatial Structure of Immigrant Residential Districts in the Late Nineteenth Century," *Geographical Analysis*, 1 (1969), 337–353. See in general, Larry Bourne, ed., *The Internal Structure of the City* (New York: Oxford University Press, 1971); Gerald Suttles, *The Social Construction of Communities* (Chicago: University of Chicago Press, 1973); Karl E. and Alma F. Tauber, *Negroes in Cities: Residential Segregation and Neighborhood Change* (Chicago: Aldine, 1965).

variably were also home to large numbers of literates of the same group.
For example, in three Hamilton wards, St. Lawrences', St. Mary's, and
St. Patrick's, lived 85% of these illiterates and over two-thirds of their
literate countrymen. Finer, district-level data reveal the same pattern
(e.g., Census Districts 9 and 14 held 19 and 14% of Irish Catholic illiterates, 13 and 11% of literates, respectively). Some clustering did occur,
of course, following the ethnic base of communities (such as Hamilton's
Irish "Cork Town") and the availability of affordable housing stock.
Overall though, the cities were residentially mixed and the illiterates
were neither more isolated nor more segregated than any others.

This lack of segregation, even in the gross level, leads to important
implications for the social, cultural, and economic integration of those
unable to read or write. The illiterates lived in close proximity—sometimes in the same dwelling—to others who could read and write. They
shared work places and frequented the same taverns, shops, and streets,
walking the same routes. Information and news were undoubtedly exchanged informally. Constant contact with literates would moderate
any loss in which illiteracy, in theory, may have resulted. (Recent evidence, in fact, shows that the most dramatic influence of the press and
other mass media is through the diffusion of its message by personal
contact, and not by the media's direct impact. Other data further suggest that illiterates use print media; they often purchase newspapers and
magazines and have them read to them. Even in underdeveloped places
today, as in the mid-nineteenth-century cities, few households do not
contain at least one literate person [see pages 7, 104]). Local leaders
and neighbors, moreover, not the media, are considered to be the best
sources of information. It was little different a century ago.) Print culture may or may not have been an important source of the basic data
for living; regardless, illiterates were not excluded from that source.
Newspapers were read aloud and discussed in shops and pubs. Oral
culture, by which much news was transmitted, was equally available to
them; it may have been more important than other sources, too. As
Robert Webb concluded, "in any estimate of the newspaper audience,
it must be emphasized that it extended far beyond the limits of the
reading public. There was also a hearing public." The integration and
adjustment of illiterates, then, need not have been significantly hampered
by their own inability to read.[49]

---

[49] See the studies of John E. deYoung and C. L. Hunt, and E. M. Rogers and
William Herzog cited in the introduction. For the nineteenth century, see Brian
Harrison, *Drink;* Robert K. Webb, *The British Working Class Reader* (London: Allen
and Unwin, 1955), 34, *passim;* E. P. Thompson, *The Making of the English Working
Class* (New York: Pantheon, 1963), 712–719, *passim.* See also, Introduction, Chs. 5, 7.

V. Family Formation: Urban Adaptation (2)

The family-formation strategies of the illiterates also reveal illiterates' resourcefulness in dealing with the challenges raised by their disadvantages and poverty in the urban environment. Contradicting the opinion that saw the poor, the immigrant, and the uneducated as disorganized—especially in family life—the illiterates displayed adaptive strategies in domestic life, too. Modifying their family organization in useful ways was another effort to temper the effects of structural inequality and poverty; in controlling the size, shape, and composition of their domestic units, they attempted to counteract both poverty and demographic pressures.[50] Through choice or necessity, illiterates could and did act to protect themselves and their dependents. There is little evidence, moreover, that illiteracy led to demographically or familially dangerous behavior or unsound vital decisions. Their responses to urban conditions are seen in the structure of their families and in their approach to family formation, in this final section.

Household status and domestic position were distributed among illiterates differently from the way they were distributed among literate adults in these cities. Most importantly, illiterates were heads of household or spouses more often (71 to 63% of all adults); in addition, they were more often married, rather than single, regardless of age or ethnicity (Table 2.17). The differences, in fact, were greatest among the youngest, aged 20–29—the consequence of an earlier age at marriage. Marriage, as is typically assumed, is regulated by the age at which a potential husband judges himself, or is judged by others, somewhat independent or secure economically (at least considering his prospects); in Hamilton, this commonly occurred in one's late twenties (around age 27), while brides were a few years younger (on the average, aged 23), with no major ethnic distinctions. Illiterates, the distributions suggest, married earlier in all groups, however. Contrasting starkly with the marital experience of those who remained in Ireland whose age at marriage got higher throughout the nineteenth century, the behavior of these men and women, predominantly Irish Catholic and predominantly poor, had significance for their lives.[51]

[50] See for example, M. Anderson, *Family Structure*; W. J. Goode, "The Process of Role Bargaining in the Impact of Urbanization and Industrialization on Family Systems," *Current Sociology*, 12 (1963–1964), 1–13; Sidney Greenfield, "Industrialization and the Family in Sociological Theory," *American Journal of Sociology*, 67 (1961), 312–322; F. F. Furstenberg, "Industrialization and the American Family: A Look Backward," *American Sociological Review*, 31 (1966), 326–337; David Levine, *Family Formation in an Age of Nascent Capitalism* (New York: Academic Press, 1977).

[51] Kennedy, *The Irish*.

Table 2.17
Marital Status by Age, 1861

	20–29	30–39	40–49	50–59	60–69	70+	Total
Single							
Literates							
N	1,885	432	145	48	23	6	2,539
%	57.8	17.7	9.4	6.0	5.7	3.9	29.5
Illiterates							
N	142	53	23	20	13	5	256
%	35.4	10.3	5.7	7.8	9.8	8.3	14.4
Married							
Literates							
N	1,330	1,886	1,225	550	210	56	5,257
%	40.7	77.1	79.3	68.2	52.1	36.8	61.0
Illiterates							
N	244	423	302	166	85	15	1,234
%	60.8	81.8	75.3	64.6	60.7	25.0	69.5
Widowed							
Literates							
N	49	127	175	207	170	90	818
%	1.5	5.2	11.3	25.7	42.2	59.2	9.5
Illiterates							
N	15	41	76	71	42	40	285
%	3.7	7.9	18.9	27.6	30.0	66.7	16.1

Contradicting the traditional relationship between poverty and later marriage, illiterates' marital actions reflected a shift in behavior toward a more direct, rather than an inverse, relationship between class and marriage-age during early industrialization. Further, they may have derived from traditional rural Irish practices before the demographic effects of later marital ages and a higher incidence of celibacy were felt. In addition, as examined later, earlier marriage could bring negative demographic repercussions in higher (age-specific and lifetime) rates of fertility. Yet marriage may have aided the illiterates' adaptation, adjustment, and acculturation. Solace could be found in sharing a life with a spouse—benefits whose importance need not await some minimum of success. Marriage added stability in the chaos of the city, a stability that might have carried more importance to one who could not read and who was also poor. Illiterates, in fact, married other uneducated persons only 50% of the time; marriage, then, had direct advantages for communication and information from printed sources, when and if required (Table 2.18). Not all illiterates, for that matter, resided in households headed by other illiterates. Wives of course could also work and contribute to

Table 2.18
Illiterate–Literate Marriage Patterns, Residence Patterns, 1861
(Heads and Spouses)

A. Marriage patterns

	Male and female illiterate		Male illiterate–female literate		Male literate–female illiterate	
Hamilton	185	54.4%	36	10.6%	119	35.0%
Kingston	66	41.2%	35	21.9%	59	36.9%
London	81	51.9%	17	10.9%	58	37.2%
Total illiterates	332	50.6%	88	13.4%	236	40.0%

B. Co-residence: Number of illiterates in a household headed by

	Hamilton literates				Hamilton illiterates				Kingston illiterates				London illiterates			
	Male		Female		Male		Female		Male		Female		Male		Female	
0	3,110	99.3%	2,949	94.1%	86	24.0%	53	14.8%	29	18.4%	65	41.1%	33	21.7%	32	21.2%
1	21	0.7%	171	5.5%	248	69.3%	253	72.1%	117	74.1%	84	53.2%	107	70.4%	107	70.4%
2	2	0.1%	9	0.3%	19	5.3%	31	8.7%	11	7.0%	7	4.4%	12	7.9%	12	7.9%
3			3	0.3%	3	0.8%	14	3.9%			2	1.3%			1	0.7%
4+					2	0.6%	2	0.6%	1	0.6%						

the family economy, reducing the impact of poverty, whether this work was registered in the census or not. To get married was a decision that illiterates made often, and a step taken earlier for them than for many others.

Despite the potential for stable family life, illiterates nevertheless exhibited a high incidence of female-headed, single-parent households. Twenty-eight percent of illiterate-headed households were female-headed, compared with 13% of literate-headed units. Some of this disproportion undoubtedly followed from the preponderance of women among the illiterates, but not all. Much of it reflected their more common widowhood (18% of illiterate heads-of-households, 11% of literate), which plagued all ages, not merely the oldest. Virtually all ethnic groups were affected, as illiterate women were more often heads of households and widowed. Among the Irish, who also dominated in female headship among the literate (16%), illiterates suffered more often (23%). Poverty was the most pronounced of the causes of this plight; the poorest ethnic groups had the greatest frequency, and for the illiterates this frequency was increased. These circumstances reinforced the disadvantaged position of women in this society, striking hardest among the poor illiterates.

For domestic life, the most important consequence was the single-parent family (Table 2.19C). Twenty-seven percent of all illiterate-headed families had a single head compared with 20% of the literates. Overwhelmingly, these were women, with their frequency paralleling that of female heads; the Irish, literate or not, faced this situation most often. Blacks, however, did not share this condition; despite their depressed economic status, their rates of female-headed and single-parent families were about half that of the Irish, and lower than most others.[52] The illiterates' families, in their common poverty, confronted these threats to their stability and cohesion. Single- and female-headedness, nevertheless, did result in smaller families, through the loss of the spouse, which moderated their disadvantage. Illiterate female-headed families were more often small (71%), with fewer than three children, than either literate female-headed units (62%) or male-headed ones (56% and 58% of literates and illiterates, respectively). The illiterates' overall stability in rates of male-headed and two-parent families (admittedly a normative measure), which fell *only* 15 and 7%, respectively, below those of the literates, is more significant than these complications.

[52] On the black family, see Herbert Gutman, *The Black Family in Slavery and Freedom* (New York: Pantheon, 1976); *Journal of Interdisciplinary History*, 6 (Autumn, 1975), special issue on the history of the black family, among an important revisionist literature.

Table 2.19
Household Characteristics, 1861

	N	%	N	%	N	%	Mean	Total
A. Family size (number of children)	Small 0–2		Medium 3–5		Large 6+			
Hamilton literates	1,768	56.4	1,094	34.9	272	8.7	2.4	3,134
Total illiterates	406	60.7	220	32.9	43	6.4	2.2	669
B. Household size	Small 1–3		Medium 4–6		Large 7+			
Hamilton literates	829	26.5	1,743	55.6	552	17.6	5.2	3,124
Total illiterates	222	33.5	363	54.8	77	11.6	4.6	662
C. Number of parents	One		Two		Total			
Hamilton literates	623	19.9	2,511	80.1	3,134			
Total illiterates	180	26.9	488	73.1	668			
D. Number of families with one—	Relative		Boarder		Servant			
Hamilton literates	303	9.7	311	9.9	511	16.3		
Total illiterates	57	8.4	55	8.2	23	3.4		
E. More than one—								
Hamilton literates	208	6.5	316	10.0	195	6.2		
Total illiterates	57	8.5	45	6.7	2	0.3		
F. Number of families in a dwelling house	One		Two		Three +			
Hamilton literates	2,819	92.5	236	7.8	17	0.6		
Total illiterates	518	82.6	72	11.5	27	4.3		

We may judge it a major accomplishment in their response to urban life that the indicators of instability were no higher.

The household statuses of other illiterates add to this interpretation. Very few illiterates were grown children living at home (3 to 10% of literates). If a child remained with parents, then, he or she most likely was not illiterate; even with a smaller chance for schooling, intergenerational transmission of illiteracy was by no means certain. The paucity of children reflects also the dynamics of poverty and the illiterate adjustment process. Limited circumstances forced more children to leave home at earlier ages, for fewer parents were able to afford their keep. Relatives and boarders existed among the illiterate about as often (7 to 6%, and 9 to 12%, respectively, of illiterates and literates); their presence in the household undoubtedly contributing similarly—in additional income, care of kin and countrymen and women, shelter for the single youth or elderly.[53] The aged, especially women, were likely to be relatives in the homes of either literates or illiterates (Table 2.19D,E), while boarders were somewhat less common. Significant here, however, are the small differences among households regardless of the education of their heads. Among Hamilton's entire population, the presence of both relatives and boarders related directly to wealth, but illiterates differ relatively little (8 to 10% with one relative, 8 to 10% with one boarder, though fewer had more than one). Boarding and especially kinship also may have worked to their advantage; these persons could contribute to the family, directly or indirectly aiding in their care. This eased the perils of poverty and assisted in their adaptations.

Some illiterates—invariably women—were servants. Despite the contemporary stereotype of the illiterate servant, the fact that 7% of all literate adults were domestics and 5% of illiterates were shows that illiteracy was hardly a badge of domestic service. The Irish Catholic representation is most interesting, for they were so often branded as illiterate, dissolute, dirty, untrustworthy, and illequipped as servants, by employers and other critics. In fact, only 5% of these illiterates were recorded in service, and only 13% of Irish Catholic servants were uneducated. Of all servants in Hamilton, only 6% could not read or write. The complaints of masters and mistresses related to causes other than illiteracy alone, I suspect.

The most important aspect of the formation of illiterate-headed families, however, was their size and the dynamics that regulated size. Fam-

---

[53] See John Modell and T. K. Hareven, "Urbanization and the Malleable Household: An Examination of Boarding and Lodging in American Families," *Journal of Marriage and the Family*, 35 (1973), 467–479. M. Anderson, *Family Structure;* Katz, *The People of Hamilton,* Ch. 5.

ilies and households headed by illiterates were on the average smaller and simpler than those of literates (Table 2.19A,B). Single parents contributed to a smaller household and fewer contained boarders or servants, although 6% in Hamilton did claim a resident domestic, a sign of some status. Only in the presence of relatives within the household did their families tend toward complexity; relatives no doubt helped the family, providing resources, information, and childcare. Other kin probably resided near by.[54] The result of course was smaller households for these illiterates: 4.7, 4.4, 4.6 persons in Hamilton, Kingston, and London, respectively, to 5.2 for Hamilton's literates. Regardless of marital status, sex, race, ethnicity, occupation, or age, their households were smaller, with no important exceptions. The influence of size and composition of the household on socialization, adjustment, or success has yet to be ascertained for past or present, but, in any case, the size of the illiterates' households need not have overburdened them. Certainly they carried the potential for various kinds of important support.

The illiterates also had fewer children residing at home than the literates. In the three cities, their average family size in respect of number of children was 2.1, to the literates' 2.4—a clear if not substantial difference. Despite some small variations, this distinction held among the ethnic groups, too, as illiterates' families were regularly smaller. This finding, while very important as we will see, does conflict sharply with their tendency to marry earlier. In a time and society in which the diffusion of knowledge and use of contraception remains unknown to interpreters, we should expect earlier marriage among the uneducated to produce larger families rather than smaller ones.[55] Calculations of fertility, in fact, indicate that illiterates did have more children born to them, owing to their earlier marriages.[56] Nominal census data, deriv-

[54] On contributions of kin, see M. Anderson, *Family Structure*. Richard Sennett, *Families Against the City* (Cambridge, Mass.: Harvard University Press, 1970) also attempts to assess the presence of kin in the household.

[55] Recent research has begun to revise the traditional interpretation that contraception did not exist to any significant extent among pre- or early industrial populations. No new consensus has been produced but see Charles Tilly, ed., *Historical Studies of Changing Fertility* (Princeton: Princeton University Press, 1978); James C. Mohr, *Abortion in America* (New York: Oxford University Press, 1978); James Reed, *From Private Vice to Public Virtue* (New York: Basic Books, 1978); Angus McLaren, "Abortion in England, 1890–1914," *Victorian Studies*, 20 (1977), 379–400, "Women's Work and Regulation of Family Size," *History Workshop*, 4 (1977), 70–81, *Abortion in England* (London: Croom Helm, 1978); Levine, *Family Formation;* the seminal studies of E. A. Wrigley and Louis Henry.

[56] The difference could be greater, as more children of illiterates left home before the age of 16. If female heads were eliminated, the margins would increase as well. See Ch. 4.

Table 2.20

Fertility Ratios, 1861 [a] *(Three Cities Combined)*

Ethnic group	Urban illiterates	Hamilton literates
Irish Catholic	2.930	2.789
Irish Protestant	2.622	2.981
Scottish Presbyterian	2.818	2.565
English Protestant	2.684	2.610
Canadian Protestant	2.000	2.086
Canadian Catholic	2.000	1.929
Black	2.030	1.788
Others	2.045	2.357

[a] $\text{Fertiliity} = \dfrac{\text{Number of children (5–16)}}{\text{Number of heads (20–48)}}$

ing from one snapshot, limit calculations of specific fertility rates, permitting only an estimation of fertility by a child-head ratio.[57] These ratios show illiterate fertility to be higher than that of the literates for virtually all ethnic groups (Table 2.20). The estimates are conservative; if more precise calculations were possible, the differences might well be greater. Two of the largest ethnic groups, Irish Catholics and blacks, largely contributed to the difference. This higher marital fertility stemmed overwhelmingly from their earlier ages at marriage; there is no reason to expect illiteracy to have otherwise directly influenced the birthrates in this society.[58]

Nevertheless, we find their families smaller in size than those of literates. The explanation for an apparent paradox lies in the dynamics of their family formation. Illiterates used family size, as they did family

[57] The common procedure, the child–woman ratio, employing the population of women assumed to be fecund, those aged 16–45, could not be used since data was not collected on literate wives of illiterate male heads of household. Therefore, the heads aged 20–48 (revised upwards to account for age differences between marrying men and women) form the denominator of the ratio. The numerator derives from the number of children aged 5–16 (again a revision to reduce the distortions of possible differentials in infant mortality due to poverty). The fertility ratio therefore is the ratio of the children 5–16 divided by the heads 20–48. The results are *not* comparable with those derived by the common (0–5/16–45) ratio, but allow a realistic comparison among these illiterates.

[58] I have considered more generally the relationship between education and literacy and fertility in "Literacy, Education, and Fertility—Past and Present: A Critical Review," *Population and Development Review*, 5 (1979); David Levine is now studying the fertility and domestic strategies of illiterates in England in the eighteenth and nineteenth centuries.

structure, to ease the problems of poverty and of their adaptation in urban society. This they did through regulating the size of their families by controlling the numbers they kept at home. Consequently, families were larger in the earlier stages of the family life cycles, especially in comparison with literates, but did not increase directly and regularly with aging (Table 2.21). The process worked through their children's

Table 2.21
Number of Children by Age, 1861 (Heads of Household) (Three Cities Combined)

	Small 0–2	Medium 3–5	Large 6+	N
20–29				
Hamilton literates				
N	426	69	2	497
%	85.7	13.9	0.4	
Illiterates				
N	65	20	—	85
%	76.5	23.5	—	
30–39				
Hamilton literates				
N	578	441	46	1,065
%	54.3	41.4	4.3	
Illiterates				
N	98	72	5	175
%	56.0	41.1	2.9	
40–49				
Hamilton literates				
N	350	322	141	813
%	43.1	39.6	17.3	
Illiterates				
N	88	64	18	170
%	51.8	37.6	10.6	
50–59				
Hamilton literates				
N	211	175	68	454
%	46.5	38.5	15.0	
Illiterates				
N	89	41	12	142
%	62.7	28.9	8.5	
60+				
Hamilton literates				
N	194	84	15	293
%	66.2	28.7	5.1	
Illiterates				
N	63	23	4	90
%	70.0	25.6	4.4	

leaving home more often and earlier, as discussed in Chapter 4. The release of the young was the regulatory mechanism for many of these families, reducing family size despite higher fertility and earlier marriages and thereby not weighing too heavily upon scarce resources. Daughters, in fact, left home more often than sons, probably for domestic service, leaving families with an excess of males (110 sons to 100 daughters at home), who could contribute more to the family economy. Reduction of the family's dependency ratios (the proportion of those unable to contribute to those who were able) made for a smaller domestic unit, whose survival and adaptive capacities were increased.[59] Illiterates could and did manipulate family size and organization in their struggles to succeed in the city, in spite of the odds against them. This is a further indication of their abilities to rationally adapt and use their resources in seeking out security.

The full significance of this strategy of family formation emerges in the relationship between family size and economic achievement. Illiterates who succeeded generally had smaller families than either those who remained poor or literates (Table 2.22). They were sometimes older men, whose families decreased in size as all did, but their families remained smaller than those of the literates. Most striking is the almost total absence among illiterates of the direct relationship, found among the others, which joined large families to wealth. In efforts to succeed, large families could only be a drain; in addition, we find here another reason that family size did not relate directly to higher rates of home-ownership among the uneducated as it did among literate heads of families. Among the poorest, not surprisingly, the family sizes were closest to one another, but successful Irish Catholics and English Protestants displayed this strategy in their formation. Illiterates, in most cases, required fewer children, rather than the economic contribution of more, if they were to escape poverty or to fare even better. They regulated their family size accordingly.[60]

Surely the dynamics of family formation were even more complex

---

[59] The dependency ratio is commonly expressed as those members of family or household aged $\frac{(1-16) + (66 \text{ or older})}{(17-65)}$. It would have to be revised for nineteenth century applications of course. See Allan Schnaiberg, "The Concept and Measurement of Child Dependency: An Approach to Family Formation Analysis," *Population Studies*, 27 (1973), 69–84.

[60] The relationship of family size or structure to mobility remains quite obscure. See, Sennett, *Families;* Bernard Farber, *Guardians of Virtue: Salem Families in 1800* (New York: Basic Books, 1972); Goode, "Family Systems and Social Mobility," in *Families East and West*, ed. R. Hill and R. Konig (The Hague: Mouton, 1970), 120–131.

Table 2.22
Family Size by Wealth, 1861

Percentile	0–19	20–39	40–59	60–79	80–89	90–94	95–98	99–100
				Small (0–2)				
Hamilton literates								
N	205	344	264	339	111	72	60	30
%	62.3	56.5	55.4	57.2	48.3	51.1	51.3	54.6
Total illiterates								
N	60	54	15	12	6	1	1	—
%	65.2	55.1	45.5	52.2	54.5	100.0	100.0	—
				Medium (3–5)				
Hamilton literates								
N	102	218	171	205	92	53	42	14
%	33.4	35.8	35.9	34.6	40.0	37.6	35.9	25.5
Total illiterates								
N	27	38	14	9	4	—	—	—
%	29.3	38.7	42.4	39.1	36.4	—	—	—
				Large (6+)				
Hamilton literates								
N	22	47	42	49	27	16	15	11
%	7.2	7.7	8.8	8.3	11.7	11.4	12.8	20.0
Total illiterates								
N	5	6	4	2	1	—	—	—
%	5.4	6.1	12.1	8.7	9.1	—	—	—

than this interpretation indicates. Small numbers restrict extensive ethnic or life course analysis and investigation of other relationships. The question of motivation, awareness, and consciousness must remain open as well. Nevertheless, illiterates clearly seized a variety of approaches to adaptation and adjustment, in confronting their urban environments and in attempting to reduce the social structural forces they met. Family formation, family structure, patterns of home and property ownership, residential patterns—these were all drawn on by the illiterates, as they sought to survive and sometimes succeed in an unequal society. These were not the actions of marginal, disorganized, or isolated men and women, whose illiteracy was paralytic; they faced the world with resources and used them as well as they were able—their efforts, considering their lack of education, are impressive.

Three themes unify this analysis of literacy and illiteracy in the mid-nineteenth-century commercial cities of Hamilton, Kingston, and London (Ontario) in 1861. Each holds significance for revision and reinterpretation. These threads, as we have seen, converged in the thought and assumptions about the uneducated, the immigrant, and the poor, contributing to arguments and social theories that have dominated discussions of the importance of literacy in both the nineteenth and the twentieth century. Most significant is the evidence presented in this chapter that the facts of mid-century urban life were never completely congruous with the perceptions, claims, and expectations of commentators, reformers, or social observers. Only at the more superficial levels of understanding can confirmation for their views be found, despite the consistency and maintenance of opinion. At most there was a small, but apparently sufficient, amount of support (as in the rewards to skilled persons) for their assertions to be accepted and the school's hegemony to be developed.

To review: The first theme concerns the nineteenth-century view of immigrants, especially the Irish and Catholic, as the illiterate, disorderly, dissolute, and unwashed dregs of their society who brought their problems to North America with themselves. Despite this long-accepted conclusion, the great majority of migrants to these cities, regardless of origins, religion, age, or sex, were literate, confirming other research which directly relates distance of migration to literacy. North America received a select group of immigrants, including the Irish, who, nevertheless, often remained poor despite their education. The illiterate, moreover, were selected as well—negatively—by the disadvantage of their ascriptive characteristics, especially in ethnicity, but also in race, sex, and age.

As for the second theme: Social thought and social ideals have, for the past two centuries, stressed the preemption of ascription by achievement as the basis of success and mobility, and the importance of education and literacy in overcoming disadvantages deriving from social origins. In the three cities, in 1861, however, ascription remained dominant. Only rarely was the achievement of literacy sufficient to counteract the depressing effects of inherited characteristics, of ethnicity, race, and sex. The process of stratification, with its basis in rigid social inequality, ordered the illiterates as it did those who were educated. Only at the level of skilled work and its rewards did literacy carry a meaningful influence. Literacy, overall, did not have an independent impact on the social structure; ethnicity, primarily, mediated its role, while literacy largely reinforced that of ethnicity. Literacy's very distribution, along with its economic value, followed this pattern of ethnic differentiation. The possession of literacy alone rarely entailed occupational and economic gains; its benefits were very few in these areas, in sharp contrast to theory and assertions. Sex, ethnicity (especially Irish Catholicism), and race were far more important than literacy or education. Illiteracy of course was a depressing factor; the converse, however, did not hold true.

Within these basic limits, literacy could be important, of course, to individual men and women as well as to their society. Though most of the differences remain revealingly small, literacy did result in occupational and economic advantages. Skilled work may not always have required literacy, but literacy facilitated opportunities for entry to it and, consequently, commensurate remuneration. Literacy, to be sure, carried little independent influence and its absence precluded few kinds of work; yet the acquisition of literacy brought to some individuals potential advantages in social and cultural areas as in material ones. Access to a rapidly expanding print culture (not, though, altogether distinct or isolated from oral and community patterns), literature, additional news and information, and some channels of communication were open to those able to read and write. With ever rising levels of popular literacy and the promotion of schooling, illiteracy could, in some circumstances, become a personal or social embarrassment, although no direct evidence of this has been found. The working class, as we will observe in Chapter 5, was ambivalent about the schooling offered to them and about the promoted uses of literacy, but accepted much of its value nevertheless. Education was tied to notions of respectability and advancement; here the illiterates were surely disadvantaged and perhaps less respected by their literate peers. The promoted uses of literacy, considered in Chapter 7, were not synonymous, however, with the popular ones. The social and cultural needs for reading and writing, while growing in number and importance, competed with the needs of daily life and needs for survival. For the latter literacy was hardly central.

As for the third theme: A "culture-of-poverty" interpretation has predominated in discussions of the poor, the immigrants, and the uneducated. Generally assumed to be disorganized, unstable, irrational, and threatening to social order, without schooling their plight was assured. Illiterates in the three cities, contrary to the stereotypical expectations, proved themselves to be far more adaptive, integrated, and resourceful in confronting the urban environment with its unequal society. Using their traditions and human-material resources effectively and impressively, they strove to protect themselves and their families against the ravages of the marketplace and poverty. To this end, they purchased homes when possible and sensibly regulated their family organization and its size. Illiteracy did not prevent their adaptation or integration into the processes of stratification which discriminated against them and against so many of their literate peers. For some illit-

erates, ethnicity was an advantage which could cancel some of the
restrictions of illiteracy.

These conclusions are sweeping, especially in their implications for
historical understanding, observers' perceptions, and social theories. They
raise further important questions, too—all of which require additional
exploration and testing. For the present, however, we must ask, How
did the illiterates fare over time? How did parental illiteracy impinge
upon the future of their children? To these immediate questions the
next two chapters are addressed.

3

Persistence, Mobility, and Literacy

The years following 1861 marked continued development in the commercial cities of Upper Canada. Commerce continued to dominate their economic activities, but early industrialization, with its impact upon social and spatial structures, transformed them into more modern, more industrial cities. The decade of the 1860s, the years this chapter spans, was a relatively prosperous period; it represented in many ways the onset of a new social order, based more than ever before upon larger industry and increasing institutionalization. These of course were irregular and uneven processes of change, whose effects were differentially and relatively felt.[1] In this context, illiterate men and women continued their lives in the cities, working and striving to maintain or improve their positions. Although a short period of time, the decade provides an opportunity for further examination of the economic and adaptive abilities of those who lacked educational achievement. We may investigate the roles of literacy and illiteracy over a period of some years, testing and extending the interpretation developed from their positions in 1861. How did they fare over time? Did the restrictions represented by their lack of skills and achievement become more severe or less with time and with the social transformations of their places of residence? Was social and economic mobility available to the uneducated; did their

[1] On the relationship of modernization and industrialization, see E. A. Wrigley, "The Process of Modernization and the Industrial Revolution in England," *Journal of Interdisciplinary History,* 3 (1972), 225–259; J. Rogers Hollingsworth, "Perspectives on Industrializing Societies," *American Behavioral Scientist,* 16 (1973), 715–739; Michael B. Katz, "The Social Organization of Early Industrial Capitalism," ms. in progress (1978).

ascriptive bonds loosen or tighten in this context? These questions shape the analysis in this chapter.

The main concerns of this analysis reflect upon issues in social theory, modern social inquiry, and the understanding of the modernization process. Despite continuing debate and active dissent, a general consensus exists about the relationship of education to modern, industrial society; a conclusion stressing the heightened need for and significance of education, for individuals and for economic and social development, dominates theoretical and sociological literature and its assumptions analogous to the issues of the preceding chapter. With increased change toward a modern society, schooling becomes more central, valued, and requisite. In a volume that summarizes well many of the relevant issues, Donald Treiman makes this case in formal propositional terms. The more industrialized a society, he begins, the greater the proportion of eligible children who will be attending school—which has indeed been the case. In more industrialized societies, further, education will have a greater direct influence on occupational status and mobility, while, conversely, a father's status will have a smaller direct influence on his children's status. The direct influence of education on income, however, should lessen, but occupational status' direct impact on income should nevertheless increase in a cumulative path toward advancement. Despite ambiguities in findings and evidence of some persisting role for "background" ascriptive influences, the lines of the major interpretation are clear: with social and economic developments comes increased education, which influences social placement and mobility more than other measured factors. These connections, implanted in ideologies of educational opportunities, dominate both theory and popular received wisdom today.[2] Hauser succinctly summarizes the conclusions: "Educational attainment is a powerful intervening variable in the stratification process. Socioeconomic origins (race excepted) have rather small effects on adult socioeconomic achievements beyond those implicit in their influence on educational attainment and its influence on later achievements." Or, as Blau and Duncan state, "The chances of upward

[2] Treiman, "Industrialization and Social Stratification," in *Social Stratification,* ed. E. O. Laumann (Indianapolis: Bobbs Merrill, 1970), 207–234, *passim.* See also S. M. Lipset and R. Bendix, *Social Mobility in Industrial Society* (Berkeley: University of California, 1959); the works cited in Chapter 2, note 23 by Blau and Duncan; Sewell and Hauser; Sewell, Hauser and Featherman. For dissenting views, see Boudon; Bowles and Gintis; Berg; Collins; Squires (cited in Chapter 2, Note 3). The empirical dimensions of the controversy are by no means settled for the present, quite aside from earlier periods. On educational developments, see Ian Davey's Ph.D. Diss., Univ. of Toronto, 1975 (Chapter 1, Note 9).

mobility are directly related to education. . . ." [3] Set within the mainstream of evolutionary social theory, this interpretation derives from the past two centuries of western development and links the past century of educational expansion directly with the present.

In the developing urban context of industrial and educational growth, these conclusions strongly suggest that the position of the uneducated should deteriorate, especially in occupational attainments but also in access to wealth and property. Their lack of schooling should be an increasing barrier to individual progress, with time and with social change, attenuated only by experiential gains. An assessment of the performance of the illiterates from 1861 to 1871 must address this conclusion and its historical evaluation, reducing the limitations of the initial "static" view of 1861 by the addition of the dynamic of time, through the decade.

The experience of the illiterate adults who persisted in the cities over the course of the decade contradicts important aspects of these expectations, complicating the normative interpretation but also increasing our understanding of the nature of education and literacy in processes of attainment and adjustment. In occupation, little change occurred, while in wealth and homeownership important upward and improved shifts were made. Illiteracy did not block progress for those illiterates who persisted in each city, as the significance of ascriptive characteristics was reduced, but by no means erased. The stratification process had not changed in ways that made education mandatory for mobility or a requirement for success, despite theory and expectations to the contrary.

Presenting this analysis and interpretation will involve three closely related topics: first, the nature of geographic persistence and the identity of "persisters" will be examined; second, linking persistence with mobility, the status of illiterates in 1871 and the extent of movement from their earlier positions will be assessed.[4] This allows further exploration of the nature of inequality and stratification and the effects of age and time. Finally, patterns of mobility will be discussed. In these ways, the meaning of literacy may be elaborated and the case for a revision of dominant expectations advanced.

[3] Robert M. Hauser, "Educational Stratification in the United States," in *Social Stratification*, ed. Laumann, 111; Blau and Duncan, *Structure*, 155–156; Sewell and Hauser, *Education*, conclusions, *passim*.

[4] On the crucial relationships of transciency and mobility see Michael B. Katz, *The People of Hamilton* (Cambridge, Mass.: Harvard University Press, 1975), Ch. 3; Stephen Thernstrom, *The Other Bostonians* (Cambridge, Mass.: Harvard University Press, 1973); Sune Åkerman, "Swedish Migration and Social Mobility: A Tale of Three Cities," *Social Science History*, 1 (1977), 178–209.

This was an important decade in the social and economic development of these cities, signalling the emergence of a modern industrial order. The fullest effects of this complex of changes, in mode and scale of production, social relations, institutional maturation, and spatial differentiation, were not felt for another decade or more, but the transformation had nonetheless begun. The rise of heavy industry, the use of technology and mechanization, the arrival of larger firms, and the persistence of commerce and crafts all marked the onset of early industrialization. The process, 1871 census data show, was uneven, and the three cities of Hamilton, Kingston, and London exhibit differential patterns of development. Hamilton with a population of 27,000 counted 317 industrial establishments, Kingston (population 12,500) had 202, and London had 205, with economic development accompanying population and commercial growth (Table 3.1). Many of these establishments were small, of course, employing few hands, and artisanal in nature of production. Larger work settings and factories were increasingly common by 1871, however, especially in Hamilton with its greater development, but also in the other cities. The more modern sectors expanded markedly and the ratio of hands to firms ranged from 6.4 to 14 across the cities, despite the many small shops. Substantial numbers of men,

Table 3.1
Industrial Development, 1871 (Published Returns, Census of 1870–1871, Vol. 3)

A. Number of hands		Capital invested ($)	Number of establishments
Hamilton	4,456	1,541,264	324
Kingston	1,298	526,855	203
London	2,261	1,001,789	206
Ontario	87,281	37,874,010	—

B. Types of industries	Hamilton		Kingston		London	
(census classification)	N	Hands	N	Hands	N	Hands
I. Manufactures (1)	182	2,329	143	760	144	1,749
II. Manufactures (2)	64	642	35	263	36	466
III. Manufactures (3)	26	252	11	49	10	30
IV. Manufactures (4)	25	278	8	107	9	49
V. Miscellaneous	20	894	5	16	6	46
Total	317	4,395	202	1,195	205	2,340
Average number of hands	13.75		6.39		10.98	

women, and children worked in industry: 4,500 in Hamilton, 1,300 in Kingston, and 2,300 in London, representing perhaps 40 to 50% of the workforce.[5] Education also expanded in this period, with more facilities and higher enrollments. In sum, modernization and industrialization reshaped the cities in which the illiterates had to work, make their livings, house, and maintain their families.[6]

I. Persistence and Transiency

In recent research, historians have discovered the tremendous volatility of population movements in the past, particularly the extent of mobility in and out of nineteenth-century cities. Population turnover was apparently so common and frequent that students now grant that only a minority of individuals persisted in one place *over even one decade*. Studies in this period, despite methodological and conceptual weaknesses, demonstrate, typically, a geographic persistence rate of about one-

[5] On industrial work and the meaning of its changes, see E. P. Thompson, "Time, Work-Discipline, and Industrial Capitalism," *Past and Present*, 38 (1967), 56–97; Sidney Pollard, *The Genesis of Modern Management* (Cambridge: Cambridge University Press, 1965); Herbert Gutman, "Work, Culture, and Society in Industrializing America, 1815–1919," *American Historical Review*, 78 (1973), 531–588. For Canada, see The Royal Commission on the Relations of Capital and Labor (Ottawa, 1889); W. T. Easterbrook and H. G. J. Aitken, *Canadian Economic History* (Toronto: Macmillan, 1970); Harold Innis, *Essays in Canadian Economic History* (Toronto: University of Toronto Press, 1956); G. S. Kealey and P. Warrian, eds. *Essays in Canadian Working Class History* (Toronto: McClelland and Stewart, 1976).

[6] Several different subpopulations of illiterate adults form the basis of the following analysis. I ask readers to note these groups and their changing compositions, at the relevant points in the text. 1. Heads of household linked from the 1861 census (January) to the 1861 Assessment (April in Hamilton, March in Kingston); 2. Illiterates linked from the 1861 census to the 1871 census (January); 3. Illiterate heads of households linked from the 1871 census to the assessment of 1870–1872 (Hamilton: April, 1872 [1871 fire-damaged]; Kingston: March, 1870 [1871 not located]; London: April, 1871); 4. Illiterate heads of household linked in the 1861 Census and Assessment and in the 1870–1872 census and assessment (four-way links). Care will be taken to identify each population and to note changing bases in the pages that follow.

On the record linkage, which was totally manual, See Appendix E. On nominal record linkage in theory and practice, see Ian Winchester, "The Linkage of Historical Records by Man and Computer," *Journal of Interdisciplinary History*, 1 (1970), 107–124; papers by Winchester and Katz in the *Reports of the Canadian Social History Project;* E. A. Wrigley, ed. *Identifying People in the Past* (London: Arnold, 1973); Katz and John Tiller, "Record Linkage for Everyman," *Historical Methods Newsletter*, 5 (1972), 144–150.

third, to two-fifths, between censuses, with some variation by class, status, wealth, ethnicity, age and sex. Transiency and persistence were, nevertheless, very complex processes.[7]

In assessing the dynamics of persistence and transiency, we consider the evidence from three experiences: short-term persistence, from census to assessment-taking in 1861 *and* 1870–1872, and decade-long, census to census, from 1861 to 1871. All four linked populations of illiterates are used; comparative data derive from Hamilton's literate and total populations, as available.

Studies of migration and population persistence, if imperfect, do point to certain regularities despite their commonly inconclusive nature. For example, fairly high levels of geographic mobility are found throughout the west since at least the early modern period; rates of movement also seem to vary quite regularly by individual and family life cycles, wealth, property ownership, and ambition. Sex, ethnicity, culture, and occupation in some cases and contexts bear on migration, but overall their relationship has proved relatively elusive to investigators. Migrants, moreover, reveal a propensity for moving frequently from place to place. Research on the nineteenth century, in particular, shows that with such high rates of transiency virtually *all* types of persons were moving regardless of these general probabilities.

In general, two implicitly contradictory patterns are seen to tie education to migration. On one hand, there is evidence (such as that discussed in Chapter 2) that migrants are better educated and more aware of opportunities than nonmigrants, while the uneducated (more often poor as well) are immobilized and trapped in their predicaments. The uneducated, the poor, and the unskilled, on the other hand, are often seen as moving frequently, perhaps almost randomly, searching for work and subsistence in an almost rootless and restless

---

[7] See Thernstrom and Peter Knights, "Men in Motion: Some Data and Speculations about Urban Population Mobility in Nineteenth-Century America," *Journal of Interdisciplinary History*, 1 (1970), 7–36. Other historical studies of transiency and geographic mobility include, Katz, *People;* Thernstrom, *The Other Bostonians;* Knights, *The Plain People of Boston* (New York: Oxford University Press, 1971); Howard Chudacoff, *Mobile Americans* (New York: Oxford University Press, 1972); Katz, Michael Doucet, and Mark Stern, "Migration and the Social Order in Erie County, New York, 1855," *Journal of Interdisciplinary History*, 8 (1978), 669–701, "Population Persistence and Early Industrialization in a Canadian City: Hamilton, Ontario, 1851–1871," *Social Science History*, 2 (1978), 208–229, among a burgeoning historical literature. See also the studies by Åkerman, Long, and Anderson cited in Chapter 2; Julian Wolpert, "Behavioral Aspects of the Decision to Migrate," *Regional Science Association, Papers,* 15 (1965), 159–169; James W. Simmons, "Changing Residence in the City," *Geographical Review*, 58 (1968), 622–651; Sidney Goldstein, *Patterns of Mobility, 1910–1950: The Norristown Study* (Philadelphia: University of Pennsylvania Press, 1958).

manner. Higher mobility rates for poor and disadvantaged individuals lend credence to the latter view, although it is not difficult to locate expectations or evidence that both patterns have existed in some form. Recent studies in fact point to a phenomenon of a "U"-shaped curve: high rates of movement for the highly educated and the uneducated. Long's 1960s U.S. data and Åkerman's 1870s–1880s Swedish evidence each show the most frequent movers to be among the highest and lowest in education, but, importantly, the common experience of movement breaks down with the distance of migration. Longer distance migration is much more common for those with greater amounts of schooling.[8] What was the experience of the urban illiterates, most of whom had already made at least one major migration in their lives?

The answer is short and simple: the rate of transiency among illiterates was very high. Both in absolute terms and in relative ones (i.e. relative to literates), the illiterates persisted in each city dramatically less often, over both short and long time periods. Over a 3–4-month period in 1861, one-half of illiterate heads of household were located in the same city, while 80% of literate heads were found in Hamilton. Over a full decade, one-fifth of all illiterates remained, compared with one-third of literates. Differentials in mortality, the possibility of underenumeration, and problems in locating women whose names may change (with marriage or remarriage) make these rates only approximations of reality. Yet the major conclusion is inescapable: illiterates were more mobile, more transient men and women, and the differences stand regardless of ethnicity, age, sex, life cycle, marital status, or economic position. Persisting at rates of about 60% of those of others, their experiences were structured by the same variations and regularities.

Clearly, the uneducated were not trapped in paralytic poverty. Like others in nineteenth-century urban places, they were highly mobile; and illiterates of all types moved, and moved frequently. Illiteracy did not trap them in one place; it did not function so as to narrow visions of opportunity outside the cities. Many undoubtedly were forced by circumstances to pack up and leave while some few were perhaps immobilized. Some learned about possibilities of employment, or nurtured hopes of greater success, elsewhere and took their chances. Even if they tramped, working irregularly or seasonally, illiteracy did not prevent them from learning the ways of the roads and the sources of work and opportunity.

[8] B. Anderson, Long, and Åkerman as cited in Chapter 2, Note 11; Åkerman, Per Gunnar Cassel, and Egil Johansson, "Background Variables of Population Mobility," *Scandinavian Economic History Review*, 22 (1974), 32–60. See also, Ronald Freeman and Amos H. Hawley, "Education and Occupation of Migrants in the Depression," *American Journal of Sociology*, 56 (1950), 161–166.

Although we do not know their paths or destinations out of the cities, there is no reason to assume their movements were errant and aimless.[9]

The experience of these men and women supports other findings that uneducated persons, past or present, were (or are) very mobile, contributing to the massive population turnover and moving in response to job opportunities. As elsewhere, they often were among the most frequent movers, and we may well suspect that their travels were more of short distance than long. If unable to settle successfully in one place, illiterates were more likely to respond in physical terms, within a more restricted geographical circumference perhaps—probably within the limits of a regional labor market about which they could readily gain information from others. Although they moved most often, this was still an experience they shared with other poor and unskilled members of disadvantaged groups. Lack of education, we may conclude, did not relate to *non*movement; rather it contributed to specific forms of migration. What they learned in the cities may have aided their searches for security, but as long as we remain ignorant of their destination, we cannot know if these forms of transiency brought greater success.

More-frequent movers, and less persistent, than literates, the illiterates' patterns of movement were not entirely fortuitous, as students of other populations have also found. The variations in persistence and the determinants of the probability of staying or leaving linked their experiences to those of others; illiteracy did not restructure the processes of persistence and transiency. Both short-term and the longer-term movements illustrate the common process. Consider first, the three-month period between the census and assessments of 1861 (Table 3.2). Regardless of attributes and characteristics, achieved or ascribed, the illiterate heads of household were more frequent movers. Persisting at a rate of 50%, they remained with only 60% of the literates' frequency. In spite of this wide differential, sex and the life cycle contributed similarly to each. Women persisted far less often than men, even over a period too brief for many to remarry and change their names; the proportional difference is quite close among the two groups. Women's insecurity continued to be greatest. Variations among those of different marital status show the same parallels and the effects of the life cycle. Single persons moved most frequently. Married ones remained most often, regardless of education—those with family ties being more rooted. The life cycle exerted the largest force, in fact, among the factors that determined

⁹ E. J. Hobsbawm, *Labouring Men* (Garden City, N.Y.: Doubleday, 1967); **Raphael** Samuels, "Comers and Goers," in *The Victorian City*, ed. H. J. Dyos and Michael Wolff (London: Routledge, Kegan Paul, 1973), 123–160. Daniel Calhoun, "The City as Teacher," *History of Education Quarterly*, 9 (1969), 312–325 is also suggestive.

Table 3.2

Persistence: Heads of Household, Census 1861—Assessment 1861
(Three Cities Combined)

	Literates		Illiterates	
	N	%	N	%
Total	2,551	81.4	332	49.6
A. Ethnicity				
Irish Catholic	399	82.8	189	50.9
Irish Protestant	445	80.7	27	43.5
Scottish Presbyterian	569	82.7	9	39.1
English Protestant	832	82.9	40	64.5
Canadian Protestant	266	80.8	8	36.4
Canadian Catholic	32	71.9	3	42.9
Black	45	93.3	24	45.3
Others	463	76.3	32	45.7
B. Occupation				
Professional/proprietor	207	87.4	1	50.0
Nonmanual	395	85.5	19	57.6
Skilled	870	85.2	60	55.6
Semiskilled	170	77.8	28	43.8
Unskilled	374	77.8	173	54.2
None	535	74.5	51	35.9
C. Age				
20–29	370	74.5	37	43.5
30–39	907	85.2	89	50.9
40–49	675	83.0	79	46.5
50–59	360	79.3	81	57.0
60–69	174	79.1	36	47.4
70+	60	82.2	9	52.9
D. Sex				
Male	2,290	83.6	276	53.9
Female	261	66.1	55	35.3
E. Family size				
0–2	1,425	80.6	190	47.1
3–5	897	82.0	117	53.2
6+	229	84.2	22	51.2
F. Household size				
1–3	641	77.3	100	45.0
4–7	1,437	82.5	190	52.3
8+	473	85.7	42	54.5
G. Marital status				
Single	104	64.2	7	35.0
Married	2,115	84.2	261	54.3
Widowed	331	72.3	64	39.0

migration; its impact was quite distinct and regular among both groups.[10] Marriage and a larger household and family weighed in favor of persistence; this is also reflected in aging's ties to migration, albeit to a smaller and less direct extent. The youngest, in search of their niches and success, were the least likely to remain, but among others there were no major variations. Yet, it is also clear from these data that among the illiterates, many of these factors diminished in significance. Their greater propensity to move reduced the force of these influences. Larger families among the illiterates persisted no more often than middle-sized ones; they could overburden limited resources and not be correlates of success, as we saw in the last chapter.

Ethnicity did not influence persistence as directly. The Irish and the blacks, poorest groups among the literates, persisted no less often than the more advantaged, although the patterns are much less distinct. Among the literates, the English, who fared the best, did remain in the cities most often (65%), far more often than the Irish Catholics (51%). The latter nonetheless ranked second in propensity to remain. Ethnic advantages made some difference, but more-common acquisition of property for members of these groups tied them to the cities. Occupation also made very little difference, especially for illiterates. If some small variations distinguished literates, yet for illiterates occupational ranking simply did not influence persistence. The unskilled, at 54%, remained as frequently as those at nonmanual or skilled positions, 58 and 56% of the time, respectively. Other factors were more important than these in shaping the migration and persistence patterns of the uneducated. With their greater proclivity for moving, the illiterates continued to feel the same forces that shaped movement for others; in these processes, as in others, they remained integrated into the social structure and its functions.

The same dynamics shaped persistence and transiency over the longer time span of a decade, 1861–1871 (Table 3.3). The propensity for migrating more often and the determining factors remained distinct and constant. Over ten years, a small number of illiterate and literate adults continued residence in the cities; illiterates, however, were again only about 60% as likely to stay as the others: 21% of them were linked, to 33% of all adults in Hamilton. These crude persistence rates are undoubtedly underestimations. If we adjust them, by estimating the effects of women's name-changes (through the sex ratio) and mortality,

10 See Roger Schofield, "Age-Specific Mobility in an Eighteenth-Century English Parish," *Annales de Demographie Historique* (1970), 261–274. This has been a common feature of mobility studies, and relates of course to marital status; see also, Katz, *People,* Ch. 3, for example.

Table 3.3

Persistence: Illiterates, 1861–1871 (Census to Census)
(Three Cities Combined)

	Illiterates	
	N	%
Total	365	20.5
A. Ethnicity		
Irish Catholic	239	23.4
Irish Protestant	38	19.2
Scottish Presbyterian	5	9.3
English Protestant	25	20.5
Canadian Protestant	4	6.6
Canadian Catholic	4	12.1
Black	21	17.6
Others	29	17.1
B. Age		
20–29	58	14.5
30–39	121	23.2
40–49	91	22.5
50–59	64	24.9
60–69	25	22.9
70+	5	8.5
C. Sex		
Male	167	24.5
Female	198	18.1
D. Marital status		
Single	15	5.9
Married	314	25.4
Widowed	35	12.3
E. Household status		
Head	182	26.8
Wife	154	26.4
Child	2	4.3
Relative	9	7.1
Boarder	12	7.8
Servant	5	5.8
F. Occupation		
Professional/proprietor	1	25.0
Nonmanual	8	20.0
Skilled	34	25.2
Semiskilled	21	10.9
Unskilled	97	23.8
None	6	0.6

we may approximate persistence rates for the illiterates at about 26% and for the total population at 37% (literates should be slightly more persistent).[11] Admitting the limits of approximation, the conclusion is unchanged. Illiterates maintained their greater likelihood of migrating with the same differential when compared with the others. The uneducated were more transient, in their quests for survival and security; few were trapped for a period as long as one decade.

The processes of persistence and transiency continued to be regular, in some of their features, punctuated especially by the life cycle. The life cycle played an even more pronounced role over the course of the decade, inasmuch as it continued to influence the experiences of both literates and illiterates. The youngest illiterate adults, those aged 20–29 in 1861, persisted least often (15%), with aging and families tying more of the others to the cities. The differences, while constant, remained very small among other age cohorts, and less than those of literate adults. Marital and household status also contributed directly. The married were most likely to stay (25%), with few widows (12%) and even fewer single persons (6%). Husbands and wives, at 26%, persisted far more frequently than others. The youngest, the unmarried, those less attached to work, homes, and families were much more transient (and harder to trace) than illiterates with roots and ties, despite the commonality of movement for all types of individuals. Women persisted less frequently than men (25 to 18%), as among literates. On all measures, illiterates remained less often than literates, although their experiences remained shaped by similar processes.

Ethnicity and occupation, as before, contributed less distinctly. No clear pattern differentiates the experience of the ethnic groups, but the poor Irish Catholics persisted most often (23%). Followed by the English (21%) and the Irish Protestants (19%), their success in homeownership tied these groups to the cities, as we will see again. Among the occupational classes, higher rank brought no results in persistence, and the skilled remained no more often than the unskilled (25 and 24%). Neither ethnicity nor occupational status directly influenced persistence and transiency; their (to us) blurred and ambiguous roles were felt among the educated as well as the uneducated. While the life cycle added an independent determinant to the processes that sorted and moved the population, ethnicity and occupation did not.

Data on persisting heads of households, traced from census and assessment rolls at each end of the decade, allow us to explore the process further with regard to wealth and homeownership. The number

[11] See Thernstrom, *The Other Bostonians,* Ch. 9; Katz, *People,* Ch. 3, for the problems of comparing persistence rates.

of four-way-linked illiterate persons is, expectedly, quite small: 82 from the three cities, representing a persistence rate of about 25% of the 1861 linked heads of household. As expected, their transiency rate exceeded that of all four-way-linked household heads in Hamilton, who remained at a rate of about 37%, the consistent difference of a ratio of three-fifths to two-thirds remaining. As we should expect, among this group, sex and the life cycle remained major determinants (Table 3.4). Male household heads, at 28%, were more than two and one-half times as likely to persist; many women undoubtedly found it difficult to continue as heads due to economic pressures, but remarried, or became boarders of relatives. Age in fact played no clear role, as the youngest two cohorts of adults remained most frequently, about 30%, but persistence did not increase with age after this point. The effects of aging were felt earlier by illiterates. The married far exceeded the single or widowed in propensity to remain: 28 to 14 and 13%, respectively. Family and household size, as determined at the earlier date, continued to act directly and positively, reflecting the major influence of the life cycle. Rates of persistence increased directly with family size, from 19% for small families to 30 and 33% for middle- and large-sized ones; household size acted similarly. The life course of the household head and his or her family served as major and independent factors.

Wealth and homeownership also played major roles within the processes of persistence and transiency. Homeownership, especially, provided a direct and independent impetus to staying in the cities,[12] as those owning a home in 1861 remained one-third more often than renters. In fact, the power of property was shared by these illiterates to the same extent as among all persisters in Hamilton; 29% of illiterate owners persisted and 30% of all owners. To these persons, whose drive for property has already been noted, persistence followed from the fact of ownership; this tie, a roof in the city and a measure of security, rooted them and certainly marked their success. Homeowning Irish were among the most likely to stay, followed by the English. For others, to be discussed presently, persistence led to increased opportunities for property of their own and the social mobility it represented. Irish Catholics and English Protestants led among persisting owners. Through this action they were most likely to persist among these heads of households, as homeownership played a very large role in influencing ethnic rates of persistence, too.

The influence of wealth on continuing residence, while distinct, was less clear and powerful for illiterates than for literates. Among the

[12] See Katz, *People,* Ch. 3.

latter, persistence increased linearly with wealth, from 29% among the poor to 35% among the middle ranking, to 44% among those in 80th–89th percentile rankings of wealth. Among illiterates (as Table 3.4, Part 5, shows) the probability of remaining did increase with wealth, but far less regularly. This pattern is highly suggestive, nevertheless; once more, it illustrates the limitations eventuating from illiterates' frequent poverty. Thus, it was those just above the poverty line (40th–59th percentiles) and those in the second quintile, with rates of 30 and 33%, who continued. And of course, these were the household heads most likely to purchase homes. With illiterates' disadvantages and their adaptive strategies, wealth's influences became muted; it was a less important determinant of persistence or migration, and a means for subsistence and adaptation within their larger limits. The life course and home-ownership, in part assisted by wealth, are clearly the most important independent influences on illiterates' persistence over the decade; this pattern closely approximated that which bound literates and their households, as common processes integrated these experiences despite the illiterates' greater mobility.

With the powerful and independent impact of these major factors, it is hardly surprising that the illiterates' proclivity for migrating had sharply declined, after 10 years of persistence. Over the shorter term, from census to assessments, 1870–1872 (a range of from 3 to 14 months in the cities), the dynamics of frequent movement reversed: 84% of illiterates now persisted. Continued residence over the long-term of a decade almost assured the short-term persistence; if this rate were corrected for the effects of mortality and other biases toward underestimation, virtually all would be accounted, I suspect. As a result of this new stability in their ties to the cities, the influence of most factors was tremendously reduced; neither age, sex, marital status, family or household size, nor occupation or ethnicity contributed directly or importantly. In fact, women were more likely to continue than men (100 to 75%) and the widowed more than the married (96 to 75%). Death of course made the major distinctions now. Long-term residence, with its much greater chances for stability, success, and even social mobility, was indeed possible for the uneducated; the forces which impelled their transiency and frequent movements were dramatically reversed. Their propensity for transiency, which marked short-term experience a decade earlier, and the experience of a decade as well were erased. The disadvantaged and uneducated need not be seen as either rootless or paralytically rooted; more mobile they were, but most likely in structured responses to their environments with their opportunities and inequalities. Regular variations must have influenced and ordered their move-

Table 3.4

Persistence: Illiterate Heads of Household, 1861–1871 (Four-way Linkages)

	N	%		N	%		N	%
1. Ethnicity			4. Home ownership			8. Household Size		
Irish Catholic	54	28.6	Own	30	28.6	Small	15	15.0
Irish Protestant	8	29.6	Rent	42	22.9	Medium	51	26.8
Scottish Presbyterian	0	0.0	No information	1	33.3	Large	16	38.1
English Protestant	11	27.5	5. Wealth–percentiles			9. Marital Status		
Canadian Protestant	2	25.0	0–19	17	18.5	Single	1	14.3
Canadian Catholic	0	0.0	20–39	29	29.6	Married	73	27.9
Black	4	16.7	40–59	11	33.3	Widowed	8	12.5
Others	3	9.4	60–79	4	17.4			
Total	82	24.7	80–89	3	27.3			
2. Age			90–94	0	0.0			
20–29	11	29.7	95–98	0	0.0			
30–39	28	31.5	6. Sex					
40–49	18	22.8	Male	76	27.5			
50–59	17	20.9	Female	6	10.9			
60–69	6	16.7	7. Number of children					
70+	2	22.2	Small (0–2)	36	18.9			
3. Occupation			Medium (3–5)	35	29.9			
Nonmanual	5	26.3	Large (6+)	11	33.3			
Skilled	16	26.7						
Semiskilled	10	35.7						
Unskilled	45	26.0						
Unemployed	6	11.8						

ments much as they ordered the paths of others. The disabilities of their ascriptive characteristics, which reduced their opportunities for educational achievements and left them more often poor and disadvantaged, also contributed to their more common transiency and more regular search for a place in which to settle and survive. Gaining the initial foothold depended on ethnic and class advantages denied to most of them. For those able to persist, however, another path toward greater rewards was open; for if they remained, some success was indeed possible.

II. Literacy and Social Mobility

Central to understanding the meaning of literacy in this society are the experiences of those able to persist across the decade. How did they fare in occupation, wealth, and property? Did they lose whatever progress they had made earlier; did most remain poor; or were opportunities available, in this context, to the illiterate? We have reviewed the sociological expectations for their futures, lacking as they did the skills and other attributes that accompany the acquisition of literacy and the process of education. With society becoming ever more modern, industrial, commercial, and institutionalized, the illiterates who remained should have had, in theory, major obstacles to their progress. If this were true, expectations should have been met and additional documentation for the link between education and mobility found. As the preceding pages have indicated, the actual workings of the social process, even with its firm basis in the dominance of ascription, are far from self-evident: the role of literacy continues to be complex. Illiterates did experience significant opportunities for improvement during this period; the implications of this major discovery will be raised after we review the evidence.

Before proceeding, however, the limitations on this analysis must be noted. We lack information, first, about the futures of the majority of illiterates who did not persist in Hamilton, Kingston, or London. This of course remains the central weakness of all mobility research, which students have thus far proved unable to surmount. Most assume that the least successful are most likely to be transient, thus biasing upward the findings of record-linkage studies. Certainly the common results of persistence studies reinforce this conclusion. Nevertheless, evidence can be located that at least suggests that outmigrants may be more likely to improve their positions than others.[13] Until much more evi-

---

[13] Knights, *Plain People*, 118; Blau and Duncan, *Structure*, 243–275.

dence is gathered, any conclusions must remain tentative; for the present, we point to the prevalence of mobility among all components of these populations and the general representativeness—in ethnicity, occupation, and wealth—of these persisters as legitimating the following conclusions. The second issue is both conceptual and methodological. A concentration on occupation as the major dependent variable has marked most studies of mobility, especially those set in the nineteenth century. Recent work, especially that of Michael Katz, has revealed the quite basic limitations of this focus: not only do individual occupations or broader occupational strata mask wide ranges of differences in prestige or reward as well as task, but occupational mobility does not correlate well with economic, property, or other kinds of mobility.[14] This study, consequently, assesses movement on the three scales of occupation, wealth, and property and their relationships. We begin with the dimension of occupational changes.

The conclusion is straightforward: over the 10 years, occupational class positions were remarkably stable for persisting adult male illiterates (Table 3.5). In the three urban centers, almost 115 men (80%), did not change rank; 15 moved up at least one level (10%) while 18 (12%) slipped downward. This is very little movement for a decade, and certainly provides no evidence of mass occupational decline due to illiteracy. By 1871, therefore, slightly fewer workers were unskilled and semiskilled than had begun the decade at these lowly levels (66 to 71%); and of those occupationally stable ones, only 74% remained in those ranks. Of those who slipped, only 9, or 26%, fell from skilled positions, as illiterates overwhelmingly maintained that status. Only one person, in fact, dropped from nonmanual status to unskilled, an unambiguous decline. Of those who moved upward in rank, almost all (13 of 15) had started as unskilled laborers; 6 achieved skilled work and 2 rose to nonmanual positions, marking real gains. Overall, the amounts of upward and downward movement were the same in total mobility and in levels gained and lost.

Compared to Hamilton's population, the illiterates were more stable, with fewer changing their occupational rank. Despite this greater movement, similar proportions of the linked population remained within each rank at the end of the decade, as with the illiterates. The likelihood of maintaining unskilled or semiskilled positions was the same: 70% of the total linked work force and 66% of the illiterates. At the skilled level, 84% of the total and 71% of the illiterates remained, and among both groups, most movement was of a short distance. A lack of literacy

[14] See Katz, *People*, Ch. 3, esp. 134–141. Compare with the amount of movement discovered by Katz from 1851 to 1861.

Table 3.5
Illiterate Occupational Mobility, 1861–1871 (Males) (Three Cities Combined)

	1871					
1861	Non-manual	Skilled	Semi-skilled	Unskilled	None	*N*
Professional/proprietor						
N	—	—	—	1	—	1
%	—	—	—	100.0	—	0.6
Nonmanual						
N	4	2	—	1	1	8
%	50.0	25.0	—	12.5	12.5	4.8
Skilled						
N	1	24	1	5	3	34
%	2.9	70.6	2.9	14.7	8.8	20.4
Semiskilled						
N	—	1	10	8	2	21
%	—	4.8	47.6	38.1	9.5	12.6
Unskilled						
N	2	6	5	77	7	97
%	2.1	6.2	5.2	79.4	7.2	58.1
None						
N	—	2	—	3	1	6
%	—	33.3	—	50.0	16.7	3.6
Total						
N	7	35	16	95	14	167
%	4.2	20.9	9.6	56.9	8.4	

Mobility summary (with occupations, 1861, 1871)

	N	%
Stable	115	77.7
Upward	15	10.1
Number of ranks	25	
Downward	18	12.2
Number of ranks	24	

had no pronounced impact in differentiating the groups' occupational experience over this decade; stability was most frequent, regardless of education, and illiterates could hope for some small gains. Importantly, of course, they did not plummet downward from earlier attainments of nonmanual or skilled occupations, although they did not have quite the hold that literates had. Illiteracy, in the context of a society industrializing and modernizing, proved itself no insurmountable barrier to maintaining position or even to gaining. Persistence and adaptation surely were more important. By this time—at least, for these workers—there was little truth in Charles Clarke's stereotypical claim that "the uneducated are sinking, more rapidly and certainly than ever, into the position of mere 'hewers of wood and drawers of water,' socially, mentally and politically. To be more condemned to the galleys for life, to sink into the mud which clings to the wheels of progress and to be at a disadvantage, at every turn, in whatever the world finds for man to do." [15] The uneducated who remained in these cities did not succumb to such pressures; without the promised benefits of education, they did not sink. The upper ranks remained restricted to them, with their origins and lack of literacy skills; their decade-long experience, nevertheless, was far from a negative one, comparing favorably with that of others.

Aging paralleled adjustment, as most movement took place among the youngest cohort of adults. For most workers in this society, the twenties were a period of searching for careers. Almost one-half (44%) of illiterates aged 20–29 in 1861 changed occupational rank, consequently, with more able to rise (25%) than fall (18%) in position. For others, stability was dominant. Ethnic ascription made no more difference than age in these slight variations in occupational rank. Stability was shared by each of the major groups, including the advantaged English Protestants and the disadvantaged Irish Catholics. These Irish held on to their few higher-ranking positions, as downward mobility equalled but did not exceed upward (10%). Blacks were stable as well. Small distinctions due to age or ethnicity were quite minimal in the face of stability. If anything, ethnicity's links with stratification were slightly reduced, as the English, for example, suffered some small downward movement (20%) and no corresponding gains. Small numbers limit this analysis of intragroup differences, however, but do not preclude the conclusion that there was stability and maintenance of position at all levels, and some rises over the decade. Illiteracy, while undoubtedly limiting the attainments of many, did not mean loss of skilled or higher-ranking attainments or no improvement; conversely, for many others, literacy did not guarantee upward mobility.

Occupation, we now recognize, is only one dimension of mobility, and not the most revealing one. Other measures, such as servants, property, and wealth, provide necessary and significant perspectives, which supplement and broaden understanding. To consider wealth, or measures of economic standing, is a more precise and sensitive way of estimating change. In respect of wealth, illiterates displayed much more

[15] Clarke, *Teachers and Teaching (and) Then and Now* (Elora, Ont., 1880), 1.

movement, as did literates too. More importantly, much of their mobility was upward in direction. The base for the discussion of wealth and property mobility narrows to the small group of four-way-linked heads of households from the three cities. With such small numbers, conclusions can only be tentative and suggestive. The total assessed population of Hamilton serves as a control group and as the basis for the percentile ranking of the wealth-holders.[16]

In sharp contrast to stability in occupational rank, upward economic mobility was the dominant experience of the urban illiterates. In Hamilton and Kingston (recall the lack of a comparable category in London in 1861), *almost 60%* of the linked heads of household (38 of 64) moved upward in standing (Table 3.6). Of these mobile but uneducated persons, 18 rose one level, 15 two levels, and 5 three levels. Only 7 household heads, 11%, suffered downward mobility over the span of the decade 1861–1871; 30% remained the same. Not only is this a great deal of movement, but it is an impressive accomplishment for any group, especially for those who lacked education and who had often suffered from other disadvantages as well. Clearly and unambiguously, persisting illiterate heads of households progressed economically over this period, providing important evidence that their lack of literacy did not depress their status as the society changed. The representativeness of these persons is not certain, and their very persistence was probably biased in the direction of increasing wealth, but the improvement is too definite to require qualification. Only 34% of the illiterates who persisted remained poor, but over 70% of them had begun the decade in poverty. The top ranges of wealth (80th–99th percentiles) remained largely closed to the uneducated, as had the top of the occupational hierarchy. Within these limits, though, upward mobility came to the majority of persisters, and downward to a small number. Illiteracy neither resulted in mass decline nor precluded significant progress; undoubtedly illiterates were greatly assisted by their time in the city and their ability to adjust to its ways.[17]

The illiterates' mobility compared favorably with the experience of the linked population of Hamilton. Of those who started poor, 43% remained poor; 57% of the total population who started the decade in poverty were immobile. The proportion of the poor among the entire

---

[16] The assessment of wealth changed its basis from 1861 to 1871 as well. *Total value*, rather than *total annual value*, became the most inclusive category; this is a larger sum of course, but comparable across the cities. Percentile rankings, and not absolute amounts, form the basis of analysis.

[17] A fascinating analysis of "reading" a city is provided by Steven Marcus, "Reading the Illegible," in *The Victorian City*, ed. Dyos and Wolff, 257–276; see also Daniel Calhoun, "The City as Teacher."

Table 3.6
Illiterates: Economic Mobility, Four-way Linked Heads of Household (1861–1871) (Percentiles, Total Annual Value, 1861—Percentiles, Total Value, 1871)

	1871						
1861	0–19	20–39	40–59	60–79	80–89	90–94	*N*
0–19							
N	2	6	6	3	—	—	17
%	11.8	35.3	35.3	17.6	—	—	25.6
20–39							
N	2	10	9	8	—	—	29
%	6.9	34.5	31.0	27.6	—	—	45.3
40–59							
N	—	2	6	2	1	—	11
%	—	18.2	54.5	18.2	9.1	—	17.2
60–79							
N	—	—	2	1	—	1	4
%	—	—	50.0	25.0	—	25.0	6.3
80–89							
N	—	—	1	—	1	1	3
%	—	—	33.3	—	33.3	33.3	4.7
Total							
N	4	18	24	14	2	2	64
%	6.3	28.1	39.1	21.9	3.1	3.1	

Economic mobility summary

	N	%
Stable	19	29.7
Upward	38	59.4
Number of levels	63	
Downward	7	10.9
Number of levels	8	

linked population fell from 28 to 24%; among illiterates it fell from 71 to 34%. In the middle ranges of wealth (40th–79th percentiles), illiterates increased their standing from 24 to 61%; the total Hamilton group fell from 48 to 40%. Some small movement was possible at the top for the larger group, to which of course only the most exceptional and tiny number of uneducated persons could realistically aspire. Nevertheless, the persisting illiterates proved a special group; less stable than others, they made, relatively, much greater gains. Considering their beginnings, this was no small achievement.

Economic progress, not surprisingly, was shared by virtually all ethnic groups. The Irish Catholic illiterates, in contrast to those in the total population, moved clearly ahead from their earlier positions. Sixty-three percent of them increased their economic standing (11 individuals by two levels, 3 by three); only 4% fell. Fewer than one-third of these persisters remained poor after one decade. The English Protestants also fared very well, although they were now few in number. Of the eight who were four-way linked across the decade, six (86%) improved (three by two levels, two by three), only one declined in economic rank, and only one remained poor. The total extent of their gains was greatest; their ethnic advantages were hardly erased. More importantly though, other groups, especially the Irish, also progressed. Disabilities—of ascription and achievement—were undoubtedly reduced for these illiterates with time, experience, adaptation, and social changes. Persisting illiterates adapted well in this changing society, dominated as it was by the literate and by a social structure still rooted in inequality and in ascription. Their improvement in the context of moderately decreasing economic mobility for the total population and continuing structural rigidity is impressive; it also contradicts common expectations about the roles of literacy and education in economic success. On the one hand, experience and stability in continuing residence obviously attenuated limitations of education and origins, as contemporary studies report.[18] This is important. The nature of their progress, with upward mobility for the majority and departure from poverty, especially compared with the greater stability among the total population, strikes against notions of both the relative and absolute importance of schooling for mobility. Without that achievement, these illiterates still rose, often with small steps, over the decade. Limitations of schooling were surmountable.

In the achievement of economic mobility, aging made remarkably little difference. Proportions remaining poor decreased very gradually with aging, from one-third of those aged 20–29 to 21% of those 50–59, rising again after that point. Mobility and improved position came to household heads of all ages, as persistence and adjustment assisted their progress.

Stability in occupational rank and upward mobility in economic standing were the dominant experiences of the illiterates who persisted in each of the cities from 1861 to 1871. Occupational change, as we have noted, is far less precise an indicator of mobility than change in economic position; measures of their association among the entire population of Hamilton, for example, show little correlation. Katz found that

---

[18] For example, see Blau and Duncan, *Structure,* 187.

from 1851 to 1861 the relationship between occupational and economic mobility was quite low: phi coefficient (ϕ) = .10; from 1861 to 1871, it was virtually unchanged.[19] Other indicators show that while a knowledge of occupation aids little in predicting economic rank, they were generally close to each other but did not always change together or in the same direction. Among the illiterates there was no necessary connection, or causal link, between economic and occupational mobility (this is illustrated in Table 3.7A). With common economic gains but

Table 3.7
Occupational and Economic Mobility, 1861–1871—Heads (Only Employed)

	All illiterates	Hamilton	Kingston
A.			
Stable occupationally			
Rise economically	22	14	8
Stable economically	15	10	5
Fall economically	4	1	3
Rise occupationally			
Rise economically	6	4	2
Stable economically	1	—	1
Fall economically	—	—	—
Fall occupationally			
Rise economically	4	2	2
Stable economically	3	2	1
Fall economically	1	1	—
Total	56	34	22

	N	%	N	%	N	%
B. Frequencies						
Upward	45	60.0	23	57.5	12	48.0
Stable	20	26.7	12	30.0	8	32.0
Downward	10	13.3	5	12.5	5	20.0

Scoring system (to calculate cumulative upward and downward mobility frequencies)

	Stable	Moves up 1 rank	Moves up 2 or more	Moves down 1 rank	Moves down 2 or more
Occupational	0	2	4	−2	−4
Economic	0	3	6	−3	−6

[19] Katz, *People*, 149–160. The scale employed below was suggested to me by Michael B. Katz.

occupational stability, this is hardly surprising, and also reinforces the
need of moving beyond occupation as the sole measure of mobility.
Nevertheless, gains in occupation were most clearly related to economic
improvement: six of seven rising in job level also increased in wealth
rank; a loss in occupational level, conversely, led to less likelihood of
gaining economically. With a simple additive scale, we may examine
these relationships between occupation and economic change, as summarized in Table 3.7B. Examined in this way, we find slightly more
stability (27%) with upward mobility for 60% of these illiterates. Few
of them (13%) fell. Notwithstanding no clear aggregate mobility in occupations, upward social mobility remains the major experience (and the
substance of a general conclusion) when the joint effects from these
two dimensions are combined. Mobility is undoubtedly a cumulative
and complex process, tied to the structural context, as perceptive students have discovered. Different dimensions and joint effects must be
considered; in this perspective, the rise of persisting illiterates is
unambiguous.

Home or property ownership constitutes a third dimension of social
mobility, one of special significance to the uneducated urban residents,
as we discovered in the preceding chapter, and one closely related to
their very persistence. This dimension is somewhat independent of other
forms of movement, involving choices in the use of resources, adaptive
strategies, and cultural traditions. In this dimension, as in economic
standing, the illiterates who remained in the cities made solid gains, in
Hamilton and Kingston, as well as in London. Among persisters, homeownership was an important tie; and over the decade, 77% of them
retained their holdings or owned other property (Table 3.8). This compares very favorably with the 86% stability in ownership among Hamilton's total linked household heads. A substantial number of others
(38%) who began the decade as renters advanced to ownership by 1871,
and less than 25% lost their property and became renters. Once again,
illiterates compared well with the larger population, of which 34%
gained property and 14% lost. Considering that despite their economic
gains their resources remained well below those with literacy and ethnic
advantages, they stand well indeed. Overall, their rate of ownership in
1871, at 51%, equalled that among all household heads, now 53%. In
the context of their earlier success in acquiring property, this is not at
all surprising; in the context of the structural and personal disadvantages they confronted, this level of ownership represents a significant
accomplishment.

Maintaining ownership or securing property was a central aspect
of the mobility experiences of these urban illiterates, whose emphasis
on and struggle for property can not be disputed. As part of the manner

Table 3.8

Homeownership–Property Mobility, 1861–1871 (Four-way Linked Heads)
(Three Cities Combined)

	1871			
1861	Own	Rent	No data	Total
Own				
N	23	7	—	30
%	76.7	23.3	—	36.6
Rent				
N	19	28	3	50
%	38.0	56.0	6.0	60.9
No data				
N	—	2	—	2
%	—	100.0	—	2.4
Total				
N	42	37	3	82
%	51.2	45.1	3.7	

Property summary

	N	%
Stable	51	66.2
Gaining	19	25.7
Losing	7	9.1

in which they confronted the city and faced its threats to their survival, purchasing homes signified success in adaptive strategies and a path to further mobility, as well as a major achievement in its own right. This was particularly true of the Irish, whose relatively high rate of ownership was noted by 1861. They in fact were the only ethnic group to increase substantially their proportions owning homes over the decade; their cultural emphasis, which others have discovered among Irish laborers, continued over the period, propelling their rates of ownership.[20] Fourteen of the Irish Catholics gained property, while only four lost and two-thirds were stable; their gains parallel those of other Irish.

[20] Katz, *People*, comes to the same conclusion. See also Ch. 2, above; Thernstrom, *Poverty and Progress;* Griffen, *Natives and Newcomers* (Cambridge, Mass.: Harvard University Press, 1978); K. N. Conzen, *Immigrant Milwaukee* (Cambridge, Mass.: Harvard, 1976); D. R. Esslinger, *Immigrants in the City* (Port Washington, N.Y.: Kennikat Press, 1975); M. P. Weber, *Social Change in an Industrial Town* (University Park, Pa.: Pennsylvania State University Press, 1976); Hershberg *et al.,* "Occupations and Ethnicity in Five Nineteenth-Century Cities," *Historical Methods Newsletter,* 7 (1974), 174–216.

Illiterates joined in this Irish drive, seizing an important and visible sign
of settlement, adaptation, and success. Irish Catholics, as in other dimensions of mobility, made relatively the greatest progress in this decade;
homeownership was a major object within their grasp.

Like the relationship between occupational and economic mobility,
the relationship between economic and property mobility was less than
perfectly direct. Property represented in large measure an independent
path and dimension of mobility. Measures of their association, as Katz
has found in Hamilton, were very weak, and change in property status
had rather less relation to other factors than had movement in other
dimensions.[21] Among the illiterates, there was some tendency for those
gaining in wealth to purchase homes, but it was far from universal
(Table 3.9A). Nine of those rising in economic position (30%) gained in
property. But very few lost their homes, whether they were stable or
declining economically, and a few were able to gain property while stable
or falling in wealth rank. When the joint influence of these dimensions
of mobility are examined (again with the additive system), we find that
most illiterates who persisted were able to increase both their economic
rank and their chances of ownership (Table 3.9B). Over 60% achieved a net
gain, with only 15% losing and 23% stable. The sum of the decade
experience was positive.

The mobility of these illiterates may be illustrated by several examples. The Dillon, Daylet, and Lavelle families, all resident in Hamilton in 1861 and 1871, exemplify the processes and progress that marked
the illiterates' experience. J. M. Dillon, born in Ireland and brought up
as a Roman Catholic, was a 32-year-old laborer in 1861. Residing in a
rented frame one-story house, with his wife and four children (two sons,
two daughters), he was poor. Ranking in the 20th–39th percentiles
(second quintile) of assessed wealth, he was able to send only one child,
a son, to school. Ten years later, Dillon was neither a laborer nor poor.
Working as a hotelkeeper and its caretaker, he also owned his own
house, made of brick, and sent three of the four sons who lived at home
to school (only one daughter remained at home). The decade brought
real success to the Dillons; they ranked well above the poverty line, being
now in the 60th–79th wealth percentiles, and reported real property
worth $1000. Clearly, Dillon was an exceptional person, whose illiteracy
did not block the possibility of mobility in either occupation or wealth.

The more common process of occupational stability accompanied
by gains in wealth and stability or gain in property can be seen in the
case of the Daylets. The family head, a 50-year-old Irish Catholic laborer,
lived, in 1861, with his wife and two daughters in a one-story brick

21 Katz, *People*, Ch. 3.

Table 3.9

Economic and Property Mobility, 1861–1871 (Heads)

	All illiterates	Hamilton	Kingston
A.			
Stable economically			
Gain a home	2	2	–
Stable	16	8	8
Lose home	2	1	1
Rise economically			
Gain a home	9	5	4
Stable	20	11	9
Lose home	1	1	–
Fall economically			
Gain a home	2	1	1
Stable	8	6	2
Lose home	1	1	–
Total	61	36	25

	N	%	N	%	N	%
B. Frequencies						
Upward	39	62.9	25	67.6	14	56.0
Stable	14	22.5	7	18.9	7	28.0
Downward	9	14.5	5	13.5	4	16.0

Scoring system (to calculate cumulative upward and downward mobility frequencies)

	Stable	Moves up 1 rank	Moves up 2 or more	Moves down 1 rank	Moves down 2 or more
Economic	0	3	6	−3	−6
		Gains	Loses		
Property	0	2	−2		

house that the family had managed to purchase. The Daylets, who were poor (20th–39th percentiles), not only owned a home but also kept five cows, no doubt using livestock in the manner discussed before. By 1871, Daylet and his wife lived alone in their brick house, their children having left home. He was still a laborer; but the Daylets were no longer poor. They reported property worth $650 and ranked among the 40th–59th percentiles of the assessed population.

The Lavelle family provides a final example. In 1861, Lavelle was a 36-year-old Irish Catholic laborer, who lived in a rented one-story frame house with his family of three boys and four girls. An eighth child,

another daughter, had died within the year. A female relative joined
this already large family. The Lavelles, burdened by the size of their
household, were desperately poor; they stood within the lowest quintile
of the assessed wealthholders, with a total annual worth of $18. By 1871
they owned their own home and reported real property valued at $500
(the family now numbered nine, with two parents and seven children).
None of the children attended school in either census year, but the
family now owned its place of residence and had also risen above the
poverty line. They now ranked among the 40th–59th percentiles of
the assessed population.

These three cases, I should add, are not atypical. They represent
the common experiences of many persisting illiterate-headed households
and suggest the opportunities for progress that time, stability, and adaptation made possible, even for those without education.

In all measures of mobility, the persistent illiterates fared well over
the years 1861–1871. These experiences add an important perspective
to the role of literacy in the changing society. How significant and
requisite were the skills of literacy—reading and writing—when those
without them were able to make solid, substantial gains through continuing residence in these cities? What were the benefits of education?
Occupationally, the uneducated held their own, not cascading toward
the lowest end of the occupational hierarchy as the cities continued their
transformation to modern and industrial forms. Less volatile than others
whose movement was short-range and limited, they did not lose skilled or
nonmanual positions. Economically, they progressed much more frequently, making solid progress toward the middle ranks of the population, and in property ownership they advanced as well. Of these illiterates, the Irish Catholics stand out. Beginning the decade lowest in wealth
and position, they advanced the farthest. The English, who started as
relatively high-ranking, maintained their status and gained in wealth,
notwithstanding that their ascriptive advantages probably diminished.
None of the ethnic groups, in fact, can be accurately described as down-
wardly mobile, as this progress was a shared experience. Persistence
undoubtedly contributed strongly to the determination of increased
success, but it alone provides insufficient evidence at present to account
for the accomplishments of these uneducated persons. We must emphasize, moreover, that this progress occurred in the context of continuing
structural inequality, heightening the significance and implications of
illiterate progress.[22]

[22] Other evidence exists for social mobility for illiterates. Especially interesting
is William H. Sewell, Jr., "Social Mobility in a Nineteenth-Century European City,"
Journal of Interdisciplinary History, 7 (1976), 217–233. Sewell reports that sons of

The highest ranks of wealth and occupation were closed to illiterates, in 1871 and 1861; there were definite limits on the mobility of those lacking in education, regardless of other characteristics. Larger proprietary, professional, and clerical positions were rarely possible, but skilled and smaller proprietary posts were available to attain and to hold. Similarly, the upper reaches of wealth were largely obstructed. Yet within these broad limits, illiteracy clearly did not prevent these individuals from some success in mid-nineteenth-century urban society, or from improving their places over the decade. Literacy was not a requirement, and certainly many with some schooling fared no better than, if as well as, the unschooled and illiterate. These data demand that some qualifications be applied to the promises of the school promoters and to the dire predictions for the futures of the uneducated. Having explored the limits on literacy extensively in the preceding chapter, we may now add that these limits, largely nonindependently operating ones, were reduced with the passage of time, the ability to adapt, and the experience of urban life. The significance of literacy was not a direct or sufficient one in the processes of success and mobility. For some it undoubtedly contributed; for others it made little difference, as illiterates could certainly improve their places without this achievement, and with other, more substantial disadvantages as well. The rise of ideologies of education took place in the face of this evidence, as the hegemony of the school and its moral bases were ascendant despite the real possibility of continuing social contradictions. Mobility became intertwined with schooling and so persisted inseparably from this era on, developing a

---

peasants, in-migrants to Marseilles at mid-century, were more likely to be illiterate than native-born workers' sons (33 to 21%) but in occupations "bested all categories of workers' sons by margins ranging from 30% for skilled workers' sons to over 250% for unskilled workers' sons," 222–223. Conversely, Michael Sanderson ("Literacy and Social Mobility in the Industrial Revolution in England," *Past and Present*, 56 [1972], 75–104) shows that literacy by no means guaranteed social mobility or protection from downward movement, either intra- or intergenerationally. Soltow and Stevens ("Economic Aspects of School Participation in Mid-Nineteenth-Century United States," *Journal of Interdisciplinary History*, 8 [1977], 221–243), argue that "it appears unlikely that the common school served as a vehicle for occupational mobility. Although the expectations of common school reformers may have anticipated that school enrollment would eventually result in upward social and economic mobility, it is highly unlikely that such expectations were rewarded," 242. Moreover, they conclude, "The implication is that the common school institution did not alter patterns of economic inequality, but, rather, tended to perpetuate them," 243. For a more normative, and less convincing approach, see Robert Higgs, "Race, Skills, and Earnings: American Immigrants in 1909," *Journal of Economic History*, 31 (1971), 420–428. See also, Chs. 4, 5, below.

life of its own in its reflections of popular ideology and social order.[23] As we have seen, within the perceptions of those throughout the society were sufficient evidences of advancement through achievement of literacy and schooling to lend the required support to secure its domination despite other evidence. It is this other evidence that impels us to look further and to question theoretical relationships rooted first in these perceptions.

Another aspect of the experience over the decade is not as positive as what we have seen thus far; this involves changing household and marital status. The pattern is a continuation of the prevalence of widowhood and single-headedness found in 1861, threatening the security and status of female illiterates. In each city, the ratio of household heads to spouses rose, as 13% of wives became heads of households. More than the result of normal aging, most cases of changing household status occurred before the years of greatest mortality: during the thirties (when 17% changed) and the forties (when 13% did). In addition, in each city, a 50% increase in the proportion of illiterates who were widowed took place, with 13% of those married in 1861 becoming widowed by the end of the decade. Here too, it was not only the oldest who suffered such changes, with 11 and 22% becoming widowed in their thirties and forties, respectively. Women were victimized by poverty and the loss of spouses at a rate twice that of men. An excess of women should of course be expected in this population and with the sex differential in mortality, but the effect was to complicate the lives of those so disadvantaged.[24] These changes were hardly unique to illiterates of course, for many others suffered similarly. In spite of overall success, though, these women continued to be plagued with widowhood and greater threats of poverty, alone in a society with little place for their occupational or economic independence.

III. The Illiterates in 1871

A final perspective on the place of these persisting urban illiterates derives from the nature of the aggregate changes in their position in the social structure over the decade. This brief review places their mobility more fully into context; and, while confirming their gains, it reinforces

[23] See Anselm Strauss, *The Contexts of Social Mobility* (Chicago: Aldine, 1971); Katz, "The Origins of Public Education," *History of Education Quarterly*, 16 (1976), 381–407.

[24] See, for two examples, the recent studies of S. L. N. Rao, "On Long-Term Mortality Trends in the United States, 1850–1968," *Demography*, 10 (1973), 405–419; M. R. Haines, "Mortality in Nineteenth-Century America," *Demography*, 14 (1977), 311–332.

Table 3.10

Occupational Status, 1871—Illiterates (Census–Census Linked) [a]

	Total illiterates	1861 Total %	1861 Linked %
Nonmanual			
N	9		
%	5.6	5.1	4.9
Skilled			
N	37		
%	22.8	17.4	21.1
Semiskilled			
N	21		
%	12.9	24.7	13.0
Unskilled			
N	96		
%	59.3	52.3	59.6
Total	162		

[a] Total illiterates refers to 1871 positions; 1861 total refers to positions of all illiterates located in that year; 1861 linked refers to the 1861 standing of persisting illiterates (the latter is used in the text).

our understanding of the restrictions on those without schooling and on the majority with other, ascriptive disadvantages. For despite their important opportunities to rise without benefit of literacy, which belie the contemporary and more recent emphases on the need for education, the structure of inequality persisted, rooted only indirectly on achieved characteristics.

First, consider their occupational distribution. For persisting workers came a slight overall gain in job status, compared with both all illiterates in 1861 and their own ranking in that year (Table 3.10). At the top, among smaller proprietors, virtually the same numbers remained, while the skilled level saw a small but important increase in their representation. Virtually no net change occurred at the lower levels. Gains were made, but they were very small steps, as the net aggregate shift was very slightly upward in the context of overwhelming stability. Of more consequence are the ethnic patterns. Ethnically stratified occupational differentiation, very similar to that of ten years earlier, persisted in 1871.[25] The English Protestants remained high-ranking among the illiterates. Two-thirds of them were skilled (47%) or higher (20%); only one-third were unskilled. This distribution represented no aggregate change,

[25] On the persistence of stratification systems, see Katz, *People,* esp. Ch. 2, and the literature cited there.

however; their gains were made earlier, and their advantages carried them no further. The Irish, in contrast, were able to move slightly forward, as their proportions unskilled slightly decreased (72 to 66%) and skilled or higher increased (15 to 19%). The overall context, then, was one of dominant stability, some small improvements, and the persistence of ascriptively rooted structural inequality. The stratification of the illiterates continued in occupation, as before, as the range began to narrow with industrialization and change.

Wealth provides the second measure, representing of course the dimension of greatest change and most progress for the illiterates. The decade began with over 70%, yet concluded with less than 50% below the poverty line (40th percentile) (Table 3.11). Middle-range status (40th–79th percentiles) was attained by almost 50%, a substantial accomplishment, and four persons stood even higher. As with occupation, ethnic stratification persisted in the distribution of wealth. Not one English Protestant illiterate remained poor now; all reached middle-class economic standing. The Irish Catholics, despite their impressive attainments, continued to be poorer, with 47% now above the poverty line, the others poor. Irish Protestants fared similarly. Female heads of households, who were found more often in the latter year, also improved their economic standing over the period. One-half of these heads escaped from poverty, reducing their overall plight and mediating slightly the hardships of widowhood—and that double disadvantage that uneducated women faced in this sexually-stratified society that allowed them so few opportunities for independence or economic improvement.

Table 3.11
Wealth of Illiterates, 1871 (Census–Assessment Linked Heads) [a]

Percentile	Dollars	Total illiterates		1861 Total	1861 Linked
		N	%	%	%
0–19	0–150	8	5.6	35.5	25.6
20–39	151–400	59	41.5	37.8	45.3
40–59	401–680	45	31.7	12.7	17.2
60–79	681–1,395	26	18.3	8.8	6.3
80–89	1,396–2,480	—	—	4.2	4.7
90–94	2,481–4,550	2	1.4	—	—
95–98	4,551–12,750	1	0.7	—	—
99–100	12,751+	1	0.7	—	—

[a] Total illiterates refers to 1871 positions; 1861 total refers to positions of all illiterates located in that year; 1861 linked refers to the 1861 standing of persisting illiterates (the latter is used in the text).

Even with extensive opportunities and frequent mobility, the social structure of illiteracy remained intact in its rigid structure of inequality. The extent of differentiation by ethnicity did narrow; while ascription remained strong, its impact was reduced. Perhaps achievement would rise in significance as ascription declined. Further inquiries should focus on these relationships.

As in 1861, wealth related to occupation rather imperfectly. All occupational ranks of illiterates improved their economic standing, however. Sixty-one percent of the unskilled were still poor, but most had climbed from the 0–19th into the 20th–30th economic percentiles. Many more scaled poverty's walls than had done so earlier. Of the semiskilled, a small majority (54%) stood above that line in 1871, when most had been poor earlier. Skilled workers advanced the most, moreover. Seventy percent of them ranked among the middle ranges of wealth, and none of the small proprietors were now poor, a testament to their higher occupational status. With time and experience, following from adaptation and continuing residence in the cities, came the kinds of commensurate rewards that had often been denied in 1861. This attainment no doubt came later to many who were uneducated than to those with some schooling; illiteracy, if a handicap, was not an insurmountable obstacle either to economic improvement or to hopes of securing rewards commensurate with work. By the same token, literacy by itself held no guarantees of wealth, mobility, or even fair rewards.

Homeownership represented the final dimension in which the illiterates significantly advanced over the decade. This, of course, formed one aspect of change independent of occupational and wealth shifts. In each city, by 1871, we find a net gain in the share of household heads owning their homes: from 37% (of linked heads) in 1861 to 46%. Other gains, especially in wealth, were translated into property as part of the adjustment and subsistence efforts of these illiterates. Women fared well in property acquisition and in confronting their social insecurity and frequent loss of spouses. Their rate of ownership in 1871 slightly exceeded that of male heads of households. Once again, the Irish Catholics led in the move toward more frequent ownership. Forty-three percent now owned, compared with 30% a decade earlier. The English also maintained their standing, largely through their greater economic resources, with 50% owning homes in 1871. As with wealth, though, they did not increase as did the Irish; their improvement could come earlier and presumably with less efforts to reduce disadvantages. Overall, adaptation, persistence, and improvement were possible for many illiterates, and were translated into property acquisition—their approach to security in the changing city.

Table 3.12
Household Summary Data, 1871 (Census Linked Heads) Illiterates

	Hamilton		1861 Link	1861 Total	Kingston		1861 Link	1861 Total	London		1861 Link	1861 Total	Total illiterates		1861 Total	1861 Linked
	N	%	%	%	N	%	%	%	N	%	%	%	N	%	%	%
A. Household size																
Small	30	34.9	26.7	36.0	12	27.3	25.0	31.4	12	30.0	15.6	28.3	54	32.1	68.4	23.1
Medium	38	44.2	51.2	50.3	23	52.3	52.3	59.1	20	50.0	67.5	58.6	81	48.2	54.8	59.8
Large	18	20.9	22.1	13.4	7	15.9	22.7	6.9	8	20.0	17.5	11.8	33	19.6	11.6	17.2
Mean		5.12	5.21	4.7		4.89	5.05	4.4		5.53	5.4	4.6				
B. Family size																
Small	40	46.5	47.7	61.2	23	52.3	50.0	58.5	13	32.5	42.5	61.8	76	44.7	60.7	47.1
Medium	28	32.6	38.4	31.8	15	34.1	45.5	36.5	14	35.0	42.5	31.6	57	33.5	32.9	41.2
Large	18	20.9	14.0	7.0	6	13.6	4.5	5.0	13	32.0	15.0	6.6	37	21.8	6.4	11.8
Mean		3.16	2.84	2.2		2.77	2.57	2.2		3.38	3.10	2.1				
C. Boarders																
None	73	84.9	87.2	80.9	40	90.9	90.9	84.4	37	92.5	85.0	85.5	150	88.8	85.1	86.9
One or more	12	15.1	12.8	20.1	4	9.1	9.1	15.6	3	7.5	15.0	14.5	19	11.2	14.9	13.1

D. Servants																
None	79	90.9	94.2	94.1	43	97.7	97.7	94.1	39	97.5	100.0	100.0	161	94.7	96.3	96.5
One or more	7	9.1	5.8	5.9	1	2.3	2.3	5.9	1	2.5	—	—	9	5.3	3.7	3.5
E. Relatives																
None	85	98.8	83.7	83.5	41	93.2	81.8	88.6	36	90.0	80.0	75.0	162	95.3	83.1	82.3
One or more	1	1.2	16.3	16.5	3	6.8	18.2	11.4	4	10.0	20.0	25.0	8	4.7	16.9	17.7
F. Household status																
Head	102	53.4	48.7	40.8	51	57.3	50.6	31.3 a	50	59.5	48.2	41.1	203	55.3	38.2	50.1
Wife	71	37.1	42.9	35.3	30	33.7	38.2	25.5 a	30	35.7	44.7	36.8	131	35.7	32.8	42.4
Child	1	0.5	1.0	3.4	1	1.1	—	2.0	—	—	—	1.6	2	0.5	2.6	—
Relative	2	1.1	1.0	6.4	3	3.4	2.2	6.3	3	3.6	5.9	10.2	8	2.2	7.1	2.5
Boarder	16	6.3	4.7	6.9	3	3.4	3.4	15.2	1	1.2	1.2	5.1	20	5.4	4.8	3.6
Servant	2	1.1	1.0	4.1	1	1.1	2.2	5.9	—	—	—	5.1	3	0.8	8.9	1.1
G. Marital status																
Single	4	2.1	3.1	12.5	5	5.6	5.6	17.8	4	4.7	4.7	14.2	13	3.6	14.4	4.1
Married	148	78.5	85.9	69.0	69	77.5	87.6	69.1	62	72.9	84.7	70.7	279	76.9	69.5	86.3
Widowed	37	19.6	10.5	18.3	15	16.9	6.7	12.9	19	22.4	10.6	15.1	71	19.6	16.1	9.6

a 13.7% were soldiers and their wives.

151

The size and structure of illiterate-headed families, finally, changed over this decade, reflecting larger social changes and the progress these persisters made. Families and households headed by illiterates varied principally by virtue of aging and an increase in adolescent-dependency relationships, which marked larger shifts toward more "modern" families (Table 3.12). The mean number of children at home increased in all three cities while the size of the household fell, very few now containing relatives or boarders. Larger families, consistent with other findings of prolonged adolescent dependency, also illustrate the results of adaptation, increased wealth, and more frequent homeownership. Success in these dimensions reduced the need for children to leave home as early as they had in 1861—a major shift in the experience of growing up.[26] As we shall see, there was less dependence on manipulation of the family size for adjustment and survival. Despite continued insecurity and poverty, the pressures on the family diminished with persistence and its consequences.

During a time of change and early industrialization, persisting illiterates experienced a decade of improvement. Stable occupationally, they moved forward and upward in economic standing and purchased homes and property more often than before. Their accomplishments, without the much-bespoken advantages of educational achievement, are important; they force us to recognize that such gains were made by individuals who lacked the skills of literacy and the experience of schooling. Illiterates, at least those able to spend a decade or more in a nineteenth-century city (who were not much wealthier or higher ranking than transients), did not lose earlier occupational gains, were not precluded from gaining more wealth and moving out of poverty, and were not obstructed from acquiring property. Learning to live in these cities and to succeed modestly required the education that comes of experience—of "reading" the city, of adapting and adjusting—more than the education that comes of reading and writing the printed word.

As literacy did not necessarily bring success, its absence did not guarantee failure. The force of ascription was reduced by 1871, but was still substantial, dominating over that of achievement. Illiterates, moreover, did not live in a social or cultural sphere of their own, segregated and isolated; they were strongly influenced by and suffered the inequalities of the urban social structure. Integrated into its processes, they were stratified and differentiated, as were those who were able to acquire more education but fared no better. In "skilful" and competitive times, the uneducated did not "sink"; unable to read or write, they

26 See Katz, *People*, Ch. 5; Ch. 4, below.

need not "starve outright." Some, to the contrary, moved ahead. The implications for contemporary reformers' school promotion, for their promises of education, and for the historical bases of modern social theory need not be belabored; they are obvious and clear. These findings, based on case studies, raise important questions that challenge our received wisdom and demand its qualification and re-examination. The resolution of these many essential questions sets the stage for the next chapters, and, even more, the stage for further comparative inquiries.

4

The Children of the Illiterate:

Education, Work, and Mobility

With the transformation of social and productive relations in the nineteenth century came a new concern with children and youth, the next generation of workers and citizens. Through the century, more and more parents directed heightened attention toward their children's socialization, education, and futures. Simultaneously, special systems of institutions, such as the schools, were developed, signifying a novel public concern and responsibility for the young. Under the state, educational institutions increasingly stood between family and society, as both family and institutions acquired augmented and specialized roles in socialization. As Katz has summarized, the process marked "part of a general tightening of the boundaries between social institutions and between the family and community." Part of the shift first to commercial and later to industrial capitalism, the school system along with other social institutions was centralized and expanded in the context of perceptions of massive social disorders: from urban crime and poverty to cultural diversity, changing labor-force requirements, and a crisis of the young. The school's functions lay in the confrontation of these problems and their resolution through mass education, in which literacy occupied a crucial place (as we have noted). The goals of public education were of course many; they included the inculcation of habits and values, social discipline, work preparation, cultural homogenization, literacy, and the establishment of hegemony among the population.[1]

[1] Katz, "The Origins of Public Education: A Reassessment," *History of Education Quarterly*, 16 (1976), 388, 381–407. On the development of educational systems, see also, Katz, *Class, Bureaucracy, and Schools* (New York: Praeger, 1975, 2nd ed.) and *The Irony of Early School Reform* (Cambridge, Mass.: Harvard University Press, 1968);

Prior to the complex of socioeconomic transformations that remade
North America and much of the west after the mid-eighteenth century,
social position depended overwhelmingly on inheritance and genera-
tional succession, in theory and commonly in fact. Social ascription ruled
the social order. Accompanying the changing social order, especially in
North America, and devolving especially upon the schools, was the promotion of achievement as the substitute for ascriptive continuities,
among education's other functions. Ideals and social theory reversed
their traditional expectations, as opportunities for intergenerational
mobility and socioeconomic attainments through universal schooling
acquired legitimacy, popular acceptance, and urgency. The future of
the young, and in them, the guarantees of civilization, society, and
progress, began to depend on the expected fulfillment of the ideology
of achievement, for both continuing social status at middle-class or
higher levels and for upward movement in surmounting more lowly
social origins. Conversely, those without education and literacy would
either fall into or remain fixed in lower-class positions. Upper Canada's
preeminent educational promoter, Egerton Ryerson, voiced these new
expectations, asking "Does a man wish his sons to swell the dregs of
society—to proscribe them from all situations of trust and duty in the
locality of their abode—to make them slaves in the land of freedom?
Then let him leave them without education, and their underfoot position in society will be decided upon." [2] In the present century, the

Alison Prentice, *The School Promoters* (Toronto: McClelland and Stewart, 1977); Ian
Davey, "Educational Reform and the Working Class," unpub. Ph.D. Diss., University
of Toronto, 1975; Katz and Paul Mattingly, eds. *Education and Social Change: Themes
from Ontario's Past* (New York: New York University Press, 1975); Carl Kaestle, *The
Evolution of an Urban School System: New York, 1750–1850* (Cambridge, Mass.: Harvard University Press, 1973); David Tyack, *The One Best System* (Cambridge, Mass.:
Harvard University Press, 1974); Phillip McCann, ed., *Education and Socialization in
the Nineteenth Century* (London: Methuen, 1977); and the work of Richard Johnson
cited in Ch. 1. On youth and adolescence, see Joseph Kett, *Rites of Passage* (New
York: Basic Books, 1977); Katz, *The People of Hamilton* (Cambridge, Mass.: Harvard
University Press, 1975), ch. 5; Katz and Davey, "Youth and Early Industrialization," in
Turning Points: Historical and Sociological Essays on the Family, ed. Sarane Boocock
and John Demos (Chicago: University of Chicago Press, 1978), S81–S119; John Gillis,
Youth and History (New York: Academic Press, 1974); Harvey J. Graff, "Patterns of
Adolescence and Child Dependency in a Mid-Nineteenth-Century City," *History of
Education Quarterly (HEQ)*, 12 (1973), 129–143; Michael Anderson, *Family Structure
in Nineteenth Century Lancashire* (Cambridge: Cambridge University Press, 1971);
Chad Gaffield and David Levine, "Dependency and Adolescence on the Canadian
Frontier," *HEQ*, 18 (1978), 35–47.

[2] *Journal of Education for Upper Canada*, 1 (1848), 297; Prentice, *School Promoters;* See also, Ch. 5, below, and Chs. 2–3.

emphasis on achievement has continued relatively unabated, despite an absence of justification for it to be found in empirical research, and despite persistent debate. Blau and Duncan repeat the dominant viewpoint and the democratic ideology, that "the chances of upward mobility are directly related to education. . . ." "The premise," they maintain,

> hardly a startling one, of the calculation is that education is a major factor intervening between occupational status of origin and achieved occupational status. Although the amount of education attained depended in part on level of origin, it also depends on other factors. It is quite possible, therefore, that a substantial number of men receive enough education to insure a moderate amount of upward mobility, taking into account the levels at which they start.

Other students, of course, take a much more restricted view, stressing a relative lack of opportunity and an inheritance of social-class position, the reproduction of inequality from generation to generation.[3] As traditional patterns of growing up were displaced by the process of change, anxieties about the place of young persons mounted. Observers focused upon the idle and vagrant youth, the working juvenile, the delinquent, as well as the school child. Most concluded that the best place for the young was nowhere but in school; the experience of education was the hope for the young as well as for their society.

The children of the illiterate adults whose lives, work, and adjustment we have studied grew up in this context of capitalist development and social transformation. Their opportunities for education and literacy, work and wealth, were formed in the commercial cities of Ontario that we are considering, set by the resources and decisions of their parents, and limited by the structures of inequality. Historians' knowledge about the role that parental circumstances and early influences contribute to personal and career development is severely limited, to be sure; this represents one of the most glaring gaps in social, psycho-, and educational history today. Nevertheless, to analyze the schooling, early work, and mobility patterns of the children of those without the benefit of education or literacy remains important. To further explore the meaning of literacy and the nature of the disadvantages that illiteracy carried, these data permit us to evaluate the familial and intergenerational effects of parental illiteracy. What did it mean to grow up as the

[3] *The American Occupational Structure* (New York: Wiley, 1967), 156, 155. See also, in support of this contention, the literature by Sewell and Hauser, Laumann, Lipset and Bendix, and in opposition, Bowles and Gintis, Boudon, Jencks, all cited in Chs. 2–3. There are no historical inquiries which treat the questions directly, as yet, but see Katz, *People*, Ch. 3; Thernstrom, *The Other Bostonians* (Cambridge, Mass.: Harvard University Press, 1973), Ch. 5. These issues are enormously complex.

child of an illiterate father or mother? Did the circumstances of parental illiteracy adversely affect their children's chances for schooling? Were the young forced into disadvantaged positions in the labor market, inheriting parental class and status? Where did they begin their own careers?

Patterns of school attendance, work and leaving home, and intergenerational occupational mobility form the interrelated concerns of this chapter. This analysis shows that the circumstances that surrounded parental (especially family head's) illiteracy influenced the children's experiences in growing up. Although such children were integrated into the social processes that determined life-course experiences, their patterns of education, work, and home-leaving diverged from those of the children of most literate parents. The difference, not surprisingly, was to their disadvantage. Yet the culmination of these experiences, in so far as we may judge, did not constitute a complete deterrent to the illiterates' children's futures. Their origins were undoubtedly restrictive, and ascription was important, but parental status did not debilitate the children's chance for some success in occupations, relative to their parents' achievements. As literacy and schooling did not insure success or mobility, so illiteracy did not completely obstruct the progress of the next generation, locking them into cultures of poverty or the lowest class of society.

I

Education in mid-nineteenth-century cities was not equally available to all children, despite ideologies promoting universal, free common schooling and equality of opportunities. Schooling, even as it expanded rapidly and was systematized into large bureaucracies, remained stratified: by class, ethnicity, race, and sometimes sex—the same ascriptive characteristics that dominated the social structure, as we have seen. In Upper Canada, public school systems developed from the 1840s, expanding rapidly for the next quarter century or more. Throughout the period, the proportion of children attending school (those enrolled) increased markedly, virtually all of them attending the new, public institutions. Class, along with other ascriptive factors, continued to be the primary determinant of attendance; as enrollments rose, therefore, differences between social groups remained intact. Consequently, few children of the laboring and poor class attended long enough to reach the higher grades, and never as long as children of higher-class parents.

Moreover, even when most working class children attended, the duration of their time in school and the regularity of their attendance were limited by poverty, transience, and poor health. Periodic poverty, social inequality, the rhythms of work, and irregular attendance were inseparably linked.[4]

That the children of illiterates were disadvantaged in educational opportunity should hardly surprise us. Limited by poverty and lower-class status, and frequently by their ethnicity, their attendance was simply not always possible, nor would it always be their families' first priority. By 1861 and 1871, the hegemony of the new educational system was well established, as Davey's, Katz's and Prentice's respective research documents, and these patterns of attendance reflect this social phenomenon. Yet within the restrictions of their circumstances, illiterate parents could respond in different ways to the promise of the school and achievement. With perceptions no doubt colored by their own and others' experiences—whether of success or failure—in work, wealth, and survival, *with* and *without* the benefits of schooling, the educational decisions of illiterates did not follow the common patterns in all ways. In effect, they may well have felt, and responded to, the tensions and contradictions arising from the realizations, on one hand, that a lack of schooling had not, in many cases, had a dramatic impact on their own careers and that the acquisition of some education had not aided many close to them. This they confronted along with, on the other hand, the social pressures of educational promotion, hegemony, and some acceptance of the import of education for their children's futures. Could they have completely ignored Egerton Ryerson's warning about their sons possible swelling the dregs of society, the visible (albeit limited) returns of literacy and schooling, and the ideology of opportunity for advance-

---

[4] See esp. Davey, "Reform"; Halay P. Bamman, "Patterns of School Attendance in Toronto, 1844–1878," *HEQ,* 12 (1972), 381–410; Katz and Mattingly, eds. *Education; Census of the Canadas,* 1851 (Quebec, 1853), 1861 (Quebec, 1862–63); *Census of Canada,* 1871 (Ottawa, 1873); *Reports* of the Chief Superintendent of Education for Upper Canada and Ontario (Toronto, *passim.*); C. B. Edwards, "London Public Schools, 1848–1871," London and Middlesex Historical Society, *Transactions* (1914), 14–29; F. R. Smith, "Early Schools in Kingston," *Historic Kingston,* 5 (1955–56), 25–29. Extracts of local superintendents reports, in *Reports* of the Chief Superintendent, are useful in understanding influences on attendance and local variations (original reports are kept in the Province of Ontario Archives, Toronto). See also, Kaestle, *Evolution;* Selwyn Troen, "Popular Education in Nineteenth Century St. Louis," *HEQ,* 13 (1973), 23–40; A. C. O. Ellis, "Influences on School Attendance in Victorian England," *British Journal of Educational Studies,* 21 (1973), 313–326; McCann, ed., *Education;* Maris Vinovskis, "Trends in Massachusetts Education, 1826–1860," *HEQ,* 12 (1972), 501–530. Kaestle and Vinovskis have recently completed a major study of school attendance in nineteenth-century Massachusetts.

ment and mobility that legitimated popular education's hegemony and gained for it popular assent for the imposition of the school systems? Could they simultaneously neglect the very restricted benefits of literacy to most members of their class and ethnic groups? These social contradictions formed the parameters for the illiterates' and the poor's response to the school. They permeated their educational choices and influenced their selections among the alternatives of schooling for their children, work for the support of the family economy and own experience, savings for property acquisition. Consequently, they sent their children to school, but not always as often as literate parents did, and not always with the same expectations and assumptions as the literates held. Illiterate parents, therefore, varied in their reactions to the school, and sometimes also exhibited a great desire for education and acceptance of the school.

At the aggregate level, the school attendance of illiterates' children was shaped first by the structure of local educational opportunity. Thus, in 1861, more of the school-aged children (5–16 years) of illiterates attended in Kingston (46%) and London (55%) than in Hamilton (38%). Not revealing in themselves real differences in attitudes toward schooling, however, these patterns derived from differentials in total attendance among the three cities. In Kingston, according to the census, about 62% of all eligible children attended, in London 67%, and in Hamilton 57% of all children or 59% of literates' school-aged children were enrolled.[5] In *no one* of the three cities did the percentage attendance of illiterates' children equal that of either all children or that of the children of literate parents. Their children, though, were more likely to go to school in a city in which greater numbers attended. Community behavior, more opportunities, and the concomitant hegemonic process pressed upon their actions. This intracity variation is important. The net difference between their children's attendance and that of others is relatively consistent from place to place, representing a regular disadvantage for the children of the illiterates. Differential attendance was a constant fact in the lives of these parents and their children, whereas children in different cities nonetheless received different amounts of schooling. To what extent was this a result of parental illiteracy or parental choice?

Different social groups and individuals of course responded to the

---

[5] Attending school, as the term is employed in this chapter, corresponds only to the category of the census (and also the Superintendent's *Reports*) "Attending school during the year." It is not a measure of regular (daily, monthly, etc.) attendance, but of enrollments. The Chief Superintendent's reports for this time indicate that most children attended in the range of 50–100 days each year, increasing to over 100 by the 1870s. Ian Davey's dissertation ("Educational Reform and the Working Class," University of Toronto, 1975), esp. Ch. 5, provides the best discussion of attendance available.

availability of education and its promise in different ways. In these patterns of response, the determinants of attendance are found, for the decisions made by parents or by the children themselves derived primarily from two sources. The premium placed on the value of and the need for schooling contributes one factor; the second, and perhaps more important, basis follows from the extent to which limited family resources, poverty, irregularity of work, the necessity of a child's working, and the like, permitted the necessary investments to be made. These are not mutually exclusive factors; moreover, to them may be added the discrimination, formal or informal, against some children, such as blacks or Catholics. With these considerations, we may ask, What were the determinants of attendance and how did they influence the decisions of literate- and illiterate-headed families? The mean percentage of children per family attending school, of those aged 5–16, provides the data: Of the children of the Hamilton literates, 54% attended, compared with 35% of illiterates in Hamilton, 42% in Kingston, and 50% in London. These total patterns were determined by the families' class and occupation, ethnicity, and family circumstances.

Occupational class, with its broad correlation with wealth, clearly shaped the social structure of school attendance in these cities. This held among literates and illiterates, as highest-ranking parents sent a larger proportion of their children to school (Table 4.1). As the data reveal, a direct relationship tied occupational class to proportions of children attending, from the children of nonmanual-working parents downward. This common pattern reflects the roles that the availability of surplus family resources, or poverty, played in the allocation of education and the extent to which education among the children, like literacy among their parents, was socially stratified. It reveals as well the social function of education, inasmuch as it served to reproduce the social structure intergenerationally; those ranking highest were able to secure more education for their children in the interests of maintaining social position.[6]

The illiterates, consequently, with only one exception, sent their children less often regardless of occupational class. The Hamilton comparison shows this most directly, as the intraclass differences ranged from 10 to 20%. Even the largely poor unskilled literate parents sent more of their young, and only among the semiskilled did illiterate attendance equal that of the others. This differential is especially significant, for we have seen that very little benefit accrued to literate men in unskilled

[6] See Davey, "Reform"; Katz, "Who Went to School?" *HEQ*, 12 (1972), 432–454, and "Origins of Public Education"; the literature cited in Note 2, esp. Boudon and Bowles and Gintis.

Table 4.1
School Attendance, 1861, by Head of Household Characteristics:
Mean Percentage of Children 5–16 Attending

	Hamilton literates		Hamilton illiterates		Kingston illiterates		London illiterates	
	N [a]	% [b]	N	%	N	%	N	%
Mean	1657	54.2	201	35.2	83	41.6	70	49.5
Ethnicity								
Irish Catholic	272	41.1	136	35.0	47	44.3	27	49.3
Irish Protestant	251	56.1	19	27.9	11	41.7	7	39.3
Scottish Presbyterian	282	61.1	2	50.0	3	50.0	5	53.3
English Protestant	450	57.1	17	39.2	3	66.7	11	55.3
Canadian Protestant	125	58.9	4	25.0	3	55.6	3	16.7
Canadian Catholic	15	48.9	—	—	4	41.7	—	—
Black	19	39.5	14	48.2	2	0.0	4	72.5
Others	243	52.5	9	25.9	10	23.3	13	48.6
Occupation								
Professional	125	62.5	1	—	—	—	—	—
Nonmanual	232	51.2	5	40.0	3	33.3	1	83.3
Skilled	553	59.1	31	38.9	13	56.4	12	56.3
Semiskilled	107	47.3	12	48.1	17	54.9	4	50.0
Unskilled	283	42.9	112	32.9	38	40.0	35	49.3
None	352	52.5	40	34.8	12	13.9	18	41.1
Sex								
Male	1451	54.6	153	34.4	69	43.3	49	52.8
Female	205	51.6	45	40.2	12	38.9	19	46.1
Number of children								
0–2	453	47.9	77	32.5	25	40.7	19	31.6
3–5	949	54.3	101	36.7	51	41.5	40	51.9
6+	255	64.8	23	37.4	7	45.9	11	71.4
Household size								
1–3	145	46.6	38	47.1	9	51.9	10	50.0
4–7	1079	52.4	124	42.3	63	39.2	46	47.3
8+	433	61.1	36	36.8	9	57.9	13	60.3
Number of children, 5–16								
1	587	41.2	83	45.6	34	41.2	25	30.0
2	444	57.8	50	42.3	18	36.1	22	56.8
3	329	63.5	36	38.6	18	66.1	11	66.7
4	193	64.1	18	33.5	7	17.9	7	53.6
5	72	63.9	9	30.2	3	60.0	3	73.3
6	28	62.5	2	0.0	1	0.0	1	83.3
7	4	75.0	—	—	—	—	—	—

[a] N = Number of families.
[b] % = Percent of children.

or semiskilled jobs. The children of unskilled literates attended at a rate 10% higher (43 to 33%) in Hamilton, yet they were only slightly less often poor (78 to 85%). This small difference in wealth can hardly account for the entire difference. Conversely, semiskilled illiterates sent their children as often (43%) with virtually no difference in wealth separating them from literate parents. In Hamilton and Kingston, these illiterates' children's attendance equalled or exceeded that of the skilled illiterates as well.

The contradictions of economic circumstances and social perceptions in the face of hegemony emerge clearly from these patterns of schooling. The illiterates at the semiskilled level were the one group least disadvantaged when compared with literates; to some degree, their more equal resources could be translated into more equal educational access, far exceeding the attendance of the unskilled in two cities. Yet equal resources (or a lack of differential disadvantage) do not provide a complete explanation when the unskilled are considered, although the 20% separating the literate from the illiterate skilled workers' children also reflects the important role of poverty. Poverty and scarce resources undoubtedly established the critical boundaries in which choices were made; within these parameters other factors were at work.

Ethnicity was one. Ethnic inequality and stratification differentiated the social structure of school attendance much as it had determined the structures of occupational class, wealth, and literacy itself. Not surprisingly, then, a similar ranking of groups orders the attendance patterns, as in the other dimensions of inequality in the urban society. Within each ethnic group, the illiterates sent fewer of their children, with the extent of difference relating directly to the status and wealth differentials. To be specific: English Protestants (and the Scottish) ranked high among either literates or illiterates, whereas the Irish sent their children least often (Table 4.1). Group differences show this as well, illustrating again the role of poverty and limited life chances in parental decisions.

Among the groups, the attendance of blacks is most striking, especially when the extent of parental illiteracy and the evident racial discrimination are considered. Sending more of their young than any ethnic group in London (73%) and ranking second to the more prosperous English in Hamilton (48%), they hungered for the schooling of their young, exceeding the attendance of *literate* blacks' children by almost 10 percentage points, or 25%. With the same economic resources as the literates, their actions indicate a difference in attitudes and values toward education, paralleling the great investments that Herbert Gutman has discovered among former slaves in the postbellum United States South. It is probable that these illiterate blacks were more often former

slaves than literates would have been—fugitives who had been systematically denied common schooling by the slave society of their youth.[7]
They apparently sought for their children that which they themselves
could not obtain legally, and rarely illegally, in many places. The numbers are too small for firm conclusions, yet they do suggest that these
illiterates chose to use their resources toward a different strategy of
securing schooling for their young.

The Irish Catholics, the largest ethnic group among the illiterates
and the poorest among either literates or illiterates, sent relatively few
of their children to school. Regardless of occupation or parental literacy,
their attendance rate was among the lowest, although by 1861 separate
schools were available to those wanting to escape the pan-Protestant
domination of the public school system. The literates, who were almost
as poverty-stricken as illiterate parents (64 to 78% poor), sent more of
their school-aged youth, but the difference was not large: 6 percentage
points in Hamilton, 41 to 35%. Severely limited resources, irregularity
of work, frequent movement and illness, and the need for child labor
combined with perceptions of their underfoot position in a society
stratified against their progress, to produce low attendance rates. The
awareness that achievement of literacy and some education only slightly
reduced their ascriptive disadvantages weighed among the influences on
their decisions, leading them to choose alternatives to more schooling.
Consequently, unskilled literates sent no more children than illiterates
(33%), with virtually equal proportions poor. And conversely, the skilled
literate parents, with greater wealth as a reward, sent more of their sons
and daughters. Resources to expend, and perceptions of the value of
educational advancement, made the major differences.

Semiskilled illiterate parents, however, formed a revealing exception
to the processes of inequality and decision making that resulted in less
education for the children of Irish Catholics. The major contributors
to the equal attendance rate among all semiskilled workers' children,
these illiterates (though few in number) far exceeded the enrollments of
literate Irish Catholics: 72 to 41%. Their success in wealth and especially
in homeownership (examined in Chapter 2) allowed them to free resources which might then be invested in the children's education. In his

[7] Gutman's study of black education remains unpublished. See W. R. Taylor,
"Toward A Definition of Orthodoxy," *Harvard Educational Review*, 36 (1966), 412–426;
Eugene Genovese, *Roll, Jordon, Roll* (New York: Pantheon, 1974). See Robin Winks,
The Blacks in Canada (New Haven: Yale University Press, 1971) for accounts of pro-
vision for education of blacks; local studies are sadly lacking. For evidence of discrimi-
nation, see the testimony in *American Freedman's Inquiry Commission*, 1863–1864
(National Archives of the United States), excerpts of which appear in Canadian Social
History Project, *Report*, 5 (1973–1974), 38–84. See also, Ch. 2, note 20.

Newburyport study, Stephan Thernstrom concluded that the ambitions of Irish Catholic laborers for savings and property greatly restricted the chances of their children's attending school; other studies of school attendance consistently report higher attendance rates for the children of home and property owners.[8] The question involves both the chronological ordering of savings, ownership, and school attendance among family priorities and choices, and the availability of separate (parochial) schools; schooling did not always take first place among family strategies. Rather, as in Hamilton, and in Kingston, the success of the poor and illiterate in acquiring property created an impetus toward schooling virtually unrivalled by any others, literate or illiterate. Homeownership and education were not simple dichotomous choices to these parents. To save toward purchase did not preclude their children's schooling; it could delay education, though, as the two were linked in the process of adaptation. Illiterates' reasons to doubt the school's benefits conflicted with its legitimating hegemony and ideological support. Education, if not always the first priority of the poor and illiterate, would follow upon the attainment of more immediate, and perhaps essential, goals. If they chose to neglect schooling, that was presumably a temporary decision to be reconsidered when it became more feasible and reasonable for them to do so.

Reaching the semiskilled ranks could represent a real accomplishment to illiterates. Importantly too, they were closer to skilled work, perhaps recognizing the impact of literacy on artisanal attainment and its full rewards. This would distinguish them from the unskilled illiterates, whose children attended even less often than the wealth differentials might indicate. Further away from higher levels of status and reward, with survival more difficult, and with little evidence of returns to literacy among the educated at their level, schooling for unskilled illiterates' children need not rank so high. In these ways, illiterate parents—and other poor, too—probably saw their own positions and the role of literacy in their attainments as relevant to their decisions about the future of their children in schooling. Although the hegemony of the school and the moral economy cannot be doubted, parental and familial circumstances and perceptions could either reinforce them or compete

---

[8] See Stephan Thernstrom, *Poverty and Progress* (Cambridge, Mass.: Harvard University Press, 1964), 155–157, 22–25; Davey, "Reform"; Katz, "Who Went to School." See also Thernstrom, *The Other Bostonians*, Ch. 5; the unpublished work of David Hogan, esp. his "Capitalism and Schooling: A History of the Political Economy of Education in Chicago, 1880–1930," unpub. PhD. Diss., University of Illinois, Urbana. 1978, "Education and The Making of The Working Class, 1880–1930," *HEQ*, 18 (1978), 227–270.

with them, diminishing the pressures and urgency of the children's education. In some cases, therefore, the significance of schooling was heightened; in others, circumstances led to alternative uses of resources for homeownership, savings, or simply surviving, with less pressure to secure education.

The timing of adaptation to the cities, moreover, was crucial to these decisions, as the experience of the Irish and the semiskilled indicates. Schooling, we may conclude, need not always be the most important investment or alternative to these parents, despite the power of the educational ideology and its promotion. Homeownership was undoubtedly more valuable, yet this approach need not erase all opportunities for schooling, as some have argued about the poor and immigrant. After property, savings, or gains in work and wealth had been made, education could then increase in significance. Schooling, consequently, did not always assume the highest priority, although attendance rates and their clear relationship to class and wealth show that it could be very important; wealth and resources, of course, created the parameters within which all subsequent actions took place.

The behavior of persisters' children, discussed in Section II of this chapter, reinforces this argument. Hardly exceptional in wealth, occupation, or ethnicity, illiterates who persisted to 1871 sent more of their children to school in Hamilton and London in 1861 than their more transient peers, although not as many as literates. Their distinction lay in homeownership and successful adaptation.

The McCowell family of Hamilton provides a case in point. The family, headed by an illiterate, Irish Catholic teamster, persisted through the decade. Of the five children, the three of school age (one boy, two girls) attended school in 1861. A decade later, the two remaining children (a boy and a girl), now of school age, went to school. The older children were still living at home. One daughter was a schoolteacher, one son a clerk, another daughter a dressmaker; their father was still an illiterate teamster and carter. Schooling may not have been a first priority of poor families as they faced the economic constraints on their lives, but once those constraints were reduced, schooling became more important and was adopted more frequently as a phase of familial strategies.

Schooling followed other achievements. Limited resources and the insecurity of the working class in commercial and early industrial urban society restricted schooling for the majority of illiterates, as for others in the working class. They contended with the same pressures and processes that determined educational opportunities for many others and weighed the relative advantages of schooling in the light of their own circumstances, perceptions, and its promotion; they often sent their children. They obviously saw reasons for educating their young and accepted the hegemony of the school; largely their decisions were mediated by the same forces which influenced literates. Poverty acted as the primary constraint, yet many also grasped that social inequalities restricted their opportunities beyond their lack of education, contributing to decisions that delayed, or restricted the value of their children's schooling. For some, the child's labors or assistance around the house seemed more valuable than the time spent sitting in a classroom; others simply could not afford clothing, shoes, or fees. Within this framework of inequality, severe constraints, and hopes of opportunity through education, individual families made their choices.

The factors that shaped family life, in the context of class and ethnicity, were also direct influences on schooling in the mid-nineteenth-century cities. Family cycle and size were among the determinants of school attendance. Proportions attending, for example, increased directly with the size of the family, among both literate- and illiterate-headed domestic units. Attendance varied among illiterates' children less regularly with household size, however (Table 4.1). In Hamilton and Kingston, the size of the family influenced attendance rates much less than among literates; only 5 percentage points separated large from small families. While it contributed to their decisions, reflecting age and adaptation too, size for them was a less important consideration, limited as they were so often by poverty. (London's difference probably derives from the much greater educational opportunities available in that city.) The differing significance of large families between literates and illiterates affected these patterns as well; recall that for illiterates more children were often a greater burden on limited resources, rather than the sign of wealth they represented among literate-headed families.

The variable impact of family size, and household size to a lesser extent, reflects the perceived uses of the school by different families in their educational strategies as well as the socioeconomic correlates of the domestic units' composition. For literate-headed families, the linear relationship between their size and the proportions in school illustrates at once the connection between wealth and family size and the role of the school as a baby- or child sitter for the young. This role was obviously less important to illiterates, as greater numbers of children, of school age or not, made much less difference in determining their attendance: 5% in Hamilton and Kingston to 17% for the literates. For those with very limited resources, and other approaches to family maintenance, the choice to send a child to school was more narrow, restricted

to the attendance of selected few at any one time. Of Hamilton's illiterates, moreover, a smaller number of eligible children in fact increased
the likelihood of any one's attending.

Larger families, in this way, drained precious resources, limiting
chances for schooling as they had also obstructed economic success.
Scarce resources served to limit the chances of schooling for children
from larger, illiterate-headed families. Analogously, larger households
did not function to increase attendance as directly as among literates;
here relatives or boarders, often elderly, could usefully substitute for the
school in childcare and supervision. Finally, we may note that illiterate
female-headed families, despite their prevalence and poverty, succeeded
remarkably often in sending their children to school. Youngsters from
such families attended almost as frequently as those from male-headed
units in Kingston and London (5 and 6% less) and more often in Hamilton (40 to 34%). To mothers who were also household heads, and who
had smaller families, the school served important purposes. Economic
circumstances and family factors combined to determine the school attendance strategies of these illiterates. Faced with great limitations on
their behavior and the social contradictions of schooling in an unequal
society, they sent their children when they could, choosing among the
options within their grasp.

In a study of changing patterns of school attendance in Hamilton
in 1851 and 1861, Michael Katz concluded that schooling reflected *and*
reinforced the unequal social structure of that city. He further hypothe-
sized that differential benefits from education were maintained by higher-
class groups in the face of absolute gains in attendance of the lower
class; Ian Davey has replicated and extended these findings in his analysis
of the response of the working class to educational reform.[9] The schooling of the children of these urban illiterates, importantly, fits squarely
into that interpretation which has it that social inequality was transmitted intergenerationally through differential access to education. Yet
their disadvantages in schooling were, with partial exceptions in some
cases—persisters, blacks, the semiskilled—even more nearly absolute than
relative as their children obtained less educational access than those of
literates of the same ethnic groups and occupational classes. Poverty
and its concomitants and their alternative, but strategic use of limited
resources joined to create the gap in opportunities for educational experiences for these children. We need to ask if this signified, on the one
hand, a denial of the children's chances for betterment, a sacrifice of
the child's future for the family's present condition, and Ryerson's

---

[9] "Who Went to School," 445; Davey, "Reform."

"underfoot position" of "slaves in the land of freedom," or, on the other hand, an approach to familial security that did not drastically debilitate the children and their hopes.

II

To begin to address these questions, and those with which the chapter began, we must shift the focus. We have thus far centered upon aggregates of children in their families of origin, to examine the determinants of schooling; complementing this analysis are the age-specific relationships among schooling, work, and leaving home for the individual children. Since data on career paths, and class and wealth destinations, are not available, only through the early positions of these children and the routes they took may we estimate the significance of their familial beginnings for their futures. These aspects of the process of growing up distinguished the experiences of the children of illiterate parents from those of literates, as with school attendance, and sexually differentiated them in the process, while the "modernization" of childhood and youth marked the boundaries through its homogenizing force. The result, a blend of commonality and divergence, created different patterns of maturation and socialization for these disadvantaged young persons, showing at once the poverty of their origins but also the important possibility that those origins may not have left the children "underfoot" and relegated to unskilled positions in lives of poverty. To discover this process requires first the identification of the ages at which their life courses were marked by, respectively, schooling, the onset of work, and home-leaving.[10]

Age-specific profiles of the children reveal that not only did fewer children of illiterates attend school, but that they attended for fewer years (Figure 4.1, Table 4.2). Since they probably went to classes less regularly, class and ethnic differentials were reinforced and their disadvantages exacerbated. Consequently, when the individual children's schooling is tabulated (rather than that of statistical means of families), 59% of the literates' 5–16-year-olds attended during 1861, compared with

[10] See Katz, *People*, Ch. 5; Graff, "Patterns"; Laurence A. Glasco, "Ethnicity and Social Structure: Irish, Germans, and Native-Born of Buffalo, N.Y., 1850–1860," unpub. PhD. Diss., State University of New York at Buffalo, 1973, and "The Life Cycles and Household Structures of American Ethnic Groups," *Journal of Urban History*, 1 (1975), 339–364; Richard Wall, "The Age at Leaving Home," *Journal of Family History*, 3 (1978), 181–202.

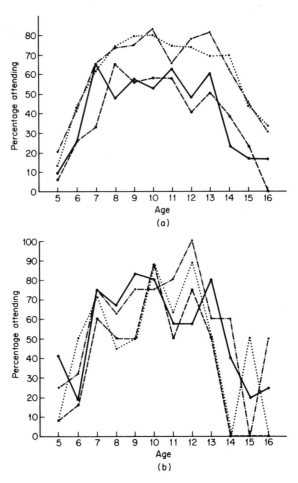

Figure 4.1   School attendance by age, 1861: males and females. (a) Hamilton: literates' and illiterates' children. (– • – •) literate males, $N = 2026$, $\% = 59.6$. (• • •) literate females, $N = 1933$; $\% = 57.8$. (——) illiterate males, $N = 228$; $\% = 39.5$. (– – –) illiterate females, $N = 202$; $\% = 36.6$. (b) Kingston and London: children of illiterates. (—— ·) Kingston males, $N = 94$; $\% = 51.1$ (– – –) Kingston females, $N = 87$; $\% = 39.1$. (– • – •) London males, $N = 73$; $\% = 60.3$. (• • •) London females, $N = 84$; $\% = 51.2$.

38% of Hamilton's illiterates' children, 46% of Kingston's, and 55% in London. In the first place, patterns of attendance diverged by sex from the near parity of the literates' children (an important new development itself) to the sexually unequal experience of the illiterates'. When illiterates were able and willing to send a child to school, most often a son was selected; his education was more highly valued than a sister's would have been when limited assets and future needs were considered. Attendance of sons thus exceeded that of daughters in each city, differentiating educational opportunities, and varying from a small, 4 percentage point difference among Hamilton's illiterates to 10 percentage points (20 and 25%) in the other cities. Indicating further differences in work and home-leaving patterns by sex, males predominated in any educational opportunities and any returns to such investments.

Overall, illiterates' children were able to attend school for a shorter period of time than other children, a result primarily of poverty, although patterns varied by class and ethnicity more than by literacy of parents. Yet, the reform of education and the process of modernizing and homogenizing childhood and youth established a series of ages of most-frequent attendance common to most children, regardless of their sex or their parents' literacy.[11] Ages 7 to 14 marked the period of schooling for literates' youngsters; these were the ages at which over one-half and more often two-thirds went to school (Figure 4.1, Table 4.2). These ages were also the time of education, when possible economically, for the children of illiterates, with local variations due to differentials in the structures of opportunity across the three cities. At very few ages (only at 7 and 11 in Hamilton) did the attendance rates of illiterates' school-aged children equal that of literates', with the child's sex also punctuating these patterns of schooling. Despite the constant differentials, a basis for a common experience existed through the age-grading of the school experience, which gave to many youngsters some shared occasions and regularity in the timing of their life courses. In addition, these data reinforce the earlier conclusion that illiteracy itself was not by any means universally transmitted across the generations; the great majority of illiterates' offspring would acquire some schooling, even if less than that of most of the literates'. The children of persisting illiterates, as expected, were able to attend even more frequently: 11 and 20% more often in Hamilton and London. Education was a path to which they could turn when more critical problems of survival were satisfied; home-owning and adaptation provided a stimulus toward increased educational participation, in attendance rates and in length of stay in school. But even these youngsters did not obtain as much exposure to the school as those of literates.

[11] On the variability of experience before this period, see Kett, *Rites* and "Growing Up in Rural New England, 1800–1840," in *Anonymous Americans,* ed. T. K. Hareven (Englewood Cliffs, N.J.: Prentice-Hall, 1971), 1–16. Katz, *People,* Gillis, *Youth,* discuss the effects of modernization on the adolescent experience. See also, for vivid presentations, Ralph Connor, *Glengarry Schooldays* (Toronto: Macmillan, 1902); Edward Eggleston, *The Hoosier Schoolmaster* (New York: Hill and Wang, 1957).

Table 4.2
Children at Home, 1861, of Households Heads

	Hamilton literates						Hamilton illiterates					
Age	N	%	M	F	Percentage in school	Percentage with occupation	N	%	M	F	Percentage in school	Percentage with occupation
1–4	2247	31.1	1121	1124	1.2	0.0	206	26.4	106	100	0.9	0.0
5	491	6.4	240	251	16.9	0.0	51	6.5	21	30	7.8	0.0
6	432	5.6	218	213	42.8	0.2	45	5.8	24	21	26.7	0.0
7	383	5.0	170	213	62.9	0.0	41	5.2	20	21	48.8	0.0
8	348	4.5	191	157	73.6	0.0	44	5.6	21	23	56.8	0.0
9	334	4.4	159	174	77.2	0.0	36	4.6	18	18	55.6	0.0
10	344	4.5	184	160	81.4	0.0	35	4.5	21	14	54.3	0.0
11	288	3.8	157	131	75.7	0.7	33	4.2	19	14	60.6	0.0
12	335	4.4	167	168	75.8	0.0	32	4.1	17	15	43.8	6.2
13	272	3.5	140	132	75.0	0.0	20	2.6	12	8	55.0	5.0
14	250	3.3	131	119	65.6	2.4	30	3.8	17	13	33.3	3.3
15	242	3.2	138	104	44.2	6.6	32	4.1	19	13	18.8	9.4
16	243	3.2	131	111	31.7	12.4	31	4.0	19	12	9.7	19.4
17	212	2.8	104	108	22.2	17.0	17	2.2	7	10	5.9	35.3
18	205	2.7	95	110	11.7	20.6	25	3.2	11	14	0.0	28.0
19	170	2.2	90	80	4.7	31.2	15	1.9	9	6	0.0	46.7
20+	882	11.5	435	447	0.9	42.0	90	11.5	48	42	0.0	55.6
Total	7678	Mean age: 9.9	3871	3802	Mean 5–16: 58.7		783	Mean age: 10.2	409	374	Mean 5–16: 38.1	

	Kingston illiterates						London illiterates					
Age	N	%	M	F	Percentage in school	Percentage with occupation	N	%	M	F	Percentage in school	Percentage with occupation
1–4	101	28.6	50	50	0.9	0.0	94	28.9	50	44	1.1	0.0
5	26	7.4	15	11	26.9	0.0	17	5.2	8	9	17.6	0.0
6	17	4.8	11	6	17.6	0.0	15	4.6	9	6	40.0	0.0
7	18	5.1	8	10	66.7	0.0	19	5.8	8	11	73.7	0.0
8	18	5.1	12	6	61.1	0.0	20	6.2	11	9	55.0	0.0
9	14	4.0	6	8	64.3	0.0	14	4.3	4	10	57.1	0.0
10	13	3.7	5	8	84.6	0.0	15	4.6	8	7	80.0	0.0
11	13	3.7	7	6	53.8	7.7	13	4.0	5	8	69.2	0.0
12	15	4.2	7	8	66.7	0.0	15	4.6	6	9	93.3	0.0
13	11	3.1	5	6	63.6	18.2	7	2.2	5	2	57.1	0.0
14	14	4.0	10	4	28.6	7.1	10	3.1	5	5	30.0	0.0
15	10	2.8	4	5	10.0	20.0	6	1.8	2	4	33.3	16.7
16	13	3.7	4	9	7.7	38.5	6	1.8	2	4	16.7	16.7
17	12	3.4	5	7	0.0	8.3	12	3.7	8	4	0.0	16.7
18	14	4.0	8	6	0.0	42.9	8	2.5	6	2	12.5	25.0
19	8	2.3	5	3	0.0	50.0	7	2.2	4	3	0.0	14.3
20+	36	10.2	23	13	0.0	52.8	46	14.2	28	18	0.0	37.0
Total	353	Mean age: 9.8	185	166	Mean 5–16: 45.6		324	Mean age: 10.6	169	155	Mean 5–16: 55.4	

Socially stratified educational systems, restricted resources, the insecurities of lower class life, and parental choices (as well as the actions of the children themselves) combined to result in less schooling for the children of illiterate parents. Beginning slightly later and concluding somewhat earlier, they spent less of their youth in the schoolroom. The same social processes, nevertheless, age-graded and homogenized most of their experiences with that of other children; and virtually all children in these cities, by 1861, gained access to some period of education, even if a restricted one. Despite the major divergence in their experiences, these elements of commonality compensated for their impoverished origins to some extent, making the school a part of their childhood and early adolescence in ways their parents had not experienced.

Schooling, especially around the mid-century and for the children of the working class, did not dominate the experience of growing up, as it so often does today. Work formed an important part of the adolescent years for many young persons; early work could contribute, and sometimes greatly, to the development and socialization of many children. Although data such as those from censuses can be misleading, much work being, no doubt, unreported or disguised, child or juvenile labor could coexist with infrequent or irregular school attendance. Casual labor, moreover, was far from regularly reported. Nevertheless, work during adolescence was very common. With employment in a wide variety of jobs, from common labor to service and clerical jobs, juvenile work actually increased with the transition from a commercial to an industrial economic base.[12]

Until they turned 16 no more than 10% of the children residing at home and of literate parents were reported to be working, although the beginnings of their work careers often came earlier, varying with family class, needs, and income (Table 4.2). Some of course had left home earlier and were working, living as boarders, or with relatives, or as resident domestics. Despite their lower rate and shorter duration of school attendance, illiterates' children did not rush into work dramatically earlier when still living at home. For them, 15 and 16 overwhelmingly marked the years at which reported work commenced, indicating another common transition in the life course. More of the illiterates' children, nevertheless, were employed at earlier ages, contributing to their families and in some cases gaining worthwhile skills and experience. This is most striking in Kingston, where 18% held jobs at 13 and 8% at 11; in Hamilton also, more of such children worked than literates': 6% at 12, 5% at 13. The children of persisting illiterates also started to work earlier. A number of factors

---

[12] See Davey, "Reform," Ch. 4; Katz and Davey, "Youth." On casual juvenile labor, see Gareth Stedman Jones, *Outcast London* (Oxford: Oxford University Press, 1971).

combined to form these patterns of earlier work. A poor family, persistent or transient, needed the additional income a child or adolescent could earn, however small that amount. The ill health or death of a wage-earner such as a father, seasonality or irregularity of work for such a one, frequent relocation, and traditional expectations for the employment of the young contributed to these patterns, as they created major family needs for additional earnings and reflected the deep insecurities of urban life. Sometimes, no doubt, parental evaluations of the common-school curriculum as perhaps irrelevant to the requirements of their children's future careers probably joined with economic conditions to reduce schooling and hasten the start of working. And the illiterates and other working-class parents who chose not to invest in further education may well have perceived in work experience a more valuable instructor in the ways of the world and a more valuable preparation for later life, and therefore encouraged—or forced—some of their children to start their working lives early. As we know, this process had benefitted some of the fathers in their careers.[13] The culmination of factors, as they intersected in the children's lives, resulted in greater proportions of illiterates' youths at work by age sixteen; 19, 39, and 17% were employed in Hamilton, Kingston, and London, respectively, to 12% of literates' children. Work consequently formed a larger and more central part in the adolescent socialization and experiences of illiterates' children, while it helped to meet family needs.

The early jobs of the sons of illiterate-headed families, not surprisingly, were often unskilled common laboring positions (Table 4.3A). After the age of 16, though, they had a better-than-even chance for higher-ranking work. In Hamilton, for example, two 17-year-olds were carpenters; one 18-year-old was a clerk and two others a lathemaker and a tinsmith; one 19-year-old was a plumber; and two 21-year-olds were a clerk and a carpenter. Across the three cities, in fact, only one-third of working sons at home were employed as unskilled laborers, as many of their fathers had been. Almost 40% of the children held skilled positions in their early careers; another 8% worked in nonmanual posts. The children of the persisters fared slightly better. For those who remained at home through the teen years, the facts of less schooling; parental poverty, insecurity, and illiteracy; and earlier work did not prevent occupational diversity and improved status. Their patterns of growing up did not foreclose all opportunities and consign them only to the ranks of the unskilled, as the McCowells illustrate. The son of Henry Wynn, an Irish Catholic laborer, also became a clerk. Obviously, very

---

[13] Ch. 2, above; Davey, "Reform," Chs. 5 and 6; Chs. 5 and 7, below.

Table 4.3
Occupations of Chilldren Residing at Home, 1861 and 1871

	Illiterates		Hamilton (total population)		Illiterate persisters	
	N	%	N	%	N	%
A. 1861						
Nonmanual	11	7.9	86	30.8	2	4.8
Skilled	53	38.4	129	46.2	17	40.5
Semiskilled	25	18.1	12	4.3	9	21.4
Unskilled	49	35.5	52	18.6	14	33.3
B. 1871						
Nonmanual	19	9.3	257	23.9		
Skilled	98	48.0	601	56.1		
Semiskilled	52	25.5	63	5.9		
Unskilled	35	17.2	150	14.0		

few traversed the line between manual and nonmanual jobs, blurred as it was, or crossed class lines; they remained overwhelmingly within the working class but were nonetheless able to progress occupationally. Their early work statuses give good reason to suppose that their socialization and experiences in the cities provided a valuable education in their own right, compensatirg in part for other ascriptive and familial disadvantages.[14]

Daughters did not fare as well in this sexually stratified society. They worked as domestic day servants (eight), seamstresses (five), milliners, dressmakers (four), and tailoresses. Before consigning them to lower status in a sacrifice for more education and better jobs for their brothers, we must note that these were the most common occupations for *all* women who worked in the urban society and especially for young women. It is hardly surprising that these daughters would secure this kind of work, if work they must, regardless of their parents' poverty or illiteracy.[15]

Many youngsters in each of the cities neither worked nor went to

[14] See, for relevant suggestions, Daniel Calhoun, "The City as Teacher," *HEQ,* 9 (1969), 312–325.

[15] On the work of women and girls, see Katz, *People,* Ch. 2; Davey, "Reform", Ch. 4; D. S. Cross, "The Neglected Majority: The Changing Role of Women in 19th Century Montreal," *Histoire sociale,* 6 (1973), 202–223; Glasco, "Ethnicity"; D. J. Walkowitz, "Working-Class Women in the Gilded Age," *Journal of Social History,* 5 (1972), 464–490; Alice Kessler-Harris, "Stratifying by Sex: Understanding the History of Working Women," in *Labor Market Segmentation,* ed. R. C. Edwards, Michael Reich, and D. M. Gordon (Lexington, Mass.: D. C. Heath, 1975), 217–242.

school in their early- or mid-adolescent years (Table 4.2). By the mid-teens, a majority of all children who lived at home were "officially" unoccupied, contributing to what many middle-class contemporaries and reformers saw as a crisis of idle and vagrant youth and a reason for increased provision of education. Some of course held casual or part-time jobs or assisted at home. The children of illiterates shared in this phenomenon of the commercial city, too, being as often on the streets as at work or in school. Commercial capitalism and urbanization, in conjunction with an increase in population, marked a decline in juvenile work opportunities, especially for the working-class youth. Illiterates' youngsters suffered at least as often as any other adolescents from this enforced idleness. With the onset of industrialization, in the 1860s and 1870s, and the further expansion of schooling, however, the children of the working class were much more often "occupied." [16]

The experiences of growing up for the illiterates' children were also differentiated by their patterns of leaving home. As indicated by the family formation strategies analyzed in Chapter 2, the early life courses of many of these young persons were punctuated by a precocious separation from their families, representing a break more striking than their less deviant paths of school attendance and work. Age-specific patterns of home-leaving began earlier and were more sexually-stratified for illiterates' children than for literates'. This is demonstrated by examining the number of children at home at each age, relative to other ages and to the sex ratios, with assumptions based in simple, stable population projections and the regularity of fertility among the female population (the estimates allow for differential infant mortality).[17] In this manner, we may isolate the key ages at which children left their homes; thus, a decline in the number of children present at some ages, regularly sustained, will illustrate the process and timing of departure from the family home.

Illiterates' children commonly left home, the data indicate, 3 to 4 years earlier than those of literates (Table 4.2). Poverty undoubtedly underlay these decisions. The ages of 9, 13 to 15 (coinciding with the start of work), and 17 were the pivotal years for them, contrasting with those of 13, 16, and 21 for the literates' children. In Hamilton, for ex-

[16] On the contemporary "crisis" of youth, see Katz, *People*, Ch. 5 and "The Origins of Public Education"; Davey, "Reform," Ch. 4; Katz and Davey, "Youth"; Kett, *Rites*.

[17] See again, Katz, *People*, Ch. 5; Graff, "Patterns"; Glasco, "Ethnicity"; Anderson, *Family Structure*, for methodological considerations in cross-sectional life-cycle and cohort analysis and for other applications. Wall, "Age" provides some caveats. The method provides approximations of course, indicating trends rather than precise movements.

ample, the percentage of illiterates' children at home fell from 5.6 to 4.6
(44 to 36) from ages 8 to 9 and from 4.1 to 2.6 (32 to 20) from 12 to 13,
similar to the changes in the other cities. The behavior of literates'
youngsters differed; their departures came several years later, but were
quite similarly marked. The persisting illiterates, as part of their strategy
of controlling family size toward survival, success and adaptation, and
allocation of the scarce resources to which their poverty limited them,
dispatched their young much the same as other illiterate-headed families.

Daughters, in fact, left home earlier than their brothers, their representation falling more sharply at these ages and creating the imbalanced
sex ratios among children at home noted above. Males predominated
among those at home at each of the major points of home-leaving. This
earlier departure, no doubt for domestic work and residence in the
home of others, constituted one significant reason for their lesser access
to schooling. With severe economic constraints, their departures were
prefigured and their "careers" the expected ones; there could be little
motivation or opportunity to invest more heavily in education for their
life preparation. The daughters of illiterates who persisted in the cities,
in sharp contrast to other illiterates and many literates, remained at
home longer; the persisting families' ratios of children at home are
nearly equal. For settled families, it was apparently less important to
send out the young females into service and thereby to further reduce
family size and dependency ratios. The others, in putting out adolescent
girls, seized an avenue of reducing family burdens while providing a
place for the child not available to sons, who were forced by limited
work and low pay to stay home longer. They could also contribute more
tangibly to the family economy. With sons' paths toward work and
residence away from home more difficult, to get more schooling was
sensible, since it could presumably aid them in a way it could not aid the
girls, especially in this sexually stratified society. Service was readily
available for daughters and was traditionally legitimated; it was undoubtedly more acceptable to parental and juvenile aspirations than
unskilled work for the sons. Strategic decisions like these informed the family economies and constraints of illiterates and other poor, in their struggles for survival and some modicum of success. One important approach,
used by those who succeeded more often, lay in the reduction of family
size while attempting to place the children in the best way possible; this
meant service for the girls and more lengthy home life for sons. Given
the narrow opportunities available to women who had to work in these
cities and the impressive early career starts of the sons, these choices do not
seem to have disadvantaged the young. In the context of widespread
poverty and the restrictions of parental illiteracy, class, and ethnicity,

their early experiences certainly did not further depress them, and in some ways may have proved compensatory, despite their reduced education.

We have no way to determine with any certainty what difference, if any, earlier home-leaving made in the socialization and subsequent careers of those who departed. Yet their experience of dependency and semidependency within the parental household was reduced.[18] Less schooling reduced the extent of dependency as well. They were probably freer to grow up, to develop by themselves, and to gain experience while working and while on the streets—the kinds of autonomy that might translate into an education of its own, both compensation and preparation. For some, complete independence or autonomy came at relatively youthful ages, through the teenage years; others moved into early semi-autonomy outside the home or a semidependent position inside it while working. For daughters, autonomy was probably found less often, as they shifted from serving their family to serving another before marriages and husbands. But some degree of freedom, to fare and fend for themselves, came early to many children of illiterates, especially to the sons; their entries into the world of work were less dependent upon their families of origin. This was the consequence of their experiences in growing up: Early work and home-leaving may have been the best preparation that their largely impoverished families and illiterate parents could have provided them.

A decade later, in 1871, popular patterns of growing up changed radically. With modernization, increased educational provision, early industrialization, and changes in family life, childhood and adolescence were transformed. In the process, the experiences of the children of persisting illiterate families changed as well.[19] The most dramatic difference was an increase in dependency and semidependency in the home, as these stages were prolonged throughout western society with the emergence of "modern" adolescence.[20] The children of illiterates, the 1871

[18] On dependency and autonomy, see Katz, *People;* Graff, "Patterns." See also, Gillis, *Youth;* Kett, *Rites.* John Bodnar, in "Socialization and Adaptation: Immigrant Families in Scranton, 1880–1890," *Pennsylvania History,* 43 (1976), 147–162, presents a somewhat similar argument.

[19] As in Chapter 3, the analysis of the 1871 data draws only upon those who were linked from the Census of 1861 to the Census of 1871: 29% of children in Hamilton, 26% in Kingston, and 33% in London. Overwhelmingly, we are concerned with children at home; of those who could be traced, over 90% still resided with parents. The others were now heads of household (12) or boarders (8). The mean age of illiterates' children was 10 in 1861; in 1871, the persisting children had an average age of 17 years.

[20] On this "modernization," see again, Katz, *People,* Ch. 5; Davey, "Reform," Ch. 4; Katz and Davey, "Youth"; Kett, *Rites.*

data indicate, remained with their families longer than had those of a decade earlier (Table 4.4). To take one example, persisting illiterate-headed families in Hamilton had 18 5-year-olds at home in 1861; 10 years later, at age 15, 17 were still to be found with their families. The patterns in Kingston and London (i.e., 8 of 9 still at home) were quite similar, although slightly fewer stayed in Kingston than in the other cities. Fewer now departed before age 13 or 15; more remained beyond that time, as young persons more frequently stayed until their later teen years, to 16 or 18. The prolongation of dependency and the delay in leaving home was shared by the sexes. Girls now remained as often as their brothers, in part a consequence of the decline in service that had begun by the early 1870s as well as a result of this transformation of youth. Comparing more closely to the patterns of literates' youngsters in respect of increased time in the parental home and longer periods of familial dependency, these young persons gained prospects of lengthened security at home. In so doing, however, they lost the earlier semi-autonomy and autonomy that more precocious departures had made possible a decade before; this was the obverse of prolonged residence. Their losses and gains, no doubt ambiguous ones, were made possible directly by their parents' accomplishments, in wealth, homeownership, adaptation and stability, and better prospects for security in these cities. The adolescents' experiences were now more like those of others, and the family formation strategies that sent many of them out earlier, a response to poverty, were no longer required.

Similarly, schooling increased for the children of these persisting illiterates over the decade, a phenomenon common to virtually all children in the cities and the province at large (Table 4.4). In Hamilton and Kingston, especially, attendance increased at virtually all ages, and more than one-half of those aged 9 to 16 were reported as attending: 48% in Hamilton, 61% in Kingston, 59% in London. The period of common schooling encompassed much the same years, to 13 or 14, and was nearly universal from 9 to 12. By 1871, then, the attendance of these children of illiterates compared very favorably with that of other children in the cities, the earlier gaps much reduced. Class differentials (and ethnic ones—which were somewhat lessened) were still firmly maintained, as illiterates' young participated much like others from the working class; few, consequently, could hope for secondary education.[21] Investments for education were more frequently available in persisting families, and as in residence at home, the divergences in experience of growing up diminished with persistence, adaptation, and social change.

---

[21] Davey, "Reform," esp. Ch. 4, *passim*.

Table 4.4
Children of Illiterates, 1871

	Hamilton						Kingston						London					
Age	N	%	M	F	Percentage in school	Percentage with occupation	N	%	M	F	Percentage in school	Percentage with occupation	N	%	M	F	Percentage in school	Percentage with occupation
9	1	—	—	1	100.0	0.0	4	4.3	3	1	100.0	0.0	1	0.9	1	0	100.0	0.0
10	14	6.1	5	9	100.0	0.0	6	6.5	3	3	83.3	0.0	7	6.5	4	3	85.7	0.0
11	12	5.3	3	9	91.7	0.0	6	6.5	1	5	66.7	0.0	0	—	—	—	—	—
12	19	8.3	10	9	68.4	5.3	7	7.6	6	1	71.4	14.3	16	14.9	6	10	75.0	0.0
13	17	7.5	7	10	59.2	11.8	9	9.8	2	7	57.1	0.0	9	8.4	7	2	66.7	11.1
14	22	9.6	10	12	27.3	22.7	5	5.4	4	1	40.0	0.0	8	7.5	2	6	50.0	25.0
15	17	7.5	7	10	17.6	35.3	5	5.4	2	3	60.0	20.0	8	7.5	4	4	25.0	50.0
16	22	9.6	10	12	0.0	59.1	2	2.2	1	1	0.0	50.0	7	6.5	1	6	28.6	42.9
17	15	6.6	7	8	6.7	60.0	6	6.5	3	3	0.0	83.3	10	9.3	6	4	0.0	70.0
18	15	6.6	8	7	6.7	33.3	9	9.8	0	9	11.1	33.3	7	6.5	2	5	0.0	85.7
19	11	4.8	5	6	0.0	72.7	5	5.4	2	3	0.0	60.0	8	7.5	6	2	0.0	85.7
20+	63	27.6	38	25	0.0	73.0	27	29.3	15	12	0.0	81.2	26	24.3	18	8	0.0	76.9
Total	228	Mean age: 17.3	121	107	Mean 5–16: 47.9		97	Mean age: 17.3	42	49	Mean 5–16: 61.4		107	Mean age: 16.9	57	50	Mean 5–16: 58.9	

Schooling, as before, followed material gains by the family; by this point, many more were able to make that choice, and for more of their children—for girls as well as boys.

More children at home worked in 1871, a function of their older age and also of the great expansion in juvenile work effected by early industrialization.[22] Increased schooling and semidependency accompanied more frequent adolescent work, as a larger proportion, over 50%, were employed in each city by age 16, a great many more after that age (Table 4.4). The extent to which juveniles worked was most dramatic in Hamilton, where industry created more places and where employment increased steadily from age 12. Industrialization absorbed these youth, and juvenile (as opposed to child) labor was undoubtedly most extensive in that city, embracing many working class adolescents. Illiterates' children now, unlike those of 10 years earlier, worked frequently, but no more often than other working class youths; family needs and insecurities continued with the onset of larger industry and its socioeconomic transformations. Work more often created a stage of semidependency at home, diluting complete dependency and replacing the forms of autonomy more common in 1861. As one result, fewer children were unoccupied, going more often to school or to work.

Early occupational placement shifted, too, with the rise of industry. Fewer children of illiterates labored in unskilled positions than a decade earlier, 17 to 33%, as family adaptation, more opportunities, and more schooling paid off (Table 4.3B). Overall, a wider variety of jobs was attained, including many skilled occupations (nearly 50% now held this level compared with 37% in 1861) in the new industries: machinists (ten), cigarmakers, coopers, printers. Clerical posts opened up too, one result of the achievement of literacy for eight sons, as 10% of the working youths acquired nonmanual occupations in their early careers. One daughter of an illiterate became a school teacher. As their early occupational profile shifted upward, most gains were made by sons; daughters largely remained in the same kinds of jobs as they in the past had. Women's sphere of work expanded less rapidly and into the new factories more slowly; service (19), dressmaking (15), tailoring (6) remained the female preserve. In sum, improvement came in the early occupations of illiterates, particularly to their sons. They were less likely to start their careers unskilled, more occupations were open to them, and these occupations compared more favorably with those of others' children. The length of family settlement in the cities, with its diminution of poverty and need, further reduced the disadvantages of their origins; by 1871,

22 Davey, "Reform"; Katz and Davey, "Youth."

education was more often available to them, too. Opportunities were less restricted, and parental illiteracy proved an even weaker obstacle to their hopes of progress and gain—although it was not insurmountable in 1861. Efforts made by fathers and families for the survival and mobility of the first generation did not foreclose opportunities to the second, at least among these persisting illiterates whose children's dependency also increased. As the parents progressed, so did their children; but the lines between classes were very rarely crossed. The leveling of society was not the purpose of education or literacy; it was not often the result of mobility, for illiterates' or other working class youths.

III

A consideration of the patterns of intergenerational occupational mobility, in 1861 and 1871, concludes the discussion presented in this chapter. The relationship of the early occupations and status of sons to their fathers' rank allows us to explore further the significance of the early work attainments of illiterates' children in the context of their childhood and adolescent experiences and of parental illiteracy. The issue, of which the data permit only an incomplete resolution, involves the extent to which the low status of fathers was transmitted to the next generation, with their achievement of less education, earlier work, and perhaps greater autonomy. Lowly origins and disadvantaged families were restrictive to, at least, the early careers of these children; mobility nevertheless was possible for many sons, and parental occupational attainments were passed on. Parental illiteracy did not necessitate the inheritance and perpetuation of the lowest occupational class or the makings of a culture of poverty.

The limitations on this analysis must be made clear before we consider the data. The measurement of intergenerational mobility is in part artificial, and the conclusions can be no more than suggestive. The data restrict the examination solely to occupations and to the early job status of sons who remained at home in each year of comparison. No other measures of mobility are available, nor is information on later or final career destinations at hand. Finally, the classification of occupations, as always, blurs some distinctions in status, prestige, or rewards. With these caveats in mind, the resulting mobility patterns of sons aged 10 years or over and at work may be reviewed.

In 1861, the inheritance of occupational status from fathers to sons was clear and strong among both literates and illiterates (Table 4.5A).

Table 4.5

Intergenerational Occupational Mobility, 1861 (Sons Older Than 10)

Father's occupation	Professional/ proprietor	Non-manual	Skilled	Semi-skilled	Unskilled	Total
A. Literates						
Professional/ proprietor						
N	5	19	4	1	—	29
%	17.2	65.5	13.8	3.4		11.3
Nonmanual						
N	2	27	20	1	3	53
%	3.8	50.1	37.7	1.9	5.7	20.6
Skilled						
N	—	16	90	1	7	114
%		14.0	78.9	0.9	6.1	44.4
Semiskilled						
N	—	—	6	8	4	18
%			33.3	44.4	22.2	7.0
Unskilled						
N	—	9	13	1	20	43
%		20.9	30.2	2.3	46.5	16.7
Total						
N	8	71	133	12	34	257
%	3.1	27.6	51.8	4.7	13.2	
B. Illiterates						
Nonmanual						
N	—	5	4	—	1	10
%		50.0	40.0		10.0	13.7
Skilled						
N	—	—	8	—	2	10
%			80.0		20.0	13.7
Semiskilled						
N	—	1	3	2	3	9
%		11.1	33.3	22.2	33.3	12.3
Unskilled						
N	—	3	10	7	24	44
%		6.8	22.7	15.9	54.5	60.3
Total						
N	—	9	25	9	30	73
%		12.3	34.2	12.3	41.1	

(continued)

Table 4.5 (continued)

	Stable	Rose	Number of levels	Fell	Number of levels
		Mobility summary			
Literates					
N	150	47	78	60	72
%	58.4	18.3		23.4	
Illiterates					
N	39	24	37	10	14
%	53.4	32.8		13.7	
Hamilton illiterates					
N	18	5	9	3	4
%	69.3	19.2		11.5	
Kingston illiterates					
N	11	16	23	3	3
%	36.7	53.3		10.0	
London illiterates					
N	10	3	5	4	7
%	58.8	17.7		23.5	

While there was less transmission of ranks than in Hamilton in 1851, as Katz has reported (a result largely of technological innovation's impact on skills and the expansion of clerical work), occupational inheritance remained distinct.[23] Thus, the sons of literate men shared parental work status at a rate of nearly 60%. The major exceptions came only at the highest level where $\frac{2}{3}$ of the sons held nonmanual clerical or small proprietary jobs, due more to their youth than to a clear loss of status. The sons of unskilled fathers inherited that status less than one-half of the time, having a 50% chance of rising; the semiskilled suffered a 25% chance of falling and a slightly greater opportunity of surpassing parental position. It was at the skilled level that occupational inheritance was greatest; nearly 80% of sons received their fathers' place, and more of them gained than fell. In the face of so much intergenerational transmission, a great deal of movement also occurred: while 58% of these sons at home took on parental levels, 18% improved rank and 23% declined, in early job status.

Among the illiterates, occupational inheritance was also strong, but, at a 53% rate of transmission, was slightly less powerful (Table 4.5B).

[23] Katz, People, Ch. 2; Thernstrom, The Other Bostonians, Ch. 5; Lipset and Bendix, Social Mobility in Industrial Society (Berkeley: University of California Press, 1959), Ch. VII; Blau and Duncan, Structure.

At the bottom, in unskilled work, illiterates' sons had a greater likelihood of starting in that rank than those of literate fathers (55 to 47%), but considering the facts of their origins the difference is not very large. Thirty percent of these sons, moreover, attained skilled or higher-ranking work early in their careers, as 45% of them improved upon fathers' places. Parental circumstances and their restricted educations did not predetermine an "underfoot" position for these sons, as Ryerson had warned. Sons of semiskilled men quite often moved up the hierarchy (44%), and sons of the skilled overwhelmingly became skilled as well (80%)—as often as those of literate fathers. Family poverty, differential educational opportunities, and early work did not combine to severely disadvantage the second generation; nonmanual work, as well, was inherited frequently. Some of them did slip, from nonmanual and skilled origins, but given their ages we should not exaggerate the significance of starts. For at no one of the occupational levels was mobility blocked for the majority of illiterates' sons. And not surprisingly, the sons of those who persisted to 1871 fared even better. The same proportion inherited their fathers' rank, but 42% (14 of 33) rose, only one falling, as they led in the progress of all these sons. As with the sons of transient fathers, though, half of these sons whose fathers were unskilled also inherited that level. Working-class membership was intergenerationally transmitted, as would be expected in an unequal society, but within that class, lowly status was by no means a certain inheritance. Skills could be transmitted in artisanal or nonmanual jobs.

Lack of schooling, familial strategies, and parental choices did not combine to curtail opportunities for the sons of illiterate men. If we count each move between occupational classes as an advance or fall, these sons improved upon the status of their fathers much more often than they fell and more often than the sons of literate men had done: 33 to 18% moving upward. Their origins were no more restrictive if the fathers were unskilled and Irish Catholic, as ethnicity proved less important to their mobility than to the sons of literates. Among illiterates, only 37% of unskilled Irish Catholics' sons worked at that rank, and 23% rose to skilled or nonmanual positions. Of the literates' sons, who attended school no more often, 65% inherited unskilled positions. Sons of Irish Catholic illiterates attained, overall, much more upward mobility in early work than those of literates: 47 to 24%. Even the most invidious of ascriptive social characteristics did not prevent improvements and did not result in intergenerational perpetuation of disadvantaged lives at the base of the social structure.

Gains over their fathers' positions, in one-third of the cases, marked substantial progress for these sons, especially in the light of their origins but also in comparison to the literates. Despite the limitations of these data (solely the early career and occupation as indicators), the patterns are highly suggestive. Parental poverty, life's insecurities for the working class, pervasive transiency; a childhood with less chance for schooling and earlier commencement of work; and the demands placed on the young from familial survival and adaptive strategies neither doomed the children's futures, relegating them to inherited places among society's castoffs and lowest ranking, nor precluded their upward occupational movement. Neither did they prohibit the transmission of parental occupational success, when it occurred, to the succeeding generation. Fewer sons began in their fathers' ranks, a clear sign of success. In their circumstances, small steps represented achievement even among the unskilled, and some of their sons made larger ones. The fuller dimensions of the effects of origins and parental status on sons' occupations are found among the children of female illiterate heads. of household. Of 56 working sons in the three cities, 22 held skilled positions (40%) and only 13 (25%) were unskilled. The poverty and burdens of these women did not prevent early job achievements; the way their sons grew up may have been the best possible preparation.

A decade later, the sons of persisting illiterates, as expected, fared better than they had in 1861 (Table 4.6). Overall, the inheritance of occupational rank, at 51%, was the same, but the transmission of unskilled status declined from 55 to 43%, with most of these sons moving upward; 20% attained nonmanual work and 30% skilled labor in the early careers. Skilled and higher-ranking positions were now inherited even more frequently: 74 and 67%, respectively. Fathers' places at all levels were more often surpassed, as almost 40% of all working sons residing at home improved upon parental occupational levels. The sons of female heads of household also worked more often at skilled jobs than those of a decade earlier had. When compared with the 1861 patterns, in which over one-half of the sons labored at semi- or unskilled ranks, by the latter date, we find a majority, over 60%, in skilled or nonmanual occupations. Irish Catholics' sons, finally, shared fully in these gains; 50% rose from fathers' levels, including 60% of the sons of the unskilled.[24]

The occupational positions of the McCowell children in 1871 illustrate these kinds of improvements in standing—one a teacher, another a clerk, a third a dressmaker—as did the son of Wynn the laborer, who

[24] In unpublished work, Katz has found great stability in the patterns of intergenerational occupational mobility in Hamilton, 1861–1871, with the influence of ethnicity declining and that of class increasing. Chances of modest gains were good, but as with illiterates, the structure of inequality was not fundamentally altered; it was reproduced through the transmission of position between fathers and sons.

Table 4.6
Intergenerational Occupational Mobility: Sons of Illiterates, 1871 (Older Than 10)

Father's occupation	Son's occupation				
	Nonmanual	Skilled	Semiskilled	Unskilled	Total
Nonmanual					
N	4	2	—	—	6
%	66.7	33.3			7.2
Skilled					
N	3	17	—	3	23
%	13.0	73.9		13.0	27.7
Semiskilled					
N	2	3	4	3	12
%	16.7	25.0	33.3	25.0	14.5
Unskilled					
N	7	13	4	18	42
%	16.7	30.9	9.5	42.9	50.6
Total					
N	16	35	8	24	83
%	19.3	42.2	9.6	28.9	

		Mobility summary			
	Stable	Rose	Number of levels	Fell	Number of levels
Total					
N	43	32		8	
%	51.8	38.6	65	9.6	11
Hamilton					
N	26	13		3	
%	61.9	30.9	32	7.2	6
Kingston					
N	6	15		1	
%	27.3	68.2	23	4.6	1
London					
N	11	4		4	
%	57.8	21.1	10	21.1	4

also became a clerk. The Irish Catholic laborer, Lawrence Kelly, had a son who became a tailor, in 1871. J. Halloran's sons (Halloran was a fellow countryman and laborer) worked as a baker and a tobacconist; both fathers were illiterate and continued to be wage laborers through the decade.

Persistence, adaptation, increased wealth, and stability; somewhat greater exposure to education; and the transformation of adolescence all contributed directly to this pattern of progress in intergenerational mobility in which so many of the sons of illiterate parents participated. In acknowledging these significant movements up from disadvantaged origins, we also need to stress that, as class lines were rarely crossed, over 50% of the sons in 1861 and almost 40% in 1871 started work at the semi- and unskilled, low levels of the occupational hierarchy.

Virtually all of the sons continued within the working class. Neither the achievement of additional education by 1871 nor their own attainment of literacy and some schooling (usually limited) could influence this result; interclass mobility, although more frequent *inter*generationally than *intra*generationally, was then quite exceptional, and probably is still not common.[25] Literacy and education did not have *that* kind of impact on the social structure, even as they became more pervasive, more frequently needed, and more freely available. Differentials were maintained between social classes; origins within classes were perpetuated from fathers to children; and, in a broadly based and quite subtle manner, the social structure with its inherent inequalities was reproduced in the next generation. To repeat these points is not to deny the realities of social mobility, for which so much empirical evidence exists; rather, it is to comprehend their context and social function. When compared with some aspects of education's ideological promotion of equal opportunities and its contribution to mobility, success has been undeniably limited. But the fact of mobility, not only within classes but across ranks or strata, such as that of the illiterates' sons, legitimates the ideology of public schooling and serves to assure its hegemony. The illiterates who sent more of their children to school for longer periods, as they were able, were only representative of much larger numbers of people in their behavior. The ideology of mobility gained acceptance from the amount of mobility, however small, that took place.[26] The school fit squarely into this conjuncture that linked the contradictions between ideology and social reality, as its promulgated place in the

[25] See Katz, *People*, Chs. 2–3, "The Origins of Public Education;" Thernstrom, *The Other Bostonians*, esp. Chs. 5, 9, *Poverty and Progress;* Lipset and Bendix, *Social Mobility;* Boudon, *Education, Opportunity, and Social Inequality* (New York: Wiley, 1974); Bowles and Gintis, *Schooling*, esp. Chs. 3–4; Jencks *et al., Inequality;* Robert Dreeben, *On What is Learned in School* (Reading, Mass.: Addison-Wesley, 1968).

[26] On the importance of even small-scale success in legitimating social ideology, see John Foster, "Nineteenth Century Towns—A Class Dimension," in *The Study of Urban History*, ed. H. J. Dyos (London: Edward Arnold, 1968), 281–299; Thernstrom, *Poverty and Progress;* Katz, *People*, Ch. 2.

processes of equality and mobility derived assent and social support. Education and literacy therefore became intimately connected with life and achievement, as the school mediated aspirations for advancement (and also promoted them) with continuing social inequality.

The function of the ideology of success and achievement and of institutions such as the schools, which were presumed to facilitate greatly the attainment of success, was to provide the public with ways of understanding and assimilating themselves to the social and economic order— in the nineteenth century, the new orders of commercial and industrial capitalism. In these complex processes of societal transformation, literacy and schooling were central; that much is certain. Yet we have increasing reason to doubt that they were in fact essential in the manner traditionally accepted and which derived from eighteenth and nineteenth century social thinking and educational promotion. One small but telling sign of the contradictions involved is the ironic fact that the education of the sons of the illiterates contributed little to the small-scale but common gains they made, much as their parents' small successes had nothing whatsoever to do with their lack of education.

Upward mobility in wealth, property, and adjustment were not made at the expense or the sacrifice of the children's futures among the illiterates in the three mid-nineteenth-century cities we are considering. Certainly these gains aided their sons' chances in early work levels and in additional schooling; but even with less schooling, these children did not begin life without opportunities for improvement and progress within their class. Like sons of illiterate parents elsewhere in the nineteenth century, mobility came to those with some preparation in their early socialization.[27] Literacy and schooling varied according to the social

[27] In an important study, William H. Sewell, Jr. shows that sons of peasants who migrated to Marseilles and who were less often literate than native-born working class sons ("clearly less qualified . . . for non-manual occupations") had a rate of mobility into nonmanual occupations "substantially higher than that of workers' sons," besting "all categories of workers' sons by margins ranging from 30% for skilled workers' sons to over 250% for unskilled workers' sons," "Social Mobility in a Nineteenth-Century European City," *Journal of Interdisciplinary History*, 7 (1976), 222–223, 217–233. Sewell concludes that this "remarkable" success can not be explained by competitive labor market advantages, and argues that it derives from a difference in culture and values. This is analogous, I believe, to the illiterates' sons in the Ontario cities, and provides important comparative support for my interpretation. We cannot be certain how many of the urban fathers were of peasant background, although some no doubt were; nevertheless, we may point to migratory selection and the implications for personal motivation, patterns of adaptation and adjustment (including homeownership), the socialization of the children, and the relative successes of parents without education

and economic contexts, of course, but comparative research supports our fundamental conclusion that their attainment, while enabling some children to surmount the lowest of origins, did not significantly alter class stratification or structural inequality. Illiteracy could prove a great disadvantage to many, but not an insurmountable barrier to survival, adjustment, or progress; conversely, literacy and education did remarkably little in themselves to aid the greatest numbers in erasing ascriptive burdens, in cancelling the disadvantages of their origins, or in gaining upward mobility.[28] The results of these comparative nineteenth-century urban case studies provide strong support for further detailed historical investiga-

---

and sons with limited schooling. The results are highly suggestive; this marks one vital path which future researchers should follow.

In a very different context, Michael Sanderson ("Literacy and Social Mobility in the Industrial Revolution in England," *Past and Present,* 56 [1972], 75–104) presents evidence that literate parents were, conversely, unable to pass along advantages and provide opportunities for occupational mobility for their sons: "With rising literacy, the mere possession of literacy would be unlikely to secure good job prospects," 95, 95–102. See below, and Ch. 5, below. See also, T. W. Laqueur's comment and Sanderson's response, *ibid.,* 64 (1974), 96–112.

[28] See also, Lee Soltow and Edward Stevens, "Economic Aspects of School Participation in Mid-Nineteenth-Century United States," *Journal of Interdisciplinary History,* 8 (1977), 221–243; Sanderson, "Literacy"; the studies cited in note 25, above. Soltow and Stevens discover, for the U.S. in 1860, clear educational differentials by wealth of parents, especially for attendance after the ages of 10 and 15, respectively, and the effect of ethnicity on both education and wealth. After raising critical questions about the relationship between enrollment and literacy, the economic rewards of schooling and literacy, and the purposes of training in literacy (which we consider in Ch. 5), they conclude that "it appears unlikely that the common school served as a vehicle for occupational mobility," in spite of the "expectations of common school reformers," and the "impact of the common school expansion was differential, with the wealth of parents being a critical factor . . . the implication is that the common school institution did not alter patterns of economic inequality, but, rather, tended to perpetuate them," 242–243. See also Soltow, *Men and Wealth in the United States, 1850–1870* (New Haven: Yale University Press, 1975), 22, 79. Sanderson, continuing his argument cited in note 27, asserts, "In an eighteenth-century commercial society unaffected by the development of the cotton factory industry, the possibility of social mobility for the educated son of a laborer was vastly greater than in the 1830s in a society considerably affected by such industrialization, even when both societies were within the same county. . . . This is simply not consistent with an interpretation of the industrial revolution that sees it as demanding more literacy, creating more literate jobs and drawing an increasingly educated labour force up the social scale into them," 101–102. Ch. 5, below, considers both the British and North American cases. The results of studies by Lipset and Bendix, Jencks, Boudon, Bowles and Gintis, Collins, and Squires (cited in Chs. 2–3, above) argue for broad continuities rather than dramatic change over time, as does Thernstrom, *The Other Bostonians,* Ch. 5.

tions of literacy and illiteracy, but more importantly for serious and sustained reevaluation and reconsideration of the "literacy myth", the social theories and ideologies that surround it, and its contemporary extensions as well.[29]

---

[29] For a different interpretation of the response of immigrant groups to education, see Timothy L. Smith, "Immigrant Social Aspirations and American Education, 1880–1930," *American Quarterly*, 21 (1969), 523–543, "Native Blacks and Foreign Whites: Varying Responses to Educational Opportunity in America, 1880–1950," *Perspectives in American History*, 6 (1972), 623–643. For a very different approach to working class educational strategies, see the interesting book by T. W. Laqueur, *Religion and Respectability: Sunday Schools and Working Class Culture, 1780–1850* (New Haven: Yale University Press, 1976). I do not find these arguments convincing. For more recent perspectives, see Blau and Duncan, *Structure;* Sewell and Hauser, *Education,* among a mammoth body of literature.

II
LITERACY AND SOCIETY

[E]veryone now knows that the best way for an illiterate worker to achieve integration into the production process and to form an idea of his place in the production chain is to internalize the linear nature of the printed text, to acquire the ability to see things laterally and to equip himself with the spatial scheme necessary in order to learn to read and write. Industrialists have fully understood that the medium constitutes the most important part of the message.

[Literacy] serves the purposes of ideological inculcation, for example, and, naturally, for the inculcation of industrial ideology, along with sharpening the appetite for individual advancement and, finally, domesticating the working class to the industrial ethos.

E. VERNE
*"Literacy and Industrialization—
The Dispossession of Speech" (1976)*

In such a context, literacy training is simply an introduction to this positivistic conception of the world. By restricting knowledge to facts and laws, under the pretense of science, it is necessarily limited to helping people adapt themselves to the established order.

ROGER GARAUDY
"Literacy and the Dialogue between Civilizations" (1976)

One important influence is the emphasis in modern linguistics research on the primacy of oral over written sources for understanding how language works. This development is important because literacy and literacy culture have for centuries been tied to social mobility, class consciousness, and cultural elitism. With print came the grammar book, "proper" speech, and linguistic snobbery.

ROBERT DISCH
"The Future of Literacy" (1973)

[Any such] "simple distinction between literate and illiterate" . . . is fuzzy at every point in the eighteenth century: the illiterate hear the products of literacy read aloud in taverns and they accept from the literate culture some categories, while many of the literate employ their very limited skills only instrumentally (writing invoices, keeping accounts) while their "wisdom" and customs are still transmitted within a pre-literate oral culture. . . .Any attempt to segregate the literate and illiterate cultures will meet with even greater difficulty.

E. P. THOMPSON
"Eighteenth-Century English Society: Class Struggle without Class" (1978)

5

Literacy, Jobs, and Industrialization

> *No amount of literary cramming will make a good, loyal,*
> *intelligent citizen out of a reluctant child. But a crafts-*
> *man who loves his work and takes pride in his work, who*
> *would rather do his work than joy-ride over the country*
> *—such a craftsman cannot be a disloyal, unintelligent*
> *citizen, even though he can neither read nor write. But,*
> *of course, he would have mastered these arts without*
> *wasting eight years of his life on them, endangering his*
> *health to boot.*
>
> FREDERICK PHILIP GROVE
> *"A Search for America" (1927)*

In 1848, Egerton Ryerson, the Chief Superintendent of Education
for Upper Canada, addressed "The Importance of Education to a Manufacturing, and a Free People." Commencing from the premise that a
system of mass public education was a prerequisite to a system of manufacturing—the symbol of the incoming social order—he proclaimed that
"education is designed to prepare us for the duties of life." Although,
as we have seen, those duties were primarily moral and social, Ryerson
did not neglect proper preparation for work. "How," he asked, "is the
uneducated and unskilled man to succeed in these times of sharp and
skilful competition and sleepless activity?" [1]

[1] *Journal of Education for Upper Canada, (J.E.),* 1 (1848), 289–301; for English
parallels, see Central Society of Education, *Papers* (London, 1837–1839). On the centrality of morality in nineteenth-century education see esp. Alison Prentice, "The
School Promoters: Education and Social Class in Nineteenth Century Upper Canada,"

One year later Ryerson elaborated his views about the relations between occupational success, formal education, and literacy. Discussing
"Canadian Mechanics and Manufactures," he claimed that the mechanic
"will be a member of society; and, as such, he should know how to read
and write the language spoken by such society. . . . This supposes instruction in the grammar or structure of his native tongue." Although
one might advance in the working world without education, Ryerson
admitted, he would remain fundamentally at a loss:

> I have known many persons rise to wealth and respectability by their industry,
> virtues and self-taught skill; but from their utter want of training in the
> proper mode of writing, or speaking, or reading their native tongue, they are
> unable to fill the situations to which their circumstances and talents and
> characteristics entitle them, and in which they might confer great benefits
> upon society.

Social order and progress were the supreme beneficiaries of all education,
and, with other Anglo-American educators, Ryerson believed that "educated labour is more productive than uneducated labour." By "productive" he meant a variety of related qualities: less disruptive, more skilled,
orderly and disciplined, punctual, and moral. Thus, the "proper education of the mechanic is important to the interests of society as well as to
his own welfare and enjoyment." [2]

As the preceding chapters have argued, the key issues are much
more complex than Ryerson's, or many others', statements allow. How
important have literacy and schooling been to occupational and economic success? Traditional wisdom, modern sociology, the rhetoric of
modernization, and nineteenth-century school promotion all celebrated
the role of education in determining success. Yet not all the evidence,
past or present, lends credence to this view. Consider these examples—
the first a help-wanted advertisement, the second an educational study:

> Wanted immediately FORTY ABLE BODIED MEN, to serve as JUSTICES
> OF THE PEACE, for the COUNTY OF HURON. A plain English Education
> is desirable but not indispensable—each candidate must be able to make his
> mark, unless he has learned to write his name, and will be expected to pro-

---

unpub. Ph.D. Diss., University of Toronto, 1974. (Published as *The School Promoters*
[1977]); Ch. 1, above.

[2] *J.E.*, 11 (1849), 19–20. Walter Eales, in *A Lecture on the Benefits to be Derived
from Mechanics' Institutes*, February 5, 1851, made much the same argument: "the
degree of credit or usefulness in this world depends infinitely more on well-directed
and temperate activity than on the difference of original capabilities." (Delivered to
the Toronto Mechanics' Institute [Toronto, 1851]).

duce a character signed by the Deputy Commissioner of the Board of Works
and the Collector of Customs Goderich.

and

For all children, except the 10 percent who will earn a living by the use of
their verbal ability there is a case for substituting practical for academic
education.[3]

The relationship of education in general and literacy in particular to
work, occupation, and their rewards remains an imprecise one, complex
and often contradictory. This chapter explores that relationship, examining both the real and the perceived connections surrounding the
economic value of literacy. The literacy levels and differentials of the
urban Ontario working class are first reviewed in this intellectual context of the economic importance of education. The views of middle-class
reformers and working-class spokesmen are examined. Finally, a case
study based on the employment-contract ledgers of an Ontario lumbering firm is presented in order to isolate the importance of literacy to
workingmen in a specific social situation. In sum, this chapter illuminates the contradictions in the perceived connections between education,
employment levels, and economic development, to argue that literacy
was not always central to jobs, earnings, and industrialization in the
nineteenth century in the manner typically assumed.

I

Ontario in the 1860s and 1870s was an overwhelmingly literate
society. Adult (20 years and older) literacy was over 90% as measured
by the censuses of those years. In respect of wealth and occupation,
there was superficially a significant degree of stratification by illiteracy;
the majority of illiterates labored as semi- and unskilled workers. Large
numbers, lacking education, also assumed positions of skill—positions
which were maintained over the decade 1861–1871.

One hundred and thirty-five illiterates in Hamilton, Kingston, and
London held skilled laboring and artisanal occupations in 1861; 44 held
higher-ranking jobs. Open to at least some uneducated persons were
the occupations of bailiff, engineer, grocer, inn-keeper, mason, merchant,

---

[3] Hamilton *Spectator and Journal of Commerce,* December 6, 1848; John Duncan,
The Education of the Ordinary Child (London, 1943), 60.

manufacturer, molder, printer, tailor, tavernkeeper, tinsmith, wheel-wright, shoemaker, and watchmaker (as is shown in Table 5.1). No single occupation in Hamilton, in fact, comprised a majority of illiterates. Only 25% of adult common laborers, 15% of seamstresses, and 5% of female servants could not read or write. The remainder—and the greatest num-bers—of those occupying these low-status positions were literate. Seventy-five percent of the unskilled and 93% of the semiskilled possessed the skills of literacy, but nevertheless were unable to climb higher in occu-pational level. The acquisition of some education, as signified by their literacy, did not enable them to overcome the dominance of ethnic and class ascription in attaining rank and status in an unequal social structure.

The distribution of wealth in these cities strikingly parallels that of occupation. The majority of illiterates whose wealth could be deter-mined (as measured by total annual value in the 1861 city assessment rolls) were poor; that is, below a poverty line struck at the 40th per-centile of the assessed population. Nevertheless, sizeable numbers of illiterate workers achieved at least moderate economic standing, and the majority of all poor were literate. Illiteracy did not consign all men to poverty, and, conversely, many literate workers remained poor. Illiteracy could be depressing occupationally or economically, but literacy proved of remarkably limited value in the pursuit of higher status or greater rewards.

More revealing than these occupational and economic profiles is the relationship of literacy to the economic rewards of occupation. Among the unskilled and the semiskilled, very little economic advantage accrued to the literates. Literacy, though, had a greater role in the attainment of skilled or artisanal work and their commensurate rewards. Some illit-erates, nevertheless, fared well, especially those few in nonmanual or small proprietary positions.

The possession of literacy did have rewards, though its benefits were hardly clear or unambiguous; overall, they were rather limited ones. The relationship of education to work and earnings was quite complex, as we have seen, complicated by other determinants, usually ascriptive social-structural ones: ethnicity, social class, race, age, and sex. Illiterates' standing, as a result, was far from uniform or homogeneous; they were differentiated and stratified in the same ways as others in the cities. Consequently, Irish Catholics (illiterate or not), women, blacks, and the aged are generally found in the lowest occupational or economic classes. More than literacy operated in the establishment and main-tenance of the rigid stratification of nineteenth-century cities. Education

Table 5.1

Illiterates: Selected Occupations, 1861

	Hamilton	Percentage of Hamilton adult workforce	Kingston	London
Barber	2	10.5	3	1
Blacksmith	8	10.3	—	2
Builder	2	7.2	—	1
Cabinet maker	1	1.9	—	—
Carpenter	14	4.7	4	4
Clergymen	1	3.2	—	—
Clothier	2	13.3	—	—
Constable	1	11.1	—	—
Customs collector	1	33.3	1	—
Dealer	1	9.1	1	—
Dressmaker	1	1.4	2	—
Engineer	1	2.1	1	1
Farmer	3	10.0	3	2
Grocer	1	1.1	1	1
High bailiff	1	50.0	—	—
Innkeeper	1	6.7	3	—
Joiner	1	5.9	—	—
Laborer	205	25.2	105	83
Mail conductor	2	50.0	—	—
Mariner	1	2.0	10	—
Merchant	1	0.9	—	—
Mason	2	3.9	3	1
Molder	2	3.6	—	—
Painter	2	3.2	—	—
Pedlar	2	6.1	1	1
Printer	1	2.5	1	—
Seamstress	8	15.1	2	—
Servant (f)	33	6.1	34	—
Tailor	8	6.2	8	—
Tavernkeeper	7	9.3	1	—
Tinsmith	2	5.1	—	—
Wagonmaker	2	18.2	—	—
Wheelwright	1	50.0	—	—
Gentleman	1	1.5	1	—
Watchmaker	1	7.2	1	—
Porter	3	4.8	1	2
Teamster	4	13.3	—	—
Plasterer	3	6.9	—	2
Clerk	—	—	1	—
Shoemaker	8	5.6	4	4

alone seldom altered class or social position dramatically; its influence was overwhelmingly a reinforcing one.

Education and literacy did not reduce the role of class or status .as the urban society was gradually transformed by modernization and industrialization. At the same time, social mobility was possible for persisting illiterates, 1861 to 1871, the usual expectations to the contrary. Occupationally, stability was the most common experience, as skilled workers maintained their positions, not falling to lower class ranks. Economically, improvement in wealth and property dominated, regardless of occupation or ethnicity.

An absence of literacy and a lack of education did not remove all opportunities for higher-ranking occupations or the acquisition of wealth. Ethnicity favored some illiterates and hindered others; factors such as chance, personality, and motivation figured, too, undoubtedly mitigating some of the disadvantages that illiteracy and ascription could carry. An illiterate could achieve some success in the working world of the nineteenth century. These conclusions form one baseline against which to assess the rhetorical claims of middle-class school promoters and by which to understand the criticisms and aspirations of the working class. Much more than the skills of literacy were at stake to them; other issues were thought to be at least as central to the curriculum of the future workers.

II

Industry, skills, and wealth could be obtained by the individual with no schooling; education, nevertheless, was viewed as fundamental to the development and the maintenance of the economic system, as it was to the social order. The claims of the schoolmen stressed educated, literate labor for productivity and benefit to both society and individuals. As Ryerson stated it, "Every man, unless he wishes to starve outright, must read and write, and cast accounts, and speak his native tongue well enough to attend to his own particular business." [4]

Egerton Ryerson long affirmed that education underlay any of the main branches of career pursuits. In his first report, of 1846, he laid the foundation for future statements: "The establishment of a thorough system of primary and industrial education, commensurate with the population of the country, as contemplated by the Government, and is

---

4 *J.E.,* VII (1854), 134.

here proposed, is justified by considerations of *economy* as well as of patriotism and humanity." With evidence from Switzerland, he argued that uneducated workers have neither the logic for, nor capacity of making sound deductions or collecting observations to aid their work. "This want of capacity of mental arrangements is shown in their manual operations." Quite simply, it was the well-informed, well-educated workers who were thought to produce the most and the best, to possess superior moral habits, and to save money. Uneducated, illiterate workers, presumably, did not.[5]

Little doubt or hesitation accompanied the proclamations of the benefits of education to the economy or the individual workers. Yet it is important to note, with Alison Prentice, that "statements relating specific occupational groups to social status tended to be vague and contradictory." To Ryerson, there were but two kinds of workers: they were either "rude, simple or uneducated" or they were educated. These were also the classes of society, as status increasingly included demeanor and gentility as well as skills attained. "And by skills, few school promoters meant manual dexterity." Literacy was just one skill, important but not the only one; education's benefits involved the transmission of the proper code of behavior, including morality and correct attitudes. Literacy revealed that the training had begun.[6]

More than upward mobility through education, Ryerson emphasized the loss of status and downward mobility, which he claimed would accompany the lack of schooling. Educated men might advance; the uneducated would surely fall. The burden he placed on the shoulders of fathers: "Does a man wish his sons to swell the dregs of the society— to proscribe them from all situations of trust and duty in the locality of their abode—to make them mere slaves in the land of freedom? Then let him leave them without education, and their underfoot position in society will be decided upon." Ryerson further taught that workers were not to be educated to despise their occupations. Not all men should aspire to the highest statuses of work; "practical" men were needed too, and the supply of farmers and mechanics must not diminish. Education therefore must not alienate labor; and it should not, for labor, he added, did not deaden the mind. The ideal mechanic would combine "in his own person, the qualifications and skills," of both the manufacturing superintendent and the operative. All members of the working class thus required that which "is essential to the successful

---

[5] "Report on a System of Elementary Instruction for Upper Canada, 1846," in *Documentary History of Education for Upper Canada (D.H.E.)*, ed. J. G. Hodgins, 6 (Toronto, 1899), 143 (emphasis added), 144–145.

[6] Prentice, "School Promoters", 150, 174; *J.E.*, V (1852), 133.

pursuit of any one of the several departments of human activity and enterprise." This consisted of "what is rudimental, or elementary in education"; in addition to reading, writing, arithmetic, and grammar, "each must learn that which will give him skill in his own particular employments." [7] Not at all inclusive of specific job skills, this training made for more productive and more easily managed labor; advancing the nation's development took precedence over the individual among education's benefits.

Ryerson was hardly an isolated spokesman for the economic contributions of education; he was joined by many others throughout Anglo-America.[8] Charles Clarke was one such reformer. His 1877 address to the South Wellington, Ontario, Teachers Association shows the persistence of the ideas Ryerson had enunciated. "No unprejudiced man," Clarke asserted, "can conceal from himself the fact that education has lightened the toil of the laborer, increased his productive ability, surrounded him with comparative luxuries, and materially increased the purchasing power of his daily wage." Recent economic and labor history describe the period very differently, of course. Regardless, he argued that uneducated men were heavily handicapped in "the race of and for life," and that they were "sinking, more rapidly and certainly than ever, into the position of mere 'hewers of wood and drawers of water.' " [9]

More so than Ryerson, Clarke, or most others, Horace Mann, the first Secretary of the Massachusetts State Board of Education, fully elaborated these ideas. Mann was Ryerson's contemporary and associate,

---

[7] *J.E.*, 1 (1848), 297. See also Rev. John May, *Essays on Educational Subjects* (Ottawa, 1880), 19; *D.H.E.*, 11, 45. It must not be ignored that education, in the Methodist view, was not only moral and occupational preparation, but it was the training for one's calling. "The Importance of Education to an Agricultural People," *D.H.E.*, 7, 141. See also, Allan Smith, "The Myth of the Self-made Man in English Canada, 1850–1914," *Canadian Historical Review*, 59 (1978), 189–219.

[8] For English examples, see Richard Johnson, "Educational Policy and Social Control in Early Victorian England," *Past and Present*, 49 (1970), 96–119, "Notes on the schooling of the English working class, 1780–1850," in *Schooling and Capitalism*, ed. R. Dale, G. Esland, and M. MacDonald (London: Routledge, Kegan Paul, 1976), 44–54; E. G. West, *Education and the Industrial Revolution* (London: Batsford, 1975), "The Role of Education in 19th Century Doctrines of Political Economy," *British Journal of Educational Studies*, 12 (1964), 161–174. For the U.S., see Alexander J. Field, "Educational Reform and Manufacturing Development in Mid-Nineteenth Century Massachusetts," unpub. PhD. Diss., University of California, Berkeley, 1974, summarized in "Educational Expansion in Mid-Nineteenth-Century Massachusetts," *Harvard Educational Review*, 46 (1976), 521–552; Michael B. Katz, *The Irony of Early School Reform* (Cambridge, Mass.: Harvard University Press, 1968), "The Origins of Public Education," *History of Education Quarterly*, 14 (1976), 381–407; Samuel Bowles and Herbert Gintis, *Schooling in Capitalist America* (New York: Basic Books, 1976).

[9] *Teachers and Teaching (and) Then and Now* (Elora, Ontario, 1880), 2.

and the Ontario reformer quoted from his reports and exchanged information with him. For this reason as well as because of Mann's overall contribution to the development of educational thought and institutions in the nineteenth century, his opinion merits discussion.[10]

Horace Mann devoted much of his *Fifth Annual Report* (1842) to the economic benefits of education; in so doing, he entered into much greater detail than Ryerson or most other promoters. Both men favored arguments for education rooted in moral principles and civic virtues, though both made appeals to the economic self-interest of their audiences. As Mann expressed it, such self-interest, of all the "beneficient influences of education, may, perhaps, be justly regarded as the lowest . . ." yet "it represents an aspect of the subject susceptible of being made intelligible to all. . . ." Mann's primary objective in the *Fifth Report* was to argue that education was the most productive enterprise that could be undertaken by an individual or a community. To make this claim was certainly not novel; Mann, however, by surveying manufacturers, collected "hard" evidence to prove his assertions. His questionnaire, sent to selected men, inquired, principally, as follows:

> Have you observed differences among the persons you have employed, growing out of differences in their education, *and independent of their natural abilities* . . . that is, [do] those who . . . have been accustomed to exercise their minds by reading and studying, have greater docility and quickness in applying themselves to work [and] greater appetite, dexterity or ingenuity in comprehending ordinary processes, or in originating new ones?

His major concern was, of course, "How do those who have enjoyed and improved the privilege of good Common Schools, compare with the neglected and the illiterate?" The answers to the queries were hardly surprising: the manufacturers responded that "the rudiments of a Common School education are essential to the attainment of skill and expertness as laborers"; "very few, who have not enjoyed the advantages of a Common School education, ever rise above the lowest class of operatives." Uneducated labor was unproductive, and the best educated were both the most profitable and the best paid. They were also more moral, loyal, cheerful, and contented as well as more punctual and reliable—or so the replies indicated.

Pleased, Mann proclaimed that these answers "seem to prove incontestibly that education is not only a moral renovator, and a multiplier of intellectual power, but that it is also the most prolific parent

---

[10] See David Onn, "Egerton Ryerson's Philosophy of Education: Something Borrowed or Something New?" *Ontario History*, 61 (1969), 77–86; Ryerson, "Report upon a System." On Mann, see Jonathan Messerli, *Horace Mann* (New York: Knopf, 1971); Katz, *The Irony;* Field, "Reform."

of material riches." Knowledge, he concluded, must precede industry: intelligence was the "great money-maker." [11] Ryerson and Mann joined in recognizing the mid-century spirit of progress and materialism, asserting in their educational promotion the productive contribution of common-school training. Proof was another issue, however, as Mann went further in providing evidence, thinking it insufficient merely to repeat the rhetoric of his witnesses.

Two of Mann's respondents attempted to estimate the wage differentials accruing to literate workmen. One manufacturer noted that literate employees (name-signers as opposed to markers) earned, on the average, about 27% more than illiterate ones; another claimed an 18½% difference. They then calculated the wage differentials between the highest paid literate workers and the lowest paid illiterate ones at 66 and 40%, respectively. Mann throughout his *Report* referred to these estimates as *conclusive* evidence to support his viewpoint, although these data were more impressionistic than statistical. Although his argument was presented in the guise of arithmetical exactness, the analysis of the rate of return to investments in primary education remained vague and overly rhetorical. The only explicit calculation he offered was a new wage difference of 50%.

There are grave problems both with Mann's method of obtaining that figure and with his use of it. He apparently simply averaged the two extreme examples of wages—not the group averages—looking solely at atypical cases. Had he used the average wages reported to him, the result would have been less than half of his 50% differential: 23%, far from such a huge variation, and still unreliable when based on a sample of only two firms. Mann also failed to show that additional education for each child was economically profitable, exaggerating differences between markers and signers, and ignoring the factors of age and ethnicity. He further confused the value of education to parents with its worth to the community, firms, or individuals—these could be very different. Finally, his use of wage rates ignored the imperfections of the labor market, social inequality, and discrimination. In sum, we must agree with Maris Vinovskis, that "it is likely that Mann's figure of 50% for primary education greatly exaggerates the actual produc-

---

11 *Annual Report of the Secretary of the Board of Education,* 5 (Boston, 1842), 81, 87–89, 90, 100. On the biases inherent in Mann's survey, see the *Annual Report, passim.;* Maris A. Vinovskis, "Horace Mann on the Economic Productivity of Education," *New England Quarterly,* 43 (1970), 550–571. Soltow and Stevens ("Economic Aspects of School Promotion," *Journal of Interdisciplinary History,* 8 [1977], 236) provide an Ohio example.

tivity of education during that period. A much more likely estimate would be in the range of 10–20%." [12] If this is the case, the contributions of education to productivity must be evaluated in very different terms.

Another perspective emerges from the pages of the *Fifth Report*. Each of Mann's respondents concentrated (as did Ryerson) on the fact that educated workers were clean, moral, better able to follow directions, more punctual and reliable, and less likely to be unreasonable or violent during periods of labor unrest. In many ways, these were the most valued, and "productive," teachings of the common school—more so than cognitive skills. Alexander Field, in examining the "coincidence" of educational reform and the development of manufacturing in Massachusetts in this period, stresses industry's need for properly socialized labor. Importantly, he discovered that manufacturing expanded in the context of (and with the effect of) declining skill requirements—*not* of increasing skill demands. Manufacturers needed a disciplined, deferential, orderly, and honest labor force, and themselves worked with and through professional school reformers for the expansion of education at state and local levels (as other manufacturers did in Canada and England).

Recent research emphasizes the same point, stressing the importance of the molding of noncognitive personality characteristics as a major aspect of schooling. Gintis, for example, found that the contribution of education to earnings or occupational status can not be explained by the relationship between schooling and cognitive achievement. He demonstrates, rather, that the noncognitive personality traits stressed in schools, such as subordination and discipline, have a more direct influence on worker earnings and productivity. "The structure of social relations in schools reproduces rather faithfully the capitalist work-environment," he concluded.[13] This was the result of the moral economy and of

---

[12] Mann, *Fifth Annual Report;* Vinovskis, "Mann", 568. This discussion is indebted to the work of Vinovskis, Part II. See also, Frank Tracey Carleton, *Economic Influences upon Educational Progress in the United States, 1820–1850* (Reprinted: New York: Teachers College Press, 1965), Ch. 4; Field, "Educational Reform." On the relationship between literacy and inventiveness, so prized by Mann, see the fascinating article by Eugene Ferguson, "The Mind's Eye: Nonverbal Thought in Technology," *Science,* 197 (1977), 827–836. See also, A. F. C. Wallace, *Rockdale* (New York: Knopf, 1978), 237 ff.

[13] Field, "Reform", esp. Chs. 8–9; Herbert Gintis, "Education, Technology, and the Characteristics of Worker Productivity," *American Economic Review,* 61 (1971), 266–279; Bowles and Gintis, *Schooling,* Part Two; Robert Dreeben, *On What is Learned in School* (Reading, Mass.: Addison-Wesley, 1968). See also, E. Verne, "Literacy and Industrialization," in *A Turning Point for Literacy,* ed. Léon Bataille (New York: Pergamon Press, 1976), 211–228; Ivar Berg, *Education and Jobs* (Boston: Beacon Press,

educational hegemony, expected from the carefully structured provision of literacy.

The contradictions between promoters' emphasis on skills and individual wages (undoubtedly central to popular acceptance of public schooling) and society and industry's behavioral requirements are extremely important in understanding the relationships between literacy, jobs, and development. Dr. Edward Jarvis' discussion of the specific ways in which education enhanced the skills of common laborers illustrates the dimensions of the connections, with his amusing and novel presentation of the manifold benefits. Jarvis analyzed the "processes of labor" of woodcutters, woodsplitters, turners, coalheavers, shovellers, and others in order to compare educated and uneducated workers. He perceived, pseudoscientifically, that

> The discreet shoveller [to take one case] carries his shovel to a point in the circle when the tangential movement, modified by gravitation, shall describe a curve which at its highest part is above the cart-wheel. . . . As the blade of the shovel is held at right angles with the plane of the curve of motion, all the contents are carried in a curve of the same radius . . . and all fall together in to the vehicle in a compact mass; none are lost on the way.

In contrast, the uneducated laborer or

> thoughtless workman, unaccustomed to noticing the exact relation to things, and having no comprehensive plan of his operations, places his cart by accident. . . . Or, as chance, not intelligent observation, governs this matter, the recepticle may be so far off as to require the workman to walk a step or two. . . . Nor is this dull laborer always mindful of the position of his shovel when he throws its contents.

Experience, knowledge acquired from others, and common sense are ignored, relegated behind the promoted benefits of schooling. Still, it remains unclear how common schooling would aid the worker in the ways Jarvis stressed. What neither Jarvis nor Mann or Ryerson revealed was how education specifically benefitted the future workers in opening their eyes, comprehending their work, or applying their powers for best effect. How many sawyers, splitters, coalheavers, or shovellers needed or

---

1971); G. D. Squires, "Education, Jobs, and Inequality," *Social Problems*, 24 (1977), 436–450; Alex Inkeles and David H. Smith, *Becoming Modern* (Cambridge, Mass.: Harvard University Press, 1974); James Bright, "Does Automation Raise Skill Requirements?," *Harvard Business Review*, 36 (1958), 85–98, "The Relationship of Increasing Automation and Skill Requirements," in *Report* of The U.S. National Commission on Technology, Automation, and Economic Progress, Appendix Vol. II (Washington, D.C.: G.P.O., 1966), 203–221. See also Note 50.

acquired much education for their jobs, and how much schooling was required to develop these vaunted mental skills? Were the skills of the common schools those necessary for productive labor? These questions went unasked and unanswered, for the primary assumption went unchallenged: "Education . . . is the economy of force, and gives it a greater power to create value. It enables the intelligent and skillful to add more to the worth of matter than the ignorant." [14] In addition, they confused knowledge and intelligence with schooling and literacy; skills from experience and what might be termed "technical literacy" were simply not considered. In this manner, promotion stressed increased skills, productivity, and returns (individual and other) from educational reform and expansion. The results of education added significantly to productivity, economic development, and social order; the process through which they were accomplished was a rather different one from that typically emphasized.

Contemporary sociological debate continues to focus on the relationship between education and occupational attainment, illustrating persisting interest in the importance of this issue. Recent data, significantly, enter into our conclusions about the role of literacy and schooling in the past, contradicting assumptions of a direct link between school achievement and job attainment. The methodological classic of the 1960s, Peter Blau and Otis Dudley Duncan's *The American Occupational Structure,* marked a watershed in the current controversy. Analyzing a special 1962 Current Population Survey, these sociologists found that "the chances of upward mobility are directly related to education," that mobility for individuals "is simply a function of their education and their social origins," and that "occupational status in 1962 apparently is influenced more strongly by education than by first jobs." Blau and Duncan, though, qualified these sweeping generalizations in three important aspects.

They argued that education, historically viewed, had been less important to occupational status than it has become in recent decades. The evidence presented here could suggest that, in some ways, this might be true. Second, they stressed the importance of social-class origins (ascription), which they found played a major role in accounting for

[14] Edward Jarvis, M.D., "The Value of Common-School Education to Common Labour," *Report of the United States Commissioner of Education* (Washington, D.C., 1872), 572–585, 577, 574, 585. On Jarvis, see G. N. Grob, *Edward Jarvis and the Medical World of the Nineteenth Century* (Knoxville: University of Tennesse Press, 1978). See also *Report* (1870) 465–466; John Eaton, *Illiteracy and its Social Political and Industrial Effects: An Address* (New York, 1882). Eaton was the U.S. Commissioner of Education.

both education and occupation, notwithstanding the amount of mobility they discovered. Finally, they concluded that "the direct effects of education and father's status are attenuated drastically with the passage of time." A compensatory effect derived from the increasing importance of the accumulation of occupational experience. Blau and Duncan, nevertheless, maintained the importance of education in their conclusions, aside from these basic qualifications.[15] Other researchers, however, have quickly supplemented their findings, revising them to conclude that education is less directly related to occupational attainment.

Ivar Berg, in particular, demonstrated that these commonly perceived relationships between education and jobs are an endemic part of modern democratic mythology.[16] Berg discovered that it is simply impossible to construct an occupational scale according to the intellectual abilities required by diverse occupations. Recent census data (1950, 1960) also contradict the Blau–Duncan findings. Instead of showing education becoming more important, they reveal "a distinct drift of 'better' educated people into 'middle' level jobs and a reduction in the number of 'less' educated people who move up into middle-level jobs. . . ." Education has expanded more rapidly than the net change in skill requirements (there may not be much more of a fit in terms of skills than in the nineteenth century). The problem then becomes whether education—at all levels—might offer less in rewards than it engenders in expectations, making underemployment a serious concern, as it is today.

Berg's, and also Squires', examination of job requirements in a number of firms found self-fulfilling prophesies of the value of educated workers to be rampant among managers. Not only is there overeducation for requirements, there has been little, if any, relationship between changes in educational level and changes in output per worker. (Ryerson and Mann would have shuddered!) And in some plants "educational

15 (New York: John Wiley, 1967), 156, 159, 170, 180, 195, 187; among a large literature (see references in Chs. 1–3, above). See also, John Porter, *The Vertical Mosaic* (Toronto: University of Toronto Press, 1965), 189–195. Revision of traditional relationships has just begun in Canadian sociology, and while there is no critical study yet published, many sociologists support the critiques elaborated below as highly relevant to the Canadian scene. The issues, needless to add, are highly controversial and value-laden, especially in their implications for the nature of modern society and social policy.

16 *Education and Jobs: The Great Training Robbery*, Ch. 1. See also, Squires, "Education," for additional evidence; Jencks *et al.*, *Inequality* (New York: Basic Books, 1972), as examples (see other references in Chs. 1–3, above). See too, David Noble, *America by Design* (New York: Knopf, 1977), esp. Chs. 8–9; Harry Braverman, *Labor and Monopoly Capital* (New York: Monthly Review Press, 1974); Bright, "Automation."

achievement was *inversely* related to performance;" "the less productive workers were slightly better educated." Education, then, may be predictive of initial salary and job title, but not promotion. Finally, in professional and managerial positions, educational achievement, Berg found, was rewarded, rather than performance! "To argue that well-educated people will automatically boost efficiency, improve organizations, and so on may be to misunderstand in a fundamental way the nature of American education, which functions to an important, indeed depressing extent as a licensing agency." [17] Schooling of course serves more of the former role among the less-well educated, but this is hardly what is usually meant by productive skills. These arguments, regardless, are a direct legacy from the nineteenth century; their veracity then and now we have good reason to doubt.

To a significant extent the spokesmen of the labor movement in Canada (and the United States and Great Britain) in the last third of the nineteenth century agreed with the voices of middle-class school promoters in their discussions of the benefits of education; they accepted much of the schools' hegemony. To an important degree, however, labor's views were scored by a tension between a hunger for public schooling and very real doubts about the value of the formal education being offered. To them, education represented something more than just the making of better workmen, in spite of their assent to schooling's value.

That workers desired educational provision can not be doubted. Their case was put forth in the first issue of the *Ontario Workman,* in 1872: "A thorough and general system of education we consider to be one of the first duties of the state; to see that in all its branches it is placed as near as possible within the reach of every son and daughter of the land." The whole body of workmen should be raised by education and mental training to a higher intellectual level, not merely to permit isolated cases of social advancement. As the Hamilton *Palladium of Labor* claimed, "An education is the practical side of American industrial success. In the industries where your working people have the best common school education, there you will find them earning the best wages." This situation, we need to note, was also related to the absence of child labor and therefore to the absence of cheap competition, in labor's didactic participation in educational promotion. For education cut two ways in its benefits for workingmen: First, education was valuable in raising and maintaining wages and standards of labor, while it

---

[17] Berg, *Education,* 40–41, 59, 80–3, Ch. 5, 87, 104; Squires, "Education", 439–440.

restricted the supply of workers. Second, "Educated workmen, skilled workmen, and moral workmen . . . [made] labor respected as well as profitable." [18]

To make better workers was not the sole emphasis of the labor press, and their educational program was not quite that which Ryerson *et al.* had urged. Education ought to be mechanical, scientific, and technical: for the hand and body as well as the mind. They recommended a combination of work and study, four hours of each per day. Having an idea of common-school education different from that of Ryerson, Clarke, Mann, and Jarvis, the spokesmen of the working class sought a preparation in job skills of a different kind, and articulated a different perspective on the place of literacy. What they wanted was in part a schooling that was practical and related to future occupations. "It is generally felt," the *Palladium* echoed, "that our educational methods are too one-sided. They do not develop the constructive faculties as they might. The adoption of industrial education would do much to enable those of the pupils who, on leaving the school follow mechanical operations to take higher positions than they otherwise occupy by reason of the training secured." Traditional forms of practical training were found wanting (vocational and industrial education, which never precisely met these desires, were not introduced into the school curriculum until the 1890s and 1900s). *Fincher's Trades Review,* a Philadelphia working-men's weekly read by and concerned with Canadian labor, reported that apprenticeship was fast declining and that regulation was required; the period of indenture had become too short and incomplete. One problem was that masters neglected the education of their charges.[19]

This neglect was not solely a U.S. concern, as an examination of Upper Canadian indentures reveals. Of the fourteen-odd documents that could be located, representing a handful of nonmanual, skilled, and semiskilled occupations, only half (servant, tailor, carpenter) made any provision for education in the contract. The issue of schooling was not mentioned for a turner, patternmaker, shoemaker, machinist, miller,

---

[18] *Ontario Workman (O.W.),* April 18, 1872; March 13, 1873; *Palladium of Labor (P.O.L.),* (Hamilton, Ontario), May 16, 1885, February 7, 1885. See also *Fincher's Trades Review (F.T.R.),* (1863–1866), a Philadelphia workingmen's weekly, read by and concerned with Canadian labor, which included letters from Canadian workmen: September 24, 1864, February 4, 1865. On the context of working-class attendance, see Davey, "Educational Reform and the Working Class," unpub. PhD. Diss., University of Toronto, 1975.

[19] *O.W.,* May 2, 1872, January 16, 1873, February 12, 1874; *P.O.L.,* December 22, 1883, February 23, 1883, September 19, 1885, August 16, 1884; *F.T.R.,* July 18, 1863, July 11, 1863, November 15, 1863, July 9, 1864, September 24, 1864, May 13, 1865.

draper, or a stonecutter. If the sample is tiny and spans without visible trend a lengthy period, the 50% neglect of schooling remains indicative.[20]

The crux of the issue, in labor's interpretation, was that masters wanted the most work for the least costs. "The desire to make his boys finished workmen, to fit them by night or day schooling for the better comprehension of the business, or to qualify them for advancing in the higher branches, of art and science, scarcely ever enters the master's mind." The sad results left youngsters conscious of their inferiority, not aspiring to any position higher than the one they had been taught, and often slipping to day labor. "Botches" were created among the industrious classes each year.[21]

Education nevertheless was not viewed primarily as job preparation; it represented a higher ideal and a different goal. A boy "should be regarded, rather as the man that will be, than as the future doctor, lawyer, tradesman, farmer or mechanic." Would such education intersect with economic productivity? The *Workman* suggests that workers were not to be educated to increase the value of capital through their labors. They were not simply *to be* educated: "They must educate themselves to think; they must also learn to think for themselves." To a large degree, education was to instill a direction, a goal, and the correct set of personal qualities—all more important than skills or a mere hunger for gold. Education was, in one sense, character-building; it enabled workers to see their calling as useful and dignified. Morals, wisdom, and honorable careers ranked above the skills of the job. Were such men the loyal, punctual, nondisruptive workers the mill-owners desired and Egerton Ryerson promised if allowed to fashion a system of common schools? Education could lead in a rather different direction as the *Palladium* saw it:

> Educate first, agitate afterwards. Ignorance, superstition and timerity [timorousness] are the weapons which our oppressors have used most effectively against us in the past. Secure an education at any cost, put the ballot to its proper use, and then the fall of the venerable structure of legal robbery, alias monopoly, will shake to its centre. . . .[22]

[20] The indentures examined are all those located in the Archives of the Province of Ontario (Toronto). See also D. T. Ruddell, "Apprenticeship in Early Nineteenth Century Quebec," unpub. M. A. Thesis, Laval University, 1969.

[21] *F.T.R.*, September 24, 1864.

[22] *O.W.*, February 13, 1873, January 22, 1873; *F.T.R.*, June 27, 1863, October 22, 1864, September 17, 1864, July 11, 1863; *P.O.L.*, November 24, 1883, November 22, 1884, January 5, 1884. See also Phillips Thompson, *The Politics of Labor* (New York, 1887), 11–14, who claimed that reading would open the eyes of the working man to the injustices of the system. Thompson, a Toronto radical journalist and autodidact, often contributed to the *P.O.L.* under the pseudonym Enjolrus.

Furthermore, the working class was more than a little ambivalent about education and its value; this tension brought contradiction to their apparent endorsement of mass public education:

"A self-made man" awakens in most all a glow of appreciation and regard which we do not feel for the man, equally distinguished for ability and learning he has got, who has been regularly taught in the schools. The latter has had the counter-sign, and has been invited into the fort, the other has scaled the ramparts and conquered his place.

Success without the assistance of education was admired above that "aided" by the schools, in sharp contrast to Ryerson's view. A curious tale related in the *Workman* indicates a further lack of esteem for education-related skills. A man in England, the story went, had been jailed. To obtain bail, he was advised that he must sign his name; overnight he taught himself to do so. The implications drawn are important; there was no a priori reason for illiterates or poor workers to be barred from the ballot. Inability to read or write need not disqualify a man from exercising his rights, nor did it signify an inability to carry them out. A final point is implied: When needed, one could quickly and easily gain some skills of literacy.[23]

Ambivalence went even deeper. For example, *Fincher's Trades Review* reprinted "Proverbs of the Billings Family," which included "If you kan't git clothes and education too, git the clothes." A more interesting notice came from the Lawrence, Massachusetts, Mutual Benefit Society. The society began its operations with a system of bookkeeping for accounts, but "We are now doing it with checks. Our checks are printed on card board, of the following denominations . . . fifty cents, white; one dollar, blue; two dollar, yellow; five dollar, orange; ten dollar, salmon color. We find that this system is much easier than booking. . . ." Store personnel and society members need not even know the decimal system or how to read numbers; the colors differentiated for them. Literacy need not figure in workers' everyday transactions.[24]

More important in understanding the working class' awareness of the contradictions of educational promotion and programs is their analysis of the "evils" of the system. The *Palladium* urged its readers to learn a trade, not to be seduced by "class" education, with its examples in school of millionaires, for "schools love to dwell too much on the achievements of professional men." The school curriculum itself was found to be class-biased, and the ideas of classical literature anti-

23 *O.W.*, April 2, 1874, October 14, 1872.
24 *F.T.R.*, June 27, 1863, February 11, 1865.

workingmen. Or, as Phillips Thompson expressed it, education "if perverted by the inculcation of the untruths and half-truths of bourgeois political economy, is a hindrance rather than a help." This he called "wrong education," tempting the worker with self-aggrandizement and wealth. The system of state education, compulsory by the 1870s, taught reading but "then [gave] them dime novels for perusal, having previously given them a taste for such reading." Such an education—and use of literacy—was hardly desirable; it would not benefit the working class.[25]

The greatest evil of all stood at the pinnacle of the educational system—the university, which all workingmen supported through taxation, but whose expense was prohibitive to most.

> It is an injustice that all the farmers, mechanics, and laborers should be taxed to teach the sons of the wealthy merchants and professional men Latin and Greek, and to support a lot of imported professors at high salaries to inculcate false and undemocratic notions of social caste, and to teach an obsolete system of political economy. As a training for practical life and usefulness, the ordinary university education is well-nigh valueless.

The educational system, from the top down, was biased against the workingman and his children. Lest the working class be falsely accused of anti-intellectualism we note that the *Palladium* urged that as good an education could be secured by well-directed reading.[26]

Reading, moreover, was often discussed in terms of amusement, enchantment, comfort, consolation, and leisure—in brief, noninstrumentally. "Let the torch of intelligence be lit in every household." The family hearth was the place for the taste for reading ("one of the true blessings of life") to commence, and where parents were to guard against the taint of bad books, magazines, or newspapers. Relief from toil came through literature, making "study the more refreshing," and the delights of reading and contemplation brought wisdom "in common with all mankind." Here lay one real value of literacy to workmen, for knowledge is always power, but not only in an economic or political sense.[27]

Similarly, there were reasons more important than book-learning in the establishment of mechanics' institutes, workingmen's reading

[25] *P.O.L.*, November 10, 1883, August 29, 1885, August 16, 1884; Thompson, *Politics,* 17, 58, 83, 151, *P.O.L.*, February 2, 1884.

[26] *P.O.L.*, December 1, 1883; see also Thompson, *Politics,* 61, 171.

[27] *O.W.*, November 22, 1872, December 19, 1872, January 2, 1873, February 12, 1874, March 19, 1874; *P.O.L.*, March 1, 1884, September 1, 1883; *F.T.R.*, October 22, 1864, September 17, 1864, July 11, 1863. See Ch. 7, below; Richard Hoggart, *The Uses of Literacy* (Boston: Beacon Press, 1961).

Reading and working—transmitting information and news through the work group.
"Reader in a work group, New York City, cigar factory," 1909, by Lewis W. Hine.
[International Museum of Photography, George Eastman House]

rooms, and ancillary public institutions. Workers needed a place to
become better acquainted with one another, where their various interests could harmonize, where committees could meet. Two hours of leisure
each day (related to demands for reduced hours) spent in mental and
physical culture "would result in the shame and discomfiture of our
opponents." Knowledge, then, could be power in the purely political
sense, much as Phillips Thompson would have it. Yet mass literacy
need not be a requirement for the development of a shared consciousness, a common political culture, or the exchange of ideas or information. Only a few readers were needed to enlighten a large number
if given the chance of congregation and the customary modes of communication. As E. P. Thompson argues, "Illiteracy by no means excluded men from political discourse." They could listen and participate
in discussion—at work, in reading circles, in pubs, or at ports of call.
Activities such as those of the Luddites and "Captain Swing" support
the argument, and contrary to the typical views of historians such as
Robert Webb, upheavals can take place without printers. It was the
areas lowest in literacy, for example, that experienced the greatest number
of "Swing" actions.

Reading and writing, *Fincher's* found, were less important than the hammer, the sign of workingmen: "Only the hammer is all powerful and peaceful. . . . Without the hammer—a symbol of toil, as the pen is of thought, and the sword is of violence—the world could not exist in comfort and refinement." "The ability to read," moreover, E. P. Thompson reminds us, "was only the elementary technique. The ability to handle abstract and consecutive argument was by no means inborn; it had to be discovered amid almost overwhelming difficulties. . . ." Much more than literacy or education alone is required for cohesion, consciousness, and activity; social structural and economic factors, leadership and organization, psychology and motivation, numbers and opportunity are equally if not more important. Easier communication, which literacy can advance, may aid the process, but literacy is hardly the key variable.[28]

Labor, in spite of its acceptance of hegemony and an apparent clamor for equal educational opportunity, deviated from the major premises of leading schoolmen who sought more education of the working class for greater productivity. Ambivalent about the proper role, form, and content of education, recognizing some contradictions, and often placing its benefits and application quite aside from their jobs, they sought to be free and independent, powerful in ways that would not have pleased the men who desired to have the masses educated. More fundamentally, they did not always equate education solely with the skills (in either an academic or a practical sense) required to gain and perform a good job.

Estimates, such as Horace Mann's, of a 50% greater return to educated laborers and corresponding increases in productivity from specific

[28] *F.T.R.*, March 18, 1865, April 8, 1865, November 7, 1863, January 16, 1864, April 23, 1864; see also October 3, 1863; *P.O.L.*, September 8, 1883. Ironically, Mechanics' Institutes in Canada, as in Britain, tended to be middle class in inspiration and in membership; see J. Donald Wilson, "Adult Education in Upper Canada before 1850," *Journal of Education* (U. B. C.), 19 (1973), 43–54; Foster Vernon, "The Development of Adult Education in Ontario, 1790–1900," unpub. Ed.D. Thesis, University of Toronto, 1969; J. A. Eadie, "The Napanee Mechanics' Institutes," *Ontario History,* 68 (1976), 209–221; E. Royle, "Mechanics' Institutes and the Working Classes, 1840–1860," *The Historical Journal,* 14 (1971), 305–321; Eales, *Lecture.* See also John Foster, "Nineteenth-Century Towns—A Class Dimension," in *The Study of Urban History,* ed. H. J. Dyos (London: Edward Arnold, 1968), 281–300, *Class Struggle in the Industrial Revolution* (London: Weidenfeld and Nicolson, 1974); Patrick Joyce, "The Factory Politics of Lancaster in the Later Nineteenth Century," *Historical Journal,* 18 (1975), 525–553; E. P. Thompson, *The Making of the English Working Class* (New York: Pantheon, 1967), 712–713; R. K. Webb, *The British Working Class Reader, 1790–1848,* (London: Unwin, 1955); Hobsbawm and George Rudé, *Captain Swing* (New York: Pantheon, 1969), Charles Tilly, *From Mobilization to Revolution* (Reading, Mass.: Addison-Wesley, 1978).

skills provided in public schooling, can not be accepted. A 10–20% differential puts the issue into a radically different perspective. Such a difference need not seem so significant to the average workingman, and major questions surround the reasons why he chose—and the majority did—to acquire some education and to send his children to school. An answer must lie in the relationships among the hegemonic functions of the school, the contradictions and ambivalence inherent in working-class attitudes toward education, the noneconomic importance of literacy, and the connection between literacy, skilled work, and its rewards. Equally important questions pertain to how much schooling made a significant difference in wages.

We must ask, moreover, why discussions of the productive contribution of education so rarely addressed specific job skills, beyond abstract thought processes, such as those so disarmingly recounted by Edward Jarvis. Certainly a major answer derives from the recognition of the moral bases of literacy—the moral virtues, attitudes, and behavioral traits—which Egerton Ryerson, Horace Mann, and manufacturers all held central to the making of a productive and malleable labor force. In this, they were undoubtedly correct. As Field and Gintis have found and Dreeben has argued, it is precisely the noncognitive functions of schooling, the concomitants of literacy transmission, which most directly relate to the creation of a workforce acceptable to modern capitalism. Schooling's contribution came from these other kinds of skills. Toward this end, the schools were designed to socialize, prepare, and assimilate the masses—and the schools were attended. Nevertheless, this does not sufficiently answer the basic query of how schooling related to the skills of specific occupations. Neither schoolmen nor labor spokesmen addressed this question to any meaningful degree, although it was a much more serious concern of the latter. So we do not yet know, beyond educated guesses or extrapolations from modern analogues, how much education a carpenter, shoemaker, mechanic, painter, storekeeper, or hotelkeeper would need to do his work. They might need arithmetic, but this could be gained without schooling.[29] Examples of the self-taught readers or writers are almost legendary, and they are central to working-class cultural traditions. But to what extent these skills, the tools based in literacy, were required remains questionable for those not employed

[29] *Massachusetts Teacher*, 15 (1862), 10, May, *Essays*, 23, reinforces the point: "Men who could neither read nor write have lived, some of them not unsuccessfully; but without Arithmetic nobody has ever lived, or can live." Not only did children come to school knowing how to count, as the *Massachusetts Teacher* reported, May implies that arithmetic literacy neither implies or correlates with alphabetic literacy. See also, Bright, "Automation."

in professional or clerical endeavors. Practical job skills were not part of the literacy-centered common school curriculum.

It is very possible that reading was not often required in the search for employment. Advertisements for jobs are rarely found amidst the plethora of announcements and solicitations in nineteenth-century newspapers. Work was most often gained informally, as Gareth Stedman Jones reports for the labor market of London, England, in the second half of the century. Workers circulated among the trades, from one to another in a seasonal pattern:

> Skilled workers could gain information about the availability of work either from press announcements or from local trade union branches. But neither of these channels was really open to the casual worker. The only way he could find out about work was either by chance conversations in pubs or else by tramping around the yards and workshops in his districts . . . being known at local centres of casual work was more important than degree of skills and where character references were not required.[30]

Reading and writing were to such men—a sizeable proportion of the workforce in nineteenth-century cities—relatively inconsequential to their searches for work, perhaps relatively unimportant in doing a good job. Stedman Jones' conclusions probably hold for many skilled workers, journeymen, and artisans as well. The economic—and other—benefits of literacy lay elsewhere.

III

The contradictions of literacy's relationship to work may be further explored in a specific work setting. In this section, we focus on one large lumbering concern, the Hawkesbury Lumber Company, located in the rich timberland of the Ottawa River Valley. Hawkesbury was in important ways a typical large-scale nineteenth-century firm. Lumbering was firstly a primary extractive industry, but it also had a large com-

---

[30] Jones, *Outcast London* (Oxford: Oxford University Press, 1971), 82–83; see also E. J. Hobsbawm, "The Tramping Artisan," in his *Labouring Men* (Garden City, N.Y.: Doubleday Anchor, 1967), 41–74. Skilled literate, and organized, workingmen could of course read about economic conditions, and therefore employment opportunities, in the working class press. The development, circulation (including oral transmission of news, group and shop reading aloud), and impact of the Canadian labor press in this period is obviously critical and merits separate and detailed study. See also, E. P. Thompson, *Making;* Webb, *Reader;* J. F. C. Harrison, *The Early Victorians* (New York: Schocken, 1971).

ponent of secondary processing (or, more properly, industrial) functions. Lumbering, certainly capitalist-based, may be viewed as a transitional operation between traditional, seasonal rhythms and the discipline and internal control of the factory that milling would represent. It was a mixture of two historical developments of economic organization. It represents the large work setting, as 795 men were employed, or rehired, during the years 1887 to 1903. The number hired varied from year to year, from a maximum of 208 in 1888 to a low of 6 in 1906. Rather than indicating the introduction of new technology or mechanization, or a drastic response to business conditions, this fluctuation illustrates the stability of the workforce, as most hands retained their positions.[31]

The Hawkesbury Lumber Company is of special interest, for its detailed records of employment contracts have survived. Ledgers of annual contracts were maintained, for 1887–1888 (Hamilton Brothers) and 1889–1903 (Hawkesbury). Exceptional records, they provide for each employee, contract date, occupation, name, wage rates, and a signature or mark—a measure of literacy.[32] From these records, the occupational and wage structure and the distribution of literate and illiterate workers may be reconstructed.

The horizontal, or functional, structure of occupations is readily established from these records. As Table 5.2 shows, the largest group of workers were the semiskilled, although the group "millmen" may well have included some skilled workers. Skilled workers constituted the

[31] The company was begun by George and William Hamilton of Quebec in 1797, and transformed into a joint-stock venture upon its sale to Blackburn, Egan, Robinson, and Thistle in 1889, taking on the new name of Hawkesbury. A few summary statistics suggest the scope: by 1885, 30 million feet of timber were cut annually and milled by 350 hands, by 1909, the annual yield was 50 million feet. Hawkesbury continued to operate until 1936. The records are found in the Archives of the Province of Ontario (Toronto). On lumber industry, see in general, Michael S. Cross, "The Dark Druidical Groves: The Lumber Community and the Commercial Frontier in British North America to 1854," unpub. PhD. Diss., University of Toronto, 1968; Edward McKenna, "Unorganized Labour versus Management: The Strike at the Chaudière Lumber Mills, 1891," *Histoire Sociale*, 5 (1972), 186–211; and A. R. M. Lower, *The North American Assault on the Canadian Frontier* (Toronto: Ryerson Press, 1938).

On work rhythms, see E. P. Thompson, "Time, Work-Discipline, and Industrial Capitalism," *Past and Present*, 38 (1967), 56–97; Sidney Pollard, "Factory Discipline in the Industrial Revolution," *Economic History Review*, 16 (1963), 254–271.

[32] On signatures and literacy, see Roger Schofield, "The Measurement of Literacy in Pre-Industrial England," in *Literacy in Traditional Societies*, ed. Jack Goody (Cambridge: Cambridge University Press, 1968), 311–325; Kenneth A. Lockridge, *Literacy in Colonial New England* (New York: Norton, 1974). Signatures, it should be noted, slightly underestimate the level of reading literacy, as some men would be able to read and not write.

Table 5.2
Occupational Classification and Literacy: Hawkesbury Lumber Company

	N [a]	Percentage literate		N [a]	Percentage literate
Nonmanual labor			Semiskilled labor		
(8.5%)			(68.8%)		
Foreman	17	88.2	Handyman	21	47.6
Clerk	27	100.0	Teamster	149	36.9
Timekeeper	6	83.3	Courier	1	100.0
Jobber	5	40.0	Lumberman	2	0.0
Lumber inspector	1	100.0	Cook	1	0.0
Contractor	1	100.0	Blockmaker	1	100.0
Total	57	89.5	Fuller	1	100.0
			Housekeeper	1	100.0
Skilled labor			Stableman	3	66.7
(17.7%)			Chainer/raker	9	66.7
Blacksmith	11	81.8	Picket	8	50.0
Carpenter	19	52.6	Spareman	3	0.0
Cutter	28	64.3	Barkman	5	40.0
Millwright	14	57.1	Pileman/piler	69	40.6
Watchman	5	100.0	Stabber	7	71.4
Mechanic	11	90.9	Slideman	16	31.3
Gardener	2	100.0	Chopper	21	28.6
Painter	1	0.0	Loader/striker	6	0.0
Saddler	6	100.0	Boorman	8	50.0
Sawyer	4	50.0	Butter	3	0.0
Trimmer	1	100.0	Millman	99	32.3
Wheelwright	1	100.0	Road Cutter	13	23.1
Miller	1	0.0	Logmaker	14	21.4
Plasterer	1	0.0	Total	462	36.8
Filer	1	100.0			
Edger	6	50.0	Unskilled labor		
Ironworker	7	0.0	(5.1%)		
Total	119	63.9	Laborer	28	35.7
			Choreman/boy	6	16.7
			Total	34	32.4

[a] $N = 672$.

second largest group, twice the number of the nonmanual, three times the unskilled. The diverse processes of work are easily seen from the list, including the extractive and the processing. The largest number of factory jobs (millman, ironworker, mechanic, millwright, etc.)—perhaps one-third of the total—shows the industrial side of operations. Large variations existed in monthly rates of earnings, from $1.00 (a day's work)

Table 5.3
Rates of Wage and Literacy

Rate/month	N^a	%	Percentage literate
$ 1–10	12	1.6	25.0
11–20	298	39.6	43.3
21–30	341	45.4	49.0
31–40	48	6.4	89.6
41–50	40	5.3	72.5
51–60	2	0.3	50.0
61–70	7	0.9	100.0
70+	4	0.5	50.0
Mean	$24.12		
Median	$22.53		

$^a N = 752.$

to $87.00. The mean wage was $24.00, the median $22.50, certainly not atypical for the area or the period (Table 5.3).[33]

How did literacy intersect with the structure of earnings and occupations? Fifty-two percent of employees were literate and 48% were not, though this measure underestimates the level of reading ability (Table 5.4). This was a high rate of illiteracy for Ontario, Canada, and North America in the last quarter of the century, but it reflects the traditionally high rates of Eastern Ontario and the Province of Quebec, and the French Canadian origins of the greatest number of workers.

As elsewhere, literacy did not always result in higher earnings, a fact supportive of the conclusions of this chapter. Among the lowest paid, at $10 or less per month, illiterates dominated (Table 5.3). The succeeding wage levels show near parity, however. These ranges, $21–$30

Table 5.4
Literacy of Workforce

	N^a	%
Literate	413	51.9
Illiterate	382	48.1

$^a N = 795.$

[33] For comparative wage data see McKenna, "Labour," 190; *Royal Commission on the Relationships of Labor and Capital* (Ottawa, 1889), Ontario Evidence. A useful compendium of its four volumes has been edited by Gregory Kealey (University of Toronto Press, 1973).

(which encompassed a plurality of the workforce) and \$11–\$20, together comprised over 80% of employees; herein illiterates were hardly disadvantaged. With the exception of the lowest paid (probably casual or part-time), literate workmen fared little better than their illiterate colleagues. Yet there was a limitation on the level of earnings to which the majority of illiterates could aspire, much as tabulations of urban assessed wealth revealed earlier: 92% earned \$30 or less, compared with 70% of literates. Here, however, it was only the top 12% from which illiterates were largely excluded, as they constituted just 20% of those earning \$31 or more each month. Nevertheless, some illiterates did make it to these higher levels (8%). What such men lacked in education or booklearning, they no doubt compensated for with skill, experience, or common sense. Presumably their employers did not find that their illiteracy made them less productive; so their work was rewarded.[34]

The rewards possible for illiterate workers are also illustrated by their shares in rising wage rates. The contracts in some cases (24% of all) include two rates of remuneration for a workman: the initial wage, used above, and a subsequent higher wage. These men were employed to hold more than one job, their jobs often varying seasonally, showing a versatility of skill if not necessarily a high initial wage or occupational status. Illiterates predominated among men exhibiting this flexibility. One and one-half times as many of them increased earnings in this way as did literate employees, constituting 70% of all increases from \$1–\$10 and 50% of larger ones (Table 5.5). These wage differentials strikingly

Table 5.5
Wage Differentials and Literacy

Change in wages	N [a]	%	Percentage literate
− \$ 1	2	0.3	50.0
0	605	76.1	57.6
+ 1– 5	125	15.7	31.5
6–10	42	5.3	30.9
11–30	20	2.6	50.0

[a] N = 794.

34 Information on workers' ages not included in these records, could be very revealing in this regard. This analysis may be confirmed and supplemented by an examination of the receipt book of the Madawaska Improvement Company (1888–1903) (Provincial Archives of Ontario). These data also show little disadvantage in wages for illiterates, although the records are less complete than the Hawkesbury material. Obviously, more studies of this kind are needed.

demonstrate the abilities of the uneducated to perform several jobs and to benefit directly in their rewards.

Skills of course relate to occupations, a subject of less significance than economic rewards in attempting to evaluate literacy's role. Occupation is also an inadequate measure of class, status, or skill, but still an important issue. As in the larger society, literacy related directly to occupational status in the Hawkesbury operation. The proportions of the literate increased regularly with occupational class, with large differences separating the nonmanual from the skilled and the skilled from the remainder. These sharp divisions did not, however, carry over into wages, contradicting analyses of social or class structure based solely on occupations, a quite common sociological procedure. In fact, skilled workers were more highly paid than nonmanual ones despite literacy differences, and several semiskilled men attained high salaries. In addition, the obvious factory occupations were not all marked by high levels of literacy. Some illiterates, moreover, were able to achieve higher-ranking occupations; 11% of nonmanual and 36% of skilled workers were unable to sign their names. Blacksmiths, carpenters, cutters, jobbers, millwrights, mechanics, millers, and ironworkers could be illiterate. Though largely disadvantaged in occupation, illiterates held a great variety of jobs and were only slightly disadvantaged in earnings. Their lack of schooling did not significantly restrict them in the pay envelope or pocket.

Ninety-six men, longer-term employees, signed more than one contract. The influence of literacy both on this form of persistence within the firm and on their changes in wage rates advances the argument. Illiterates outnumbered literate workers in this group, and they dominated among those who increased earnings (Table 5.6A). Literacy apparently was not the salient factor; more probably the key was skills and performance about which the ledgers are silent. Illiterates' greater persistence is significant; their wage changes are intriguing. Literacy's importance is seen more in the magnitudes of the changes, as literate workers gained a greater proportion of the larger increases ($11–$18), but also in the larger decreases (Table 5.6B). Illiteracy may have placed restraints once more on mobility, but these limits operated in the directions both of rising and of falling, regulating the frequency of changes.

An analysis of literacy's role in a specific work situation, the Hawkesbury Lumber Company, reveals the limits of illiteracy. These operated largely in the occupational dimension, but much less in wages, flexibility, or salary increments. Literacy related to occupation strongly, but not completely, and very little to remuneration. This case study supports and extends the conclusions from the urban inquiry. The Hawkesbury

Table 5.6
Changing Wage Rates: Employees with Two or More Contracts

	Literate	%	Illiterate	%
A. Same rate	9	20.9	7	13.2
Increasing rate	27	62.8	34	64.2
Decreasing rate	7	16.8	12	22.6
Total *a*	43		53	
B. Increase $ 1–5	15	55.6	23	66.7
6–10	7	25.9	10	29.4
11–18	5	18.5	1	2.9
Decrease $ 1–5	4	57.2	9	75.0
6–8	3	42.8	3	25.0

a N = 96.

experience, on the one hand, contradicts the expectations and perceptions of Ryerson and other middle-class school reformers along with one aspect of working class opinion. On the other hand, it provides further support for working class claims that education figured not always or necessarily in work, but could relate more directly to other aspects of life.

IV

In the partly industrial setting of Hawkesbury, literacy did not significantly relate to individual rewards or to job performance; presumably it did not relate to productivity. This section treats the more general question of the connection between education, literacy, and industrialization. Recent research in economic history and development, if far from complete, has begun to contradict the received wisdom and dominant assumption that education is at once central to the process of industrialization and that it must logically precede "take-off into sustained growth." This opinion forms yet another part of the literacy myth. Education and economic development, however, need not be seen as collateral or sequential processes. Productivity and wealth do not necessarily follow from mass literacy, as the histories of Sweden and Scotland, for example, firmly demonstrate. Both achieved mass literacy before the nineteenth century, yet remained desperately poor.

The primary issue is confronted by Roger Schofield, who remarks,

"Today literacy is considered to be a necessary precondition for economic development (and this one may question); but the historian might well ask himself whether this was so in England at the end of the eighteenth century"—or, we might add, North America in the nineteenth. Schofield continues:

> The necessity of literacy as a precondition for economic growth is a persistent theme running through many UNESCO publications [and a great many others]. Correlations between measures of industrialization and literacy both in the past and in the present are established in UNESCO *World Illiteracy at Mid-Century* (Paris, 1957), pp. 177–89. These measures are very general and throw no light on the question of why literacy should be considered essential to economic growth.[35]

In various studies, C. Arnold Anderson and Mary Jean Bowman, in particular, have attempted to demonstrate the ways in which literacy should be considered essential to economic development. Proceeding from the premise that education is one of the few sure roads to economic growth, they find an increasingly common tendency among economists and governments to "justify" education in economic terms (as "human capital"). In 1965, Anderson claimed that "about 40 percent of adult literacy or of primary enrollment [which should be conceptually distinguished] is a threshold for economic development." He added, of course, that the level of education alone is an insufficient condition in a society lacking other prerequisites. Throughout the past decade and a half, their position has been qualified and refined, as they continue to stress the necessity, if not the sufficiency, of a "literacy threshold" for sustained growth or development, a stage to be maintained until a new literacy level, of 70–80% is attained. They have not shown with any precision or direct historical evidence, however, that these thresholds have the significance that is ascribed to them.[36]

[35] Schofield, "Measurement," 312. See also E. Verne, "Literacy"; Introduction, above.

[36] Anderson, "Literacy and Schooling on the Development Threshold: Some Historical Cases," in *Education and Economic Development,* ed. Anderson and Bowman (Chicago: Aldine, 1965), 347–362; Bowman and Anderson, "Concerning the Role of Education in Development," in *Old Societies and New States,* ed. Clifford C. Geertz (New York: Free Press, 1963), 247–279; Bowman and Anderson, "Education and Economic Modernization in Historical Perspective," presented to the Fourth International Congress of Economic History, 1968, now published in *Schooling and Society,* ed. Lawrence Stone (Baltimore: Johns Hopkins, 1976), 3–19. The latter contains the best summary of their work. The roots of the human capital school of economists, largely dominated by Gary Becker and Theodore Schultz are found in these approaches. For a useful critical analysis of approaches in the economics of education, see W. G. Bowen, "Assessing the Economic Contribution of Education," in *The Economics of Education,* 1, ed. Mark Blaug (Harmondsworth: Penguin, 1968), 67–100.

Another social scientist has discovered a different explanatory approach to the literacy-and-education–development connection. From his data, David McClelland finds that investment in education at the elementary or literacy level is inadequate and does not correlate positively with growth rates. He argues that:

> Primary school attendance has a doubtful relationship to significant improvements, in the labor force or even to literacy itself. That is, the marginal product of a primary school education would seem likely to be low, because skilled artisans may function as well without being literate. Furthermore, primary school attendance is not enough by itself to lift a person to the level of being able to perform jobs characteristic of the middle class.

A strong relationship, however, derives from postprimary education, if the lag-time between training and its effect on the economy is considered. "Education is a long-term investment from the economic point of view," McClelland concludes. This approach seems more sound, for an historical context, though problems do remain, especially when it is applied to the industrial revolution. Nevertheless, distinguishing between levels of training, and critically differentiating literacy from higher and more technical education makes more sense when seeking to explicate and understand education's contribution to economic change; literacy alone should not be seen as representing the level of skills that is required for major development.[37]

What about the past, and the transition to the factory itself, in the transformation of modes of production and the work-setting for industrial capitalism? In the most general sense, as John Talbott has remarked, "in the first decades of industrialization, the factory system put no premium on even low-level intellectual skills. Whatever relationships existed between widespread literacy and early industrial development must have been quite roundabout."[38] "Roundabout" is hardly a precise

---

[37] "Does Education Accelerate Economic Growth?," *Economic Development and Cultural Change*, 14 (1966), 262, 266. See also, M. W. Flinn, "Social Theory and the Industrial Revolution," in *Social Theory and Economic Change*, ed. Burns and Saul (London: Tavistock, 1967), 9–34; David Landes, *The Unbound Prometheus* (Cambridge: Cambridge University Press, 1969).

[38] "The History of Education," *Daedalus*, 100 (1971), 141. For contrary views, see Webb, *Reader*, 15, *passim.*; Bowman and Anderson, "Education." See also D. J. Treiman, "Industrialization and Social Stratification," in *Social Stratification*, ed. E. C. Laumann (Indianapolis: Bobbs Merrill, 1970), 207–234. The most recent restatement of the normative view may be found in E. G. West, "Literacy and the Industrial Revolution," *Economic History Review*, 31 (1978), 369–383. I find it no more persuasive than other versions.

description, but it is an improvement on theories of linear, deterministic causal connections. We can improve upon that description, I believe.

Firstly, contradicting those who argue for the productive value of educated and literate labor's skills, the relationship in the first, English Industrial Revolution was less than roundabout. Early industrialization was disruptive of education, and literacy rates fell or stagnated as a result. There was little demand for new or increased labor skills, and more importantly, the demand for child labor, in England and elsewhere, greatly reduced the chances for a lower-class child to attend school. Factory schools were, on the whole, rare, ineffectual, and very irregularly attended. Secondary education was unheard of for the children of the working class.[39]

The consequence, Roger Schofield and Michael Sanderson have shown, was reflected directly in the literacy rates of late eighteenth- and early nineteenth-century England. Sanderson found that "the English Industrial Revolution cannot be seen as one nourished by rising educational standards at least at the elementary level," and from more recent research comes broader, comparative support for his conclusions.[40] The stagnation or decline in literacy, which varied regionally, did not impede the upsurge of economic growth, because the nature of this industrialization made very low literacy demands on the educational system. Or, as Schofield explains:

> Thus, insofar as economic growth in this period entailed the acquisition of a large number of practical skills by a growing proportion of the population, developments in literacy and education were probably largely irrelevant to it. And, insofar as economic growth resulted from the increased productivity of labor brought about the shift from domestic to factory production, literacy

[39] Michael Sanderson, "Education and the Factory in Industrial Lancashire, 1780–1840," *Economic History Review*, 20 (1967), 266, "Social Change and Elementary Education in Industrial Lancashire, 1780–1840," *Northern History*, 3 (1968), 131–154. David Levine, in *Family Formation in An Age of Nascent Capitalism* (New York: Academic Press, 1977), 28ff and in unpublished work, presents important additional evidence of this effect of early industrialization. The labor press cited above made many of the same points, as did both the commissioners and the witnesses in *The Royal Commission on the Relations of Labour and Capital.*

[40] "Literacy and Social Mobility in the Industrial Revolution," *Past and Present,* 56 (1972), 75, 102. See the critique of this paper by Thomas Laqueur, *ibid.,* 64 (1974), 96–107 and Sanderson's reply, 108–112; Laqueur's *Religion and Respectability* (New Haven: Yale University Press, 1976), "Working-Class Demand and the Growth of English Elementary Education," in *Schooling and Society,* ed. Stone, 192–205. In support of Sanderson's interpretation, see Levine, *Family Formation;* Richard Johnson, "Notes"; W. B. Stephens, "Illiteracy and Schooling in the Provincial Towns, 1640–1870," in *Urban Education in the 19th Century,* ed. David Reeder (London: Taylor and Francis, 1977), 27–48, among Stephens' studies.

and education were also probably largely irrelevant for many of the new industrial occupations recruited a mainly illiterate work force. . . .

"Knack," as Sanderson terms it, and new modes of organizing labor in industrial production were of greater importance than book-learning or literacy skills in the process of industrialization.

In the historical case of English industrialization, there are firm grounds on which to part company with those who must relate mass education directly to economic development. England had reached the 40% "threshold" of literacy by 1750 (at least for males), and it remains for researchers to isolate an exception to that rule of thumb for economic development. Stephens, for one, finds that literacy levels were "manifestly related to some extent to the economic function" of urban as well as industrial places. Throughout England, towns that experienced industrial development suffered declining literacy levels, as did other, large and growing centers. In France, with later and slower industrial development, the relationship with literacy and schooling, in the Départment du Nord, paralleled the English case. Furet and Ozouf conclude that "not only does modern industrialization not create a demand for skilled labour, it also tends to depress urban literacy rates." Peter Flora, finally, in a large-scale macroanalysis of literacy and modernization in 94 countries from 1850–1965, discovers that contrary to the typical assumptions, no direct connection existed between literacy and industrialization (or urbanization). Both the linear causal theories and threshold-level notions seem so vague and overly simplistic, as well as so empirically contradictory, as to be meaningless. The relationship of higher levels of education to development requires further detailed study, although postprimary education played no large role at this early stage (unless, however, it contributed to the development of inventors, technological innovators, and entrepreneurs—a very different matter from these traditionally assumed connections with the main labor force.) As Schofield aptly expressed it, "For England, at least [and we may now add "elsewhere"], the usual causal relationships between literacy and economic growth might probably be reversed. In this alternative perspective the reduction in illiteracy in nineteenth-century England would appear more as a cultural change brought about by economic growth than as the cause of growth." [41] Reversing traditional explanations is critically

[41] "Dimensions of Illiteracy, 1750–1850," *Explorations in Economic History*, 10 (1973), 452–453, 454; Stephens, "Illiteracy," 32. See Francois Furet and Jacques Ozouf, "Literacy and Industrialization," *Journal of European Economic History*, 5 (1976), 26, 5–44, for France, and their *Lire et écrire* (Paris: Éditions de Minuit, 1977); Peter Flora, "Historical Processes of Social Mobilization," in *Building States and Nations,*

important in disentangling these presumed relationships, and in understanding the historical processes of change and development. Attention to the chronological sequence of developments—in industrialization, economic growth, literacy, and education—(as is suggested presently) introduces a conceptualization that fits the historical contexts.

If not education as preparation for productive, skilled labor, then what? We must return to the alternative perspective on skills and literacy elaborated above. Sidney Pollard and Edward Thompson, in pathbreaking analyses, have shown that the laboring population had to be trained for factory work and taught industrial habits, rules, and rhythms. Traditional social habits and customs did not fit the new patterns and requirements of industrial life; they had to be discredited and replaced with new, "modern" forms of behavior, intended to transform, in part, the culture of the working class. Literacy could be far from central in the creation of an industrial (or also commercial, urban) workforce, depending on time and circumstance, although its potential for assimilation was soon recognized. As Pollard illustrates, it was not necessarily the better worker but rather the stable one who was worth more to manufacturers; "often, indeed, the skilled apprenticed man was at a discount, because of the working habits acquired before entering a factory." [42] The problem of course was one of discipline, as factory-owners experienced great difficulties in training men to "renounce their desultory habits of work, and identify themselves with the unvarying regularity of the complex automation." Discipline—and new standards of behavior—were required to produce goods on time. To orient the factory hands to these routines, rules became the norm: "Work rules, formalized, impersonal and *occasionally printed,* were symbolic of the new industrial relationships [emphasis added]." No primacy was to be accorded literacy (here and at first) in solving the most difficult of industrial capitalism's conundrums.

---

ed. S. N. Eisenstadt and S. Rokkan (Beverly Hills: Sage, 1973), I, 213–258, for additional cross-cultural, aggregative evidence in support of the argument; Verne, "Literacy."

    [42] Pollard, "Factory Discipline," 225. See also, his *Genesis of Modern Management* (Harmondsworth: Penguin, 1968), esp. Ch. 5; Thompson, "Time, Work-Discipline"; Keith Thomas, "Work and Leisure in Pre-Industrial Societies," *Past and Present,* 29 (1964); Robert Malcolmson, *Popular Recreations in English Society, 1700–1850* (Cambridge: Cambridge University Press, 1973); Herbert Gutman, "Work, Culture, and Society in Industrializing America, 1815–1919," *American Historical Review,* 78 (1973), 531–588; J. F. C. Harrison, *Victorians;* Field, "Reform"; Johnson, "Notes"; Stephen Marglin, "What Do Bosses Do?," *Review of Radical Political Economics,* 6 (1974), 60–112, 7 (1975), 20–38; Inkeles and Smith, *Modern,* Ch. 11.

To "educate" the workers was necessary. But it was not an education in reading and writing; rather it was "the need to educate the first generation of factory workers to a new factory discipline, [part of] the widespread belief in human perfectability . . . but one of their consequences was the preoccupation with the character and morals of the working class which are so marked a feature of the early stages of industrialization." [43] Toward this end—the reshaping of character, behavior, morality, and culture—factory owners and other capitalists joined with social reformers and school promoters (as in North America) seeking alternative, more effective and efficient approaches to socialization. Increasingly, we have seen, they turned to public schooling, literacy transmission, and mass institutions; the timing of the processes made for crucial differences in economic development on the two sides of the Atlantic.

Thompson highlights the transition, focusing more closely on the importance of precise and mechanically maintained clock-time in the shift to the factory. Regardless of the need for literacy to tell time, "the bell would also remind men of [time's] passing. . . . Sound served better than sight, especially in the growing manufacturing districts," as the first generation was taught the new routine by its masters. The schools could also contribute to this training; they could be useful in inculcating "time-thrift," among other industrial habits, notwithstanding that they might give virtually no attention to specific job skills. Charity schools, for example, were praised for teaching industry, frugality, order, regularity, and punctuality. By the time children reached six or seven years of age, they should have been "habituated, not to say naturalized to Labour and Fatigue;" the training of children of the poor was to begin at age four. In the attempt to establish the hegemony of the school, instruction intervened in working-class culture, to limit its reproduction in the interests of social order, properly trained labor, and normatively socialized citizens. From charity and monitorial schools to "reformed," less coercive methods in the 1830s, children were taught the moral bases. Kept constantly occupied, their ceaseless activity in the school was structured by rules and discipline in the effort to replace "that unproductive activity called play," as new forms of behavior and conduct represented the approved and rewarded standard. The parallels between the rules of the school and the rules of the factory were not overlooked by manufacturers or educators either: "Once within the gate,

---

[43] Richard Arkwright, quoted in Pollard, "Factory Discipline," 258, 258 (emphasis added), 268; Johnson, "Notes," provides additional examples.

the child entered the new universe of disciplined time. . . . Once in attendance, they were under military rule."[44] Discipline was modified with time, especially with the further articulation of the moral bases of literacy; both the school and the factory became important agents for productivity and social change, in reciprocal yet subtle balance.

In England, the value of formal education was increasingly recognized. Literacy, it was grasped, could ease the transition and assimilation of the working class and the poor to industrial and "modern" social habits, if provided in carefully structured institutions. To destroy traditional attitudes, culture, and habits of work was far from an easy or simple task, as many researchers have discovered. Nor was it accomplished in one generation or without great conflict. "Coercion," John Harrison summarizes, "had to be applied in various forms, from strict factory rules to the inculcation [in schools] of precepts of self-discipline." The latter of course were more effective and efficient in dealing with an increasing population at a time of great change; it also permitted an attempt at the reformation of adults through the inculcation of morality and self-restraints in the children. As a result, the process of assimilation was closely tied to the spread of literacy.[45] Literacy's importance can not be understood in isolation, or in terms of self-advancement or skills; rather, its significance lies in its relation to the transmission of morals, discipline, and social values. As R. P. Dore concluded for a different culture, Tokugawa, Japan:

> But what does widespread literacy do for a developing country? At the very least it constitutes a training in being trained. The man who has in childhood submitted to some processes of disciplined and conscious learning is more likely to respond to further training, be it in a conscript army, in a factory, or at lectures arranged by his village agricultural association.[46]

Training in being trained, as Dore aptly puts it, is the crucial job-preparation and a problem for industrialism. The English example is instructive in this respect, yet the North American experience differed

---

[44] Thompson, "Time, Work-Discipline," 64, 84–85; Johnson, "Notes," 46–48, *passim.* See, for example, Allan Greer, "The Sunday Schools of Upper Canada," *Ontario History* 67 (1975), 169–184. See also, Bowles and Gintis, *Schooling;* Gintis, "Education"; Field, "Reform"; Inkeles and Smith, *Modern.*

[45] Harrison, *Victorians,* 135–136; Johnson, "Notes"; Phillip McCann, ed., *Popular Education and Socialization in the Nineteenth Century* (London: Methuen, 1977); A. P. Donajgrodzki, ed., *Social Control in Nineteenth Century Britain* (London: Croom Helm, 1977).

[46] *Education in Tokugawa Japan* (London: Routledge, Kegan Paul, 1967), 292.

greatly in timing and in the sequence of change. England industrialized well before literacy reached universal proportions (not very much beyond a 40% "threshold"); formal education was not an integral part of the origins of her transition, and there is little role for a lag-time for educational investments in *early* industrialization. The transition to the factory and industrial capitalism was far from easy—marked by intense conflict, violence, riots, strikes, Luddism, Chartism. Mass schooling tended to follow this first set of changes; its impact was felt later.

On the contrary, North American development, particularly Canadian industrialization, but also that in the United States, came comparatively much later. Importantly, it followed the attainment of near-universal levels of literacy (among the white population) and the establishment and expansion of public systems for mass elementary education (though not much secondary schooling). As the result of the timing—and the linkages on several levels—between changes that were not merely chronologically coincidental, literacy and schooling were intimately related to social and economic development. Alexander Field's Massachusetts case study provides the best analysis available thus far, although it is not flawless. In this, the earliest North American industrial revolution, Field shows that manufacturers actively supported and participated in educational reform and expansion in efforts to resolve the social tensions arising from change and to secure a properly socialized work force, and not a more highly skilled one. Their reasons for promoting education were social as well as economic (the two were inextricably linked) in their response to the perceived need to confront the difficulties of the transformation. To protect society and property, as well as to organize, control, and increase production, they sought—with the school promoters themselves—more moral, orderly, disciplined, deferential, and contented workers: the expected result of the hegemony of the moral economy of literacy. Schooling of course also contributed more broadly to the socialization and formation of the urban, but nonindustrial workforce. In much of North America, moreover, education *preceded* industrialism. While other detailed case studies are urgently required, widely scattered evidence, from educational, working-class, and economic history illustrates the importance of the earlier reform of education in North America and its impact on socioeconomic development.[47]

[47] See, in support of this approach, the important recent studies of Field, "Reform"; Gutman, "Work"; Marglin, "Bosses"; Katz, "Origins of Public Education"; Daniel T. Rodgers, "Tradition, Modernity, and the American Worker," *Journal of Interdisciplinary History*, 7 (1977), 655–681; Bowles and Gintis, *Schooling*. For one representative, contemporary view, see John Eaton, *Illiteracy*.

Therefore, I advance the hypothesis that the transition to both commercial and industrial capitalism in North America was a smoother one than in England, and perhaps elsewhere.[48] Without ignoring or diminishing the significance of conflict and resistance, which certainly were present, their potential may well have been reduced as one direct consequence of the comparatively earlier and more extensive educational development and its intimate reciprocal relationship to economic change and industrialization. Schooling, in this formulation, paved the way for economic transformation, pointing to the function of lag-time at the elementary level. Industrial development apparently did not have the same destructive impact on education either. We also know that North American educational reformers and manufacturers were aware of the problems taking place abroad, and without assigning the conspiratorial or omniscient roles such as would belie their very real confusion and fears, we can allow that they benefitted from the English experience and from their not having to face the "first" Industrial Revolution.[49] This was one key purpose of the education that Ryerson and other middle-class reformers promoted, as they sought to school the masses in the cause of social and national development and greater productivity.

To do so, it was essential to break preindustrial work habits, to "Canadianize" or "Americanize" immigrants and workers, removing them from traditional origins and habits. The transmission of literacy in the interest of cognitive skills was of secondary importance. Literacy, though in its contribution to proper education and its relationship to noncognitive training was, central in schooling. Print literacy had important socializing functions, both direct and indirect ones; literacy training, for example, served to regularize and discipline behavior. So, in North America, education could replace some of the coercion of English labor to strict factory rules and internalized self-discipline. In the long run, education was more effective and efficient than overt coercion; certainly, it was less disruptive. The provision of mass schooling; the working class' acceptance of it, though a questioning one; and universal, public education all served this direction: promoting discipline, morality, and the "training in being trained" that mattered most in the creation and

[48] At this stage of research, this contention must remain largely hypothetical. We know all too little about the transition in Canada, and comparative studies of Anglo-America are sadly lacking. Recent work by Charles Tilly and Edward Shorter on strikes in France suggests one approach, though an exclusive focus on strike action would obscure many issues.

[49] The writings of Ryerson and Mann, with their frequent European references, make this clear. See also the important discussion by Thomas Bender, *An Urban Vision: Ideas and Institutions in Nineteenth-Century America* (Lexington: University of Kentucky Press, 1975).

preparation of a modern industrial and urban work force. These were the purposes of the school—and one use of literacy.[50]

[50] This is, of course, the mere sketch of a theory, for many questions surrounding the actual experience of schooling remain unanswered: the lines of future research should be clear, however. There is, for example, the problem of irregular attendance which was widespread. Did this militate against the schools' "success"? Quite simply we do not yet know how much exposure to the routine and the message of schools was required for sufficient training. The role of non-English-speaking immigrants must be considered as well. For a fascinating argument on a closely related theme, that of the sanitation movement, see Richard L. Schoenwald, "Training Urban Man," in *The Victorian City*, ed. H. J. Dyos and Michael Wolff (London: Routledge, Kegan Paul, 1973), 669–692.

The presumed effects of literacy and "alphabetization" on personality and the regularization and standardization of behavior may be important in this regard. See below, but see also the speculations of Marshall McLuhan, *The Gutenberg Galaxy* (Toronto: University of Toronto Press, 1962), *Understanding Media* (New York: McGraw-Hill, 1964); G. H. Bantock, *The Implications of Literacy* (Leicester: Leicester University Press, 1966); Jack Goody and Ian Watt, "The Consequences of Literacy," in *Literacy in Traditional Societies*, ed. Goody, 27–68; Goody, *The Domestication of the Savage Mind* (Cambridge: Cambridge University Press, 1977). There is also a large but very inconclusive psychological literature in this area. Among recent work, the most interesting include the studies of Michael Cole, Sylvia Scribner, and Patricia F. Greenfield (cited in Ch. 6, Note 34).

The experience of Quebec in the nineteenth century illustrates vividly the problems of the transition in a society without mass literacy; see *Royal Commission on the Relation of Labor and Capital*, Quebec Evidence. See also Michael Bliss' interesting attempts to explain manufacturers' lack of understanding of these problems: "Employers, as representative as anyone else of prevailing social mores, were often confused and puzzled when faced with insistence that the familiar rules of the game should not be changed, and not in their favour," "A Living Profit: Studies in the Social History of Canadian Business, 1883–1911," unpub. PhD. Diss., University of Toronto, 1972; 137, 148, 157; published as *A Living Profit* (Toronto: McClelland and Stewart, 1974), Ch. 3.

6

Literacy and Criminality

"First, such a system of general education amongst the people is the most effectual prevention of pauperism, and its natural companions, misery and vice." [1] With this statement, made early in his career as Chief Superintendent of Education for Upper Canada, Egerton Ryerson embraced a central tenet of the mid-nineteenth-century school promoter. That education could prevent criminality, if not cure it, was integral to school reformers' programs; and they marshalled reams of evidence, rhetorical and statistical, to prove the perceived relationship between ignorance, or lack of education, and criminality. In their formulations of this social problem, ignorance and crime were associated not only with each other but also with illiteracy, the visible and measurable sign of a lack of schooling.

The prominence accorded formal schooling and instruction in literacy for the masses as social insurance against criminality and disorder forms one significant example of the broad new consensus about education that emerged throughout Anglo-America by mid-century. At a time of massive social change, education increasingly was seen as the dominant tool for social stability in societies in which stratification by social class had replaced traditional paternalistic control by rank and deference and in which wage labor and its concomitant higher rates of physical mobility destroyed traditional community controls. The changing scale and bases of society, as we have seen, demanded the creation of new institutions, like mass school systems, to aid in the inculcation of restraint,

[1] Ryerson, "Report on a System of Public Elementary Instruction for Upper Canada," in *Documentary History of Education in Upper Canada (D.H.E.)*, ed. J. G. Hodgins, 6 (Toronto, 1899), 143.

235

order, discipline, integration—the correct rules for social and economic behavior in a changing and modernizing context. No longer could proper social morality and values be transmitted successfully by informal and traditional means; the transformation necessitated formal institutions to provide morally grounded instruction—aided, eased, and speeded by carefully structured provision of literacy. Literacy became the vehicle for the efficient training of the population and the maintenance of hegemony. Morality without literacy was more than ever seen as impossible; literacy alone, however, was potentially dangerous. Thus the nineteenth-century educational consensus was rooted in the moral bases of literacy; the reduction of crime and disorder ranked high among its functions of socialization. The development and acceptance of this view of education constitutes yet another aspect of the "literacy myth," its expectations permeating thinking about criminality today.[2]

Despite the existence of this unified attitude toward the place of the school in society and the goals of education, the connections advanced between education, literacy, and the reduction of crime and disorder, or conversely, between illiteracy and criminality, were often less than satisfactory or compelling. Egerton Ryerson's statements, consequently, were not always clear, especially regarding the role of illiteracy. To a significant extent, the moral importance of schooling represented the crucial factor, but especially in their use of the statistics of illiteracy, school promoters in Canada and elsewhere confused their arguments, uncertain at times about what form of schooling would best serve their purposes. Their focus on schooling, moreover, obscured the role of other factors that contributed to criminality and made their notions of causality less than convincing. In spite of their explanations, criminality—or, more properly, arrest and conviction—related to much more than illiteracy. Illiteracy, to be sure, was often symptomatic of poverty and lower-class status, which were also associated with arrest

---

[2] See, for example, The President's Commission on Law Enforcement and the Administration of Justice, *Report* (Washington, D.C.: Government Printing Office, 1967); National Advisory Commission on Civil Disorders, *Report* (Washington, D.C.: GPO, 1968); James B. Conant, *Slums and Suburbs* (New York: McGraw-Hill, 1961); R. A. Dentler and M. E. Warshawer, *Big City Drop-Outs and Illiterates* (New York: Praeger, 1965); David M. Gordon, *Problems in Political Economy: An Urban Perspective* (Lexington, Mass.: D. C. Heath, 1971); Stanton Wheeler, "Delinquency and Crime," in *Social Problems: A Modern Approach,* ed. Howard S. Becker (New York: Free Press, 1966), 201–276; I. K. Feierabend, R. L. Feierabend, and B. A. Nesvold, "Social Change and Political Violence: Cross-National Patterns," in *The History of Violence in America,* ed. H. D. Graham and T. R. Gurr (New York: Bantam Books, 1969), 632–687. Examples of this view are legion; education has long formed a central part of anti-crime social policies and of criminology.

and punishment, but it was only one element among a complex of factors. Ethnicity, class, sex, and the suspected crime, rather than illiteracy alone, determined conviction, as those with fewest resources were most often convicted. Systematic patterns of punishment, apparently, might relate to factors other than guilt alone.

The link between social inequality and the distribution of literacy, on the one hand, and factors of class, ethnicity, and sex, on the other, was vital. Ascribed characteristics determined social stratification, access to economic opportunity, social discrimination, and apparently judicial treatment, too. This contradicted much of the school promoters' rhetoric about the advantages of educational achievement in countering factors of birth—a key promise of modern society. Literacy, the evidence suggests, in spite of schoolmen's arguments and more recent restatements, did not relate directly to individual advancement or to social progress as exemplified by a reduction of criminality. Similarly, illiteracy alone did not relate solely or unambiguously to criminality, nor to poverty or immobility. The centrality of literacy in educational rhetoric and the promise of schooling itself, past as well as present, demand a revised account. The case of criminality, significantly, supports the emerging outlines of a new historical sociology of education, in countering the "literacy myth."

In view of these considerations, this chapter focuses upon the relationship between criminality and illiteracy perceived and discussed by school promoters. Their causal notions and their data are first examined; then they are tested through an analysis of a nineteenth-century gaol (jail) register that included literacy among its data.

I

The extent of criminality was among the most pressing concerns of Upper Canadians in the mid-nineteenth century. Revealing deep tensions and pervasive insecurity in a time of social change, many asked with others in Anglo-America, What has caused this apparent increase in crime and violence; what produces criminality in the populace? The complex answers given to these questions included immigration, poverty, urbanism, immorality, ignorance, and of course illiteracy. These forces, at work in Upper Canada as elsewhere, were woven into a causal explanation of criminality. In these explanations, the connections between ignorance, illiteracy, and criminality, always crucial, formed a central assumption of those who attempted to build and expand systems of mass schooling. To them, education was fundamental to the prevention of crime and disorder.[3]

Crime in Upper Canada, it was thought, was intimately connected to "an influx of criminal elements from outside the country, and particularly from Ireland." To Ryerson, immigrants were "notoriously destitute of intelligence and industry, as they are of means of subsistence." Neglect of schooling, idleness, and poverty were the causes of this social problem, and foreigners were the greatest offenders. Cities, moreover, were the scene of the greatest difficulty; they represented the seedbed of crime and were of course the centers of reform attention. Crime, according to Ryerson, "may be said in some sort to be hereditary, as well as infectious, . . . to multiply wretchedness and vice . . . [as] the gangrene of pauperism in either cities or states is almost incurable. The city, especially Toronto, provided his usual examples, and throughout his tenure in office he regularly supplied evidence from gaols and prisons to show that inmates came from the most populous places. Summarizing this widely held belief, Michael Katz has concluded, "In the lexicon of reformers the first fact about crime was its urban nature." Criminals and the impoverished were not seen as individuals; rather, they represented a new criminal and pauper class, resulting from social change, which frightened reformers and others in the middle class. There was general agreement on these points throughout Anglo-America and in much of the west.[4]

[3] J. J. Bellomo, "Upper Canadian Attitudes Towards Crime and Punishment," *Ontario History*, 64 (1972), 12, 13; J. M. Beattie, *Attitudes Towards Crime and Punishment in Upper Canada, 1830–1850: A Documentary Study* (Toronto: University of Toronto Centre of Criminology, 1977); Susan Houston, "Politics, Schools and Social Change in Upper Canada," *Canadian Historical Review*, 53 (1972), 249–271; Rainer Baehre, "The Origins of the Penitentiary System in Upper Canada," *Ontario History*, 69 (1977), 185–207. Beattie's collection of documents is very useful.

[4] Bellomo, "Attitudes," 12; *Journal of Education (J.E.)*, 1 (1848), 300; Ryerson, "Report," 143; Katz, *The Irony of Early School Reform* (Cambridge, Mass.: Harvard University Press, 1968), 170–171. See also, Houston, "The Victorian Origins of Juvenile Delinquency," *History of Education Quarterly*, 12 (1972), 254–280; David J. Rothman, *The Discovery of the Asylum* (Boston: Little, Brown, 1971); Raymond Mohl, *Poverty in New York, 1783–1825* (New York: Oxford University Press, 1971); Carl Kaestle, *The Evolution of an Urban School System* (Cambridge, Mass.: Harvard University Press, 1973); Carroll Smith Rosenberg, *Religion and the Rise of the American City* (Ithaca: Cornell University Press, 1971); Robert Mennel, *Thorns and Thistles* (Hanover, N.H.: University Press of New England, 1973); Steven L. Schlossman, *Love and the American Delinquent* (Chicago: University of Chicago Press, 1977); Katz, "Origins of the Public School," *History of Education Quarterly*, 16 (1976), 381–407; J. J. Tobias, *Crime and Industrial Society in the Nineteenth Century* (Harmondsworth: Penguin, 1972); David Phillips, *Crime and Authority in Victorian England* (London: Croom Helm, 1977); A. P. Donajgrodzki, ed., *Social Control in Nineteenth Century Britain* (London: Croom

These factors were associated with the causes of criminality; ignorance, however, was its putative source. Ryerson and many of his contemporaries urged that their systems of popular education were the most effective preventatives of ignorance, pauperism, misery, and vice.[5] How schooling was to accomplish this, and, conversely, how the lack of schooling resulted in criminality were points on which the school promoters were less clear. At least this was where their statements became vague. To document the apparent relationship and to urge prevention through education was one thing; to explain it was quite another.

Egerton Ryerson enunciated the commonly perceived connection in its starkest and most direct form in his first report.

> Now the Statistical Reports of Pauperism and crime in different countries, furnish indubitable proof that ignorance is the fruitful source of idleness, intemperance and improvidence, and these are the fosterparents of pauperism and crime. The history of every country in Europe may be appealed to in proof and illustration of the fact . . . that pauperism and crime prevail in proportion to the absence of education amongst the labouring classes, and that in proportion to the existence and prevalence of education amongst these classes, is the absence of pauperism and its legitimate offspring.

To this he would soon add the history of Upper Canada. Here, however, Ryerson succinctly stated that ignorance—the lack of schooling—was the first factor in a life of crime. Simply, "the condition of the people and the extent of crime and violence among them follow in like order" from the state of education. Among other evidence he cited English Poor Law Commissioners ("a principal cause of [Northumberland's lack of crime] arises from the education they receive") and the example of Prussia's school system.[6] Others in Upper Canada concurred. The Toronto *Globe,* which disagreed with Ryerson on many issues, declared: "Educate your people and your gaols will be abandoned and your police will be disbanded; all the offenses which man commits against his own peace will be comparatively unknown. . . ." Education was not only effectual; it was also the cheapest agency of prevention:

Helm, 1977); Phillip McCann, ed., *Popular Education and Socialization in the Nineteenth Century* (London: Methuen, 1977); Roger Lane, "Crime and the Industrial Revolution: British and American Views," *Journal of Social History,* 7 (1974), 287–303.

[5] See Alison Prentice, "The Social Thought of Egerton Ryerson" (unpub. paper, 1970), "The School Promoters: Education and Social Class in Nineteenth Century Upper Canada," unpub. Ph.D. Diss., University of Toronto, 1974. See also, Walter Houghton, *The Victorian Frame of Mind* (New Haven: Yale University Press, 1957); Susan Houston, "The Impetus to Reform," unpub. Ph.D. Diss., University of Toronto, 1974; the literature cited above.

[6] Ryerson, "Report," 143, 143–144. See also, Phillips, *Crime,* 154–158.

"The education of the people forms part of the machinery of the State for the prevention of crime." [7] Costs and public expenses were important, and often central to the school promoters' arguments. To them, schools were both cheaper than gaols and prisons and a better investment. Naturally, they felt that "it is much better to prevent crime by drying up its sources than by punishing its acts." [8] The school represented a form of police.

Ignorance and illiteracy, as Ryerson argued, were the first causes of poverty and crime, the latter two in turn being inextricably linked. Each was seen to cause the other, particularly among immigrants and in cities.[9] The result was a simple causal explanation or model of criminality: ignorance caused idleness, intemperance, and improvidence, which resulted in crime and poverty. Ryerson and other promoters saw crime not only as the inevitable offspring of this chain of factors, but they also labelled each factor a crime itself. For example, idleness and ignorance were more than causes, they were also offenses: "If ignorance is an evil to society, voluntary ignorance is a crime against society . . . if idle mendicancy is a crime in a man thirty years of age, why is not idle vagrancy a crime in a boy ten years of age? The latter is the parent of the former." [10]

Ignorance also led to poverty, and education, conversely, to success. The *Globe* agreed: "If we make our people intelligent, they cannot fail to be prosperous." The poor, therefore, were ignorant, often living lives of crime and withholding their children from school—preparing the future class of criminals. Families and parents were blamed for the prevalence of ignorance, nonattendance, and the resulting illiteracy; neglectful parents were as guilty as their children. They were "bringing up and sending abroad into the community [children] who are prepared

[7] Toronto *Globe*, Dec. 11, 1851, Dec. 11, 1862; Ryerson, *Annual Report of the Chief Superintendent of Education*, 1857, 17. On their disagreements, see J. M. S. Careless, *Brown of the Globe* (Toronto: Macmillan, 1959, 1963), 2 vols.; C. B. Sissons, *Egerton Ryerson, His Life and Times* (Toronto: Ryerson Press, 1937, 1947) 2 vols.

[8] *J. E.*, 10 (1857), 9; *Globe*, Dec. 11, 1851; "Truancy and Juvenile Crime in Cities, 1859–1860," in *D. H. E.*, 15 (Toronto, 1906), 1–5. See also, R. D. Storch, "The Policeman as Domestic Missionary," *Journal of Social History*, 9 (1976), 481–509.

[9] Katz, *The Irony*, 180, found the same in Massachusetts.

[10] *Annual Report*, 1857, 47; Prentice, "The School Promoters," 66. The stark simplicity of the causal model is striking:

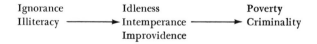

Ignorance	Idleness	Poverty
Illiteracy ⟶	Intemperance ⟶	Criminality
	Improvidence	

by ignorance, by lawlessness, by vice, to be pests to society—to violate the laws, to steal, to rob, and murder. . . ." The crime, therefore, was not only against the victim alone, for "training up children in ignorance and vagrancy, is a flagrant crime against Society," depriving it of "examples, labours, and talents . . . and inflicting upon it serious disorders and expenditures." [11]

The eradication of ignorance through education was the solution, a characteristically Victorian one. Schooling was the right of each child and the preparation of each citizen, as well as the security of the rich. Consequently, a neglect of education—and nonattendance—was itself a crime, for social order would be "better conserved by having [Toronto's] thousands of idle boys industriously and appropriately receiving instruction in her hitherto empty schoolhouses than in contracting vicious habits in the streets and on the sidewalks of the city." Nevertheless, crime persisted, especially among the young, after the founding and expansion of mass public school systems. Rather than reexamine his premises, Ryerson like most other reformers maintained that further provision for schooling was needed and that the schools, being less than full, were not reaching all of the children.[12] Arguments explaining criminality continued to be stated negatively, stressing the results of nonschooling (or improper schooling) and not the specific ways in which education would prevent crime.

In their explanations, reformers seldom considered other factors, or whether their factors might be reordered. In their disregard of the social and economic realities that determined school attendance and inequality they did not judge poverty, for example, to be a cause of ignorance or illiteracy. Upper Canada's Chief Justice Robinson made this clear in addressing a Grand Jury: "I am satisfied that no proper excuse can be given for the Children of the poor not being sent to the Schools ready to receive them in Towns and Cities." It is difficult to censure schoolmen for ignoring problems of immigration, poverty, and neglect, for they saw these as all too real. Their notions of causality, however, may be questioned, for they were unable to recognize poverty as a structural feature of capitalist society. To them pauperism and idleness stemmed from ignorance; economic failure and social deviance derived from moral

---

[11] *Globe*, Dec. 11, 1851; "Address of Dr. Daniel Wilson to the Teachers Association, 1865," *D. H. E.* 19, 48; "Truancy and Juvenile Crime," 4; *Globe*, Dec. 11, 1851; *J. E.*, 10 (1857), 9. On attendance, see the studies of Davey, Katz, and Bamman, cited in Ch. 4.

[12] *J. E.*, 1 (1848), 151; 2 (1849), 96; "Truancy and Crime," 2. See also, "Address of Wilson."

weakness, and many were considered paupers by choice, not by chance or structural inequality, blame falling especially on the lower class. By definition, the lower class family was the seedbed of paupers and criminals, with its environment of immorality and neglect.[13] Ignorance, idleness, and intemperance remained the result of individual behavior, and the reformers' typically Victorian response was to advocate education as a preventative of illiteracy, ignorance, and criminality: in one sweep this was the role of the state—to be a police force in behalf of morality.

Schoolmen were certain that ignorance and illiteracy lay at the heart of criminality. Statistical evidence was gathered as proof: data which described the educational condition of prisoners assumed guilty of criminal offenses. Ignorance of course meant more than illiteracy, but the latter was taken to be its measurable sign. From these statistics, educational promoters derived their arguments, and, reciprocally, in them they found continuing support. As a result, illiteracy itself was raised to a causal factor in their explanations, along with ignorance. Wherever in the west promoters inquired, the same results were found: the periodic examination of the literacy of the arrested and convicted served to bolster the cause of education. As direct evidence of ignorance and lack of schooling, these tabulations became the statistical foundations upon which the rhetorical house explaining criminality was built.

It is indeed significant that gaols and prisons, as well as reformatories, regularly inquired into the educational condition of their inmates, and that literacy was the universal measure chosen. Since illiteracy was accepted as the sign of ignorance, the knowledge of the prisoners' achievement or status was an essential concern. Moreover, efforts were made in Upper Canadian prisons to provide instruction in reading and writing, and J. George Hodgins, Ryerson's lieutenant, pressed for the establishment of prison libraries. Not only did annual prison reports detail the literacy of all inmates, but chaplains and schoolmasters told also of their repeated efforts to instruct their pupils, and tabulated their numbers and progress. They also linked criminality with ignorance and sought to replace it with literacy; "such being the almost barbarous ignorance in which the great majority of the convicts have been raised, it would seem an unnecessary cruelty to deprive them of the means of the 'limited education' which the humanity of Christian legislation has provided for them in this institution." R. V. Rogers, a chaplain who failed to secure funds for library, schoolroom, or schoolmaster, summed up the goal in instruction: "a Professed School of Reform, without the

---

[13] "Truancy and Juvenile Crime," 2, 1–5; "Address of Wilson." See also the studies of school attendance and urban poverty cited above; Gareth Stedman Jones, *Outcast London* (Oxford: Oxford University Press, 1971).

needed Machinery for Reformation—a Penitentiary in Name—A Jail in Fact!!" [14]

Egerton Ryerson referred to English and European statistics in his first report, and often included them in his *Journal of Education*. A decade after that report, he presented the evidence for Upper Canada itself: "How intimate and general is the connexion between the training up of children in ignorance and vagrancy and the expenses and varied evils of public crime may be gathered from the statistics of the Toronto Gaol during the year 1856, as compiled by the Governor of the Gaol from the Gaol Register." As on other occasions, he reproduced the statistics of literacy for the inmate population. For 1,967 prisoners, the registers provided this distribution:

	Male	Female
Neither read nor write	401	246
Read only	253	200
Read and write imperfectly	570	198
Read and write well	68	——
Superior education	1	——

Just what levels of skill these categories may have described will be considered below; regardless, Ryerson's conclusions from them rang familiarly in support of his stated assumptions. To him, and to most reformers, they revealed that more than 95% of the incarcerated "had grown up without the advantages of a good common school education; and that less than 5 per cent of the crimes committed, were committed by persons who could even read and write well."

Here then was the evidence for his causal model and for the centrality of illiteracy. But what was to be done? Ryerson continued, arguing prescriptively, that these were "facts which show that had a legal provision been made, such as would have secured to all these 1967 prisoners a good common school education, the number of prisoners committed to the Toronto Gaol would scarcely have exceeded one hundred, . . . their crimes would have been prevented, and the time, trouble, and expenses attending their detection and punishment would have been saved." [15] Of course there was a certain circularity in these common arguments, for it was assumed that in keeping the potential youthful offenders off the streets and in the schoolrooms the prisons would be emptied of the great bulk of their numbers (95% to Ryerson). Funds

[14] Report of the Board of Inspectors of Asylums, Prisons, & etc., Penitentiary Reports, Canada, *Sessional Papers*, esp. 1841, 1846–1849, 1852–1858, 1862; 1852–1853; 1847. See also, Baehre, "Origins." In England, see Phillips, *Crime;* Tobias, *Crime.*

[15] *J. E.*, 10 (1857), 9; see also *ibid.*, 20 (1867), 64, and "Truancy and Juvenile Crime."

saved on the one would be freed for the other. Yet no evidence of this expected result was produced to accompany the assertions.

Ryerson was far from unique in recognizing the importance of literacy in the educational prevention of crime or in the use of illiteracy statistics to support his arguments. Either summary statistics or the more prevalent practice of presenting raw numbers of prisoners, or arrested persons, at each level of education was a standard feature, significantly, of both the educational and the penitentiary reports of the last century. This was common to both the United States and Great Britain; Massachusetts reports, for example, frequently cited them, whether the discussion related to prisons, juvenile reformatories, or schools, which were all seen as weapons attacking the same social problems.[16] Standard also was the reproduction of foreign statistics to illustrate the universality of the problem, or to demonstrate that progress could sometimes be made: either to censure or to applaud the situation at home.

Others in fact went further than Ryerson in their investigations of the relations between illiteracy and criminality, continuing of course to equate ignorance in criminals with illiteracy. Reformers in the United States, in particular, scoured the records to produce statistical summaries that rang with the truth of arithmetic exactness, as part of the contemporary emergence of social research and social science. One such summary was a report by James P. Wickersham to the National Educational Association, which investigated the charge, "that a very high proportion—60 per cent, I think—of the convicts then confined in the prisons of Philadelphia, were high school graduates." His response, "Education and Crime," concluded to the contrary, in 1881,

1. That about one-sixth of all crime in the country is committed by persons wholly illiterate.
2. That about one-third of it is committed by persons practically illiterate.
3. That the proportion of criminals among the illiterate is about ten times as great as among those who have been instructed in the elements of a common-school education or beyond.

These facts led Wickersham to conclude that the amount of crime is about as uniform from year to year as the amount of ignorance or illiteracy.[17] Ten years earlier, another commentator established an even

---

[16] See Katz, *Irony;* Rothman, *Discovery;* Phillips, *Crime.*

[17] Wickersham, "Education and Crime," *The Journals and Proceedings and Addresses of the National Education Association of the United States,* Session of the Year 1881 (Boston, 1881), 45, 50; see also 45–55.

stronger relationship between illiteracy and criminality. E. D. Mansfield surveyed Europe as well as the United States, finding a high correlation between illiteracy and criminality wherever he looked. His mathematical calculations led him to conclude,

> *First.* That one-third of all criminals are totally uneducated, and that four-fifths are practically uneducated.
>
> *Second.* That the proportion of criminals from the illiterate classes is at least tenfold as great as the proportion from those having some education.[18]

Despite the certainty with which education was advanced as the best preventative of criminality and the evidence that repeatedly revealed that the criminals were largely ignorant, the eradication of illiteracy did not always seem to reduce crime. Of course, schools, as Ryerson argued, are "not responsible for defects in criminal laws, or police or municipal regulations." [19] Yet, as attendance increased (and as more police forces and prisons were established), Ryerson continued to reprint the gaol statistics, and it is revealing that he never reported a diminution in crime. The happy result of expanding educational provision in reducing offenses was not often to be found. In Massachusetts, for example, Frank Sanborn, the first Secretary of the State Board of Charities, discovered that the number of illiterates in the prison population fell by 50%, from 74 to 38%, between 1854 and 1864. In spite of such apparent progress, Sanborn was startled. First, he discovered that in England and Wales, without a system of common public schools, only 33% of prisoners could neither read nor write, and in Ireland only 50% could not. More importantly, while Massachusetts' figures led him to believe that the proportion of illiterates among the prison population was far greater than that among the entire population, the decrease over a decade in criminal illiteracy had *not* been accompanied by a corresponding decline in crime.[20]

---

[18] "The Relation Between Crime and Education," *Report of the U.S. Commissioner of Education* (Washington, D.C., 1872), 586–595; see also his "The Relation Between Education and Pauperism," *ibid.*, 596–602 on the role of poverty. Mansfield states, "Pauperism and crime are so closely allied that the same individuals belong to both fraternities. . . . The same man is a criminal or pauper depending to circumstances. He steals when he cannot beg, and begs when he cannot steal," 602.

[19] *J. E.,* 10 (1857), 9; see also "Truancy and Crime."

[20] Board of State Charities, Massachusetts, *Secretary's Report,* 1865 (Public Document Supplementary, no. 19), quoted in Katz, *Irony,* 184. These statistics must not be confused with national rates of literacy for the British Isles determined by the percentages of signatures on marriage registers. There is no necessary relationship. For other attempts to relate illiteracy with crime rates, see Phillips, *Crime,* 154–161; Howard Zehr, *Crime and the Development of Modern Society: Patterns of Criminality*

Ryerson and Sanborn were not alone in making these unsettling discoveries, which ran so counter to their models and expectations. Some sought to explain continuing high rates of crime by referring to improved enforcement and enlightened judicial systems. Usually, however, the result was a confused, sometimes contradictory posture by school reformers and public officials who used the illiteracy statistics to demonstrate that ignorance was a primary cause of criminality. Witness the efforts of Wickersham, for example, in this quandary, as he discussed the hypothetical possibility that Prussia possessed more criminals than France in spite of its better schooling and higher literacy rates. "It will be found that the cause is not in her schools but in spite of her schools, for in Prussia, as in all other countries, an illiterate man is many times more likely to commit crime than one who is educated." This alone was not a sufficient reason for continuing criminality; the cause could also be "a crime-producing factor in his nature or in the circumstances that surround him which his education has not been able to eliminate." Education would then fail to achieve its goal. With this information in mind, however, Wickersham could conclude securely and optimistically, "Were it not for the restraining effects of intellectual, moral, and religious factors, our opinion is that [crime] would completely disrupt society and resolve its broken fragments into chaos." [21] Ryerson, of course, argued the same point.

In effect, school promoters hedged their positions nicely. If education failed to decrease criminality, as they predicted, they retreated to explanations that stressed a poor environment, immigration, poverty, heredity, the wrong sort of education, or nonattendance. If, however, ignorance, as discovered by the statistics of illiteracy, was the cause, educational provisions would protect order, with training in literacy the essential aim. Some spokesmen attempted to use both arguments and to have their claims accepted both ways, seemingly unaware of the potential for circularity or contradiction. The way around problems of argument and evidence often centered upon their definitions of ignorance, and as a result the applicability of literacy statistics varied according to the meaning chosen. Illiteracy, then, represented either *the fact* of ignorance or merely *one possible* symptom of the lack of a proper education. To the former, statistics of prisoners' literacy were relevant and germane evidence. To the latter, measures of literacy—or of intellectual

---

in *Nineteenth Century France and Germany* (London: Croom Helm, 1976), 59, 167; V. E. McHale and E. A. Johnson, "Urbanization, Industrialization, and Crime in Imperial Germany," *Social Science History*, 1 (1977), 236–237.

[21] Wickersham, "Education and Crime," 50.

education—were insufficient and inappropriate proof to connect illiteracy with ignorance and criminality. Literacy, if unrestrained by morality, could be very dangerous; an individual's literacy alone was hardly a guarantee of his orderliness and proper socialization. In spite of the clear differences in the role of literacy in their discussions of criminality, schoolmen turned to both models, revealing their confusion and the contradictions inherent in their use of literacy.

By the mid-nineteenth century, the school was more than ever before recognized as the vehicle required to replace the traditional roles of moral training by family and church, and its success was sometimes determined by the proportion of literate men and women produced for the society. Literacy, then, indicated that the expected training had occurred; illiteracy, conversely, meant a lack of schooling or the presence of a deeper ignorance rooted in personal deviance such as schooling could not eradicate. The provision of schools to teach literacy properly was sufficient for the *Globe*: "Give the child the *simple rudiments* of education and to him all else is opened . . . if we make our people intelligent, they cannot fail to be prosperous: intelligence makes morality, morality industry, industry prosperity as surely as the sun shines." The process was automatic; intelligence, morality, and prosperity followed, in order, from literacy. Prison chaplains and masters agreed. J. T. Gardiner claimed, "Reading and studying of books is a powerful means of leading men to consider and abandon the evil practices by which their youth may have been contaminated." Or, as a Kingston Penitentiary schoolmaster exclaimed, "To be a reading man, is to be a powerful man, . . . a moral man and a useful member of society." [22] Here, illiteracy was equated with ignorance, and statistics of prisoner illiteracy were relevant and necessary to the arguments.

Simultaneously, arguments were advanced that stressed the insufficiency of literacy as a preventative of crime. Ryerson, for one, remarked that schooling did not always end in moral training, as "much of this moral degradation and social danger must be charged on the neglected or perverted, culture of the Schools." False education, "which severs knowledge from its relations to duty," could be found in many schools, and as a result, "a reading and writing community may be a very vicious community, if morality be not as much a portion of education as reading and writing." Henry Hayhew in England was even more vehement in his critique of Ragged Schools. These institutions, he concluded, "may be, they are, and must be, from the mere fact of bringing so many boys

[22] *Globe*, Dec. 11, 1851 (emphasis added); *Report* of the Board of Inspectors of Asylums, Prisons, & etc., 1857, 1860. See Ch. 1, above; Baehre, "Origins." For similar confusion in England, see Phillips, *Crime*.

of vicious propensities together, productive of far more injury than benefit to the community. If some boys are rescued . . . many are lost through them." [23] Some schools could stimulate rather than prevent crime, and if schooling prevailed without morality at its core, illiteracy could diminish while crime increased, much as Frank Sanborn had discovered. The result of the expansion of this sort of education, it was argued, could be no more than the production of more clever and skillful criminals.

The issue, usually implicit, was confronted directly by the *Christian Guardian,* which under Ryerson's editorship addressed earlier doubts about the dangers of overeducation. Responding to the question "Does Mere Intellectual Education Banish Crime?" the *Guardian* noted that "the only ascertained effect of intellectual education on crime is to substitute fraud for force, the cunning of civilized for the violence of savage life." To increase intellectual power without inculcating moral principles would make a man restless and dissatisfied, "hating those that are above him, and desirous of reducing all to his own level." To convince its audience of the truly conservative nature of proper schooling, as Ryerson continued to do as Chief Superintendent, the *Guardian* explained that intellectual and secular education alone were insufficient. The formation of the Christian character was the only proper end, and literacy itself did not erase the crucial ignorance. The fault of the age, they concluded, was that "men have hitherto been prone to take for granted, that it was only necessary to teach the Art of reading, and before this new power all vice and error would flee away." Education such as this might not cause crime, but it did not prevent it. This was the argument which Ryerson made central to his discussions and promotions in the succeeding decades. Schooling, he often urged, included the moral as well as the intellectual; literacy, the tool of training, was to be provided in carefully structured institutions. The pace of social change demanded no less a solution; the maintenance of the social order and hegemony mandated it. Prison chaplains and instructors agreed, too, contradicting their other statements. Reading and writing, while important, were not education; accompanying instruction in morality was necessary and the moral faculties must be trained directly.[24] The role of literacy was to provide the vehicle for the efficient transmission and reinforcement of morality and restraint.

[23] Ryerson, "Report," 150, and Thomas Wyse, *School Reform,* as quoted, 151; Mayhew in the *Morning Chronicle,* March 29, 1850, quoted in Tobias, *Crime,* 207. See M. Hill and C. F. Cornwalles, *Two Prize Essays on Juvenile Delinquency* (London, 1853), 220, quoted in Tobias, *Crime,* 207. See also Stedman Jones, *Outcast London.*

[24] *Christian Guardian* (C. G.), July 2, 1834; see also *The Church,* Oct. 12, 1839, May 15, 1851; *Reports* of the Inspectors, 1862, 1852–1853. See also, Ch. 1, above.

These were the principal lines of argument regarding the relationships joining ignorance and criminality. Forming two poles in the elaboration of the perceived connections, they were *not* seen as exclusive or contradictory. Each was used as it fit the circumstances: definitions 'and processes differed with the argument chosen, with both functioning toward the same end. School promoters vacillated between the two, but they continued in many cases to employ the statistics of literacy regardless of their line of argument. If the first formulation were expounded—that learning to read led naturally to the inculcation of restraint and morality—the use of literacy and the prisoners' statistics was both necessary and appropriate. If, however, the second argument were advanced—that morality is distinct from literacy or intellectual training—the use of literacy as a measure of proper education was highly problematic and unsatisfactory. For "the moral [man] must advance contemporaneously with the intellectual man, else we see no increased education, but an increased capacity for evil doing." [25]

In this formulation, literacy was hardly the crucial element—or an appropriate test: its role was unclear, and individuals could be ignorant whether literate or illiterate. Its importance instead lay in its usefulness for effective and efficient mass schooling in a growing and changing society. Nevertheless, those who argued in this way continued to draw upon the statistics of criminal literacy, while their words denied the relevance of this evidence. Thus, Egerton Ryerson, within the span of several pages, could both recognize the potential immorality and viciousness of the literate and employ the gaol registers as proof for his explanations, thereby contradicting himself with his own data. So did Wickersham, Mansfield, and British reformers. Apparently, very few ever realized that the literacy statistics simply could not be used to prove both arguments. In attempting to do so, school promoters confused and contradicted their own efforts, reducing their credibility and forcing us to reexamine both their assumptions and their explanations. The questions about which they were so certain bear reopening.

Some contemporaries realized the contradictory use of literacy tabulations, and not all accepted the use of this evidence. From Great Britain, for example, came a scathing attack on their application to demonstrate the relationship between education and crime. W. B. Hodgson, addressing the Social Science Association in 1867, declared that although there may be "fallacies more palpable than that . . . ignorance of reading and writing is productive of, or accompanied by, a greater amount of crime . . . there can be few more gross and serious." While granting that the inability to read or write may represent the ignorance of all

[25] *C. G.,* July 2, 1834; see also Ryerson, "Report," *passim.*

that lies beyond, he concluded that "the ability . . . (not to cavail about the degree of ability), by no means as gives the knowledge of aught beyond. Negatively, the ignorance implies múch, positively the knowledge implies little." Twenty years later, another English commentator, Rev. J. W. Horsey, continued the attack on the role of literacy and education in the equation which accounted for criminality. "One can get no clear evidence or trustworthy statistics," he discovered, "to prove that the greater attention to educational matters has largely diminished even juvenile crime. There are fewer boys and girls sent to prison happily, but this arises from various causes, and *not entirely from their increased virtue and intelligence* [emphasis added]." [26] The statistics did not prove the case; the explanation was faulty. The expansion of educational provision, it would seem, did not prevent crime. If the convicted were and continued to be illiterate or if more were literate, there must be other causes, or the factors must be ordered differently. Illiteracy by itself could not represent the first cause of criminality, and their relationship must be mediated by other factors.

Other problems also result from the use of literacy statistics in the usual manner. First, and most superficially, school promoters naturally found what they were looking for; the statistics became part of a self-fulfilling prophecy. And, they could be manipulated. For example, if one-third of prisoners were illiterate, it was then claimed that (at least) one-third of all crimes were committed by the illiterate—a questionable deduction in itself and an assertion of group culpability disproportionate to the group's share of the population. This does not negate, however, the possibility that the criminals may have had a lower rate of literacy than the population at large. But the degree of difference could vary radically from place to place and year to year. To compare prisoners with others whose abilities exceeded the level of "neither read nor write" is very difficult, and entire populations, enumerated only by censuses or evaluated by signature frequencies on marriage registers, were never questioned about their *levels* of education, but only about literacy or illiteracy. The very ambiguity of the classifications for the different levels of ability obscures their meaning as well as their comparability, for nowhere are they defined. [27]

Several difficulties are apparent here. First, we are never told how prisoners compared with the population at large on levels of education

---

[26] Hodgson, *Exaggerated Estimates of Reading and Writing as a Means of Education* (London, 1867), 6–7; J. W. Horsey, *Jottings from Jail* (London, 1887), 57, quoted in Tobias, *Crime*, 206 (emphasis added).

[27] David Phillips' comments on classifications and categories in England is revealing. *Crime*, 155.

above that of simple literacy or illiteracy. Nor are we told how they compared with the arrested-but-not-convicted or with the unapprehended criminal. The reinforcing role that the statistics played obscured attention from these questions. Furthermore, there is no a priori reason for contemporaries' ceaseless combination of illiterates with those of imperfect education in applying this evidence to support their explanations. This was also done without regard to the wider distribution of educational skills in the society.

Problems with the employment of criminal statistics are exacerbated by the irregularity of the statistical relationships found for the past century. Stability in rates of crime could be accompanied by increases or decreases in rates of inmate (or popular) literacy. Similarly, rises or falls in rates of crime do not correspond unvaryingly to changes in either criminal or popular literacy rates, which seem to have been remarkably stable in the face of movement in rates of other relevant factors.[28] As the century passed, more children enrolled in and attended school, and rates of adult literacy increased, yet there was no corresponding discussion of crime's reduction as a result. At best reformers claimed that more offenses would have been committed or that the situation was worse elsewhere. Regardless, the asserted beneficent role of literacy and education was never proved. In sum, too many ambiguities and contradictions exist among the relationships within the simple causal models of Ryerson and other reformers, who consequently failed to establish convincingly that illiteracy caused criminality and that the association was either direct or causal, unmediated by other factors of potentially greater significance.

II

The data used by the reformers, the detailed nineteenth-century gaol registers, have survived for places in Upper Canada (and elsewhere), allowing us to move beyond the rhetoric and to directly reexamine the relationships claimed by educational promoters. In discussions of the connections between education and crime, the low level of literacy of the criminal-inmate population represented, as we have seen, the most

[28] See V. A. C. Gattell and T. B. Hadden, "Criminal Statistics and their Interpretation," in *Nineteenth-century Society*, ed. E. A. Wrigley (Cambridge: Cambridge University Press, 1972), 363–396, Statistical Tables and *passim.;* Zehr, *Crime;* McHale and Johnson, "Urbanization"; Phillips, *Crime.* The entire issue requires far more serious study; see, for example, Lane, "Crime."

frequently cited item in the annual tabulations of prisoners' conditions, to the neglect of other regularly collected information about them. The registers, on an annual and individual basis, also inquired about birthplace, religion, age, sex, occupation, moral habits, crime or offense, and judgment by the authorities, all in addition to the educational status of each arrested person.

With this information, patterns of arrest and conviction may be re-created. As we will see, conviction was in fact associated with illiteracy, but the clearest patterns of successful prosecution related directly to ethnicity, occupational class, and gender, when the effects of illiteracy are statistically controlled. These important factors, largely ignored in nineteenth-century explanations of criminality and key features of social stratification, blur a direct connection between illiteracy and conviction, for they intervened to form patterns of systematic discrimination and prosecution by the judicial system. Illiteracy, of course, was often symptomatic of factors that made for high rates of punishment, as both were rooted in social inequality; however, the most illiterate groups did not always fare the worst in judgments. Illiteracy's role was in many ways a superficial one, acting through its links with poverty and structural inequality, and not necessarily with guilt. The interaction of the major factors was more complex and subtle than the causal explanations of men like Ryerson would allow, forcing us to develop a new, more sophisticated understanding of crime and punishment in the past and a reevaluation of the role played by literacy. School promoters' and reformers' use of aggregate tabulations obscured the complex interrelationship of variables; in their certainty, the literacy statistics served as blinders.

The manuscript gaol registers of Middlesex County, Ontario, for the year, 1867–1868, were selected for this analysis. The earliest registers to be located, they provide complete information on all persons arrested, permitting us to distinguish between the convicted and the acquitted, and to analyze their characteristics. Urban crime and prosecution form the core of this discussion, as Middlesex County was dominated by the fledgling metropolis of London, a source of the majority of the county's criminals, although its population represented less than one-fourth of the county's 48,000 inhabitants in 1861. The city and the country were growing, prosperous centers of trade and transportation in western Ontario.

In the 13 months the register spans, 535 men and women were arrested, their profiles and characteristics recorded. Overwhelmingly urban residents, 64% claimed London as their home, with an additional 3% reporting other Ontario cities as theirs. They were arrested for a broad

Table 6.1
Literacy of Middlesex Criminals (in Percentages)

	All arrested	Convicted	Acquitted
Neither read nor write	17.8	22.7	7.2
Read and write imperfectly	62.6	63.5	60.8
Read and write well	16.3	11.9	25.9
Read and write very well	3.2	1.7	6.0
Total	535	362	173

range of crimes (over 60 in all) and two-thirds of them were convicted. Arrest and conviction, however, were far from random, as certain groups (the Irish and English) were disproportionately arrested and one group (the Irish) were most often convicted. Similarly, those holding lower-class occupations, the officially unoccupied, and women were dealt with severely, as were those arrested for crimes associated with drink and vagrancy.[29] Literacy related to these patterns in both reinforcing and contradictory ways.

Differences in educational background existed among the convicted, the acquitted, and the arrested (Table 6.1). Among the arrested, for example, the number who read well or very well exceeded the number of illiterates ("Neither read nor write"), as more educated than uneducated persons were apprehended as suspects. Reformers, of course, would not accept this distinction, for as we have seen they readily combined the numbers with an imperfect grounding in literacy with the illiterates. For Middlesex, they would have observed, rather, that 80% of those arrested and 86% of those convicted lacked a "good common-school" education. If their combinations were justifiable, it remains interesting that 68% of those acquitted had not been well educated and that over 60% of those arrested were imperfectly educated; many supposedly ignorant individuals, in other words, had not been found guilty. More important than that is the slight difference in educational achievement between those suspected and those convicted as criminals; the proportion largely unedu-

[29] I acknowledge my gratitude to Edward Phelps, Regional History Library, University of Western Ontario, who not only saved these records from destruction, but also drew my attention to them and made them available to me. I have discussed the general patterns found in the analysis of the registers in "Crime and Punishment in the Nineteenth Century: The Experience of Middlesex, County, Ontario," Canadian Social History Project, *Report*, 5 (1973–1974), 124–163 and have described the registers in "Crime and Punishment in the Nineteenth Century: A Note on the Criminal," *Journal of Interdisciplinary History*, 7 (1976–1977), 477–491. The latter includes a listing of all crimes and their classification.

cated ("neither" or "imperfectly") diverged marginally from one group to the other, although somewhat more from those released. Ignorance, as defined by those who assumed it to be the first cause of crime and signified by a lack of education, apparently did not significantly differentiate suspects from convicts. It was only slightly better in distinguishing the acquitted from the accused, much as David Phillips also found in England's Black Country.[30]

It is far from evident, nevertheless, that the reformers' combination of the lowest educational classes was justified in the first place. The representativeness of the imperfectly educated, in comparison with the larger population, is the main point at issue; and, in fact, there is little reason to consider them very much overrepresented among either suspects or convicted criminals. They were arrested, convicted, and acquitted with the same frequency as those who were better educated. In addition, the published tabulations of prisoners' illiteracy in the province's *Sessional Papers* did not include them in its statistical tables, providing only county totals of those who could not read or write at all. It is possible, moreover, that the imperfectly educated were broadly representative of popular levels of literacy and schooling. As the next chapter argues, the high statistical level of literacy in Upper Canada may well belie a lower qualitative level of achievement and usefulness.

Direct evidence on this question comes from research in progress in the extraordinary Swedish sources, conducted by Egil Johansson, of Umeå University. The parish catechetical examination registers include, for some years and on an individual basis, measures of both oral reading ability and comprehension. For Bygdeå parish in 1862, Johansson discovered that of those who achieved the highest grade in oral ability, 77.6% comprehended only partially at best. Of those who read orally with less proficiency, 28% had poor comprehension, while less than 4% read with "passable" understanding. The ability to read well did not correlate highly with an ability to understand or to use that ability;

---

[30] Phillips, *Crime*, 158–161, Tables 18–19. Phillips concludes, "This shows that there was a higher degree of illiteracy among those committed to trial than among the population as a whole (bearing in mind that three-quarters of the accused were male)— *but not very much higher,* even by the mid-1850s. The criminal offenders of the area were slightly less literate and less educated than the population of the area, *but not very much less; certainly not enough to sustain the thesis that their delinquency was directly attributable to their want of adequate education.* . . . But then, they came from the working classes, in an area where the working classes were ill-provided with the facilities for education," 160–161 (emphasis added). Note that he combines "neither read nor write" with "read only" but not with "imperfectly" in comparing gaol records to marriage registers. Phillips' is a modest but important study which stands out among recent historical studies of crime.

regardless of literacy level, few comprehended even passably and only a tiny proportion totally understood what they read.[31]

The implications of these findings for a country with a long heritage of high levels of literacy can not be minimized. Not only do they effectively contradict the efforts of Ryerson and others to join the imperfectly literate with the illiterate as being without education, they also suggest that the imperfect range was a broad one, which encompassed a large proportion of the population. In this way, the close correspondence of the imperfectly skilled's distribution among the arrested, convicted, and acquitted persons is significant and should be expected. In all likelihood, they were men and women broadly representative of the city's and county's educational condition. They can not simply be combined with the illiterate in the effort to prove that a paucity of schooling, or ignorance, contributed directly to criminality, its apprehension and conviction. A rejection of the school promoters' categorization radically revises the statistical relationship that purportedly linked ignorance and illiteracy with criminality. No longer may it be claimed that five-sixths of the convicted were exceptional persons without education; only 23% remain fairly within those ranks. The evidence leads us to concur in David Phillips' conclusion that it is "certainly not enough to sustain the thesis that their delinquency was directly attributable to their want of adequate education." [32]

That fewer than one-fourth of the convicted criminals were illiterate, and that fewer than one-fifth of the arrested were uneducated, severely modifies the contentions of reformers. The weight of numbers shifts to individuals who were at least partially educated, and who may now be seen as the great majority of the supposed offenders. Among the arrested, as noted, the well-educated equalled the illiterates; among those convicted, the illiterates outnumbered those with a good education, but the margin is not large (10 percentage points). The illiterates who were convicted only slightly overrepresented their distribution

[31] Johansson, "Literacy Studies in Sweden: Some Examples," in *Literacy and Society in a Historical Perspective: A Conference Report,* ed. Johansson (Umeå: Umeå University, 1973), 56. The incomparable Swedish parish registers provide data on annual examinations on the quality of literacy as determined by either oral ability or comprehension. Sponsored by the state church, the examinations record individual and community progress over the years as well as demographic and socioeconomic data. Available from the seventeenth to the nineteenth centuries, they allow more detailed analysis of literacy's transmission, dimensions, and correlates, as well as distinguishing levels of literacy, than any other Western sources. Johansson has begun a large-scale project, but unfortunately little work has focused on the relationship of reading to comprehension. See also, Ch. 7, below, for more evidence and discussion.

[32] Phillips, *Crime,* 160.

among all arrested persons. The balance swings, however, when the convicted are compared with the acquitted: the illiterates constitute a small portion of those released, representing only one-third of their proportion among the convicted. But this difference must be qualified too; the illiterates, significantly, were not underrepresented among the acquitted, for their proportion corresponded closely to the 1861 rate of adult illiteracy in London, home of the majority of those persons arrested. Although they were somewhat overrepresented among all arrested, a direct causal relationship linking illiteracy with criminality, as promoters claimed, should have led to a far greater underrepresentation of illiterates among those found innocent and released rather than only a proportionate representation.

Illiterates in Middlesex and London were not the most frequent offenders; nevertheless, they were punished with greater regularity than others.[33] While their place in the criminal population was far from the extraordinary one reformers claimed, 5/6 of them were convicted if brought to trial—the frequency of conviction seemingly related directly to education. Does this signify some measure of truth in reformers' arguments, that although the convicted were not overwhelmingly illiterate, the uneducated suspects were almost certainly guilty? Their incredible rate of conviction, in fact, was related first of all to patterns of discrimination and social prejudice against the Irish, the lower class, and women—individuals in these groups were convicted most often regardless of their level of literacy. Punishment was of course more frequent for the least educated members of these groups, for good reasons, as we will see; and illiteracy related more directly, perhaps, to arrest and successful prosecution than it did to guilt or criminality. Social inequality was the root of both illiteracy and conviction, and the actions of the courts were based in the social hierarchy.

We can not doubt, moreover, that the agencies of law enforcement and justice, the constabulary and the courts, accepted the dominant explanations of criminality, naturally accusing the ignorant and the illiterate, who were very often poor, and expecting them to be guilty. The ideology of criminality and its causes, and the mechanisms of inequality were operationalized as illiterates, with supposedly unrestrained ignorance and immorality, were perceived as a threat to social order. Their other characteristics—of class, gender, and ethnicity—only reinforced their social marginality and the severity with which respectable society would react to them. As a result, their vulnerability increased.

---

[33] Conviction rates for each group are as follows: Neither read nor write, 86.3%, Read and write imperfectly, 68.7%, read and write well, 49.4%, read and write very well, 35.3%.

No doubt they were visible, not hidden in ghettos like the poor today (given the patterns of residence of these cities), laboring outdoors when employed, living amid other classes, or perhaps begging in the streets.

Illiterates would have few resources to employ for their defense, whether for legal aid or in a bribe attempt. They also lacked the kind of formal training and experience to deal effectively with the procedures and the language of a courtroom. Prepared by family, work, and life, rather than by the organizational context of the school, illiterates could perhaps be intimidated, uncomprehending, unable to respond properly or usefully or to make themselves understood in a situation where their guilt might be presumed. Class and cultural differences in language and perception could reduce their chances for a fair hearing and frustrate their efforts, too.[34] Some of them also might welcome the gaol as a refuge,

[34] The cognitive consequences of illiteracy and literacy are far from clear, although *formal training* in literacy does seem to be closely associated with more abstract thought processes, generalization of solutions, classification and association, changes in concept formation, use of language in description, *in some contexts and some tasks.* As Scribner and Cole put it, "differences in the social organization of education promote differences in the organization of learning and thinking in the individual . . . the school represents a specialized set of educational experiences which are discontinuous from those encountered in everyday life and that it requires and promotes ways of learning and thinking which often run counter to those nurtured in practical daily activities," "Cognitive Consequences of Formal and Informal Education," *Science,* 182 (1973), 553, 553–559. Among a large and generally murky literature, see also, Scribner, "Cognitive Consequences of Literacy," unpub. paper, 1968; Scribner and Cole, "Research Program on Vai Literacy and its Cognitive Consequences," *Cross-Cultural Social Psychology Newsletter,* 8 (1974), 2–4; Jack Goody, Cole, and Scribner, "Writing and Formal Operations: A Case Study Among the Vai," *Africa,* 47 (1977), 289–304; Patricia M. Greenfield, "Oral or Written Language: The Consequences for Cognitive Development in Africa, the United States and England," *Language and Speech,* 15 (1972), 169–178. See also, H. E. Freeman and G. C. Kassebaum, "The Illiterate in American Society," *Social Forces,* 34 (1956), 371–375; Don A. Brown, "Educational Characteristics of Adult Illiterates: A Preliminary Report," *New Frontiers in College-Adult Reading,* 15th Yearbook of the National Reading Conference (Milwaukee, 1966), 58–68. However else illiteracy may have handicapped urban residents in these nineteenth-century cities and however else their experiences may have prepared them, the conclusion that they were not prepared to stand well in the formal context of judicial proceedings seems warranted.

To this we must add the important function of class and cultural differences in speech patterns, which may well have contributed further to a poor showing and disadvantagement in courts. See, among his many writings, Basil Bernstein, "Some Sociological Determinants of Perception," *British Journal of Sociology,* 9 (1958), 159–174; Doris R. Entwhistle, "Implications of language socialization for reading models and for learning to read," *Reading Research Quarterly,* 7 (1971–72), 111–167, "Developmental Sociolinguistics: Inner-City Children," *American Journal of Sociology,* 74 (1968), 37–49. These areas obviously require further attention, perhaps in a situational, phenomenological, or ethnographic actor-oriented framework.

a warm shelter with food regularly provided. Expectations, ideology, inequality, and physical circumstances all combined to result in patterns of conviction.

Ethnicity was one factor upon which the wheels of justice turned, as the courts meted out judgments of varying severity to arrested members of different groups. With extraordinary frequency, the Irish (Catholic as well as Protestant) were arrested and convicted (86%), well above the mean rate of conviction (68%), and more often than any other ethnic group (Table 6.2). Significantly, the Irish were not marked by the highest levels of illiteracy. Among the arrested, five ethnic groups had greater proportions unable to read or write than the Irish Catholics and three counted more than the Protestants; yet these groups were not convicted as regularly (Table 6.3). Conversely, native-born Canadians (Protestant and Catholic) were most often illiterate, but they were acquitted most frequently. Conviction clearly was determined by more than measurable ignorance.

Within each ethnic group, rates of conviction corresponded to level of education, illiterates being most often convicted. Nevertheless, Irish Catholics, and Protestants to a lesser extent, were convicted most frequently regardless of their educational attainment. Catholics who read and wrote well, in fact, were successfully prosecuted with slightly higher frequency than those who were imperfectly skilled (91 to 85%). These patterns imply biased judicial proceedings against Irish men and women in mid-nineteenth-century London and Middlesex, and discrimination against them regardless of their literacy. Illiterates of course were selected for severe prosecution, and Irish illiterates, especially Catholics, were almost certain to be convicted. Ethnicity, however, was the key, as it was in the economic and occupational stratification of mid-nineteenth-century urban society. As social inequality often derived from the facts of ethnic ascription, successful prosecution apparently did too. Irish men and women, especially Catholics, faced inequality in courtroom as in marketplace. Concomitant poverty and illiteracy could only reinforce their precarious position; illiteracy was hardly a prior or first cause in itself. Their acquisition of literacy, thus guaranteed neither their economic success nor their security from undue criminal prosecution.

Class, status, and wealth, as signified by occupational rank, represented a second factor that determined the course of justice.[35] Lower-class workers, the unskilled and the officially unoccupied (predominantly

---

[35] The occupational classification is, as in Part One, based on the IASHP-Five Cities Project Scale. Of course, as evidenced above, we know that occupation is an imperfect proxy or approximation of social class, status, or wealth. The literature cited in Ch. 2 is again relevant.

Table 6.2

Rate of Conviction for Each Ethnic Group, Controlling for Level of Literacy

	Irish Catholic	Irish Protestant	Scottish Presbyterian	English Protestant	Canadian Protestant	Canadian Catholic	Others	Total
Neither read nor write								
N	5	7	3	3	24	16	24	82
%	100.0	87.5	100.0	75.0	75.0	94.1	92.3	86.3
Read and write imperfectly								
N	35	29	13	38	39	23	53	230
%	85.4	80.6	72.2	63.3	54.9	51.1	82.8	68.7
Read and write well								
N	10	4	1	7	15	0	6	43
%	90.9	66.7	16.7	50.0	46.9	0.0	37.5	49.4
Read and write very well								
N	1	0	2	2	0	1	—	6
%	50.0	0.0	100.0	40.0	0.0	33.3	—	35.3
Total arrested								
N	59	53	29	83	137	64	110	535
Total convicted								
%	86.4	75.5	65.5	60.2	56.9	60.9	77.3	67.7

Table 6.3
Middlesex Criminals: Ethnicity by Literacy

	Irish Catholic	Irish Protestant	Scottish Presbyterian	English Protestant	Canadian Protestant	Canadian Catholic	Others	Total	Percent convicted
Neither read nor write									
N	5	8	3	4	32	17	26		
%	8.5	15.1	10.3	4.8	23.4	26.6	23.6	17.8	86.3
Read and write imperfectly									
N	41	36	18	60	71	45	64		
%	69.5	67.9	62.1	72.3	51.8	70.3	58.2	62.6	68.7
Read and write well									
N	11	6	6	14	32	2	16		
%	18.6	11.3	20.7	16.9	23.4	3.1	14.5	16.3	49.4
Read and write very well									
N	3	3	2	5	1	—	3		
%	3.4	5.7	6.9	6.0	1.5		2.7	3.2	35.3
Total arrested									
N	59	53	29	83	137	64	110	535	
%	11.0	9.9	5.4	15.5	25.6	12.0	20.6	100.0	
Total convicted									
%	86.4	75.5	65.5	60.2	56.9	60.9	77.3	67.7	

women), were arrested and convicted far more often than those higher ranking (Table 6.4). Here there was a direct relationship with illiteracy, for literacy corresponded to occupational class as it did in the larger society: within each occupational rank, the uneducated were punished most frequently. The class convicted most often, however, the semiskilled, was not the most illiterate (10.3% illiterate). The unskilled, with slightly higher illiteracy (13.3%), were punished far less often, while those with no occupation, and much greater illiteracy (30.5%), were convicted no more often.

As with the Irish, lower-class workers were selected for severe judgments; the poor and the unemployed, with least resources for defense and subsistence, were disproportionately arrested and convicted. Their numbers included many Irish and women as well as illiterates; these factors combined, cumulatively, to produce swift pronouncements of guilt. They were by and large precisely the individuals expected to be offenders by popular opinion and theories of criminality. Lower-class status and poverty could be synonymous conditions, and they could often result in illiteracy as well as a need to resort to crime. Simultaneously, the lower-class family was also believed, due to its supposed immorality, lack of restraint, and failure in socialization, to be the breeding grounds of criminality and pauperism. Idleness was equally an offense, for in the formulations of the reformers, poverty or the structural features of society and economy did not cause illiteracy or ignorance. Despite prevailing notions (with their impressive continuity), social inequality, with its base in class and ethnicity, was an important source of convictions, whether reinforced by illiteracy or not.

The courts' decisions to convict also pivoted upon the gender of the suspect, as women were convicted in 80% of their cases compared with 60% of men (Table 6.5). Regardless of literacy, ethnicity, or crime, women received harsh judgment; this was related to both their lack of occupation (and earnings) or idleness and their high rate of illiteracy (27%). Falling into categories which were severely adjudged (10% were semiskilled too), they no doubt were seen as failing in society's expected standards of truly feminine behavior.[36] They were not at home, nurturing a family or being properly domestic; their perceived deviance endangered the maintenance and propagation of the moral order, the family, and the training of children. While Irish and illiterate women were convicted most often, women were punished more often than men

---

[36] See, for example, Barbara Welter, "The Cult of True Womanhood," *American Quarterly*, 18 (1966), 151–174, and the literature on women and the family cited in Chs. 2 and 3.

Table 6.4
Rate of Conviction for Each Occupational Category, Controlling for Level of Literacy

	Professional/ proprietor	Nonmanual, small proprietor, farmer	Skilled artisanal	Semiskilled	Unskilled	None	Total
Neither read nor write							
N	—	0	2	6	15	59	82
%	—	0.0	66.7	100.0	83.3	88.1	86.3
Read and write imperfectly							
N	—	8	27	37	59	99	230
%	—	44.4	65.9	86.0	59.6	73.9	68.7
Read and write well							
N	1	4	17	2	8	11	43
%	100.0	30.8	51.5	28.6	57.1	57.9	49.4
Read and write very well							
N	0	5	1	0	—	—	6
%	0.0	62.5	20.0	0.0	—	—	35.3
Total arrested							
N	4	40	82	58	131	220	535
%	0.8	7.5	15.4	10.7	24.5	41.2	
Total convicted							
%	25.0	42.5	57.3	79.3	62.5	76.8	67.7

Table 6.5

Rate of Conviction for Each Sex, Controlling for Level of Literacy

	Male	Female	Total
Neither read nor write			
N	33	49	82
%	76.7	94.2	86.3
Read and write imperfectly			
N	132	98	230
%	62.6	79.0	68.7
Read and write well			
N	37	6	43
%	50.0	46.2	49.4
Read and write very well			
N	6	—	6
%	35.3	—	35.3
Total arrested			
N	345	190	535
Total convicted			
%	60.3	81.1	67.7

within each ethnic group and for virtually all crimes. Pervasive inequality had deep roots in sexual stratification.

The crimes for which individuals were often arrested and found guilty, not surprisingly, were moral offenses. The most prominent of these was vagrancy: an offense marked by high rates of conviction and often linked with illiteracy (Tables 6.6, 6.7). This was of course the crime of idleness, to which ignorance and illiteracy were presumed to lead directly. Perceived as dangerous, rather than sympathetically as the poor in need of aid, arrested vagrants were largely women (77%, while only 35% of all arrested) who were visible and seen as moral failures. Vagrancy would be a charge quite easy to prove, and it is unlikely that poor, homeless women unaware of legal subleties could plead other than guilty. The shelter of the gaol might often be welcome, too, for there were few other institutions to care for them.

Crimes related to drink, the offense of intemperance, which could also be easily proved, illustrate the discrimination against the Irish. Perhaps as a function of the myth of the drunken Irishman, these offenses received serious attention; the Irish were arrested for drunkenness twice as often as they were for all other crimes combined (43 to 20%). Those suspected of drunkenness, however, were among the least illiterate of all arrested (11.4%), yet they were among the most often convicted (82%).

Table 6.6
Rate of Conviction for Each Category of Crime, Controlling for Level of Literacy

	Against property	Against persons	Related to drink	Related to prostitution	Vágrancy	Against by-laws	Others	Total
Neither read nor write								
N	16	7	5	7	39	7	1	82
%	72.7	77.8	100.0	70.0	100.0	77.8	100.0	86.3
Read and write imperfectly								
N	41	42	22	22	82	10	11	230
%	43.6	70.0	81.5	61.1	95.3	76.9	61.1	68.7
Read and write well								
N	10	11	7	1	6	2	6	43
%	33.3	57.9	77.8	12.5	85.7	66.7	54.5	49.4
Read and write very well								
N	1	0	2	—	—	—	3	6
%	16.7	0.0	66.7	—	—	—	42.9	35.3
Total arrested								
N	152	89	44	54	133	25	38	535
Total convicted								
%	44.7	67.4	81.8	55.6	96.2	76.0	51.5	67.7

Table 6.7
Middlesex Criminals: Crime by Literacy

	Against property	Against persons	Related to drink	Related to prostitution	Vagrancy	Against by-laws	Others	Total	Percent convicted
Neither read nor write									
N	22	9	5	10	39	9	1	82	
%	14.5	10.1	11.4	18.5	29.3	36.0	2.6	17.8	86.3
Read and write imperfectly									
N	94	60	27	36	86	13	19	230	
%	61.8	67.4	61.4	66.7	64.7	52.0	50.0	63.5	68.7
Read and write well									
N	30	19	9	8	7	3	11	43	
%	19.7	21.3	20.5	14.8	5.3	12.0	28.9	16.3	49.4
Read and write very well									
N	6	1	3	—	—	—	7	6	
%	3.9	1.1	6.8	—	—	—	18.5	3.2	35.3
Total arrested									
N	152	89	44	54	133	25	38	535	
Total convicted									
%	44.7	67.4	81.8	55.6	96.2	76.0	51.5		67.7

A severe moral offense, intemperance was punished regardless of the literacy of the suspect.

Even the relationship among immorality, illiteracy, and criminality, so central to explanations of deviance, was ambiguous. Moral offenses were certainly judged harshly, but contrary to Ryerson's formula, immorality was not always related to illiteracy. When the moral habits of the arrested are noted, the "intemperate", significantly, included fewer illiterates (14%) than the "temperate" (22%).[37] Prostitution, in fact, clearly a moral offense, was marked by neither high rates of illiteracy nor a high rate of conviction. (Females arrested were of course convicted more often than their male clients.) Prostitutes were among the most literate of arrested women, and they were convicted less often than virtually all other female suspects.

Importantly, too, the offenses in which these illiterate men and women were overrepresented, along with the poor, the Irish, and women, were precisely those cases in which the police, the magistry, and other authorities had their widest discretionary latitude. With regard to the offenses against public and official morality, which met with highest rates of conviction, the authorities could choose whether an actual offense or crime had been committed and whether to move toward arrest and prosecution. In other words, largely involved here were "victimless" offenses against public order. In such cases, the character and characteristics of the supposed offender and the observation and evaluation of the officer interact in determining whether a crime has been committed and an arrest should be made. Vagrancy, for example, consists of the apprehension in a public place of one who often has no means or right to enter a private place. Sociologically, then, the nature and forms of offenses and the authorities' responses contributed directly to the processes of arrest and conviction.

The fact that for any crime illiterates were disproportionately convicted obscured the ambiguities and contradictions behind this first and most obvious relationship. Blurred from school promoters' and other reformers' vision, or ignored perhaps as contrary to expectations or even as incomprehensible, were the literacy of the suspected and acquitted as well as that of the convicted, patterns of discrimination, and differing rates of conviction for various offenses. Indeed, the crime for which most arrests were made, property offenses, was least-often convicted and was marked by the literacy, not the illiteracy, of the suspects. Most judicial action seemingly was focused upon crimes of idleness, intemperance,

---

[37] All arrested men and women were classified by moral habits, on the registers: specified as "temperate" or "intemperate."

and disorder (by-law violations), crimes which were expected to follow directly from ignorance, even though they did not constitute a majority of supposed offenses. Both educational promoters and the judiciary in accepting and disseminating the "literacy myth" presumed the illiterate (or ignorant), the Irish, and the idle to be guilty of social offenses and criminality. It is not surprising that they were found guilty so often. Expectations—then and now—influenced justice, even though the perceived connection between illiteracy and criminality was neither the only nor the important relation. The "literacy myth" continues to influence thinking about criminality, the operations of the criminal justice system, and social policies.[38] Education alone, like literacy by itself, does not provide an answer.

---

[38] See the literature cited in Note 2, above. This is not to suggest that approaches have not become more sophisticated; rather, I stress the continuity of ideas and explanations regarding the role of education. The parallels are especially striking and are more than coincidental. See also, "Study links life of crime to illiteracy," *Dallas Times Herald,* 13 November 1977.

7

Literacy: Quantity and Quality

> *The only literacy that matters is the literacy that is in*
> *use. Potential literacy is empty, a void. Literacy is not*
> *merely the ability to read; it is the act of reading.*
>
> M. M. LEWIS
>
> *The Importance of Reading (1953)*

> *Schooling has been transformed into a quantifiable com-*
> *modity. . . .*
>
> E. VERNE
> *"Literacy and Industrialization—*
> *The Dispossession of Speech" (1976)*

> *It is evident that despite the lavish production made for*
> *education, a large class of the rising generation is growing*
> *illiterate, for a few weeks schooling in the year is prac-*
> *tically of no value.*
>
> HAMILTON
> *Palladium of Labour (1884)*

Reviewing his experiences in Canada and the United States during the last third of the nineteenth century, Frederick Philip Grove, novelist, laborer, and schoolmaster, drew particular attention to the schools and their transmission of literacy.

Alas! Our schools! We worship the fetish of reading and writing. Useful arts they are, of that there is no doubt. But—I speak from manifold experience— show me the grown-up who wishes to master the arts of reading and writing and cannot do so in a short time—in one-hundredth the time we waste on them in our schools, incidentally making our children into verbalists and spoiling them for reality—and I will show you a mental laggard. We say that

269

there is an age for these things; that beyond that age it becomes nearly impossible to acquire their knowledge. That is simply one of the superstitions of
the ages. Reading and writing and similar inessentials have formed the curriculum of our schools since time immemorial. Why?

Why do our children break away from school as soon as they can? Because
they are forced to follow what seems to them futile, silly, purposeless routine.
The children are right. Convince yourselves by going to the schools yourselves;
by acquiring some art which is taught there in the same deadening way in
which it is presented to them. I believe I should soon catch you in playing
truant. We are ever-lastingly hitching the buggy in front of the horse; and we
think that unfortunately it cannot be helped. A more systematic, organized,
wilfully cruel waste than that conducted in our world-wide systems of education no genius of perversity could invent.[1]

To Grove, who was only one of many critics, the process of schooling
was not succeeding: time was wasted in the classroom, time that dulled,
deadened, and literally repelled the young scholars. A child subjected
to this routine, Grove averred, would either become a verbalist, unprepared to use his or her education, or would flee, presumably with even
fewer useful skills. Observations like these, so common during the last
decades of the nineteenth century, redirect our attention to the question
of the *quality of literacy,* rather than the *quantity* alone: the level of
the skills achieved through schooling and the congruence between that
ability, the uses to which it was put, and the needs of the society.

This complex issue forms the basis of the final chapter in this exploration of literacy in the mid-nineteenth century. It is, in many ways,
the most difficult problem in the historical analysis of literacy—tran-
scending the treatment of literacy as a dichotomous (either-or) attainment, as the sources typically report it whether by signatures and marks
or by census responses. Despite the required artificiality of such an assessment of literacy, general measures of qualitative levels of literacy skills do
not exist for entire populations, outside of Scandinavia, making it exceed-
ingly difficult to discover accurately the distribution of abilities, rather than
the distribution of the possession or the lack of literacy. The problem
is largely unamenable to systematic or quantitative analysis for this society.
The few sources that might inform the question of readership, such as
library or local institute subscription, membership, or circulation lists,
are limited in their availability, representativeness of coverage, and utility. Membership, for example, need not mean use, and borrowing a book
does not mean reading or understanding it—despite the assumptions
often implicit in studies. Another potential indicator, circulation totals

[1] Grove, *A Search for America* (Toronto, 1927; reprinted: McClelland and Stewart,
1971), 302–304.

of newspapers or journals, is similarly restricted. Not only are circulation figures often quite unreliable, but they are also difficult to find for Upper Canada in this period. Comparing numbers of copies to the size of a potential audience is often no more than guesswork and certainly no more than that considering the number of readers who might hear their contents read aloud. This is not, of course, to say that such studies should not be attempted; they may tell us much about attitudes toward institutions, associations, membership, and values, and about borrowing habits, too. Nevertheless, their value to those raising basic questions about levels of literacy is limited.[2] The problem requires, instead, the use of a broader stroke and a wider search for indicators and opinion bearing on the *quality* of literacy and the uses to which that literacy could or should be put, successfully or unsuccessfully.

In previous chapters, the distribution of literacy and its limited, sometimes contradictory meaning to individuals of differing ethnicity, class, sex, and age were explored. We can not neglect the basic fact that this was an overwhelmingly literate population, with levels of adult literacy around the 90% mark in each of the cities, and perhaps in Upper Canada as a whole. What does this signify about that literacy *qualitatively,* other than that its possession did not reduce social inequality and was not a requirement for adaptation or some success?

As suggested in Chapter 6, a statistically *high* level of literacy possession may in fact obscure attention from a *lower* qualitative level of ability to use that literacy. In mid-nineteenth-century Sweden, as noted, the ability to read well orally did not always represent an ability to understand what was read. Of all those examined in one parish, only 10% read with passable to good comprehension; of those who read orally with "achievement," only 23% understood passably or better. Most literate individuals were limited in their potential for active employment of

---

[2] See the Introduction, above. The work of Paul Kaufman, Robert Winans, and Victor Neuberg is representative of this genre. See, for example, Kaufman, "The Community Library: A Chapter in English Social History," *Transactions of the American Philosophical Society,* 57 (1967), "Readers and their Reading in Eighteenth Century Lichfield," *The Library,* 28 (1973), 108–115, *Borrowings from the Bristol Library, 1773– 1784* (Charlottesville: University of Virginia Press, 1960); Winans, "Growth of A Novel-Reading Public in Late-Eighteenth Century America," *Early American Literature,* 9 (1975), 267–275; Neuberg, *Popular Education in Eighteenth-Century England* (London: Woburn Press, 1972); Alvar Ellegard, *The Readership of the Periodical Press in Mid-Victorian Britain,* Vol. 63, No. 3, Goteborgs Universitets Arsskrift (Goteborg, Sweden, 1957). See also, Michael Harris and Donald Davis, eds., *American Library History: A Bibliography* (Austin: University of Texas Press, 1978), for further examples. For one useful corrective, see Raymond Williams, "The press and popular culture: an historical perspective," in *Newspaper History,* ed. George Boyce, James Curran, and Pauline Wingate (Beverly Hills: Sage, 1978), 41–50.

their literacy skills, and there is no reason why such an examination, if possible, should uncover very different results in North America— revealing that literacy was, commonly, imperfect. The available evidence, as this chapter details, when evaluated as an indicator of the level of popular skills, points to a similar conclusion. We will consider, in the first two sections of the chapter, the question of ability and its quality.

Secondly, the necessarily related question of the uses of that level of skill and the correspondence between abilities and needs is confronted. No inclusive, systematic answer is now possible. The evidence and the logic of inquiry, nevertheless, do indicate that levels of popular literacy were at once sufficient to satisfy many of the demands of society yet inappropriate for others. The meaning and value of literacy to individuals and to the society was complex and in some ways contradictory. In the relationship between promotion and everyday uses and the primarily nonutilitarian bases of mass employment of literacy, needs were incompletely satisfied by abilities. The officially stated importance of literacy only partially corresponded to literacy's social roles.

I

The experience of schooling at mid-century provides one set of indicators that inform us about the level of literacy skills in the society. The history of public education in one of the cities examined above, Kingston, illustrates the number of complications militating against effective early learning and the development of proficiency in literacy. Problems of physical conditions, attendance, teacher ability, and instructional method intersected in the classroom. The reports of the local superintendent in the 1850s reveal the scope and magnitude of the factors that obstructed successful learning and the development of superior skills.

The description begins in 1850 with the simple, stereotypical comment "Our schools are obviously susceptible of much improvement." The physical setting of learning was identified as one impediment, for suitable school accommodations were a presumed prerequisite of successful education. In Kingston, however, "no one can teach, no child can learn, if exposed to a current of air from every side of a building, while the thermometer ranges from 20° to 25° below zero." Not only were classrooms unsuited climatically for effective education, but they were overpopulated as well. Schoolrooms were crowded; "children of all ages, are packed in their seats as close as one's fingers." The schools, local Superintendent R. S. Henderson urged, were improving in efficiency, yet they continued to be plagued by "the want of suitable school-houses with furniture, books, and other requisites of study, and a proper classification of the pupils." Children of all ages were huddled in crowded, low, and ill-ventilated rooms, with insufficient numbers of desks and few aids "to assist in developing the intellect or lure the mind to study."

"Bodily health is essential to a vigorous mind," Henderson knew, "but this cannot be long retained in an atmosphere reeking with the impurities of sixty or seventy bodies." Teacher and student alike felt their minds benumbed; languor, inactivity, and impaired health were pervasive. The natural consequence, he judged, was not only an aversion to study but also sickness and disease. As these conditions turned children away from the school and all associated with it, so they negatively influenced parental actions, too, "A parent who cares for the health of his child, who has learned to value the inestimable blessing of 'a sound mind in a sound body,' will not send him to such a school and hence, perhaps, in some measure the alleged fact, that hundreds of grown-up children about Kingston never attend school."

Tied to these circumstances were problems of attendance. Henderson found, in 1851, that "the statistics of the number in daily attendance could scarcely be credited, and astonishment and incredulity were manifested at the large number said to be growing up without education of any kind to fit them to discharge the duties of life." The next year enrollment actually declined; daily attendance was at 50% or less. This, of course, was but one-half of the children enrolled, not the eligible ones; nor were the same children in school day after day. Individual attendance was very irregular. While gratified that so many sent their children (with "undiminished confidence"), Henderson still concluded that "as many as were in daily attendance at the common schools, were growing up ignorant of even a knowledge of reading." His own calculations, in fact, indicated that perhaps fewer than 20% of 5- to 16-year-olds attended regularly.

Bad teachers were another obstacle to successful instruction. Many were poorly qualified; many had difficulties in passing the second- or third-class certification examinations. "With such a staff of teachers in a large city to conduct the education of some thousands of children, many above the age of 15 years, it is not unfair to conclude that our schools can never arrive at a higher degree of perfection." With teachers like these, the children "may continue to move backward and forward over the same ground for a number of years; but they must finally retire from school in comparative ignorance of all but the elements of a very common education."

The organization of the curriculum further interfered with even a good teacher's work. As instruction was designed, each teacher was required to teach all branches of the common-school curriculum, "involving an amount and variety of labor in a crowded school-room that cannot but be superficial and unproductive to any extent, of a thorough knowledge of any one of the branches taught." Only first class teachers, of whom there were too few, were qualified to teach all these subjects. Good teachers were not only exceptional, they also were insufficiently commended or rewarded for their abilities and efforts; rather, "they are employed today, dismissed tomorrow, and forgotten the next day." [3]

Finally, there is the question of how the teachers taught. In Kingston, each day instructors faced classes averaging seventy pupils, classified or unclassified by age and attainment, with a potential numbering twice that if all those enrolled were to attend simultaneously. The faces undoubtedly varied daily and monthly as schooling remained an irregular and discontinuous experience for many youngsters. Family mobility also uprooted pupils. Among those present, problems existed that centered on reading instruction. Henderson did not attempt to hide this, admitting that "probably there is no branch in which the pupils attending our schools are more deficient than in the art of good reading." This arose, he continued, not so much from incapacity on the teachers' part as from the inattention to and lack of appreciation of the importance of teaching children to read English fluently and correctly. Too often the other branches of study were permitted to encroach upon the time allotted to reading instruction.

At fault appeared to be the pedagogical method as well as the lack of time given to it. The old system of teaching the alphabet first, then advancing to the spelling of syllables of two or three letters remained the rule in Kingston's schools. The need to replace this "pernicious system" with teaching by whole words and the sounds of the words was recognized; its supposed endorsement by the Chief Superintendent and its applicability to the new National Readers were noted. But the old mode prevailed in the schools, only to "eventually be superceded." For better training in reading, Henderson was certain, the new "word method" must be instituted. In 1851, it was to replace teaching by letters and syllables "in none of which are the elementary sound of these letters heard," and in 1852 to supplant reading taught by the sounds of the letters. His confusion about instructional methods is imporant, as

---

[3]"City of Kingston," Excerpts from Local Superintendent's Reports, *Annual Report of the Chief Superintendent . . . for Upper Canada*, 1850, 1851, 1852. For English parallels, see R. D. Altick, *The English Common Reader* (Chicago: University of Chicago Press, 1957), 150. See also, Ian Davey, "Educational Reform and the Working Class," unpub. PhD. Diss., University of Toronto, 1975.

we will see; but regardless, "scholars were growing up in ignorance of even a knowledge of reading."

What Henderson decried was "children reading what they evidently do not understand, and hence the habit of what is called school reading." To Henderson and to many of his generation, good reading was primarily reading which sounded good: "The essential characteristics of a good reader are a just enunciation of sounds as well as words. . . . Children naturally speak correctly—their language is simple—they use only words of which they comprehend the full meaning," it was assumed. Their reading should be the same as their speaking: clear, distinct, emphatic, natural, and comprehending. Contradictions and differences between the language of the home and the street, on the one hand, and that of the school and the book, on the other, in style and diction, were apparently overlooked. Also neglected was the fact that reading adequate in terms of enunciation did not imply comprehension, even if a slight relationship did exist. Surely, though, that style of reading alone formed a limited goal, but not even this kind of reading prevailed in Kingston's schools at mid-century.[4]

Classroom management constituted another aspect of the inadequacy in pedagogical technique. "The most valuable part of a child's time" was wasted, for, on the average, pupils were called upon for a recitation of their ABCs twice daily, "the rest of the time spent in listless activity and stupor, if order is maintained in the school." Five of each six hours spent daily in class went unoccupied, the schoolroom becoming "a prison from which [the child] gladly escapes, and to which he unwillingly returns." The children dared not speak or ask questions; this would violate classroom order. "His active little mind, playing in his healthy body, looking for and desiring knowledge, is curbed, depressed, broken, under the discipline of the present system." Fondness for learning and study were presumed to depend on the nature of early encounters with the school. From the beginning, then, desire was being crushed.

Obviously, there were many impediments to learning, especially learning to read well either orally or comprehendingly, in Kingston during the 1850s. An account of such problems has a significance that transcends the experience of Kingston alone. As anyone familiar with the history of education (or inner-city schools today) will immediately recognize, these problems were hardly unique to that city. They repre-

[4] See Daniel Calhoun, *The Intelligence of a People* (Princeton: Princeton University Press, 1973), 80; "City of Kingston," *Annual Report*, 1851, 1852, 1853; Local Superintendent's Reports, RG-2, Box 21, Provincial Archives of Ontario. For a twentieth-century analogy, see H. R. Huise, *The Illiteracy of the Literate* (New York: Appleton-Century, 1933).

sented the common complaints of school reformers and many teachers at mid-century. In its educational condition, Kingston was typical; it highlights the manner in which these common difficulties converged and impinged upon the transmission of literacy and its resulting quality. In some places, urban or rural, the situation would be better, in others worse. Yet in these accounts are found important indicators which inform our assessment about the quality of literacy skills in the middle years of the nineteenth century. Even when one proceeds cautiously and allows for the effects of promotional aims on the published descriptions penned by schoolmen, the main conclusion is inescapable: Common schooling experiences were not in most cases likely to produce more than imperfectly skilled individuals.

This conclusion derives support from other indicators, as we will soon see. And, importantly, an imperfect level of popular literacy ability was peculiar neither to Kingston nor to the 1850s. In the face of improvements in a number of the contributing factors, contemporary evaluations and other indicators reveal the persistence of less than perfect qualitative abilities. During the three succeeding decades, facilities changed, as larger, more commodious, better-lit and better-ventilated schoolhouses, stocked with more modern, up-to-date learning aids and equipment accompanied the expansion and systematization of education. This was especially true in urban areas. The quality and preparation of the teaching force grew more satisfactory, too. More first-class teachers were produced by the normal schools, and increasingly only first- and second-class teachers were hired by the city systems. The stabilizing of the instructional force accompanied the professionalization and the bureaucratization of education. Finally, by the 1870s enrollment levels among children aged 7–12 or 5–14 years rose to near universalistic proportions, especially in the cities of Ontario, and pupils were more efficiently classified and graded by age.

Along with this modernization of schooling, problems that were identified in Kingston and elsewhere persisted, blocking progress in elementary instruction. One obstacle was low daily school attendance—rather than total enrollment. In Hamilton, for example, in 1851 only at the ages 9 to 11 were even a majority of children enrolled, and by 1861 still fewer than two-thirds attended. Of course, more and more children were successfully herded into classrooms for longer periods, as the hegemony of the school was more firmly established. But little progress was made in the frequency of attendance, as Ian Davey has shown. From the 1850s through the 1870s, daily attendance remained at about 50% of the enrollment levels. On any given day, little more than half of those enrolled were found in the classrooms, despite the growth in the population of pupils from less than half of those eligible to nearly all.[5] With common attendance of 100 days or less for most children, we must ask how infrequent and irregular attendance exacerbated the other problems of instruction. Reading specialists today remain uncertain about the amount of time required for learning good reading skills, but there is agreement that irregular attendance is one important obstacle to progress toward more satisfactory levels of literacy.[6]

Classroom conditions, even if improving physically, continued to militate against the acquisition of proficiency in literacy. The pupil–teacher ratios found in Kingston were representative of those across the province and in the other cities. Ratios exceeding 100 enrolled pupils per teacher, and about 70 daily, remained common throughout the 1850s to the 1870s at least. Age-graded instruction, intended to homogenize the learning experience and narrow the disparate range of abilities within a group of youngsters, had little impact on class size, especially among the younger pupils. In addition, female teachers increasingly taught the youngsters, and they were underpaid, often with lower qualifications than men. Classroom management was expected to be as central to their work as instruction.[7] The need to combine the two in daily practice could result in the stultifying routine censured by Superintendent Henderson. Whether discipline was harsh or soft, the 70 bodies and minds had to be kept occupied, often in rote exercises of recitation and imitation. Consequently, grouped activities, military-like drills, mechanical exercises, and rigid timetabling increasingly became common practice, so that no pupil would be unoccupied or become restless. This was one result of the "new" learning theory or "soft" pedagogy that replaced the older style of enforced inactivity and strict discipline, forming the classroom setting in which reading was to be learned.[8] This was hardly a forum conducive to the acquisition of skills of a high quality.

The rates of adult literacy provide concrete evidence that some

[5] See the *Annual Report of the Chief Superintendent*, 1850–1871, for documentation of change. See also Davey, "Educational Reform"; Michael B. Katz, "Who Went to School?" *History of Education Quarterly*, 12 (1972), 432–454.

[6] For example, see Cyril Burt, "The Education of Illiterate Adults," *British Journal of Educational Psychology*, 15 (1945), 23, 20–27; Jean Chall, *Learning to Read* (New York: McGraw-Hill, 1967); Chall and J. B. Carroll, eds. *Toward A Literate Society* (New York: McGraw-Hill, 1975).

[7] *Annual Reports;* Alison Prentice, "The Feminization of Teaching in British North America and Canada," *Histoire sociale*, 8 (1975), 5–20; Keith Melder, "Woman's High Calling," *American Studies*, 13 (1972), 19–32; R. M. Bernard and M. A. Vinovskis, "The Female School Teacher in Ante-Bellum Massachusetts," *Journal of Social History*, 10 (1977), 332–345.

[8] Ryerson, "Report on a System of Public Elementary Instruction for Upper Canada," in *Documentary History of Education*, ed. J. G. Hodgins, 6 (Toronto, 1899); *Annual Reports*. See also Katz, *The Irony of Early School Reform* (Cambridge, Mass.: Harvard University Press, 1968), Part II, for the context of the Massachusetts discussion.

degree of instruction was assimilated by almost all children, yet these manifold complications and the continuing infrequency of attendance force us to consider that the common level of reading ability was far from perfect. Exposure to teaching, correction, practice, drill, and reinforcement was limited for a great many children in the years most essential for gaining the basic skills of education. No doubt the quality of literacy suffered as a result; this was not lost to contemporaries.[9]

II

Methods of reading instruction, considered by Henderson among the impediments, provide an especially revealing indicator of the obstructions to effective learning and of the quality of the literacy skills gained in the schools. Reading-instructional methods were a matter of great concern to educators throughout the second half of the nineteenth century. Several approaches, in particular those favoring either the letters or the words first, competed for attention and adoption in the classroom. Each had its supporters and detractors, ready and able to prove the success of what they championed and the failure of the other; each was tied to a style of pedagogy. This rivalry, often bitter and producing exaggeration and hyperbole in the context of the different values of pedagogical schools, makes an analysis of the debate very tricky. What does emerge clearly, nevertheless, is the common dissatisfaction with reading instruction and its results, which bears significantly on the quality of the literacy transmitted by the schools. The problem of teaching children, or even adults, to read is very complicated and less than satisfactorily resolved, as present-day research and teacher opinion continue to make evident. In the past century, controversy raged at least as often as it does today, and understanding lagged behind. Furthermore, the style

---

[9] Reports from Commissioners, Popular Education, Great Britain, 1861, *Sessional Papers,* 21, Part I, esp. Sections II and III. Roger Smith, "Education, Society and Literacy: Nottinghamshire in the Mid-Nineteenth Century," *University of Birmingham Historical Journal,* 12 (1969), 42–56, poses this question in an opposite but complementary way: "Our only general conclusion, therefore, must be that no simple relationship existed between school attendance and minimum literacy. . . . Considering the proportion of children in each district who had received a schooling of one sort or the other, we must be surprised that there were such high proportions of illiterates. Part of this may reflect the sheer inefficiency of many of the schools." Of course, his measure was the signature, whose learning we may presume required a period of schooling longer than that for the barest mechanical reading. See also, Calhoun, *Intelligence.*

of reading that usually formed the explicit goal of educators was one
that confused oral with cognitive ability, reinforcing our conclusion that
reading with comprehension was an accomplishment not always
achieved.[10] The debate over methods was widespread throughout Anglo-
America with much of it conducted outside of Canada, but it was followed closely by men like Ryerson who made their contributions within
the terms of the controversy.

In his omnibus report of 1846, Egerton Ryerson devoted seven
pages to the importance of reading-instructional methods. Revealing his
debt to his own and Horace Mann's observations in Prussia and to debates in the United States, he claimed, "I have thus adverted to this
subject, not with a view of advocating any particular theory, but to
show how much importance is involved in this first step of elementary
teaching, and how much may be done." Primarily, he censured the
dominant practice of teaching the alphabet first, as Henderson did six
years later. This approach he found tedious to the teacher, stultifying
to the student—"protracted for many months" in its purely mechanical
process. Lacking were, in his opinion, meaning, ideas, and applications.
Indignantly, Ryerson asked, "Is it not calculated to deaden rather than
quicken the intellectual faculties? Is not such irrational drudgery calculated to disgust the subject of it with the very thoughts of learning?"
In the rote repetition of the letters, sometimes extending to years, the
intellectual side—the meaning of what was read—was neglected; obscured were "the meanings of the words used, the facts narrated, the
principles involved, the lessons inculcated." Children learned neither
useful skills nor fluency; they learned little more than indifference or
aversion to reading, and with "so few pleasant recollections, that they
engaged in it with reluctance, and only from necessity." Although he

[10] On reading instruction, see H. B. Lamport, "A History of the Teaching of Be-
ginning Reading," unpub. PhD. Diss., University of Chicago, 1935; M. M. Matthews,
Teaching to Read Historically Considered (Chicago: University of Chicago Press, 1966);
N. B. Smith, *American Reading Instruction* (Newark, Del.: International Reading
Association, 1934); F. Adams, L. Gray, and D. Reese, *Teaching Children to Read* (New
York: Ronald Press, 1949); E. B. Huey, *The Psychology and Pedagogy of Reading* (New
York, 1908, reprinted, Cambridge, Mass.: MIT Press, 1968); W. J. F. Davies, *Teaching
Reading in Early England* (New York: Barnes and Noble, 1974); W. S. Gray, *The
Teaching of Reading and Writing* (Paris: UNESCO, 1956); Chall, *Learning;* Chall and
Carroll, *Literate Society;* "Reading, Language, and Learning." *Harvard Educational
Review,* 47 (August, 1977); Calhoun, *Intelligence.* Calhoun's work is particularly
valuable, although my conclusions about reading instruction in the nineteenth century
were formed before his volume was published. See also, José Ortega y Gasset, "The
Difficulty of Reading," *Diogenes,* 28 (1959), 1–17. We should note also the persisting
problems and controversies over reading methods.

was convinced that the prevailing alphabetic method had to be replaced, Ryerson, revealingly, felt unprepared to advocate any specific substitute.[11]

With Ryerson's comments, we enter the debate at midpoint. His comments were largely derivative, and Upper Canadians did not make novel or original contributions. They followed the discussions in the United States and usually sided with proponents of the new, so-called "soft" pedagogy: the "natural" way for learning to advance.[12] Henry Esson, Canada's first theorist of instruction, for example, followed this organic, natural view of language-learning in his *Strictures on the Present Method of Teaching the English Language and Suggestions for its Improvement.* Languages, in this view, represented nature; words carried the simple ideas, conceptions, and notions that were the indigenous productions of the mind. Following nature's order, the pupil should be taught "to dispose words, the signs of thought, as nearly as possible, in the order of the things signified, that is, in the order of the system . . . so as to fit it to the end of education." Learning in a progressive, organized way, the pupil would advance easily, rather than plodding "in darkness and disgust through the to him, unintelligible metaphysics of language coming . . . before his knowledge is such as to admit of the possibility of his understanding it" as in the other method. Understanding would therefore systematically and scientifically replace mechanical, unnatural, and preposterous instruction, as knowledge of the words fostered intellectual education and the act of thinking.[13] In this perspective on learning theory and on reading approaches, Esson's conception paralleled the criticisms of older modes and the pedagogical innovations that swept Anglo-America and elsewhere in the west by mid-century. The recognition that the alphabetic method and the style of pedagogy associated with it produced individuals who, though technically literate, read poorly at best led to bitter controversy.

In the United States, the debate was more widespread, the criticism sharper, and the elaboration and defense of both methods more detailed. From these statements and descriptions, the level of reading ability may be assessed. Criticism of method and results, in fact, surfaced well before

[11] Ryerson, "Report on a System," 167, 163, 168.

[12] See George Combe, *The Constitution of Man* (Hartford, Conn., 1845) on the philosophical bases of the new pedagogy, as well as Katz, *The Irony.* See also Nelson Sizer, *How to Teach According to Temperament and Mental Development* (New York, 1877). For England, see Richard Johnson, "Notes on the Schooling of the English Working Class," in *Schooling and Capitalism,* ed. R. Dale, G. Esland, and M. MacDonald (London: Routledge, Kegan Paul, 1976), 48. On the fallacies in such approaches, see Frank Smith, "Making Sense of Reading," *Harvard Educational Review,* special issue, 386–395.

[13] (Toronto, 1852), 12, 14–15, 19, 23, 24.

the escalation of debate in the 1840s and 1850s. In 1830, William Russell foreshadowed the controversy in a lecture to the American Institute of Instruction, and several years later, Thomas Palmer discussed educational failings in an address to the same body. Both found too little attention paid to fundamentals like reading. Consequently, Palmer asserted, "not one out of twenty—nay, . . . not one out of fifty—who had no further privilege of education than our district schools afford, has derived that advantage which they ought to confer on every individual, the ability of going forward alone with his education." Very few were able to make practical use of their education, whether on the higher level at which reading and thinking reciprocally joined or on the level of a mind disciplined by reading to be able, for example, to follow the "chain of reasoning" of a minister. The causes were many, as in Kingston, as classroom instruction and "the result of the vicious habits acquired in learning to read" were blamed for the low quality of literacy. Not only did the younger pupils copy the bad habits of the older ones, but also reading represented little more than "a mere utterance of sounds," and "a mere affair of memory." "[A]s to the comprehension of the *meaning*," Palmer concluded, "the language might as well have been Greek, Arabic, or Chinese, as English." [14]

These criticisms, though revealing, were no more than a preamble to the major debate in Massachusetts, which erupted in the 1840s, between Horace Mann and the Association of Boston Schoolmasters. Constituting an important chapter in the reform of the schools, the rich detail of their exchanges provides a rare opportunity to examine midnineteenth-century reading instruction and practices. They permit us to focus specifically on the faults found inherent in each system and the problems involved in instruction for good reading skills. Importantly, the difficulties were more than matters of age-grading, physical conditions, or materials, all of which were eventually improved.

Mann's *Second Annual Report*, of 1839, frontally attacked the alphabetic method and the pedagogic values it represented. With others, he was impressed by the lack of mental activity and the "obvious want of intelligence, in the reading classes, respecting the subject matter of the lessons." Finding pupils unable to spell or understand, Mann estimated that fully eleven-twelfths of the reading students in the schools of Massachusetts neither understood the meanings of the words they uttered nor mastered the sense of their lessons nor grasped the ideas or feelings intended by the authors. Age-grading, contrary to the hopes of

14 Russell, "The Infant School System of Instruction," *Proceedings*, The American Institute of Instruction, 1 (1830), 98; Palmer, "Evils of the Present System of Primary Instruction," *ibid.*, 8 (1837), 211, 212, 214, 216.

many, had not countered the instructional problems, for (as today) "it is probable also, that this mischief may have been aggravated, in those places where there is a gradation of schools, by the conditions, prescribed in their regulations, for advancing from one school to another." To advance, fluent or good-sounding reading was required; yet "there is a great danger that the value of *intelligent* reading will be sacrificed to the worthlessness of mere fluent reading." [15]

Confusion about the sound of reading plagued schoolmen throughout the period. Fluency or naturalness represented good reading and supposedly symbolized understanding; yet, as Mann admitted, it could too easily obscure a lack of comprehension. Promoting students from level to level exacerbated these dangers, as the English Royal Commission on Popular Education discovered. Inspection there involved hearing each pupil read; 150 were examined in an hour and a half, a rate of one each 36 seconds—hardly a test assuring good reading ability. Parents, Mann emphasized, asked not "What have you read about?" but "How many times and how much have you read?" Comprehension and quality were subordinated to the number of pages "mechanically gone over." Inquiries centered on the amount of labor, "done by the organs of speech," the quantity of pages—not the skills learned and practiced.[16] The result was pretending to read what was not understood, a fluency and articulation that did not represent comprehension but that could be taken for literacy.

Mann's colleague Cyrus Peirce, former principal of the Normal School at Lexington, continued the criticism of traditional methodology in his 1843 lecture "On Reading." Echoing Mann's disapproval, he censured repetition and the length of time spent learning the letters and their sounds, finding reading usually poor in understanding and enunciation ("nasal, drawling, twanging or the hurried slurring, indistinct utterance"). Ignoring that such speech habits were rooted in ethnic linguistic diversity, he apparently did not relate them to the applauded, natural, language of children. Rather, oral errors were signs of noncomprehension, from compelling children to read what they did not understand or to read words with which they were not familiar. Knowing only the letters, they were totally "occupied in deciding what to *call the word*; they have nothing to bestow upon the meaning, the understanding of which is necessary to bring out the proper tone and inflection," he presumed. They read neither intelligibly nor intelligently.

[15] *Second Annual Report of the Secretary of the (Massachusetts) Board of Education* (Boston, 1839), 37, 39.

[16] Commission, Popular Education, *Sessional Papers,* 239; Mann, *Second Annual Report,* 39–40.

Instead, Peirce, Mann, Esson, Henderson, among others, urged that *words* be taught first: short, simple, familiar words that could be combined to form sentences. This would be pleasing to the pupils, and the "form or appearance" of the word would be learned together with its pronunciation and meaning. In this manner—consistent with reason, philosophy, and common sense (they claimed)—up to one thousand words should be learned before the letters, with their names and "powers," were introduced: "Children begin to *talk* with words, and why should they not begin to *read* with *words?*," Peirce asked. The relationship between print and sound, and the connections between sight and speech, as bases for learning to read, were simply never considered.[17]

The final, and provocative, round in this attack on the alphabetic method began in the primary schoolrooms of Prussia, as was noted in observations made by Horace Mann and later by Ryerson. They found active, interested pupils, learning to read quickly without knowing the names of the letters, only their "powers." Pupils neither echoed the alphabet nor waited vacantly between recitations; they were taught reading simultaneously with spelling, grammar, and drawing. The letters were ignored, and the error of giving pupils names that were not elements in the sounds of words was avoided. Learning the letters contradicted children's normal habits, as Mann exaggerated; "were it not for keeping up [the pupil's] former habits of speaking, at home and in the playground, the teacher, during the six months or year in which he confines him to the twenty-six sounds of the alphabet, would pretty much deprive him of the faculty of speech." Words, it was concluded, must replace letters and even sounds in reading method, for the Prussian phonic system was considered ill-suited to the English language.[18]

Many schoolmen joined in criticisms of the "old method," finding it productive of readers who did not understand what they read. Yet alphabetic instruction did not swiftly disappear, as Henderson's and Ryerson's testimony shows. Some instructors remained convinced of its success, especially when they compared it to the word method. Challenging the claims advanced against their approach, they responded that the newly proposed method did not train children to read well, a claim for which they found support. Opposed to the pedagogical values the new learning represented, the Boston school masters, in particular, counterattacked Mann and Peirce, devoting special attention to problems of

[17] *Lectures,* American Institute of Instruction, 1843 (Boston, 1844), 143–184; 144, 159, 153, 157–158, 149–153, 156, 160–161. On problems with this approach, see Smith, "Making Sense," 388, ff.

[18] *Seventh Annual Report* . . . (Boston, 1844), 86–90, 93, 99. See also Ryerson, "Report"; "City of Kingston," 1851, 1852.

reading instruction. They stressed, on the one hand, that the proponents of "words first" offered no good reasons to deviate from the scientific rule that "the elements should be taught first," and, on the other, that the new method did not even succeed. "Primary school teachers, who have tried the system," Samuel Greene wrote, "testify that when children learned a word in one connection, they are unable to recognize it in another, especially if there be a change of type." The masters were not persuaded that instruction in letters deprived children of their knowledge of language gained from hearing, speaking, and observing. Rather, "reading aloud is nothing less than translating *written* into *audible* signs, a knowledge of the latter, whatever may be the system of teaching, is presupposed to exist, and is about as necessary to the one learning to read, as would be a knowledge of the English language to one who would translate Greek into English." Surely there were no differences between the claims of the rival methods here, they urged, although the masters suggested that the word method confused written and spoken language, to the detriment of reading—an assertion supported by recent studies, in fact.[19]

Much of the attack on their method, the masters argued, was no more than a confusion of the names of letters with their "powers." Mann's oversight lay here, as he misunderstood the Prussian instruction which provided the form and "power" of each letter. These were then combined into written and spoken words, respectively—precisely the way they themselves taught, except that they added the letters' names as well: "to teach the alphabet . . . is to teach all that belongs to it." They simply could not understand how the Prussian example led Mann to promote such a change, "one which converts our language into Chinese," for they found the new method vastly inferior. It made the process of instruction more difficult, increasing the task tenfold if the alphabet were not known. Similarly, the new method, by avoiding letters, failed to escape the ambiguities and perplexities of the language— against the claim of its supporters. Enunciation, moreover, so important to all methodologists at this time, would suffer too. Only drill in elementary sounds could correct the habits of inarticulate speech, universally brought to school, especially by children from uneducated families. To the masters, the feelings and natural ways supposedly instinctive to

---

[19] See Association of Masters of the (Boston) Public Schools, *Remarks on the Seventh Annual Report of the Honourable Horace Mann, Secretary of the Massachusetts Board of Education* (Boston, 1844), 56–103; Samuel Greene, "On Methods of Teaching to Read," American Institute of Instruction, *Lectures*, 1844 (Boston, 1845), 211, 213–216, 207–235. See also, Smith, "Making Sense"; Chall, *Learning*, on the problems associated with these common methods, as well as continuing failings today.

the children and applauded by "soft" pedagogues were more detriments to good reading than assets.[20]

Behind these methodological differences were opposing conceptions of human nature and motivation. For example, the masters emphasized the importance of duty and discipline, contrasting with reformers' stress on activity and pleasure.[21] In its own terms, each side found the other wanting; each urged, however, the value of the pleasure arising from apprehending meaning in reading. The masters thus denied that pleasure arose from the new method; to them the teacher provided the meaning in giving the word and its sound, neither teaching children to read for themselves nor providing a source of motivation. The testimony of teachers who had used both methods was sought, leading to the conclusion that "in the end, nothing is gained, but much is lost; that the task of teaching the alphabet, and the art of combining letters into words, are more difficult, and less satisfactory, than if the child had begun with the letters." [22] Failure was also likely with the new system; children were not learning to read well, to understand, or to use their reading ability.

Regardless of the values inherent in the views of each side, the explicit criticisms and descriptions constituting the two sides of the debate join on one central issue: *children were not learning to read well, either fluently or comprehendingly.* Each argument employed the weight of science, philosophy, nature, and human nature; cited the opinion of teachers; recognized the importance of proper articulation, spelling, drill, and repetition; and valued reading for meaning. Yet each persisted in contending that children learned to read a language that they did not understand. Rivalry and competing values and methods must not obscure the major issue; both methods were condemned as failing in their goals. In this regard, Ryerson's inability and unwillingness to advocate any one method was telling. He had seen the Prussian technique, he had read Mann's critiques, and he had made observations in Upper Canada. But no one method would he support for instruction in either oral reading or the skills of comprehension. Failure to achieve good reading— for meaning—was, at the very least, quite possible regardless of the method adopted and the prevailing style of pedagogy.

The alphabetic method in fact was most common during the 1830s

[20] Masters, *Remarks,* 77–78; Greene, "Methods," 233.

[21] See Katz, *Irony,* esp. 139–146, for larger pedagogical implications of the debate.

[22] Greene, "Methods," 220, 221; Masters, *Remarks,* 56, 83–87, 99. The debate continued; see Mann, *Reply to the "Remarks of Thirty-one Schoolmasters"* (Boston, 1844), *Answer to the "Rejoinder" of Twenty-nine Boston Schoolmasters* (Boston, 1845); Masters, *Rejoinder to the Reply* . . . (Boston, 1845).

and 1840s. This was the time at which the future adult residents of Upper Canadian cities had their schooling, however limited, in Canada, the United States, or (for most) in the British Isles. English reports, importantly, stress the same problems in learning to read and in the quality of reading ability. A report to the Council of Education in 1851–1852, for example, maintained that instruction in reading was such that "the subject-matter of the book becomes practically of little importance," and that both teacher and pupil "remain equally ignorant of what it was intended to teach; and it is degraded into a mere implement for the mechanical teaching of reading. . . ." As elsewhere, comprehension was hardly the predominant result of reading instruction. Leaving school by age 10 or 11 was common, limiting exposure for many middle-class as well as working-class children. Even in the "best schools," less than one-third reached the standards; "a fair elementary education," the Commission on Public Education reported in 1861, was attained by only one-fourth of those who attended, or one-eighth of all children. Of those who reached the first class of the primary school, moreover, many had neither an ability nor a taste for reading; they soon forgot what they learned and relapsed into the condition of the uneducated, it was claimed. The large National Schools, furthermore, made proper education impossible; "in some reading is not taught at all in any real or sufficient sense." [23]

The problem, as in North America, hinged on the concentration on oral reading and neglect of attention to meaning. Reading was the most deficient subject, and little proficiency was found in either aspect, as pupils learned by memory and were unable to connect the meaning with the sounds of the words. Pupils, in fact, could "often reach a comparatively high position in the school, reading inarticulately, spelling incorrectly, and with the vaguest notions of numeration." To many of the children, the language of books was a foreign language; "the children are baffled, confused, and disheartened, and as a natural conse-

---

[23] Rev. Moseley in *Minutes of Committee of Council of Education* (1851–1852), 1, 288, as quoted in J. M. Goldstrum, *The Social Context of Education, 1808–1870* (Shannon: Irish Universities Press, 1972), 148; Commission, Popular Education, 239, 244, 248. Their goal for primary education is noteworthy too: a pupil should "spell correctly the words he will have to use; he shall read a common narrative—the paragraph in the newspaper that he cares to read—with sufficient ease to be a pleasure to himself and to convey information to listeners . . . write his mother a letter . . . legible and intelligible; he knows enough of ciphering to make out, to test the correctness of a common shop bill. . . . Underlying all, and not without its influence, I trust, upon his life and conversation, he has acquaintance with the Holy Scriptures . . . to know what are the duties required of him toward his Maker and his fellow men," 243.

quence, they subside into stolid indifference." [24] The quality of literacy that immigrants brought to North America was apparently no higher than that acquired there.

In England, damning reports such as that of the Popular Education Commission were instrumental in changing the structure of school support, with the immediate effect of instituting the system of "payment for results" to promote an emphasis on basic skills. Yet this change brought no reports of progress in reading. Criticism remained harsh, as the Council on Education reported in 1865–1866: "If their reading is to mean not only the correct utterance of the printed words, but an intelligent comprehension of what is uttered, then I fear that the percentage of children whom I can pass will be very small indeed." The ascerbic critic W. B. Hodgson reviewed the reading progress also, finding no stimulation or success, only that "it has injuriously affected . . . all that deserves the name of education, while it has not generally succeeded in ensuring even mechanical proficiency in the three arts specifically fostered." [25] Skill in reading, even mechanically, remained to many observers at a low level, and what verbal fluency there was obscured the absence of comprehension. Much was wanting in the transmission of the quality of literacy in the places that were the original homes of many Upper Canadians.

Regardless of the location of primary schooling, then, failure to achieve good reading skills was quite common. No doubt pupils learned something that could be called reading, for over 90% of them considered themselves able to read. Yet given the circumstances in which they were educated, the irregularity of attendance, and the methods that prevailed, we may well conclude that their literacy skills were quite frequently imperfect. Additional evidence shows the persistence of "school reading," older methods, and poor reading regardless of approach for the next several decades.[26] This was one important meaning of literacy in the society.

Taught either by the words or the letters first, children did learn to mechanically reproduce what they saw, whatever their proficiency in articulation or comprehension. Whether requiring a short or lengthy

[24] Commission, Popular Education, 246–261.

[25] Report, Committee, Council of Education, 1865–1866, 23, quoted in Goldstrum, Context, 166; Exaggerated Estimates of Reading and Writing as a Means of Education (London, 1868), 4–5. See also, M. M. Lewis, The Importance of Illiteracy (London: Harrap, 1953), 40–43.

[26] See Ryerson, Annual Report, 1871; William Russell, "On Teaching the Alphabet," Massachusetts Teacher, 15 (1862), 209–212; "Methods of Teaching to Read," Ibid., 16 (1863), 87–90; "Reading Made Easy," Ibid., 17 (1864), 328; Calhoun, Intelligence, Ch. 2; "The Cultivation of the Expressive Faculties," American Journal of Education, 3 (1857), 328; "City of Kingston."

period of instruction, the rudiments of reading could be and were claimed by many. In his original and brilliant essay, *The Intelligence of a People,* Daniel Calhoun arrives at the same conclusion about learning problems at the time. He found that while children gained the bare mechanics regardless of instructional method,

> pupils, once they progressed to more complex matter, relied on these elements and little more. They called out the words in a selection rapidly, and articulated them plainly for a listener who had the printed words to follow. But whether a pupil understood all the words he could pronounce was doubtful enough, and whether he understood whole passages and ideas was hardly doubtful. He did not.

They could prattle through their lessons and be promoted through the system. They had difficulty, nevertheless, in talking about what they read, for the lack of training in the meaning of words or passages was common to the results of instruction, as Ryerson and others also reported. Further, the inability to read with understanding adversely affected all other attempts at learning, Calhoun reports, indicating even more the limits on the uses of literacy in the second half of the nineteenth century. Students continued to leave school early with imperfect and deficient skills, as Ryerson repeated in 1871.[27]

By the 1870s and 1880s, pedagogical emphasis centered largely on the organic and natural in learning and particularly in reading, stressing natural articulation—one crucial element in the "new learning." This focus only exacerbated the sources of failure and confusion. While attention to pronunciation and tone had been a concern of all instructional methods, the balance shifted even more through the 1850s and 1860s as the new style of pedagogy gained acceptance and was institutionalized. This emphasis continued until the rise of silent reading in the last decade of the century. Natural, expressive, emotionally committed behavior was elicited from the pupils by their teachers. Good reading meant, more and more, reading that sounded good, and this was equated with comprehension, one of Ryerson's and others' primary aims. This was the meaning of the common expression "intelligent reading." [28] Instruction directed toward that goal not only erred in equating oral proficiency with comprehension, but educators made it

[27] Calhoun, *Intelligence,* 80, 85, Ch. 2; Ryerson, "Report," *Annual Report,* 1871; N. A. Calkins, "Primary Reading," *New York Teacher and American Educational Monthly,* 8 (1870), 34–35; T. P. D. Stone, "Reading in Common Schools," New York Regents, *Annual Report,* 83 (1880), 529–535.

[28] Ryerson, *Annual Report,* 1871; "City of Kingston"; Calhoun, *Intelligence;* Ryerson, *Annual Report,* 1877, "Report on a System." See also Katz, *Irony.*

even more difficult to judge how well the pupils understood what they articulated.

How easily confusion could occur is seen in Superintendent Henderson's list of the characteristics of a good reader: "a just enunciation of sounds as well as words; a careful regard to distinctness of pronunciation, and a proper fullness and modulation of voice. A clear and correct enunciation is of the highest importance." This was reading fluent and correct, supposedly corresponding to natural speech, for it followed, in theory, from children reading only what they understood. When newer methods were presented, such as phonetics, it was their ability to improve oral performance, not comprehension, that was applauded. Yet in Ontario, debate and discussion over method and criticisms regarding failures persisted, with no endorsement of any one successful approach. Ryerson, by 1871, continued to express dissatisfaction with reading instruction; even among advanced public and high-school students, oral ability was poor—deficiencies in articulation were threatening to become a national characteristic. Inattention to reading reflected, as earlier, inattention to meaning. If anything, the newer emphasis only further confused attempts at improvement in skills.[29]

Failings in instruction, we must recognize, need not signify that the school was not achieving many of its aims: in fostering hegemony and in socializing pupils. The presence of books, for example, was seen as a weapon against profanity and levity; and the movement led by Ryerson and J. George Hodgins to establish libraries in schools, towns, and even prisons represented another thrust. Books' "bindings and illustrations," Prentice notes, "were considered as important as their contents . . . in humanizing and refining the minds of young readers." Training in literacy involved more than understanding all that was read. The moral bases could be transmitted and reinforced in a number of ways, symbolically and orally, in conjunction with literacy. The uses of literacy included oral training as cultural conditioning; understanding was only one goal among many. Respectability, manners, taste, morality, and

---

[29] "City of Kingston," 1852; *Journal of Education,* 18 (1865), 152; *Annual Report,* 1871. Rev. John May repeated these criticisms a decade later, revealing the continuing failure to teach good reading and the stress on articulation. Reading was not taught as it "deserved" to be; the result was "a sort of cross between reading and a Gregorian chant." Moreover, "good reading is not only a pleasing and elegant accomplishment, but also an excellent intellectual exercise." The issue of intelligence, of understanding, continued to be confused with articulation: "You must understand a passage and enter into its spirit before you can read it in public," as if this were a goal for all pupils. *Essays on Educational Subjects* (Ottawa, 1880), 21. Present-day problems and practices should be compared; see Chall, *Learning;* Smith, "Making Sense"; *Harvard Educational Review, passim.*

speech habits would be inculcated in the process of instruction. Good reading in this sense was a highly valued accomplishment, greatly desired by reformers and educators. The Reverend John May summarized these goals when he wrote, "If we cannot have intelligent reading, let us have at least distinct and audible reading . . . even from a fool." [30]

One significant use of training in literacy was to homogenize the speech of the pupils. When schoolmen sought to foster natural patterns of expression, it was not the language of the streets or of the homes of the pupils that was to be instilled in the classroom and practiced in drill. The stress upon proper articulation was an aspect of the socializing function of the school, for the drawls, twangs, and slurring tones of children resulted from more than inattention to pronunciation. In an immigrant society, these were the distinctions of culture, class, and ethnicity; city streets heard a cacophony of vocal sounds and accents. By proscribing differences in speech under that comprehensive term of condemnation "school reading," reformers could then justifiably move to Canadianize or Americanize the children of the immigrant and the laborer. This strategy is clearly seen in the diction used to describe "school reading." For example, to Gideon Thayer, a former Boston principal, "a coarse style of pronouncing degrades the reader, and gives one a low idea of his breeding and his taste." As Prentice's work, in particular, has illustrated, schools in mid-century Upper Canada were promoting a class society, and one of the ways to ease social tensions was through homogenizing language, erasing some of the visible signs of diversity. Differences in acquired abilities and knowledge would persist behind the mask of similarity, as would those of class and status, but values of order and respectability could be inculcated through speech and language training. Analogously, Ryerson characterized poor spelling as discreditable; Mann asserted that an inability to spell "justly stamps the mind with the stigma of illiteracy." [31]

One use of literacy was thus to unite the heterogeneous peoples of new nations and to eradicate the *superficial* distinctions that separated classes and cultures. For this, instruction in literacy could be a valuable tool—inasmuch as classroom drill in articulation promoted cohesion and hegemony—in assimilating the values and manners of one class to those of the other classes. Simultaneously, linguistic differences readily

[30] Prentice, "The School Promoters . . . ," unpub. PhD. Diss., University of Toronto, 1974, 120; May, *Essays*, 20.

[31] "Letters to a Young Teacher, XIII," *American Journal of Education*, 4 (1857–1858), 226; Prentice, "Promoters," esp. Ch. 4; *Journal of Education*, 6 (1853), 175; Mann, *Second Annual Report*, 40.

identified the untrained, unassimilated, and uneducated, who were seen as threatening to unity and order. Moreover, and probably unknowingly, problems of reading instruction were 'complicated by an unsympathetic approach to these distinctions and their implications for learning.[32]

The available indicators together suggest strongly that the reading ability commonly attained was deficient. A literate society statistically, this was also a society in which individuals could read only after a fashion. How well they read and understood is to be distinguished from their possession of nominal literacy. Yes, instruction in reading had been provided to virtually all, and they were able to mechanically reproduce words, presumably understanding the simple and familiar either by sight or by sound. Many other words, though, and combinations of words into sentences and pages were beyond the comprehension of many readers. The literacy with which many left the schoolroom and entered the world was a restricted one—which present-day observations indicate is still the case in the twentieth century.

Reading for understanding, knowledge, and advancement was difficult given these foundations. Yet that might not interfere with many aspects of daily life. In lacking reading that was truly proficient, literate men and women would in many ways be indistinguishable from illiterates; the advantages which imperfect skills brought to them may have been indeed limited. Verbal ability could be quite another matter, however; to this, schooling had more to contribute. If Calhoun is correct that nineteenth-century culture tended to be wordy and compulsive, that "the needs of American families led children to rush through that verbalism in a mechanical way, never having the time to develop a relaxed involvement with their school words" the results of schooling could mesh with the needs of society. Verbalism, rather than high-quality skills, may well have been more attuned to social settings and needs for literacy. Calhoun discerns an inability among children to accept learned ideas and techniques as having much to do with ongoing life. Literacy of a highly qualitative level apparently was not a need felt by many. What the young mind did demand, and presumed to need, was "automatic responses and rule-of-thumb techniques by which it became a productive

[32] On literacy and nationalism, see among a large literature, Glanmour Williams, "Language, Literacy and Nationality in Wales," *History*, 56 (1971), 1–16. On the language differences of class and culture and their contributions to "learning problems," see D. R. Entwhistle, "Implications of language socialization for reading models and for learning to read," *Reading Research Quarterly*, 7 (1971–1972); Basil Bernstein, "Determinants of Perception," *British Journal of Sociology*, 9 (1958), 159–174, "Social Class, Language and Socialisation," *Current Trends in Linguistics*, 12 (1973).

member of society." Levels of useful literacy were not high, perhaps
because many saw no need for them to be high. Herein illiterates were
not severely disadvantaged, and could succeed. Those without literacy
suffered, however, a disability in verbal skills and in skills acquired in
formal or institutional settings.[33] Perhaps this was one cause of their
restricted occupational distribution and their inability to escape criminal conviction; certainly it could have hindered their social and occupational progress, although it did not debilitate all illiterates.

Training at home, at work, or on the streets could not prepare
them for all exigencies. This deficiency in preparedness, coupled with
class and ethnic stratification, blocked the paths of many. They also had
greater difficulties in acquiring the responses and techniques learned by
others in school; for them it would be perhaps harder and take longer
to learn, restricting some kinds of success and threatening their positions.
The importance of literacy *in practice* was limited, paralleling the level
of skills, but even the imperfect levels commonly possessed had their
social uses, not the least of which was the promotion of hegemony.
Literacy in this society therefore functioned on several levels, for while
the quality of literacy was adequate for many needs, it was inadequate
for others, and not necessary for all aspects of life.

III

"Illiteracy is relative," observed the English psychologist M. M.
Lewis. "The level of illiteracy is the extent to which an individual falls
short of the demands of literacy current in his society." Conversely, the
level of literacy demanded by society is also relative. The meaning of
literacy in mid-nineteenth-century urban society can only be understood
in context; it can be established neither arbitrarily nor abstractly nor
uniformly for all members of the population. It cannot be determined
realistically without reference to the structures of demands, needs, and
uses for literacy skills, which themselves vary and change. Constructing

[33] Calhoun, *Intelligence*, 130–131. On the relevance to Canada, see Grove, *Search;*
Ryerson, *Annual Report*, 1871. While there is no reason to consider illiterates disadvantaged in basic skills or in the ability to communicate, there are grounds to find
them less able in higher verbal skills and especially in formally learned cognitive
skills, perhaps useful (if not required) to gaining responsible work, performing some
jobs, conducting themselves in formal settings, such as courtrooms, etc. See the work
of Scribner and Cole and Greenfield, cited in Ch. 6, Note 34; Entwhistle, "Developmental Sociolinguistics: Inner City Children," *American Journal of Sociology*, 74 (1968),
37–49.

an index, typology, or etiology of needs and uses, as noted in the Introduction, is a task not yet accomplished for any modern society; this reveals as much about the impact of the "literacy myth" as about the relativistic position of literacy itself. Societies make demands which are felt, met, and responded to differentially by various men and women; material, economic, social, and cultural needs for literacy vary from group to group, person to person. These may be either real or perceived needs. Expectations, anticipations, and the actual employment of one's literacy vary as well. As Lewis explained, "The pressure on [a man] to become more literate will depend not only on his ability, but on the attitude of those whom he lives with, and how strongly he himself is moved by ambitions which demand literacy. If the people about him— his family, friends, neighbors—set little store by literacy, when he leaves school, he is more likely to move backward than forward." [34] "Potential literacy," as Lewis termed it, may indeed be a void, but the very potential of that literacy can be valuable to the society and to some within it.

In the past century, literacy, even on an imperfect level, existed on a wide scale. How often it was needed and how frequently and in what ways it was employed are questions too seldom asked. Yet questions like these must be raised if we are to understand the meanings of the distribution and the quality of literacy explored in these pages. Through an approach to culture and society in mid-nineteenth-century urban centers, the place of literacy may be further specified and the outlines of its varying significance sketched. To do this, several principles must be established. First, we need to consider issues of needs and uses in the context of high levels of popular possession of some skills—but skills of an imperfect nature. Second, we must distinguish the uses and needs, in so far as possible, by class and sex, at least. And third, the conclusions reached before about the social and economic limits of literacy must form the demarcations of further discussion. The latter, especially in reference to nineteenth-century comments, points to the primarily noninstrumental but still important roles that literacy played in the daily life of individuals and in the culture of the nineteenth-century city. Recognizing the contradictions between the promoted values of literacy (the basis of the "literacy myth") and its more restricted place in actuality (reconciled by its hegemonic functions) allows us to assess the relationship of literacy to life and culture. In this context, we consider the needs and uses of literacy on several levels.

Contemporaries who valued and promoted the possession and use of literacy provide important indicators for evaluation, which illustrate

[34] Lewis, *Importance,* 160, 16.

the uses and nonuses of literacy, and which also reinforce our conclusions regarding quality. With few exceptions, they observed that the literacy popularly possessed was not always employed, and if it were, then it was not properly or most effectively used. Comments and complaints such as these represent one important measure (recognizing their normative bias), complementing the other evidence. Differential needs for literacy and the levels of skill that correspond to their fulfillment can be derived from these discussions, which are found, significantly, in very different perspectives: the religious and working-class press, in particular. These comments indicate that individual literacy was imperfect, neglected, or, if used, not employed in ways perceived as best by promoters. On the one hand, we find in them a tension between the ways in which many individuals found literacy useful to themselves and the purposes that others thought literacy served. On the other hand, we find that regardless of this discrepancy, uses of literacy were primarily noninstrumental ones, while popular skills were at once appropriate for many of the demands made on them and insufficient for others.

Despite the literacy claimed by members of the society, commentators concluded that in practice literacy was insufficiently used. Its value was barely recognized; available time for reading was not seized. Individuals, it was felt, needed to be told to read, told how to read, and told why to read. " 'I have not time to read' is a complaint," the *Ontario Workman* reminded its audience, "especially of women, whose occupations are such as to prevent continuous book perusal. They seem to think, that because they cannot devote as much attention to books as they are compelled to their avocations that they cannot read anything." It was not the time that was lacking; it was the habit of reading that was absent. Others agreed. The average workingman, the *Palladium of Labor* claimed, did have enough time to read, but instead of using that time "he neglects mental culture." From labor's viewpoint, changes in patterns of work and movements to limit daily and weekly work hours freed time that could be well used for reading or other forms of mental culture. Furthermore, libraries in industrial areas were often underutilized by their working class patrons. Aside from other criticisms of improper use of literacy, this opinion indicates a neglect of the skills possessed. Of course there were other important reasons for little reading, especially by the working class: little time, poverty, exhaustion, alternative recreational habits, peer culture, poor lighting at home, unavailability or costliness of materials.[35]

[35] *Ontario Workman* (*OW*), April 2, 1874; *Palladium of Labor* (Hamilton) (*POL*), Sept. 1, 1883; *Fincher's Trades Review* (*FTR*), Oct. 3, 1863; Alastair R. Thompson, "The Use of Libraries by the Working Class in Scotland in the Early Nineteenth Cen-

In these common complaints, shared by many observers, the neglect of reading stemmed principally from two equally revealing sources. Despite—or because of—some schooling and self-reported literacy, individuals needed to be taught, or at least, reminded, how to read; they also needed to be told the importance of exercising their literacy. It seems that many had acquired a distaste and aversion to books and reading—a fact that implies the inefficacy of their schooling. Thus, the *Workman* provided its readers with complete instructions on how to read. "Read slowly; read understandingly," it advised, for cursory reading left little impression. The meaning of each word must be understood, its spelling noted. An atlas must be at hand, and used; each idea noted as well, and only one book read at a time. The men and women who presumably gained this tutelage by perusing a newspaper were seen as readers whose literacy required improvement and who needed reeducation in reading skills. The ability of gaining information from a newspaper, it seems, told little about one's level of literacy. Those who read this much apparently needed further instruction in how to read effectively; nothing in their schooling had prepared them to continue their reading to advance themselves. They did not even know where to begin.[36]

If some men and women were reading, official opinion was far from pleased with what they chose to read. Nevertheless, the popular habits revealed by typical criticisms are at least as revealing as the censure itself. It was usually agreed that "no part of education is of greater importance than the selection of proper books for perusal or study. . . ." Many, though, chose to exercise their literacy with materials considered either worthless or dangerous; thus, complaints focused on a literacy low in quality and unrestrained by morality or wise choice. "All the common, everyday reading that falls into a young man's hands is quite sure to be bad." Not surprisingly, censure most often fell on novels and other works of fiction—taking the definition of fiction in its most inclusive sense. To *The Church,* it included newspapers, periodicals, reviews, and romances—all classes of writing not conducive to the "welfare" of readers.[37]

Regardless of its value to those who chose it, fiction-reading repre-

---

tury," *Scottish Historical Review,* 42 (1963), 21–29; Alec Ellis, "Influences on the Availability of Recreational Reading for Victorian Working Class Children," *Journal of Librarianship,* 8 (1976), 185–195; Altick, *Reader;* Gareth Stedman Jones, "Working-Class Culture and Working-Class Politics in London, 1870–1900," *Journal of Social History,* 7 (1974), 460–508.

[36] *OW,* Nov. 21, 1872; *POL,* Mar. 1, 1884; *FTR,* Oct. 3, 1866; *The Church (TC),* Oct. 27, 1843; *Christian Guardian (CG),* Dec. 13, 1837.

[37] *CG,* July 31, 1850; *TC,* Oct. 27, 1843.

sented, to social commentators, an unwise use of literacy, wasteful to the individual and harmful to society. Novel-reading was pernicious; novels made few appeals to the intellect and they were habit-forming. Good men did not write novels; therefore, good men and women should not be their readers. Not only threatening to thought, intelligence, religion, and morality, "no dissipation can be worse than that induced by the perusal of exciting books of fiction . . . a species of experience of a monstrous and erroneous nature." The danger was perhaps greatest to young unmarried women and to children, whose innocence it was most important to protect. The *Workman* advised the parents in its audience that "a bad book, magazine, or newspaper is as dangerous to your child as a vicious companion, and will as surely corrupt his morals and lead him away from the paths of society." Schoolmen added their voices to these cries against novel-reading; yet, as we saw in Chapter 5, the working class press blamed the public school system for this state of affairs. Making attendance and reading instruction compulsory, schools gave the children "dime novels for perusal, having previously given them a taste for such reading." This, obviously, was not desirable.[38]

Beneath the heavy layers of censure and reform efforts, we find examples of the uses to which literacy was popularly put. The early to middle years of the nineteenth century saw the rise and easier availability of cheap, popular literature, aimed at the pleasure and amusement of the lower as well as the middle class. Many found this reading material quite well-suited to their tastes. Street literature, in particular, was easy to buy, sold on corners and hawked on the pavements; it could be bought by all but the very poorest. This was literature, moreover, which was short, easy to read and understand, appealing, and exciting, as well as socially and politically current. Illiterates also heard the broadsides and pamphlets read by others and cried out in public; this material was integrated easily into popular traditions and oral culture, without sharp discontinuity. This was one part of daily street education, for which popular skills were sufficient, aimed overwhelmingly at noninstrumental aspects of entertainment, amusement, and common culture.[39] The

[38] *CG,* Jan. 28, 1852, July 31, 1850, Nov. 7, 1849; *OW,* Feb. 12, 1874; *POL,* Feb. 2, 1884.

[39] On street literature, see Leslie Shepard, *The History of Street Literature* (Detroit: Singing Tree Press, 1973); Victor E. Neuberg, "The Literature of the Streets," in *The Victorian City,* ed. H. J. Dyos and M. Wolff (London: Routledge, Kegan Paul, 1973), 191–209; Martha Vicinus, *The Industrial Muse* (London: Croom Helm, 1975); Richard Hoggart, *The Uses of Literacy* (Boston: Beacon Press, 1961). See also, Altick, *Reader;* R. K. Webb, *The British Working Class Reader, 1790–1848* (London: Allen and Unwin, 1955). On the middle class, see Peter Baily, "'A Mingled Mass of Perfectly Legitimate Pleasures': The Victorian Middle Class and the Problem of Leisure."

middle-class criticism (an outgrowth of the reforming instinct) directed at this class of literature and its readers must not detract from its significance, as an important employment of imperfect literacy skills. Popular literacy was of value to many ordinary men and women, which contemporaries were not prepared to accept: when they pleaded for people to read, they had other uses of literacy in mind.

Even the form of literature most frequently attacked, novels, had significance to the lives of contemporaries, especially to middle-class women. The Victorian sentimental novel, according to Sally Mitchell, "supplied for women of the middle classes both a means of filling leisure time and a mode of recreation in the true sense of the word." Popular novels gratified common needs, providing vicarious experience, which gave repressed feelings a form of acceptable release and made the novels a source of pleasure. Fantasy supplied a needed, socially conservative outlet. In other words, the "women's novel provides satisfaction which real life lacks. It offers vicarious participation, emotional expression, and the feeling of community that arises from a recognition of shared dreams. . . . sensibilities about her own character, her virtues, and her moral values are not violated." Literacy in this way also had many uses: from socialization, satisfaction, entertainment, amusement, self-identification, and legitimation, to expression, escapism, or therapy. Though certainly neither praised nor considered as exercising useful skills, this mode of literacy and consumption of literature no doubt occupied a valued place in many women's—and men's—lives.[40]

While men and women of the working and middle classes used their imperfect skills in ways like these and other common employments relevant to their daily lives, the promotion of loftier uses of literacy continued. The two seldom intersected in practical applications, whether instrumental or noninstrumental ones. "Never read to pass away time," The Church instructed; "always read with a view of learning something." Read for information, they urged, not for opinions. Some persons undoubtedly did; tales of the self-educated, the improved and improving— artisans or clerks, and the respectable reader (working or middle class)— are hardly rare. Their representativeness and typicality, however, remain to be assessed.

In response to reforming impulses the religious and labor presses joined in urging the populace to read. That they felt the need to pro-

Victorian Studies, 21 (1977), 7–25, Leisure and Class in Victorian Society (Toronto: University of Toronto Press, 1978).

40 Sally Mitchell, "Sentiment and Suffering: Women's Recreational Reading in the 1860s," Victorian Studies, 21 (1977), 29, 34, 40, 45; Ann Douglas, The Feminization of American Culture (New York: Knopf, 1977), 61–63.

mote reading, even to those exposed to the press, speaks again of a situation in which the habit of reading was seen neither as common enough nor as properly employed. To promoters, reservoirs of potential literacy had to be tapped and filtered. Thus, commentators preached the advantages of approved reading. "The truth is," *The Church* explained, "the love of reading is just as much a natural bent or desire, as other habits." Selection of reading matter was like the choice of food; good reading nourished the mind as good food did the body.[41]

These uses of literacy had to be promoted. They were not the everyday practice, and they required a level of literacy different from and beyond that necessary to read newspapers and novels. To the *Christian Guardian,* for example, there were certain proper advantages of reading: Readers would acquaint themselves with the "affairs, actions, and thoughts of the living and the dead, . . . something from all parts of mankind"; and reading would teach them their place in history and civilization as well as in the present society. How very different from the typical kinds of reading these are and even from the more pragmatic ones; but at once, these would be no more practical or instrumental employments of individual literacy than many of the others. Fully understanding such lessons, the press realized, required a higher level of skills. With this practice, though, the readers could improve their abilities, as the proper use of literacy would provide examples and stimuli to advancement and social integration. And of course, wise and refined sentiments would be learned, with reviewing the lessons recommended for their reinforcement. These uses had to be taught; they represented both a level of skill and an employment of literacy quite distinct from popular abilities and uses. To religious and labor promoters and reformers of reading habits, these were the proper uses of literacy. The expected and desired use of literacy was to support the moral bases of society and order.[42] But even a lower level of ability could serve that purpose. Gaining inspiration and learning sentiments and morality need not presume total and reflective comprehension or deep involvement with the words.

The agents of promotion such as the *Guardian* apparently knew the common habits, for while they condemned novel reading, they supported newspaper reading. Though of course, only "well conducted" or religious journals should be read. This involved a selection much like that of the choice of books, but it is likely that newspaper reading was far more common than reading of books. Significantly, these comments were often aimed at poor families, who were told of the value of a religious paper for enjoyment and quiet entertainment on a Saturday night. As

41 *TC,* Oct. 27, 1843.
42 *CG,* Nov. 11, 1835, Feb. 19, 1840, May 28, 1848.

opposed to the amusement that reading fiction would bring, a religious newspaper instructed in values and morality, while easing the pains of poverty. Never was it suggested that poverty would be alleviated through reading, however. The instructional role of the press benefitted children too. Assisting them in acquiring education, it "brought them intelligence from the four corners of the globe." In this way, newspapers—cheap and widely-read—were promoted; habits of reading already in use should be shaped to encourage the proper use of literacy. And, as Ryerson and Mann had done, the *Guardian* could also appeal, if rarely, to economic self-interest.[43] No doubt important, practical daily information was thereby acquired.

The working class press similarly instructed its audience in the advantages of reading. "A taste for reading is one of the true blessings of life," the *Ontario Workman* urged. To readers, the benefits were three: as a resource, an amusement, and a solid gain. "As a resource, it is preeminent . . . the 'Open Sesame' which admits us to realms of enchantment. . . ." This was not an instrumental approach to literacy; in fact, in Scotland, workingmen who used libraries were disinclined to borrow vocational or utilitarian books, preferring instead imaginative literature. This was reading on a higher plane, too, which required advancing well beyond the foundations typically laid in schools, for the superstructure of knowledge was gained in books. (The base of it, however, was lacking.) Indeed, to the working class press, the promotion of reading was complex. Reading brought enchantment; it also brought comfort in lonely hours and consolation as well as amusement. To satisfy these needs required varying degrees of ability, some of which would not be held by all literate individuals. Recognizing this, both the *Workman* and the *Palladium* provided instruction in reading skills, and they inveighed against recurring illiteracy and the degradation of education.[44]

[43] *CG*, Jan. 16, 1850, Jan. 8, 1834, Oct. 17, 1849; see also *FTR*, Feb. 4, 1865. Revealing in this regard is the observation of Isabella Lucy Bird: "It is stated that thousands of the subscribers to the newspapers [in cities] are so illiterate as to depend upon their children for a knowledge of their contents. At present few people, comparatively speaking, are more than half-educated. The knowledge of this fact lowers the tone of the press, and circumscribes both authors and speakers, as any allusions to history or general literature would be very imperfectly, if at all understood." *The Englishwoman in America* (London, 1856; reprinted, Toronto: University of Toronto Press, 1966), 317. Aside from her tone of condescension and inaccurate labelling of many as illiterate, Bird pointed to the imperfect level of skills possessed and the wide audience of the press.

[44] *OW*, Nov. 21, 1872, Dec. 19, 1872; A. Thompson, "Use of Libraries"; *POL*, Feb. 7, 1884, Mar. 1, 1884, Feb. 7, 1885, May 16, 1885. See also Phillips Thompson, *The Politics of Labor* (New York, 1877); Ch. 5, above.

The working class press also pointed to uses of literacy beyond the commonly held low levels of ability, for example in discussing the selection of materials for family reading. When they wrote about entertainment, information, or amusement, they spoke of uses of literacy that a less-than-perfect grounding in skills could meet. Simultaneously, popular literacy could meet some demands and fail at others; a low level of ability would serve "the poor man who can read, and who possesses a taste for reading, [who] can find entertainment at home without being tempted to repair to the public house for that purpose." It could also provide relief from toil, and a cheap means of communication, preventing economic losses which resulted from a lack of information.[45] The prevailing levels of literacy could meet many of these practical and important needs much as they could generally satisfy the demands of the religious press. The literacy popularly possessed was typically sufficient for the requirements of daily survival, most work, and hegemony, if it were employed in ways related at least peripherally to those promoted. The experience of schooling may well have laid an adequate foundation for the society and culture. Illiterates, of course, suffered greater—if not insurmountable—obstacles in meeting these needs.

Nevertheless, there were other demands that this ability simply could not meet. Higher intellectual demands would not be satisfied. It would not necessarily serve to promote labor's cause as the *Palladium* felt it must, for in their view, one "must be a Reader and a Thinker." Reading critically was the the key to thought, and workingmen, the *Workman* emphasized, "must educate themselves to think; they must learn to think for themselves." Thought of course can progress without reading, but reading itself does not result naturally in the habit of thinking. That would require much more practice and attention, as they constantly remarked. The ability of abstracting information was not the ability of critically analyzing, or of creating, as E. P. Thompson, among others, concluded. "The ability to read was only the elementary technique. The ability to handle abstract and consecutive argument was by no means inborn."[46] In urging men and women to read, the labor press

---

[45] See, for example, *OW*, Jan. 2, 1873; *FTR*, July 11, 1863, Sept. 17, 1864, Feb. 4, 1865, Jan. 16, 1864, Apr. 29, 1863, April 29, 1865; P. Thompson, *Politics*, 11. See also, Chs. 1 and 5 above.

[46] *POL*, Jan. 5, 1884; *OW*, Jan. 22, 1874; P. Thompson, *Politics*, 11; E. P. Thompson, *The Making of the English Working Class* (New York: Pantheon, 1963), 713. See also, Webb, *British Working Class*, 122, 160; Ortega y Gasset, "Difficulty"; Paulo Freire, *Pedagogy of the Oppressed* (New York: Herder and Herder, 1971), *Education for Critical Consciousness* (New York: Seabury Press, 1973). See also, Jonathan Kozol, "A New Look at the Literacy Campaign in Cuba," *Harvard Educational Review*, 48 (1978), 341–377; Richard Jolly, "The Literacy Campaign and Adult Education," in *Cuba: The*

certainly realized that the usual reading skills did not meet such demands. They also saw that one needed a "deeper and broader intelligence," and that too much reading and too little thinking were of little active value. Yet in their stress on reading habits and the uses of literacy, they also lost sight of the limits of reading itself. They erred in the way many others erred as Hodgson illustrated in his *Exaggerated Estimates of Reading and Writing as a Means of Education*. Reading and writing— literacy—were just one means of gaining knowledge and ideals, Hodgson reminded his audience. They were not the only means: "It ought never to be forgotten that the power to read does not in the least determine the use to which it is put." [47] If we admit such distinctions today, we may begin to understand and to supplant the "literacy myth."

The potential uses of literacy, then, were diverse: gaining useful information; inculcating values of morality and culture; maintaining hegemony; pursuing entertainment and amusement; as well as labor's quest for organization, economic knowledge, and action; further self-guided education, higher learning, inspiration, and thought. A low level of literacy might well be suitable for the first four aims, but probably not for the last two. And, as Phillips Thompson understood, the level of literacy generally transmitted was one which bolstered the present political and economic system. Acceptance of capitalism was

> traceable to the wrong ideals of life and worldly success which are held up before the young from their very cradles. The whole tendency of modern education—not merely in the sense of book-learning, but in the broader significance which includes every influence which shapes men's thoughts and contributes to their intellectual and moral development—is to make rascals.

This spirit, he maintained, was taught in school, and by the newspaper, platform, and fireside.[48] Literacy of the common quality had its social uses and was taught in that manner. This was the purpose of its moral bases and its central contribution to hegemony. To go beyond required much more than only the ability to read, to gain information or sentiments. Transcendence of mechanical literacy involved independent thought and criticism, which were not encouraged or practiced in in-

---

Social and Economic Revolution, ed. Dudley Seers (Chapel Hill: University of North Carolina Press, 1963), 190–219.

[47] *POL,* Sept. 1, 1883, Jan. 5, 1884; Hodgson, *Exaggerated Estimates,* 11. On the relationship of literacy to intelligence, see Lewis, *Importance;* Burt, "Education of Illiterate"; see also Alex Inkeles *et al.,* "Some Social Psychological Effects and Non-effects of Literacy in a New Nation," *Economic Development and Cultural Change,* 16 (1967), 3.

[48] Phillips Thompson, *Politics,* 195.

struction and which were largely lacking in a population with few good readers.

IV

Demands for a higher literacy failed, as Daniel Calhoun's work implies, because the young mind was "not empirical in the higher active sense: it could not set up an interchange between ideas, needs, and external reality." It was empirical in another sense, as automatic responses and rule of thumb techniques could be easily assimilated.[49] Into this process, literacy and schooling fit. Demands for higher qualitative levels of ability did not have broad appeal; their uses were not obvious to most members of the society, and they were required for the activities of even fewer. Calhoun found that most children's inability to perform such an interchange related simply and directly to the needs of their lives. Book-learned ideas had little place in survival; the relationship between needs and realities was satisfied on a lower level.

We need only pause to reflect, even briefly, on the daily needs, uses, and requirements for literacy in nineteenth-century cities. The society and culture were not dominated by print; access to information and to work did not often demand much literacy. Consider the normal affairs of an unskilled or semiskilled worker. Doing his or her job seldom, if ever, required the use of reading and writing: no applications were required; print materials were rarely part of the work process; peers and community supplied important stimuli and information. At higher levels of skilled work, such as the artisanal level, literacy was more often needed; this appears clearly in the differential access to this occupational level and to its rewards which separated the experiences and attainments of some literate workers from most uneducated ones. While a real difference appears here, the evidence presented forces us to evaluate it cautiously, for the uses and demands made on literacy can all too easily be exaggerated and taken out of context. Much skilled work consisted of practical knowledge, job experience, and good work sense and abilities; these must not be confused with the potential, but not necessarily required, contributions from literacy.

Nonmanual workers, of course, often, if not always, had a more pressing and instrumental need for literacy skills; clerical work, book- and recordkeeping, billing, inventorying, and ordering all depended to

---

[49] Calhoun, *Intelligence*, 130–131.

some degree on the ability to read and write. Yet, here the "automatic responses" and "rule of thumb techniques" may well have played a more common role than higher, more advanced literary skills. The differences separating the very literate, the imperfectly literate, and the illiterate were in practicing more relative than absolute, much less than in theory or in potential. Simply, high degrees of literacy were often not required for work or welfare. We can not neglect, however, to recognize their important potential uses in gaining further knowledge and enrichment, facilitating access to culture and learning, and influencing social standing, self-esteem, and respectability. These were the areas in which illiterates suffered most, and in which a lack of abilities could lead to personal losses and to embarassments.

Demands for a higher literacy also failed because the culture neither required nor desired it. Despite the criticisms of contemporaries, and present-day commentators too, I suspect that the society and the culture *did not need* a qualitatively high level of popular skills. A corrective to the usual viewpoint seems justifiable for a number of reasons—for the present as well as the past—as I shall sketch here. But first, several comments are necessary. Most generally, as a result of the promotion and acceptance of the "literacy myth," literacy's social and cultural role is neither well understood nor systematically evaluated, even in terms used in the preceding section. Rather, it is often (but certainly not always) overvalued, its significance in some areas exaggerated. Critics might well benefit from reading nineteenth-century observers like W. B. Hodgson. In censuring popular uses or neglect of literacy, in reporting the ubiquitous declines in literacy which remain largely undocumented and recur at least generationally, we typically fail to ask how important and in what ways literacy is related or central to different aspects of life and culture, such as I have attempted in a preliminary fashion in this study.[50] Without denigrating the potential of literacy or neglecting the very real contribution and value it may have to individuals, society, economy, or culture—which are crucial to note—we need, however, to look at literacy

[50] On the myth of the literacy decline, see my comments in "Literacy Past and Present," *Interchange*, 9 (1978), 1–21; Richard Ohmann, "The Decline in Literacy Is a Fiction, If Not a Hoax," *Chronicle of Higher Education*, Oct. 25, 1976; "He doesn't think reading skills have dropped," *Dallas Times Herald*, Apr. 28, 1978; Egil Johansson, "The Postliteracy Problem," Department of Education, Umeå University, 1977; Calhoun, *Intelligence;* the inconclusive 1977 report, *On Further Examination* (New York: College Entrance Examination Board, 1977); George Douglas, "Is Literacy Really Declining?," *Educational Records*, 57 (1977), 140–148; Roger Farr, *et al., Then and Now: Reading Achievement in Indiana* (Bloomington: University of Indiana, School of Education, 1978). See also, my comments and selections in a forthcoming anthology on "understanding literacy," which I am preparing for publication.

in new ways and put reading and writing into perspective. Breaking from the pervasive "literacy myth" which has spawned a great deal of concern and renewed speculations about the presumed (and unverified) transformations wrought by print and literacy (e.g., those associated with McLuhan), we may begin the long-required reconsideration.[51] While granting their significance—both real and ideal—we must simultaneously recognize the limits of literacy alone, re-examine its conceptualization, and also remind ourselves of the distinctions in literacy between the medium, the message, the process of training, and the different effects and uses.

The history of the west since about 1800 or 1850 is usually written in terms of the rise of mass institutions and mass communications; and the decline of community, the family, interpersonal relations, and small (primary) groups. The rise of mass society and the media are seen as separating and privatizing individuals and destroying communities, local societies, and traditional cultures. "Other-directedness," consumerism, and pluralism are considered among the results of these many and re-lated changes. Literacy and print ("the rise of the book") are held to be closely connected to and an integral part of these consequences of modernization and their presumed alterations of social and psycho-logical consciousness. New paradigms of culture, thought, and awareness are assumed to have replaced traditional oral and localized patterns. Writing, for example, is said to create new means of communications among individuals, objectifying speech and transmitting it over time and space. More generalized and abstract relations replace earlier forms of oral relations; attitudes toward history and the past are fixed and fundamentally reshaped; distinctions between myth and history arise. Logical procedures accompany literacy, it is argued, as visual culture replaces an oral–auditory one; standardization proceeds with alphabetiza-tion and literacy. Psychic rootlessness, alienation, and privatized–individualized relations become more likely. The works from which these speculations derive are fascinating and important; yet they remain largely undocumented—and, I believe, somewhat overstated and exag-gerated as well.[52]

[51] For two recent and revealing attempts to evaluate modern literacy, which end in accepting *more of the literacy myth* than they reject, see David R. Olson, "Toward A Literate Society: Book Review," *Proceedings* of the National Academy of Education, (1975–1976), 109–178; H. S. Stout, "Culture, Structure, and the 'New' History," *Computers and the Humanities*, 9 (1975), 223–225. See also, the essays in Leon Bataille, ed., *A Turning Point for Literacy* (New York: Pergamon Press, 1976); Joyce Appleby, "Modernization Theory and the Formation of Modern Social Theories in England and America," *Comparative Studies in Society and History*, 20 (1978), 259–285.

[52] See, for example, Stout, "Culture, Structure"; Thomas Cochran, *Social Change in America* (New York: Harper and Row, 1972); Olson, "From Utterance to Text,"

In fact, researchers have only recently begun to reconsider the dimensions of modern (nineteenth and twentieth century) society and culture. Among our discoveries—insufficiently assessed, I feel—is the persistence of traditional oral means of communications. In the nineteenth century, for example, print media, while gaining in importance, had hardly achieved dominance. Oral communications, symbols, and visual signs abounded; sharp dichotomies between the visuality of modern life and the orality of traditional societies are unacceptable. As E. P. Thompson argues for the eighteenth and nineteenth centuries,

> Both practices and norms are reproduced down the generations within the slowly differentiating ambience of 'custom'. Hence people tend to legitimate practice (or protest) in terms of customary usage or of prescriptive rights and perquisites. (The fact that—from rather different premises—such arguments tend to control the high political culture also acts to reinforce this plebian disposition.) Traditions are perpetuated largely through oral transmission, with its repertoire of anecdote and of narrative example; where oral tradition is supplemented by growing literacy, the most widely circulated printed products (chapbooks, almanacs, broadsides, 'last dying speeches,' and anecdotal accounts of crime) tend to be subdued to the expectations of the oral culture rather than challenging it with alternatives. In any case, in many parts of Britain—and especially those regions where dialect is strongest—basic elementary education co-exists, throughout the nineteenth century, with the language —and perhaps the sensibility of—what is then becoming the 'old culture'.

The parallels to Richard Hoggart's classic *The Uses of Literacy* and many linguistic analyses are powerful. Oral culture and its fundamental sig-

---

Harvard Educational Review, 47 (1977), 257–282; Jack Goody and Ian Watt, "The Consequences of Literacy," in *Literacy in Traditional Societies,* ed. Goody (Cambridge: Cambridge University Press, 1968), 27–68; G. H. Bantock, *The Implications of Literacy* (Leicester: Leicester University Press, 1968); the works of Walter J. Ong, Eric Havelock, Harold Innis, Elizabeth Eisenstein, and Marshall McLuhan; David Reisman *et al., The Lonely Crowd* (New Haven: Yale University Press, 1961 ed.); the writings of Peter Berger and his associates; Chall and Carroll, *Literate Society,* among a huge literature including textbooks as well as specialized studies.

But see also, for recent attempts at reconsideration, Raymond Williams, *The Country and the City* (New York: Oxford University Press, 1973); Thomas Bender, *Community and Social Change in America* (New Brunswick, N.J.: Rutgers University Press, 1978); Jack Goody, *The Domestication of the Savage Mind* (Cambridge: Cambridge University Press, 1977); Lucien Febvre and Henri-Jean Martin, *The Coming of the Book: The Impact of Printing, 1450–1800* (London: NLB, 1976); François Furet et Jacques Ozouf, *Lire et Ecrire* (Paris: Les éditions de Minuit, 1977), among others. Recent anthropological and sociological studies of modern societies—of community, social organization, family, communications, etc.—point to many areas of necessary revisions of the "received wisdom," including those of the decline of community, family, face-to-face communications, primary groups, and the gemeinschaft/gessellschaft dichotomy. Historians and contemporary researchers have much to learn from recent studies of early modern society and culture, especially those in France.

nificance do not simply vanish under the attack of print, schooling, and modernization; rather, it dialectically accommodates the impact of them, one neither assimilating nor replacing the other. Too often, they are dichotomized, seen as in constant conflict with one another. Instead, in recognizing the persistence and the daily significance of oral communication, we need to study their relations: the ways in which, in some settings, one dominates or conflicts with the other, and, in others, they reciprocally support one another. A better understanding of their changing relations is required, too.

Oral patterns still form a crucial base for socialization, education and training and the learning of attitudes, norms, and habits, as well as skills; they are important to much cultural transmission and to entertainment—not just locally and regionally but nationally too. On local levels, personal contacts are daily affairs, vital to the livelihood of the community and those within it. Oral relations bind individuals and groups to each other and to their larger society while preserving distinctions; literacy often tends to reinforce these processes. With modern media—dependent on sound and sight rather than on printed texts—differences between oral and literate communications further diminish. Film, television, and radio have their foundations more in nonliterate than in print sources, although a rigid separation would distort more than advance understanding. They may integrate people, rather than isolate them—as print may as well. The telephone, for example, has facilitated oral communications over distances vast and small, allowing family and community to spread and widen rather than simply decline or disappear. The electronic media not only support older modes, but they can also reinforce the newer ones and assist in their communicating, integrating, homogenizing, and controlling functions. The use of radio and television by political leaders, and the cinema for news and "novelizing" are among the most familiar examples. At the least, oral patterns continue; and the impact of print is mediated by both older and newer forms of communication.[53]

[53] Thompson, "Eighteenth-century English society," *Social History*, 3 (1978), 153; Hoggart, *Uses of Literacy, On Culture and Communication* (Oxford: Oxford University Press, 1971); Henri-Jean Martin, "Culture écrite et culture orale, Culture savante et culture populaire dans la France d'Ancien Regime," *Journale des Savants* (1975), 225–282; Natalie Davis, *Society and Culture in Early Modern France* (Stanford: Stanford University Press, 1975), 189–269; David Reisman, *The Oral Tradition, the Written Word, and the Screen Image* (Yellow Springs, Ohio: The Antioch Press, 1955); Stout, "Culture, Structure"; Gerald Suttles, *The Social Order of the Slum* (Chicago: University of Chicago Press, 1968); Charles Tilly, *An Urban World* (Boston: Little, Brown, 1974); Alejandro Portes, "Rationality in the Slum," *Comparative Studies in Society and History*, 14 (1971–1972), 268–286; the work of Michael Young and Peter Wilmott; that

Reading the city's streets—print and lettered signs were not primary in knowing the city and using its facilities and services. *"Dundas, Ontario: King Street looking East from 50 feet east of Sydenham St. c. 1856."* [Archives of Ontario, S11902]

Reading the city's streets—symbols and icons supplemented and competed with signs and letters in identifying businesses and other urban places. "*Guelph, Ontario, St. George's Square, 1874.*" [Archives of Ontario, S8392]

Reading the city's streets—in large urban centers print, while more pervasive, continued to compete with and be supplemented with other visual symbols and markings. *"King Street, Toronto, looking East from Church Street, 1870s."* [Archives of Ontario, S13376]

In the nineteenth century, oral and visual (but not literate) means of communications and existence were even more important than in the present century, as Thompson suggests. Taverns, stores, and other buildings were often demarcated by symbols as well as lettered names. Pubs with their charming as well as socially significant signs are just one example (tools, animals, ethnic symbols). They were social and cultural centers, places of communications, news, debate, and dialogue. There is little reason, in fact, to suspect that the daily culture of a nineteenth-century city overly emphasized the printed word, or that much literacy was required to learn its ways. Residence, commerce, and industry intermingled more than not; walking was sufficient to dissect and "read" the city. Oral directions were quite adequate to find one's way about. The city was a place of sights and sounds more than of print and text, with structures both obvious and hidden, to be "read" and explored with all of the senses.

Experience was as much, and probably more, the teacher for everyday life than the school: "the urban setting is itself educative, and . . . it may have far stronger effects than do any specific schools," Calhoun reminds us. In this regard, we need new, conceptionally imaginative examinations of the influence of specific environments: the family and child-rearing, religion, community, and other learning settings, both formal and informal, as well as that of the press and institutions. As he suggests, "the urban environment has had an educative effect, independent of formal schooling. But the independence . . . has imposed difficulties and challenges that men could often accept only by buffering their consciousness with indirection, with defense mechanisms, even with outright cultural lies. . . . As part of those particulars, men have continually reconstructed and repictured the bits and pieces of the environment that came their way." As the school, mass literacy, and the printed word joined the environment, the "literacy myth" was added to those cultural lies.[54]

For communications, work-places and mixed residence as well as

---

of Elizabeth Bott; Howard H. Irving, *The Family Myth* (Toronto: Copp Clark, 1972); Kozol, "A New Look." See also, the discussion in Chs. 2 and 5, above. For different views, see the literature cited in Note 51, 1st part; Donald Gordon, *The New Literacy* (Toronto: University of Toronto Press, 1971); the writings of Edmund Carpenter; David Reisman, "The Oral and Written Traditions," *Explorations*, 6 (1956), 22–28.

[54] See the work of Brian Harrison on pubs, cited in Ch. 2, above; Jon Kingsdale, "The 'Poor Man's Club': Social Functions of the Urban Working-Class Saloon," *American Quarterly*, 25 (1973), 472–489; Daniel Calhoun, "The City as Teacher," *History of Education Quarterly*, 9 (1969), 313, 319, *passim*; Steven Marcus, "Reading the Illegible," in *The Victorian City*, 257–276. The latter two offer brilliant, original suggestions for new approaches.

recreational settings like pubs provided news and daily information. They also provided contact points, culture, and learning. The import of oral media also derives support from new studies of religious revivals and the American Revolution, contrary to the usual emphasis on literacy and reading by the few. The functions of spoken and everyday language can be very influential: for widespread communications, raising consciousness, and transmitting ideology. As Harry Stout comments, "The link between print culture and the people, between pamphlets and popular ideology, is assumed, not demonstrated." [55] This important revision, true for the American Revolution, holds as well far beyond the events of the 1770s, as the foregoing suggests. The rise of literacy and the school, as important and powerful as they are, do not negate the ongoing, traditional processes of communications.

Other information could be easily gleaned from a brief perusal of the newspapers, broadsides, or printed notices for which a high level of reading comprehension was not required. Pictures and other symbolic representations frequently adorned these forms of printed matter, too, adding both to their appeal and to their meaning; in this way, the visual sign corresponds to but is not synonymous with the letters of literacy. Advertisements were also, and continue to be, simply worded and highly stylized, with pictorial presentation of the product often featured. Handbills, flysheets, and even many schoolbooks followed the same mode of presentation, the first two generally with a minimum of print and text. Despite the growing encroachment of print, politics, religion, leisure, and other forms of cultural expression—both new and old—remained within the oral and visual focus. Hearing and seeing persisted along with the new literate culture and society. For many persons, they were undoubtedly more valuable and more regularly employed in daily affairs than the literacy virtually all were taught, and by which they certainly were influenced. Literacy and its impact can only be understood within this context—not abstractly, all powerfully, or in isolation.

Styles of social and cultural life reveal the same patterns, especially for the working class but also for the middle class. From the seminal analysis of Michael Anderson, we can point first to work, family, and critical life situations, in industrializing Lancashire in the mid-nineteenth century. None of these was much affected by the concomitant rise of

---

[55] See Rhys Isaac, "Dramatizing the Ideology of Revolution: Popular Mobilization in Virginia, 1774 to 1776," *William and Mary Quarterly*, 33 (1976), 357–385; H. S. Stout, "Religion, Communications, and the Ideological Origins of the American Revolution," *ibid.*, 34 (1977), 519–541; Calhoun, "The City as Teacher"; Ch. 5, above. It is revealing that Isaac and Stout incorporate undocumented elements of the literacy myth into their otherwise original interpretations.

literacy and schooling. Most interesting are the life crises that he inter-
prets; they reveal that the basic means of survival and assistance to families and individuals came from informal, traditional means, and not
from bureaucratic, institutional settings in which literacy could be more
significant. The Poor Law, the agency of bureaucratic aid, was avoided
as the last resort. Rather, it was kin, co-villagers, neighbors, the community, and voluntary societies (burial, friendly, building associations),
probably in that order, to which those in need turned. This included
assistance for the young and the old, the orphaned and the sick, widows
and the deserted, as well as those seeking employment.[56] In these basic
aspects of ongoing life, literacy, even if more significant, was at best
secondary.

In other areas of life—culture, leisure, recreation—literacy was also
limited as a direct influence: in its impact and in its employment. We
must distinguish, at the least, between different strata of the working
class and between the hegemonic functions of mass literacy and schooling and their role in daily life, in offering even these preliminary comments. Literate and other patterns intersected in complex ways. Consider,
for example, broad cultural patterns in the mid- to later-nineteenth
century. As Stedman Jones, along with other researchers on both sides
of the Atlantic, has recently argued, working class culture was transformed under the impact of the many changes of the nineteenth century,
including commercial and industrial capitalism, efforts at reform (by an
insecure, anxious middle class), the rise of institutions, and patterns of
urban growth. Yet none of these forces had simple, unmediated impacts.
While traditional patterns of social integration and control were replaced by more modern ones, the results were not only those that reformers and educators desired. The changes were related, albeit unclearly,
nevertheless. Some members of the working class seized elements of the
middle-class habits of morality and respectability (the moral bases of
literacy) as they were able—like those marginal members of the lower-
middle ranks. The promoted values of education and literacy were accepted least critically in their quests for security and mobility, limited
of course by their means. To them, possession of literacy took on a
greater importance.

For the greater numbers of the urban working class, however, the
direct use of reading and writing remained peripheral to many, if not
most, everyday activities. The pub, while shorn of many of its economic
functions and frequented more often by women, served still as a focal

[56] Michael Anderson, *Family Structure in Nineteenth Century Lancashire* (Cambridge: Cambridge University Press, 1971), esp. Ch. 10. I do not accept Anderson's
theory of a rational, economic calculus dominating these relationships, however.

point, perhaps more narrowly associated with leisure than previously. Drink remained important. Respectability and morality, inspired by schooling and other reform efforts, were assumed without the strictly middle-class habits of religious observances, rational recreation, or teetotalism. Leisure and recreation changed, too, but in ways that did not necessarily put a primacy on literacy or print. Earlier behavior was replaced by gaming, betting, sports (participant and observer), railway excursions, the popular theatre, fairs, pleasure gardens, and especially the music hall. These all became much more important than the new libraries or persisting institutes to the vast majority of workingmen and their families. Public lecturers flourished, too, the most popular seeking to entertain at least as much as instruct. Working-class society did become more stable and orderly; cleanliness and order, dress and decency, and familial and home-centered activities were observed more frequently by the last third of the century. This reflected not only some rise in living standards (though hardly a deterministic or constant element), an increase in leisure time, and basic alterations in places and forms of production, but also the impact of the hegemony of the moral bases. Its effect took hold, however, without completely remolding the working class into the image of their would-be reformers and without totally permeating this culture with print and literacy. Demands for entertainment and amusement increased in the last decades of the century, but the kinds of reading activity whose endorsement and promotion were considered above had little to do with the new forms of recreation. The culture shifted toward the family and the home, on the one hand, and the new leisure habits of entertainment and sport, on the other. In some measure, entertainment and family even replaced politics. To these overall patterns, education certainly contributed, more importantly and subtly than Stedman Jones' characterization as "the deadening effects of elementary education" would suggest it could.

Yet the results were not only the reformers' intended ones. More reading probably did take place, but it was not based on desires for either virtue, morality, or knowledge. Street literature, the increasingly illustrated "penny" press, cheap and entertaining fiction, sporting news, and magazines proliferated; mass markets for the consumption of cheap literature developed rapidly in the second half of the century, as did the installment novel and books of knowledge, too. This is what the people read, if contemporary reports and sales and circulation figures can be trusted. This was the popular use of literacy. Forming one component of domestic recreations, reading was nonetheless shared with indoor games, music, arts and crafts, and handiwork as time and means allowed. We can not dispute the significance of this use of reading, but neither can we neglect its more limited role in life and leisure. Nor was it the road to organization and power that Phillips Thompson and other leaders hoped it to be. The impact of literacy was much more mixed than either a Thompson or a Ryerson had hoped would result from their promotion of it—more mixed in its consequences perhaps than some present-day speculators would expect as well.

The full complexity of these issues emerges most clearly in the case of the "labor aristocracy," the upper stratum of the working class, the interpretation of which has divided many scholars. The so-called "aristocrats of labor" were those most likely among the working class to secure for themselves and their children a greater exposure to the school and the moral bases of literacy. Of its impact upon their behavior and attitudes, furthermore, there is little doubt. Yet the question remains of the degree of influence and of their resulting independence: this is the area of scholarly controversy. Judging from the available evidence, this group illustrates especially well the issues at hand and the impossibility of simple statements of literacy's historical legacy. Although they clearly sought respectability, independence, morality, and distinction from many beneath their social position, artisans and "aristocrats" did not merely mimic those above them. Rather, they sought their social and cultural goals overwhelmingly within the working class, but struggled to separate themselves from both the middle class (whose habits and attitudes they nonetheless resembled, and to some degree adopted) and the poorer, less conscious workers below them. Thus, they rejected patronage but courted social approval and status confirmation.

As ambiguity marked their social status and ambitions, it also influenced their uses of literacy and education. Respectability and morality therefore meant more than passive acceptance of the moral economy, yet their very actions reveal the process of cultural hegemony in operation, with its contradictions and complexities, as R. Q. Gray's analysis of nineteenth-century Edinburgh illustrates most clearly. To gain the rewards of respectability, separation without isolation, homeownership, security, and status required a basic commitment to such valued Victorian characteristics as morality, character, industry, sobriety, and thrift. Discipline, decorum, restraint, and proper manners signified to them, however ironically, the marks of the respectability for which they strived. The desire for education, in schools and by one's self, accompanied and was linked to this process. Consequently, basic attitudes, values, and habits were shared by both the middle class and labor aristocrats, even though motivations and the meaning of the beliefs could differ (e.g., working class collectiveness versus middle class individualism). The values and their relationship to literacy differed, too, in efforts to exist and to contend with their experience of the world around them. Despite these crucial differences, the results with regard to literacy and its social functions deviated much less.

This element of the working class defined itself less by badges of education, degree of literacy skill, and what was read than the middle-class members did. Yet its members also valued their schooling, sought it for their children, and considered it more instrumentally than others within the working class. To a significant degree, regardless of the realities or contradictions of their daily use of literacy (probably not too different from others) and its economic value to them, they accepted the "literacy myth," and aided in its promotion and endorsement. They did partially mediate, however, the maintenance of hegemony within the social and cultural system.[57] The contribution of literacy and hegemony itself is neither simple, direct, nor crudely obvious, as the process functioned within divided and changing societies: this is one meaning of literacy, subtle, dialectical, and mediating.

The place of literacy in middle-class society and culture is at once more difficult and easier to outline. In some ways, the differences between the classes can be all too easily exaggerated; in others, however, one hundred years of easy generalization and Victorian stereotypes, in addition to material and ideological variations, intrude to blur the issues. Little research has thus far penetrated the ideology and the veneer, respectively, of the Victorian middle class. To complete this sketch, a

[57] Gareth Stedman Jones, "Working-Class," 488–489, *passim*, *Outcast London* (Oxford: Oxford University Press, 1971); Geoffrey Best, *Mid-Victorian Britain, 1854–1875* (New York: Schocken, 1972), Ch. 3; Bruce Laurie, " 'Nothing on Compulsion': Life Styles of Philadelphia Artisans, 1820–1850," *Labor History*, 15 (1974), 337–366; Paul Faler, "Cultural Aspects of the Industrial Revolution: Lynn, Massachusetts, Shoemakers and Industrial Morality, 1826–1860," *ibid.*, 367–394; Alan Dawley, *Class and Community: The Industrial Revolution in Lynn* (Cambridge, Mass.: Harvard University Press, 1976); Herbert Gutman, *Work, Culture, and Society in Industrializing America* (New York: Knopf, 1976), esp. Ch. 1; Gregory Kealey and Peter Warrian, eds., *Essays in Canadian Working Class History* (Toronto: McClelland and Stewart, 1976); R. Q. Gray, "Styles of Life, the 'Labour Aristocracy,' and Class Relations in Later Nineteenth Century Edinburgh," *International Review of Social History*, 18 (1973), 428–452, *The Labour Aristocracy in Victorian Edinburgh* (Oxford: Oxford University Press, 1976); Geoffrey Crossick, "The Labour Aristocracy and its Values: A Study of Mid-Victorian Kentish London," *Victorian Studies*, 19 (1976), 301–328; Crossick, ed., *The Lower Middle Class in Britain* (New York: St. Martins, 1977); Standish Meacham, *A Life Apart* (Cambridge, Mass.: Harvard University Press, 1977); Paul Thompson, *The Edwardians* (Bloomington: Indiana University Press, 1975); Williams, "The press," among others. I hardly need to note that the issues raised in this sketch and that which follows are much more complex and require further detailed study. See also, Ch. 1, above. I plan to extend this analysis in a social history of literacy in the west, in progress.

few comments are in order. In the first place, there can be no doubt that middle-class parents and their children acquired much greater educational opportunities, especially in years of enrollment and in regularity of attendance. It was the middle class that constituted the source of reform and reformers, in their social, cultural, and economic anxieties about social change and about the present and future conditions of their youths. They, of course, sent their children to the schools, although to private schools when possible, and collected the benefits from education's socially stratifying and reproducing functions.

The middle class virtually came to wear education and literacy as a badge of status and identification. Literate culture and book culture are associated primarily with the bourgeoisie: in readership, scholarship, and in domestic life, as well as in forms of commercial and professional life. There is much truth in all of this, to be sure. As education expanded, at elementary, secondary, and university levels, so did the clerical and professional spheres of work; their relationship is not monocausal, but it is nonetheless distinct. The middle class dominated in opportunities for postprimary schooling as its members did in literacy-based employment and in literacy-oriented cultural expression and cultural life. They led in the rising incomes and time for leisure associated with these and other related changes. The values of the moral bases of literacy—morality, character, respectability—were theirs, of course; their identification and close affiliation with education and literacy should not surprise us. The achievement of education, after all, was more than ever before a requirement for the maintenance and transmission of their class and status in those times of insecurity.

Yet there is, I think, more to the question than these important truisms. The literacy acquired at school by many middle-class children was less than a perfect skill. For the great majority who were unable to afford private schooling for their youngsters, the educational conditions discussed before prevailed. Learning problems and teaching problems were not an issue for working-class pupils alone; they pervaded the educational system and included schools in middle-class districts and private facilities, too. Low-quality education did not produce highly skilled readers; parents who realized this and who wanted better for their children would have had a very difficult time finding it. The uses of that literacy are less clear, but the available indicators suggest that their literacy was often neglected and that it was typically employed in reading for amusement, entertainment, and the like—noninstrumental and censured uses of literacy, instead of or in addition to promoted or pragmatic uses. Novel- and fiction-reading, newspapers and magazines were much more popular than educational, religious, and serious literature and journals of opinion. While they surely read more frequently and in greater quantities than the working class, the middle class, as today, probably read not very often and not very edifyingly. Some of course did read voluminously and seriously, and took delight and benefit in exercising their literacy—they, however, may not have been typical.

For the middle class, there were many alternative forms of leisure that competed with private reading or family reading circles. With the spread and lengthening of leisure time came the family excursion, the holiday or vacation to the seashore, the theatre, concerts, lectures, choral societies, gardening, clubs and associations, conspicuous consumption, church and chapel, and of course middle-class sports. In the prized, sentimentalized domestic refuge, there were also activities from which to choose: music (the status-symbolic piano), toys and games, crafts and sewing, in addition to reading. Some of these activities could relate to uses of literacy, while others provided attractive diversions and competition. Literacy, in other words, must be considered in such a context of variety and choice. Even for the bourgeoisie, there was more to life than literacy; their culture spanned beyond the use of reading and writing.

By mid-century contemporary reformers in fact were quite concerned about the new opportunities that leisure presented to the middle class. Their efforts to control and rationalize their own class' recreation paralleled the reformers' attack on the working class, illustrating their anxieties and the perceived threat which morally uncontrolled activities represented. The existence of a "problem of leisure" among the middle class is revealing; the forms of enjoyment and entertainment in which individuals apparently took pleasure were seen as improper and dangerous, in the period in which opportunities for leisure first expanded. With the rise of leisure came the problem of leisure, as with the rise of literacy came the awareness of a similar problem. As leisure was severed from its traditional bases in work, community, and custom, and removed to more private settings, it stimulated fears of excessive freedom from restraints and controls. Critics of middle-class recreations, thus, inform us that this class also found more to occupy themselves than reading and other approved activities, and that when they read the material was often other than that promoted as acceptable, even after we allow for reformers' moral exaggerations. Compromises were made, and otherwise improper recreations, such as billiards, were tolerable if they took place at home, were done in moderation, and prepared without distraction for one's work and duty. Despite reformers' efforts, diverse forms of leisure grew more and more popular during the second half of the nineteenth century; they became more assured and luxurious as well.

How well this fit within the veneer of respectability and morality we can not be sure.[58]

By the end of the century, recreations and leisure pursuits in all their variety were common and accepted; they were shared by members of all classes. In many respects, patterns of cultural activity among the middle and working classes (albeit within material limits) were becoming more similar and less disparate: the homogenization and standardization of culture were increasing. Literacy and print media contributed distinctly to this vital transformation; their role was played much more at a lower than a higher level of skill and comprehension. Education and literacy naturally remained one sign of the middle class, more valuable for status and work opportunities than for their active use, I suspect, while others increasingly sought its certification. Real differences declined, though they were certainly not erased, with the arrival of universal schooling and literacy and the mass media. Newer media only exacerbated this trend. Thus, we may conclude that literacy is important to modern culture and its impact, but that it need be neither always dominant nor central to make its contribution. Furthermore, a high level of skills is not required for literacy's manifold significance to be felt.

Consider next, work in the nineteenth century. A constant use and a high quality of reading and writing were required only by clerical workers and professionals. As society bureaucratized and modernized, record-keeping functions were concentrated in the care of a small number of hands. Formal procedures and printed applications were not yet used or needed by many, and in fact not a great deal of literacy was demanded to cope with them, from either side of the counter or ledger. Commercial literacy demanded copying, recording, and tallying, at best automatic responses and rule-of-thumb techniques. Much professional work also demanded a similar empiricism, but one more practiced and on a higher level of skill, involving more comprehension and consistency

---

[58] Baily, "'A Mingled Mass'"; Best, *Mid-Victorian;* Crossick, ed., *The Lower Middle Class.* See also, Crossick, "The Labour Aristocracy"; Gray, *Labour Aristocracy;* H. J. Perkin, *The Origins of Modern English Society* (London: Routledge, Kegan Paul, 1969); Michael R. Marrus, ed., *The Emergence of Leisure* (New York: Harper and Row, 1974); J. F. C. Harrison, *The Early Victorians* (London: Weidenfeld and Nicolson, 1971); S. G. Checkland, *The Rise of Industrial Society in England* (London: Longmans, 1964); Edward Pessen, *Riches, Class, and Power Before the Civil War* (Lexington, Mass.: D.C. Heath, 1973); Rush Welter, *The Mind of America* (New York: Columbia University Press, 1975); F. C. Jaher, ed., *The Age of Industrialism in America* (New York: Free Press, 1968); John Cawalti, *Apostles of the Self-Made Man* (Chicago: University of Chicago Press, 1965); Irwin G. Wyllie, *The Self-Made Man in America* (New York: Free Press, 1966).

than creative thought or originality. It was the very few, no doubt, who needed or who succeeded in achieving a truly intellectual employment of their literacy. They, in most cases, responded to a different range of demands and needs, perceptions and expectations.

For most people work was not yet taught in a formal sense. It was learned on the job, sometimes by apprenticeship, always by experience. Few forms of employment required much literacy either, and illiterates were spread throughout the occupational spectrum, even if few rose above semi- and unskilled labor. In nineteenth-century cities, needs were little different from M. M. Lewis' 1953 description: "For the great majority of workers the order of importance is: first to grasp what is heard; then, to be able to speak; next, to be able to read; and only last, to be able to write. . . . Spoken literacy makes a greater demand than written. . . ." [59] Certainly this hierarchy of needs is even truer for the mid-nineteenth than the mid-twentieth century, as few kinds of work demanded extensive or high quality acquaintance with the printed word. The imperfect skills and the verbalism which pupils took from school were well suited to their careers. Learning by doing, following instructions, and occasionally using literacy constituted what was required. Virtually all possessed this much skill by the seventh or eighth decades of the century.

Surely though, literacy could benefit workers, particularly some skilled and nonmanual employees, for whom it related in some ways to their jobs. Imperfect reading skills were no hindrance to many of them, however. They were sufficient to read building plans, for example, or follow machine or shop instructions, complete a shop bill, or take an inventory. Not all workers on a job site, in a shop or factory, or in a commercial establishment were in positions that demanded the use of their reading or writing abilities. More perhaps needed to sign their names or to count. Schoolmen, significantly, stressed that even those who left school with a merely mechanical proficiency in reading knew how to sign and knew how to count. Even if literacy were unused and neglected and the imperfect skills deteriorated, evidence suggests that the decline was least in the arithmetic of everyday affairs.[60] Numerical ability ("numeracy") apparently had more practical uses to a worker— artisan, nonmanual, or even semiskilled—than an ability to read well, whether it involved the drawing of plans, measuring, simple counting, or keeping accounts. The training in mechanical and automatic responses

[59] Lewis, *Importance*, 138. See also, Ortega y Gasset, "Difficulty"; Ch. 5, above.
[60] T. P. D. Stone, "Reading," 529; Burt, "Education of Illiterate," 20. See also the discussion and references in Ch. 5 above and the contemporary comments in Note 23, above.

and in rule-of-thumb techniques, a product and concomitant of instruction in literacy, was more important in getting the job done than high levels of reading comprehension would be.

This empiricism was ideally suited to most work and a low level of literacy put few restraints on most aspects of people's lives. Aside from its utility in gaining basic information from the press or handbills, it opened to many the burgeoning quantities of cheap literature available for amusement, leisure, entertainment, and sometimes information about current events and politics. Changing patterns of work provided more time for this form of recreation—and the others—too. The common level of literacy, thus, while it limited most literate men and women from higher goals and higher demands, was quite functional for work, recreation, and daily living; it satisfactorily met most needs as it simultaneously met many of the society's and economy's needs.

The place of the illiterate in this society, interpreted in the preceding chapters, broadens our perspective. Illiteracy undoubtedly hindered people's advancement culturally, materially, and occupationally (in normative sociological terms), but the level of literacy demanded for survival was not one to block all progress or adjustment. Class and ethnicity primarily determined social position—not literacy or education by themselves. Literacy exerted an influence which worked cumulatively; entry into skilled work was more difficult, and even some of the limited demands placed upon literacy skills could not be met by such disadvantaged individuals. The responses and techniques useful to work, institutional contacts, and other activities were more difficult for them to acquire. Nevertheless, demands made on individual illiterates who persisted in the cities seldom precluded occupational stability, economic and property mobility, or the transactions that homeownership entailed. Nor did illiteracy prevent successful adaptation to new urban environments, access to channels of communication, or opportunities for intergenerational mobility. Demands made on literacy for practical uses in this society were insufficient to deter some success, limited as it was, by these illiterate adults. Illiteracy was restrictive, but its limits were surmountable. Class, ethnicity, and sex were the major barriers of social inequality. The majority of Irish Catholic adults, for example, were literate—and selected migrants—but they stood lowest in wealth and occupation, as did laborers and servants. Women and blacks fared little better, regardless of literacy. Possession of literacy was not in itself an achievement that brought material rewards to individuals; it guaranteed neither success nor a rise from poverty. In practice the meaning of literacy was more limited, mediated by the social structure and narrowly circumscribed for many individuals; social realities contradicted the promoted promises of literacy. The potential uses of literacy were many, but in common activities potential literacy alone carried few concrete benefits while an imperfect literacy was sufficient for many needs. Literacy's uses were very often noninstrumental ones. Yet, the higher uses of literacy and the corresponding benefits and status were often precluded.

On the larger, societal level, literacy even if imperfect was especially important. This related directly to the moral bases of literacy and to the reestablishment and maintenance of social and cultural hegemony. Literacy was more central to the training, discipline, morality, and habits it accompanied and advanced than to the specific skills it represented. In this way, we can understand the significance of literacy's perceived contribution to attitudinal and value preparation and socialization, relatively unchanging from the mid-nineteenth to the late twentieth century. Here as well, we may locate the full meaning of the contradictions between the perceived and promoted influences of literacy and schooling and the existential reality. Literacy, it seems certain, was not the benefit to individuals that it was promised to be; nevertheless, it had sufficient impact at the level of skilled work and in its consensual acceptance for its larger limitations and other purposes to be blurred and largely ignored. Consequently, on the basic level of social and economic progress and those who determined it, literacy was more valuable to the society's goals and needs than to those of most individuals within it. Conceptually, as should be clear, the meaning, needs, and assessment of literacy shift as the focus moves from one level of society to another. The needs for literacy, and the demands made, differed not only from the larger unit to the individual, but also from individual to individual, much as the ideals for literacy's role and the practical needs and uses of literacy were not always synonymous. Individual employment of reading and writing and the uses that reformers promoted for popular literacy were not the same, as we have seen; and, in fact, they could be contradictory, as nineteenth-century reading habits indicate. These contradictions or conflicts, however, did not interfere with the everyday employment of literacy or its social purposes.

V

It is not part of our intention to revive the ridiculous thesis that the Reformation was the child of the printing press. It is perhaps the case that a book on its own has never been sufficient to change anybody's mind. But if it does not succeed in convincing, the printed book is at

least tangible evidence of convictions held because it em-
bodies and symbolizes them; it furnishes arguments to
those who are already converts, lets them develop and
refine their faith, offers them points which help them
triumph in debate, and encourages the hesitant.

LUCIEN FEBVRE AND H-J MARTIN
The Coming of the Book (1976)

What would happen if the whole world became literate?
Answer: not so very much, for the world is by and large
structured in such a way that it is capable of absorbing
the impact. But if the whole world consisted of literate,
autonomous, critical, constructive people, capable of trans-
lating ideas into action, individually or collectively—the
world would change.

JOHAN GALTUNG
"Literacy, Education, and Schooling—For What?" (1976)

The parallels and continuities between past and present discussions and concerns about the importance of literacy, its uses, and its quality are especially striking. How repetitive so many of the comments and observations seem. They are not in the least surprising, however. After reviewing the transmission of literacy in England in the second half of the nineteenth century, M. M. Lewis exclaimed, "How familiar all this sounds today! There is the same belief that illiteracy is on the increase, as shown by the retrogression of children after leaving school. There is the same belief that the mischief is due to teaching methods in vogue, countered by an equally robust faith in these very methods." Written in 1953, this observation seems even more pertinent today. Lewis con-cludes, "Society today insists upon the importance of illiteracy without realizing why it is important." [61] Controversy continues to rage over instructional methods, the quality of education, the influences on learn-ing, the disuse and misuse of literacy skills, the low quality and declining levels of abilities, the negative impact of broadcast media and leisure activities, and the moral and social components of schooling. Studies show adults not reading very often, children not learning to read, and pupils graduating without useful levels of literacy.

Yet we reside in a society in which literacy, as measured by the

[61] Lewis, *Importance*, 43, 98. See also, Chall and Carroll, *Literate Society;* Chall, *Learning;* Bataille, *A Turning Point* (esp. The Declaration of Persepolis: Final Report of the International Symposium for Literacy, September, 1975); "Illiteracy in the U.S.," *New York Times,* Spring Survey of Education, Apr. 30, 1978; Olson, "Toward A Literate Society." See also my "Literacy Past and Present"; Introduction and Preface, above.

census and comparable instruments, is universal: 98 to 99% of adults are "literate." At the same time, other indicators point to something else: 20 to 50% of adults and high school students are, according to some estimates, without *functional* literacy. Ironically, the recent movement toward competency-testing in schools constitutes the first concrete effort at specificity in the matter. The point is that we are in the grips of the "literacy myth." We do not know precisely what we mean by literacy or what we expect individuals to achieve from their instruction in and possession of literacy. As a result of this severe and long-standing conceptual failing, we flail out at schools, teachers, parents, and the media and make dire predictions about the future of civilization and the conditions of people's lives. We continue to apply standards of literacy that—owing to our uncertainties—are inappropriate and contradictory, and usually far beyond the basics of reading and writing that literacy literally signifies.[62]

The underlying assumptions of the importance of literacy, which we have studied as they were manifested in the nineteenth century, have been maintained to the present, uncritically accepted, for the most part, and constantly promulgated. These assumptions, tied to modern social thought and theories of society, of social change, and of social development, form the basis of the "literacy myth." The paradigms of progressive, evolutionary social thought have outlived their usefulness and are in a state of crisis, as more and more critics and commentators illustrate. This does not mean of course that literacy has not had its uses, whether socially, culturally, economically, or individually—or that it has not been important or can not be potentially more important.[63]

If we are to understand the meanings of literacy and its different values, past and present, these assumptions must be criticized, the needs reexamined, the demands reevaluated. The variable and differential contributions of literacy to different levels of society and different individuals must be confronted. Demands, abilities, and uses must be matched in more flexible and realistic ways, and the uses of literacy seen for their worth, historically and at present. Literacy, finally, can

---

[62] See, for example, Robert Disch, ed., *The Future of Literacy* (Englewood Cliffs, N.J.: Prentice Hall, 1973); Joseph Gold, ed., *In the Name of Language!* (Toronto: Macmillan-Maclean-Hunter, 1976); U.S. Department of Commerce, *Social Indicators, 1976;* Robert Escarpit, *The Book Revolution* (Paris: UNESCO, 1965); Mary Johnson, *Programmed Illiteracy in the Schools* (Winnipeg: Clarity Books, 1970); Chall and Carroll, *Toward A Literate Society.*

[63] See, for example, Kozol, "New Look," Freire, *Pedagogy;* Bataille, *A Turning Point.*

no longer be seen as a universalistic quantity or quality to be possessed however unequally by all in theory. Needs, aspirations, and expectations must be best met for all members of society. And literacy must be accorded a new understanding—in historical context. If its social meanings are to be understood and its value best utilized, the "myth of literacy" must be exploded.

Appendix A_____
Sources for the Historical Study
of Literacy in North America
and Europe[1]

[1] This is a modified and greatly expanded version of Table A, in Kenneth A. Lockridge, *Literacy in Colonial New England* (New York: Norton, 1974).

Source	Measure of literacy	Population	Country of availability	Years of availability	Additional variables
Census	Questions: read and write, read/write; Signature/mark (Canada 1851, 1861 only)	Entire "adult" population (in theory): ages variable, e.g., over 20 years, 15 years, 10 years	Canada, United States	Manuscripts: Nineteenth century	Age, sex, occupation, birthplace, religion, marital status, family size and structure, residence, economic data
Wills	Signature/mark	20–50% of adult males dying; 2–5% of adult females dying	Canada, United States, England, France, etc.	Canada, eighteenth century on, U.S. 1660 on, others from sixteenth–seventeenth century on	Occupation, charity, family size, residence, estate, sex
Deeds	Signature/mark	5–85% of living landowning adult males; 1% or less of females	Canada, United States	Eighteenth century on	Occupation, residence, value of land, type of sale
Inventories	Book-ownership	25–60% of adult males dying; 3–10% of adult females dying	Canada, United States, England, France, etc.	Seventeenth–eighteenth century on (quantity varies by country and date)	Same as wills
Depositions	Signature/mark	Uncertain: potentially more select than wills, potentially wider. Women sometimes included	Canada, United States, England, Europe	Seventeenth–eighteenth century on (use and survival varies)	Potentially, age, occupation, sex, birthplace, residence
Marriage records	Signature/mark	Nearly all (80%+) young men and women marrying (in England)	England, France, North America	From 1754 in England; 1650 in France	Occupation, age, sex, parents' name and occupation, residence (religion—North America)

326

Source	Measure	Population	Location	Period	Information recorded
Catechetical examination records	Reading, memorization, comprehension, writing examinations	Unclear, but seems very wide	Sweden, Finland	After 1620	Occupation, age, tax status, residence, parents' name and status, family size, migration, periodic improvement
Petitions	Signature/mark	Uncertain, potentially very select, males only in most cases	Canada, United States, England, Europe	Eighteenth century on	Occupation or status, sex, residence, political or social views
Military recruit records	Signature/mark or question on reading and writing	Conscripts or recruits (males only)	Europe, esp. France	Nineteenth century	Occupation, health, age, residence, education
Criminal records	Questions: read, read well, etc.	All arrested	Canada, United States, England	Nineteenth century	Occupation, age, sex, religion, birthplace, residence, marital status, moral habits, criminal data
Business records	Signature/mark	1. All employees 2. Customers	Canada, United States, England, Europe	Nineteenth, twentieth century	1. Occupation, wages 2. Consumption level, residence, credit
Library/mechanics institute records	Books borrowed	Members or borrowers	Canada, United States, England	Late eighteenth, early nineteenth century	Names of volumes borrowed, society membership
Applications (land, job, pensions, etc.)	Signature/mark	All applicants	Canada, United States, England, Europe	Nineteenth–twentieth century	Occupation, residence, family/career history, etc.
Aggregate data sources [a]	Questions or direct tests	Varies greatly	Canada, United States, England, Europe	Nineteenth–twentieth century	Any or all of the above

[a] Censuses, educational surveys, statistical society reports, social surveys, government commissions, prison and jail records, etc.

Appendix B ⎯⎯⎯⎯⎯⎯⎯⎯⎯⎯⎯

Literacy and the Census[1]

Despite their common contemporary use (both in the nineteenth century and today), manuscript censuses have not been employed by historians in the study of literacy, nor have scholars researching other questions from this source often inquired into its literacy data. This is most unfortunate, for there are a number of reasons for accepting census information regarding literacy and illiteracy; it is, I believe, a very valuable source, especially for the nineteenth century. This is particularly true of the 1861 Canadian census, the document on which Chapters 2, 3, and 4 are based. This use requires some explanation and comment.

Of the many sources employed in the historical study of literacy (outside Scandinavia), the census has potentially the broadest coverage (see Appendix A). Surveying, in theory at least, all persons resident in the Canadas, the 1861 census distributed printed schedules to each household in the cities, which inquired into the literacy of each person aged 20 years or more, collecting data for the analysis of adult literacy. At a time of educational reform and expansion, these returns provided the first systematic and direct information on the educational level of this population; they asked the respondent to indicate "persons over 20 who cannot read or write" on an individual level. Thus, the manuscripts provide a basis, first, for the estimation of adult literacy rates, and, second, for the study of variations in the social distribution of literacy and its value. The census, in addition to wider coverage than many other sources, also supplies a greater amount of information on

---

[1] This brief note is based upon my "What the 1861 census can tell us about literacy," *Histoire sociale,* 8 (1975), 337–349. Readers wishing an extended discussion of these issues should consult that article.

each individual (e.g., occupation, age, sex, marital status, birthplace, religion, family status). Important in themselves, these data also facilitate linkage with other sources, such as wealth reports. For literacy study in mid-nineteenth-century Canada (and probably elsewhere), the census manuscripts hold the greatest potential in coverage, representativeness, and versatility—certainly more than the alternatives of wills, deeds, certificates, etc. The census category also forms one definition of literacy; it is flexible and broadly comparable among the population and with other sources. The procedure and the definition strongly suggest that the authorities were cognizant of the high levels of literacy and acted accordingly. The definition, while ambiguous in not separating reading from writing, specifies a minimum level of attainment, allowing readers to respond as well as those who held other abilities. Here as elsewhere, reading was taught before writing; that skill provides the foundation for a definition of literacy and a presumption of its presence.

A number of factors point to the imprudence of the all too frequent and abrupt dismissal of these censuses for literacy research. These include external evidence, the practice of urban enumeration, and the internal patterns.

1. Explicit legal sanctions against giving false information were printed on each form. It is doubtful that the fine of $8–$20 was strictly enforced, but these sums were not insubstantial to many. In the absence of evidence to the contrary, we can not assume that the threat of penalty carried no weight.

2. The press and pulpit conducted campaigns for public acceptance and compliance with the census. These included the review of the schedule and its instructions, and exhortations to comply honestly. Interest in the census was promoted and a climate of opinion in its support was created by leaders.

3. A presumed stigma of admitted illiteracy need not have compromised the accuracy of the data, as some have argued. As Webb found in England, and all students have seen, "a good many people would admit to illiteracy." Illiterate gentlemen and wealthy individuals, some with high status occupations, are located regularly in historical research.

4. The enumeration procedure complicated easy hiding of illiteracy. An illiterate head of household was unable to complete his or her own schedule; another party would have to substitute, with the awareness of the first person's inability. A second party, whether enumerator, neighbor, or coresident, could have little or no reason to obscure the fact of illiteracy or to perjure him or herself, especially since his or her own signature would often go on the form. Urban enumeration procedures

(as distinct from rural ones, which brought an enumerator with his book from door to door) encouraged rather than deterred the admission of illiteracy.

5. Some underenumeration must be expected with any source like the census, as we find today. The lesser amount of residential segregation and more common mixing of class and ethnic groups, however, may have allowed coverage to be more complete. Regardless, we must recognize that rates of literacy derived from historical sources must be considered approximate. Further, in the analysis presented here, the individual, and not rates, forms the more important unit of analysis; with this emphasis, the problem of underenumeration is less acute: the census differentiates the literate and illiterate, and provides their characteristics.

6. The census is a collection of reports of and by individuals in response to a series of questions, in which literacy was included. Research on literacy in widely varied places has discovered high levels of accuracy: in the Philippines, Columbia, Bangladesh, for example.[2] Agreement not unusually ranges up to and above 90%; exaggeration is slight.

7. A census requires a conscious act of the individual in responding to the inquiry, an evaluation and assessment. To signify literacy in 1861 required leaving a column empty, a statement as direct as the completion of any other category and a measure of conscious intent (the literacy column fell in the middle of the schedule too). The individual creates a record of his or her literacy ability, whether the column is marked or left unmarked.

8. Internal evidence provides a check on the accuracy of this self-reported data. In some cases, especially those involving the literacy of the head of household who was to sign the form, self-reports may be compared with the presence or absence of a signature. The correlation, though, is not a simple and direct one; it nevertheless may be interpreted consistently with the validity of the measure. In Hamilton, Kingston, and London, 40, 70, and 60% of heads, respectively, admitting illiteracy made their mark. For others, there is no such simple check. However, many readers would not be able to sign; the absence of a mark on the schedule of an illiterate does not affect that status; other markers could be readers. (Research by K. A. Lockridge and R. S. Schofield supports

[2] J. E. deYoung and C. L. Hunt, "Communication Channels and Functional Literacy in the Philippine Barrio," *Journal of Asian Studies,* 22 (1966), 69–70; E. M. Rogers and W. Herzog, "Functional Literacy among Columbian Peasants," *Economic Development and Cultural Change,* 14 (1966), 194; Alex Inkeles *et al.,* "Some Social Psychological Effects and Non-effects of Literacy in a New Nation," *ibid.,* 16 (1967), 2; Inkeles and D. H. Smith, *Becoming Modern* (Cambridge, Mass.: Harvard University Press, 1974), 254.

this pattern and its interpretation.) An obsession with signatures or marks alone is unwarranted, and further, it would force a test of literacy employed with other, signatory types of sources that is not wholly appropriate to the census' measure. Thus, unsigned schedules and those signed by another individual (often an enumerator) are equally consistent with the interpretation of self-reported testaments of accuracy. The admission of literacy or illiteracy carries a greater evidential and interpretive weight than other indications—none of which is contradictory or inconsistent with the procedures of census-taking.

9. The results of the tabulations of individual illiterates provide strong additional evidence that the admission and indication of illiteracy was very far from random or spotty. Literacy rates were quite similar among all the cities of Ontario, and rates varied by age, sex, ethnicity, and occupation and wealth, as familiarity with the historical background would predict. Regional patterns are consistent, too. The meaning of these patterns forms the matter of Part One; nonetheless, the presence of these patterns lends support to the census' credibility and validity.

The census' evidence on literacy and illiteracy, it must be stressed, while important and valid, is not directly equatable with the status measured by a signature (perhaps the most common of historical measures used thus far by researchers). Its standard for comparison is the person's own evaluation of his or her literacy skills; that from a signature is no more comparable from person to person. Both sources (and all others) require interpretation as to what ability they in fact represent; each provides a direct test, but we must note that the ability to read varies widely. Those researchers working from signatory documents (marriage registers, wills, deeds, etc.) must assume that some fluency in reading accompanied, or preceded, the ability to sign a name; those using the census base their studies on an individual's statement of a personal assessment of the possession of an ability to read or write, a usable level. This measure of literacy therefore has an important evaluative and practical aspect, and it relates to the ability to use literacy in daily life and work in nineteenth-century places. Problems of comparability among sources undoubtedly remain, and comparisons must be conducted cautiously.

The census, finally, does suffer from problems. Most important are those of underenumeration and of the short span of its present availability to researchers. Other sources also present their complications. Deeds and wills, for example, provide an increasingly unrepresentative sample, with population growth, stratification, landlessness, and the infrequent appearance of women narrowing and limiting their representativeness. Both are biased in the direction of wealth, and probably in ethnicity and occupation too. Wills, of course, suffer from the bias of age, which may well lower significantly the signature rates, although the extent of this remains to be estimated accurately. For Ontario, and elsewhere, in this period, neither of these sources provides the amount of information, the representativeness, or the coverage that the census does. Even marriage registers, the most popular source to date are restricted to those legally marrying, perhaps 80% of the population.

Census reports of literacy and illiteracy from the 1861 urban manuscripts provide an important and valid measure. They share with all other indices some advantages and some disadvantages, and, as with all measures, their meaning and utility must be interpreted and understood before the data are exploited. In representation and coverage, census data is far more broadly based than any other measure available to historians of nineteenth-century Canada and probably for the United States as well. I hope that this use of the census will stimulate others to follow suit.

Appendix C

Classification of Occupations

Professional/ proprietor	Nonmanual/ smaller proprietor	Skilled, artisanal	Semiskilled	Unskilled
Clergy	Agent	Baker	Bartender	Farm laborer
Commission	Bookkeeper	Barber	Boatman	Lab man
merchant	Broker	Blacksmith	Carman	Laborer
Gentleman	Builder	Boat captain	Carter	Railroad worker
Lawyer	Chemist	Boiler	Chair factory	Waterman
Merchant	Dentist	Bookbinder	Coachman	Washer-woman
Physician	Druggist	Brewer	Drayman	Hewer
	Dry Goods/	Bricklayer	Driver	
	fancy	Brickmaker	Ferryman	
	Farmer	Butcher	Fisherman	
	Grocer	Cab maker	Furnaceman	
	Hotel keeper	Carpenter	Gardener	
	Innkeeper	Carriage maker	Hostler	
	Jeweler	Cigar maker	Mariner	
	Liquor dealer	Conductor	Porter	
	Manufacturer	Confectioner	Quarryman	
	Sales agent	Cooper	Sailor	
	Salesman	Cordwainer	Seaman	
	Storekeeper	Dealer	Servant	
	Student	Dyer	Teamster	
	Tavern keeper	Engineer	Waiter	
	Teacher	Gas fitter	Watchman	
	Tobacconist	Glass blower	Yardman	
	Victualer	Saddle maker	Cook	
	Clothier	Hatter	Huxter	

(continued)

(continued)

Professional/ proprietor	Nonmanual/ smaller proprietor	Skilled, artisanal	Semiskilled	Unskilled
	Yeoman	Joiner	Livery-stable	
	Vinegar maker	Machinist	keeper	
	Superintendent	Mason	Nurse	
	Clerk	Moulder	Cab driver	
	Boarding house	Nail maker	Cab owner	
	keeper	Operator	Midwife	
	Toyshop	Painter	Sawyer	
	Constable	Paperhanger	Soldier	
	Customs	Pattern maker	Roller	
	collector	Peddler	Messenger	
	High baillif	Piano maker	Lumberman	
		Plasterer	Woodcutter	
		Plumber	Housekeeper	
		Printer	Milkman	
		Puddler	White washer	
		Saddler	Mail conductor	
		Ship carpenter	Dressmaker	
		Shipwright	Seamstress	
		Shoemaker		
		Stonecutter		
		Stonesmason		
		Tailor		
		Tanner		
		Tinsmith		
		Turner		
		Typesetter		
		Upholsterer		
		Weaver		
		Wheelwright		
		Broom maker		
		Chandler		
		Harness maker	Caulker	
		Wagon maker	Brakesman	
		Watchmaker	Miller	

Appendix D

Illiterates: Occupations, 1861

A. Hamilton

	N	%		N	%
None	41	4.5	Innkeeper	1	0.1
Barber	2	0.2	Joiner	1	0.1
Blacksmith	8	0.9	Laborer	205	22.7
Bricklayer	1	0.1	Livery-stable keeper	1	0.1
Brickmaker	1	0.1	Mail conductor	2	0.2
Broom maker	1	0.1	Mariner	1	0.1
Builder	2	0.2	Mason	2	0.2
Cabinet maker	1	0.1	Merchant	1	0.1
Carpenter	14	1.6	Dairyman	1	0.1
Carter	1	0.1	Molder	2	0.2
Chandler	1	0.1	Painter	2	0.2
Clergyman	1	0.1	Peddler	2	0.2
Clothier	2	0.2	Plasterer	3	0.3
Constable	1	0.1	Printer	1	0.1
Cook	3	0.3	Harness maker	1	0.1
Customs collector	1	0.1	Seamstress	8	0.9
Dealer	1	0.1	Servant (f)	33	3.7
Dressmaker	1	0.1	Servant (m)	2	0.2
Engineer	1	0.1	Stonecutter	1	0.1
Farmer	3	0.3	Tailor	8	0.9
Fruiterer	1	0.1	Tanner	1	0.1
Gardener	2	0.2	Tavern keeper	7	0.8
Grocer	1	0.1	Teamster	4	0.4
High bailiff	1	0.1	Tinsmith	2	0.2
Hostler	2	0.2	Vinegar maker	1	0.1
Huxter	3	0.3	Wagon maker	2	0.2

(continued)

(continued)

Washer-woman	11	1.2	Unemployed	4	0.4
Wheelwright	1	0.1	Porters	3	0.3
Gentleman	1	0.1	Nurses	3	0.3
Wife	336	37.2	Prisoner	2	0.2
Shoemaker	8	0.9	Cab driver	1	0.1
Spinster	15	1.7	Lunatic	1	0.1
Waiter	4	0.4	Superintendent	2	0.2
Watchmaker	1	0.1	Not given	6	0.7
Widow	111	12.3			

B. Kingston			C. London		
	N	%		*N*	%
None, wife	261	51.7	None, wife	214	57.5
Baker	2	0.4	Baker	3	0.8
Barber	3	0.6	Barber	1	0.3
Butcher	2	0.4	Blacksmith	2	0.5
Carpenter	4	0.8	Bricklayer	1	0.3
Carter	5	1.0	Builder	1	0.3
Caulker	1	0.2	Butcher	1	0.3
Clerk	1	0.2	Carpenter	4	1.1
Cook	3	0.6	Cook	3	0.8
Cordwainer	1	0.2	Cooper	3	0.8
Customs collector	1	0.2	Dentist	1	0.3
Dealer	1	0.2	Engineer	1	0.3
Dressmaker	2	0.4	Farmer	2	0.5
Engineer	1	0.2	Gardener	1	0.3
Farmer	3	0.6	Grocer	1	0.3
Grocer	1	0.2	Laborer	83	22.3
Huxter	1	0.2	Mason	1	0.3
Innkeeper	3	0.6	Miller	1	0.3
Laborer	105	20.8	Pedlar	1	0.3
Livery-stable keeper	1	0.2	Pensioner	3	0.8
Mariner	10	2.0	Plasterer	2	0.5
Mason	3	0.6	Shoemaker	4	1.1
Midwife	1	0.2	Spinster	2	0.5
Pedlar	1	0.2	Yeoman	1	0.3
Printer	1	0.2	Porter	2	0.5
Sawyer	1	0.2	Nurse	2	0.5
Seamstress	2	0.4	Messenger	1	0.3
Servant (f)	34	6.7	Brakesman	2	0.5
Servant (m)	5	1.0	Housekeeper	1	0.3
Storekeeper	1	0.2	Woodcutter	1	0.3
Tailor	8	1.6			
Tallow chandler	2	0.4			
Tavern keeper	1	0.2			

(continued)

(continued)

B. Kingston

	N	%
Washer-woman	2	0.4
Gentleman	1	0.2
Shoemaker	4	0.8
Soldier	15	3.0
Spinster	2	0.4
Widow	1	0.2
Porter	1	0.2
Cab driver	1	0.2
Ladies	1	0.2
Boarding-school keeper	1	0.2
Cab owner	1	0.2
White washer	1	0.2
Roller	1	0.2
Toyshop keeper	1	0.2

Appendix E _____

A Note on the Record Linkage

As noted in Chapters 2, 3, and 4, techniques of nominal record-linkage were employed in this study to join records of individuals from several distinct sources. The linkage conducted for this research was totally manual, as opposed to computer-based procedures. To proceed by hand was a requirement rather than a choice, for my search for individuals identified in the 1861 manuscript census involved a relatively small proportion of the population of any given place, and not entire lists of inhabitants. (The census-to-assessment linkage of literates, however, had been accomplished through use of a semiautomated system by the Canadian Social History Project.) Consequently, the linkage was based on an examination of complete lists of census-enumerated and assessed individuals in each of the three cities in 1861 and 1871. (For references to the literature on nominal record-linkage in history, see the footnotes to Chapter 3.) My system was based upon the rules for computer-assisted linkage developed by Ian Winchester and the Canadian Social History Project; however, I did not compute weighted scores or additive totals to judge each potentially linked pair of records.

Two types of linkage formed the structure of data-collecting for this study: that over a short time span (census-to-assessment, 1861, 1870–1871–1872) and decennial searches (census-to-census, 1861–1871, four-way census-to-assessment linkages, 1861–1871). While both were conducted manually, the basis of the search and the rules for acceptance of records as truly linked differed.

The criteria for judging possible records as linked and selection or rejection were based upon a hierarchy of individual characteristics. For census-to-assessment linkage, the surname of the individual (heads of household only in this case) was obviously the most important identifiable variable. For a record to be accepted, then, the name had to be either the same or a close approximation in spelling or pronunciation. Initials, or in some cases, first names, were important too, although as expected they were a less reliable indicator. Age, when given in both sources, was important as well. For a link to be made, age had to be approximately the same in both sources (with some allowance for age-heaping at 5-year intervals; i.e., 30, 35, 40) unless all other variables were the same. Occupation and ward of residence followed in importance, as I assumed that there would be little residential or occupational mobility within a short time span. Generous allowance, however, was made for cases of occupational equivalence, and if name and age were the same in both sources, a link was made, regardless of occupation or residence. Moreover, the 1871 assessments included family size and school support (public or separate: an indication of Protestantism or Catholicism) adding important variables to the roster of comparison. If it was impossible to choose between two cases, especially in those involving a common name like Sullivan, none were selected; this rule, however, was seldom applied. In all cases, these criteria were stringently employed; consequently, all links were made with a relatively large degree of confidence, and the rates of persistence must be considered conservative ones.

The census-to-census search involved all illiterates, regardless of household status, and all children present in their families in 1861. With these links, name was also the key variable for selection, followed by sex, birthplace, religion, age, and initials. More liberal allowance was made for aging, as far from all "aged" a full 9 or 10 years over the decade, as was reported by them. Nevertheless, when considered as a whole, those linked did age between 9 and 10 years from 1861 to 1871. Sex, however, had to be the same for a link to be accepted. Birthplace and religion, importantly, were the same in virtually all cases, excepting some children who were reported as native-born Canadians by 1871 when they had been foreign-born a decade earlier. These involved few cases. If religion and birthplace were not identical, a match was not made unless all other variables agreed. For heads of households, and for most children, information on the family was important. For example, a head of household's match was supported by the presence of the spouse, unless marital status had changed from married to widowed. Names and ages of spouses and children as well as their birthplaces were useful in selection, if children aged 9 years or older remained at home, which of course the majority did. Similarly, the decision to link a child depended upon his or her parents' or parent's identity in both years as well as that of siblings. If, however, household or marital status changed (and these could not be used as independent criteria for judgment), name, age, sex, initials, birthplace, religion, and other family data (such as for a woman who became a widow and head of household) were the only judgments for a link. Therefore, the fewer the variables, the more rigorously the rules for equivalence and exactness were applied.

In census-to-census linkages, neither occupation nor place of residence could be used in making the decision to link. Comparison of change in these variables was the object of the linkage, and therefore they were ignored in judgments to accept or reject a potentially linked pair. As with the other linkage, these rules were rigorously applied, and the resulting set of matched pairs of records must be considered conservative. If biased, then, the linkage results would be in favor of greater transiency rather than persistence, a choice for caution and not greater numbers.

Finally, the four-way linkage was in many respects the simplest, involving the fewest possible matches, the shortest lists, and the greatest number of useful variables. The rules were much the same as those employed above; however, as with occupation and residence in census-to-census linkages, neither wealth nor homeownership was used in accepting or rejecting a record: their changes were the object of study. I refer the concerned reader to the work of Ian Winchester, the files of the *Historical Methods Newsletter,* and to E. A. Wrigley, ed., *Identifying People in the Past* (cited in Chapter 3), for both theoretical and practical discussions of nominal record-linkage and the problems encountered by researchers.

Subject Index

STUDIES IN SOCIAL DISCONTINUITY

Under the Consulting Editorship of:

CHARLES TILLY
University of Michigan

EDWARD SHORTER
University of Toronto

William A. Christian, Jr. Person and God in a Spanish Valley

Joel Samaha. Law and Order in Historical Perspective: The Case of Elizabethan Essex

John W. Cole and Eric R. Wolf. The Hidden Frontier: Ecology and Ethnicity in an Alpine Valley

Immanuel Wallerstein. The Modern World-System: Capitalist Agriculture and the Origins of the European World-Economy in the Sixteenth Century

John R. Gillis. Youth and History: Tradition and Change in European Age Relations 1770 – Present

D. E. H. Russell. Rebellion, Revolution, and Armed Force: A Comparative Study of Fifteen Countries with Special Emphasis on Cuba and South Africa

Kristian Hvidt. Flight to America: The Social Background of 300,000 Danish Emigrants

James Lang. Conquest and Commerce: Spain and England in the Americas

Stanley H. Brandes. Migration, Kinship, and Community: Tradition and Transition in a Spanish Village

Daniel Chirot. Social Change in a Peripheral Society: The Creation of a Balkan Colony

Jane Schneider and Peter Schneider. Culture and Political Economy in Western Sicily

Michael Schwartz. Radical Protest and Social Structure: The Southern Farmers' Alliance and Cotton Tenancy, 1880-1890

Ronald Demos Lee (Ed.). Population Patterns in the Past

David Levine. Family Formations in an Age of Nascent Capitalism

Dirk Hoerder. Crowd Action in Revolutionary Massachusetts, 1765-1780